Counseling and Gender

Marie L. Miville • Tatiana Vera • Nic Bensmiller

Counseling and Gender

Intersectional Approaches for Practice, Research, and Advocacy

Springer

Marie L. Miville
Department of Counseling and Clinical Psychology
Teachers College
Columbia University
New York, NY, USA

Tatiana Vera
Department of Counseling and Clinical Psychology
Teachers College
Columbia University
New York, NY, USA

Nic Bensmiller
Department of Counseling and Clinical Psychology
Teachers College
Columbia University
New York, NY, USA

ISBN 978-3-031-69171-3 ISBN 978-3-031-69172-0 (eBook)
https://doi.org/10.1007/978-3-031-69172-0

This Springer imprint is published by the registered company Springer Nature Switzerland AG
The registered company address is: Gewerbestrasse 11, 6330 Cham, Switzerland

Marie L. Miville
Thank you Tatiana and Nic for being amazing co-authors in the long journey of writing this book. I could not have asked for more responsible, caring, and competent individuals to join me in this project. Thank you Jill (and Alli), your loving patience and joyful presence is felt each day. Thank you to my parents and family, your love, devotion, and many gifts are ever present in my heart.

Tatiana Vera
Thank you, Dr. Marie Miville, for having faith in me during my academic career, trusting me with meaningful projects, and allowing me to finish my PhD with valuable academic contributions. Thank you also to Nic: your impact on me in our short time knowing each other has been invaluable and mind expanding. To my best friends Aisha, Amanda, Jay, Mikiko, and many others: thank you for our conversations at length about the topics written in this book. And of course, to my parents and sister: thank you for your unconditional support and helping to make my journey what it is today.

Nic Bensmiller
Thank you to Dr. Marie Miville for trusting me with this material and always welcoming my perspective. Thank you also to Tatiana, who has taught me so much and continues to be a fiercely loyal friend. To Robert, my family, my friends, and my comrades: thank you for your constant support and collaboration in learning and doing radical things.

Preface

In light of recent societal events (e.g., #MeToo movement, public policies for transgender/gender nonconforming individuals, Black women's pregnancy health), gender once again has become a salient topic in the mental health professions. Today, gender remains an impactful component of both mental and physical health, as evidenced in recent statistics that show that girls and women demonstrate significantly higher levels of mental health concerns, particularly depression (NSDUH, 2024), whereas boys and men are vastly overrepresented in the commission of violent behaviors (APA, 2018). The psychological and emotional impacts of both historical and current sociopolitical events have led to a refocusing of research and practice on how gender intersects with other important aspects of functioning that may help account for these unique gendered experiences and outcomes.

This book focuses on gender and mental health and is geared toward practitioners as well as undergraduate and graduate students in the mental health professions (i.e., counseling, professional psychology, and social work). We present important counseling issues that apply for individuals of a variety of gender backgrounds and identities, primarily women, men, and transgender/gender nonconforming (TGNC) individuals. We present research and practice considerations regarding gender through an intersectional and inclusive lens. Our intention is not to comprehensively summarize all the literature pertaining to gender but to highlight key issues that help readers become oriented to current thinking and research, as well as describing common concerns that may be present for many clients seeking mental health treatment. Chapters 2 through 11 each contain a case study and discussion questions that help apply important constructs and processes in a specific situation related to that chapter's themes.

Much discussion, even controversy, continues today regarding what gender is and how it affects people, including people who are mental health professionals and their clients. We utilize an intersectional framework as an effective way to better understand gender, addressing the available evidence for defining and measuring gender and gender-related psychological processes, as well as discussing the sociopolitical implications of gender for individuals, families, communities, and the larger society. Racial-cultural and ethnic underpinnings are described as key to understanding the definition and impact of gender. Other important social group experiences, based, for example, on socioeconomic status (SES) and sexual orientation, are presented as well. Topics covered in the book include the cultural bases of gender, especially gender roles; experiences of privilege and oppression; and prejudice and discrimination, as based on gender. Finally, therapeutic frameworks helpful for understanding key attitudes, knowledge, and skills for dealing with gender and its intersections in counseling settings are described.

Our book is arranged along a variety of important dimensions related to mental health, including the history of gender both in the larger society and within psychology; specific issues arising from gender and its intersections with race, ethnicity, SES, and sexual orientation; gender identity; the assessment of gender; education and career; relationships and families; physical and mental health; and violence. The last chapter is dedicated to providing gender-affirmative and liberatory counseling interventions.

Specific objectives addressed in the book include:

(a) Important demographic trends and historic bases regarding gender
(b) Cultural/ethnic/spiritual bases of understanding gender, particularly traditional gender roles
(c) Critical social group experiences, as based on race, ethnicity, socioeconomic status (SES), and sexual orientation, that may influence definitions, norms, and practices surrounding gender
(d) Attitudes, beliefs, understandings, and acculturative experiences, including clinical cases for each chapter
(e) Conceptual, diagnostic, and intervention strategies for working with gender in counseling and other settings
(f) Professional role development in social justice, advocacy, and gender self-awareness as these address various systems, especially institutional and social barriers that impede access, equity, and success for clients
(g) The nature of biases, prejudices, processes of intentional and unintentional oppression and discrimination, and other culturally reinforced behaviors that are detrimental to the growth of people
(h) Theories of gender affirmative counseling, liberation and resistance in counseling practices, theories of identity development, and multicultural/gender competencies
(i) Importance of research and assessment, including the opportunities and difficulties of conducting research and assessment

We believe the book will be helpful for individuals who want to become familiar with the wide range of counseling issues that are relevant to gender in clinical work with individuals, families, and communities. The book also is a helpful introduction to undergraduate and graduate students interested in how psychology has investigated gender as well as available counseling frameworks and interventions. Finally, in taking an intersectional and inclusive approach to counseling, we hope to expand current thinking around gender that typically separates discussion of individuals based on their gender (e.g., exclusively woman, man, or TGNC) to more clearly illuminate how gender affects all individuals, albeit in substantively different ways.

New York, NY, USA

Marie L. Miville
Tatiana Vera
Nic Bensmiller

References

American Psychological Association. (2018). *APA guidelines for psychological practice with boys and men: (505472019-001)* [dataset]. https://doi.org/10.1037/e505472019-001

Substance Abuse and Mental Health Services Administration (SAMHSA). (2024, January). *NSDUH data brief: Gender differences in mental health among young adults aged 18 to 25* (Vol. 1, No. 1). Retrieved from https://www.samhsa.gov/data/sites/default/files/reports/rpt44475/2021-nsduh-data-brief-1.pdf

Acknowledgments

The authors would first like to thank Yasmin Butt for her outstanding organizing contributions in putting this book's citations together. Her commitment to handling these intricacies and material structure while negotiating the difficult doctoral program application process has been genuinely priceless. We also thank our Springer publishing editor Sharon Panulla, whose patience, understanding, and flexibility facilitated this volume being published in light of the impact of pandemic times and major caregiving responsibilities.

Contents

About the Authors

Marie L. Miville is a Professor of Psychology and Education and Vice-Dean for Faculty Affairs at Teachers College, Columbia University. She is the author of three books exploring intersectionalities of gender with other aspects of identity, and over 60 publications dealing with social justice and multicultural issues in counseling and psychology. Professor Miville has engaged in multiple leadership and advocacy positions that have promoted the needs of diverse communities as well. Major accomplishments include serving as the Associate Editor of the *Journal of Multicultural Counseling and Development*, the Book Series Editor for American Psychological Association (APA) Division 44, the 2015 President of the National Latinx Psychological Association (NLPA), past-President of the Council of Counseling Psychology Training Programs, and Vice-President for Education and Training for the APA Division 17; she also is an APA Fellow (Division 17 and 45). In addition to being a Full Professor, Dr. Miville is a Vice-Dean for Faculty Affairs (VDFA) and coordinates many aspects of faculty work life, such as the New Faculty Orientation, mentoring committees for pre-tenured faculty, professional development programs, and other support services for faculty. Prior to her current administrative appointment as Vice-Dean for Faculty Affairs at Teachers College, Professor Miville served as the College Ombuds, the Chair of the Department of Counseling and Clinical Psychology, and Director of Training/Program Director of Counseling Psychology, all at Teachers College. Professor Miville has been involved in multiple major federal grant projects that provided training support for students of various backgrounds.

Tatiana Vera is a Ph.D. candidate in Counseling Psychology at Teachers College, Columbia University, serves as the Student Representative of the National Latinx Psychological Association, and is an Interdisciplinary Minority Fellowship Program fellow for 2023–2024. Her research focuses on the mental health impacts of educational systems on STEM Latina Doctoral students, utilizing a Mujerista and Latine Critical Theory lens. Tatiana also co-authors work on counseling psychology at the intersection of racial and gender minorities. Clinically trained in trauma-informed care, she works with Latinas and immigrants affected by relational trauma, and has contributed to CDC efforts to shape policies preventing violence against immigrants. As she completes her final Ph.D. year in San Diego, California, Tatiana aims to develop mentorship practices for Latinas in STEM and advocate for policy changes benefiting monolingual and bicultural Latines in the USA.

Nic Bensmiller is a Ph.D. student in Counseling Psychology at Teachers College, Columbia University. They are also a Licensed Mental Health Counselor in private practice in New York City. Their clinical work focuses on providing intersectional Feminist therapy for communities who are positioned at multiple points of marginalization, particularly LGBTQI+ communities. Nic's research work incorporates social justice theory, philosophy, and psychology to analyze matrices of power and work toward radical praxis that aims to target systemic violence through honoring the material reality that people live within.

Chapter 1
Constructions and Sociohistorical Considerations of Gender

Historical Underpinnings of Gender

Gender as a serious sustained area of research in psychology has only been around for a little over a century, beginning in the early 1900s when the first wave of women psychologists entered the field. However, it was not until September 1970 that women psychologists formed a major advocacy group that surged to prominence, on the momentous day when a newly formed group, the Association for Women in Psychology (AWP), protested at a town hall meeting of the American Psychological Association (APA) (Johnston & Johnson, 2018). The protests centered on how the field of psychology up to that time had played a significant role in promoting and maintaining the subordination of women in society. The protesters, who represented several generations of psychologists, demanded $1 million dollars in reparations for APA's "criminal treatment and imprisonment of women, to be used for battered women and feminist alternatives to asylums" (Johnston & Johnson, p. 3). Although the funds were never disbursed, APA formed a task force on the status of women, which led to other important developments, such as a new APA Division focused on women (Division 35), the Committee on Women in Psychology, and a new APA journal, *Psychology of Women Quarterly* (PWQ), all of which remain active today. Thirty years later, similar kinds of protests erupted once more regarding the invisibility of individuals who have transgender, non-binary, and gender nonconforming gender identities (TGNC), leading to another APA Task Force focused on TGNC people, and eventually another division (Division 44) that changed its name to reflect a more inclusive focus on both sexual orientation and gender diversity.

Today it seems puzzling, even frustrating, that a discipline focused on mental health and functioning could have missed out on the specific concerns, needs, and interventions for over half of the human population. However, the invisibility and subordination of women and TGNC people from primary discourse in society has been ongoing for far longer in many parts of the world. Although a historical

M. L. Miville et al., *Counseling and Gender*,
https://doi.org/10.1007/978-3-031-69172-0_1

recounting of gender across the ages and cultures is well beyond the scope of this book (for an excellent comprehensive historical perspective on gender, please see Wiesner-Hanks, 2011), suffice to say that many, though not all, societies throughout history, have generally centered their sustained attention (e.g., mythologies, histories, forms of governance, laws, and so on) on men and their perspectives and accomplishments. Indeed as Wiesner-Hanks notes, this near exclusive male focus on all aspects of human functioning and achievement, such as art, politics, sports, and science, including psychology, has not only hidden the histories and experiences of women and transgender/gender nonconforming (TGNC) people, this focus has prevented a clear understanding of men's unique experiences as well. Moreover, taking a gender inclusive stance on all aspects of psychology and mental health, not just those specifically affecting women and TGNC people, profoundly changes theories, investigations, and interpretations of the human psyche and functioning. Gender shapes much of what people think about each other based on their particular gender, as well as people and the larger society in general (Wiesner-Hanks, 2011). Today gender remains "a constitutive element of social relationships based on perceived differences between the sexes, and gender is a primary way of signifying relationships of *power*" (emphasis added, Scott, in Wiesner-Hanks, p. 2). These relationships have often been characterized along a binary dimension, with dominant individuals being perceived or described as masculine and dependent or submissive people as feminine. There are historical exceptions to this binary perspective throughout human history, with some cultures engaging with gender through a three-or-more-gender system of categorization, though these systems have not remained dominant through modernity and have largely been repressed through various means, particularly colonization (Wiesner-Hanks, 2011).

A key distinction between and among genders has focused on presumed biological differences between women and men, or what in short hand has come to be known as sex differences. However, much debate continues today about what truly are biological differences, especially as these are "real" versus cultural interpretations of or societal impositions on that reality (e.g., Spence & Buckner, 2000). In other words, does it make sense to ask which came first, sex or gender? This question is not meant to deny the basic physical existence of different types of genders, but to query whether this existence laid a pathway for so-called innate gender (psychological) differences, or whether these differences were presumed to exist, and then exaggerated, for social-organizational, economic, and political purposes; a hybridization of these two processes may be more likely the case. Some scholars even doubt whether it is meaningful or an investigable empirical question of whether there is a true sex vs. gender distinction (Wiesner-Hanks, 2011). These scholars suggest that perhaps it is gender (or psychological assumptions thereof) that led to the presumption of *some* biological differences among genders coming to mean that *all* was different among the genders. That is, is it possible that destiny, for example, being born a woman or an intersex person, becomes anatomy, rather than the other way around, as Freud originally posited. As Simone de Beauvoir famously noted, "One is not born, but becomes a woman," because of widely held presumptions about gender.

Additionally, it is important to consider recent advances in biological sex categorization in human beings. The majority of these biological assumptions arise from the myth that humans are purely sexually dimorphic. Sexual dimorphism is the tendency for a species to be either one sex or another; in humans, this is often posited as male/female leveraging either genetic/chromosomal or genital/reproductive characteristics as one-or-the-other. However, research indicates that humans are not as sexually dimorphic as previously hypothesized, primarily due to the prevalence of intersex people at approximately 2% (Blackless et al., 2000; Fausto-Sterling, 2000; Hyde et al., 2019). Intersex people are those whose genetic "sex" or genital/reproductive characteristics do not fall into the conception of either "male" or "female" as they are currently utilized and understood (Hyde et al., 2019). Historically, these differences were seen as exceptionally rare, though recent evidence indicates this may not be the case. Biological evidence shows the possibility of more than 5 biological sexes naturally occurring in humans (Fausto-Sterling, 1993). Another significant note here is that intersex people are often subject to non-consensual forced gender assignment or reconstructive surgery, which the intersex activist movement has fought diligently against, but still occurs (Dreger & Herndon, 2009; Hyde et al., 2019). Unfortunately, the traditional view of biological sex dimorphism holds strong as a belief, even by the scientific community, due largely to the pervasive need to categorize people into gendered groups as a form of perpetuating the structure of sexism (Fausto-Sterling, 2012).

The traditional view of the biological bases of sex and the resultant male dominative patterns goes something like this: Although there is clear evidence across history and cultures of third and fourth genders (of up to 5 to 6 genders) as well as intersexed and transgender individuals, the majority of human societies created social structures that differentiated among only two genders, each of which were imbued with distinctive roles, purposes, qualities, and so on. Over time, this distinction became associated with other dualities, such as light/dark, yin/yang, public/private, sun/moon, and so on (Wiesner-Hanks, 2011). Major reasons cited for the persistence of patriarchal (male-dominated) social hierarchies are that the gestational and caregiving period for humans is relatively long, and has been the responsibility of women. Some psychobiologists have argued that this kept women in a more dependent position, while men, empowered through their upper body strength, became aggressors within the natural world and each other (Geary, 2021). Another important social and economic evolution for most societies was the change over time from nomadic gatherer-hunters to domesticated lifestyles that emphasized agriculture and staying in place. The common myth surrounding gatherer-hunter societies in prehistory is that women were gatherers and men hunters, providing an evolutionary argument for the differentiation of observable biological differences between men and women. This view, however, has been discounted in recent archeological research, which found that women and men participated in both hunting and gathering activities (Anderson et al., 2023).

About 10,000 years ago, more domesticated lifestyles emphasizing growing and managing one's own food supply among most human societies led to profound social and economic change that may have included a change of focus from mother-child relationships as the basis for cultural values and social relationships to father-son relationships that emphasized the passage of land and valuable resources across generations (Brown, 2024; Wiesner-Hanks, 2011). Women's work became concentrated in smaller areas and more easily monitored by their male counterparts. An important consequence of this shift was men beginning to emphasize their control over women, at times with violence, in order to ensure a smooth transition across generations through their male heirs, what Engels has described as "the world historical defeat of the female sex" (in Wiesner-Hanks, p. 17).

Women became defined primarily by their relationships and roles with men, eventually becoming excluded from mythological/spiritual/religious and political systems, and as was seen in ancient Roman times, being publicly decried and treated as inferior. In many parts of the world (though not all), women had lesser access to resources on their own (e.g., land, trade-based skills, money), and became more dependent on men for survival in their communities. Many of the earliest known societies around the world, including Europe, Asia, and Latin America, heightened these gender distinctions as societies grew larger and focused on monopolistic hereditary forms of power, leading to norms and laws specifying and enforcing gender-based behaviors, such as requiring "purity" or virginity before marriage and outlawing adultery for women, but not for men (Wiesner-Hanks, 2011). Even the cosmos became gendered in many spiritual belief systems, with a balance of "male and female" energies being emphasized; male forces were seen as more powerful and the original human form was presumed (incorrectly) to be male. To be sure, there have been multiple exceptions to a patriarchal gender structure across time and place, for example in Africa and the Americas. However, as humans became more interconnected and dependent on each other, particularly through trade, war, climate events and other upheavals, patriarchal societies became the general norm around the world. Colonization has thus far played a significant role in mobilizing the spread of patriarchy; an example of this is colonization through the tool of missionary work (Lugones, 2007).

Science and the Scientification of Gender

In light of this brief world history, it is not surprising that the evolution of scientific inquiry also reflected patriarchal systems of knowledge and thinking. For much of human history, areas of thought, as might be seen in history, philosophy, and the natural sciences, were written by elite educated men (Wiesner-Hanks, 2011). These men often wrote of women as a large undifferentiated mass of people, ostensibly in order to better understand what made them unique and ideal (though often in direct downward comparison to men), whereas most male scholars did not think this was possible for themselves. In other words, "men saw women as a group as the Other, an object for their analyses, but saw themselves as the One, about whom generalizations which extended to the whole sex were either impossible or unnecessary" (Wiesner-Hanks, 2011, p. 86). Instead men focused on distinctions among themselves (e.g., nobles, clergy, and peasants during medieval Europe) which usually did not fit most women's experiences. In more recent times, scholars focused on how differences among genders might be overcome, as in the suffragist and anticolonial movements that began in the 1700s.

The intentional exclusion of women and TGNC scholars and their perspectives led to the presumption across many disciplines that male experiences are the normative or universal experiences, not needing any further discernment, resulting in a skewing of perspective that remains today in many areas of learning and investigation, including the natural, medical and social sciences (Arredondo et al., 2022). What relatively little attention was paid to women and TGNC people in many forms of scholarship typically was relegated to subjugated gendered experiences as inferior representations of the male as well as in dependent relationships with males (e.g., the mother/caregiver). For example, Laqueur (1990), rather controversially, has posited two distinct views of gender over the last 2000 years within Western thinking. He suggested that prior to the Enlightenment period, women and men were thought to be of one sex, with women being considered the same as men, except "theirs (sexual features) are inside the body, not outside", or as captured in an old song "women are but men turned outside in" (Laqueur, p. 4). Within the one-sex framework, men were considered to be imbued with a "vital heat" that had led to their features being turned outward, and thus "more perfect" (Laqueur, p. 4). By 1800, with the discovery of biological differences (e.g., sexual organs), this thinking changed to a two-sex modality emphasizing total differentiation between "male"s and "females" that scientists began to highlight:

> All parts of her body present the same differences: all express woman; the brow, the nose…if we sift our view to the inside, and with the help of the scalpel, lay bare the organs…we encounter everywhere…the same difference. (Laqueur, p. 5)

As noted earlier, in other cultures, such as several American Indigenous societies, there was an emphasis on gender complementarity, leading to resources and other sources of power and privilege to be passed to all children, rather than only sons (Wagner, 2020). Unfortunately, in Latin America, these egalitarian practices were outlawed with Spanish colonization, which reflected the Western/European emphasis on women's exclusion from possession of resources and power (Wiesner-Hanks, 2011). Indeed, with the onslaught of European colonization of many nations and racial-cultural groups around the world, the racial implications of male gender dominance became more complex, as in the case of a woman European Queen (e.g., Elizabeth I) and male members of a racially diverse colony over which she presumably ruled. Such was the concern about the potential impact of these questions that beginning in the 1600s, science came into usage to affirm gender, and what were quickly becoming racialized, social hierarchies in Europe, the Americas, and elsewhere. For example, Emile Durkheim, considered the "father" of sociology executed studies on skull sizes of humans from around the world to display both the racial and gender superiority of French (White/European) men, when he found that French women had among the smallest skulls of all people, in contrast with French men. Thus, a number of scientists engaged in research that highlighted gender distinctions within and among racial groups seemed to affirm both the gender and racial hierarchies that were being developed and legalized along political and economic frameworks (Wiesner-Hanks, 2011; see Chaps. 2 and 3 for more discussion of intersections of gender). The publication of Darwin's *The Origin of the Species* further cemented essentialist (i.e., representing an unconscious bias) biological constructs in which "sex differences predict sex differences" as represented in his theory of sexual selection (Gowaty, 2018).

In light of these histories, as well as the leveraging of scientific inquiry to confirm extant societal structures, it is not surprising that psychology as a discipline and a practice also came to reflect distinct gender biases in many theories and areas of inquiry. For example, early personality theorists such as Freud and Erickson all provided negative or pessimistic views of women regarding their propensity for true maturation and development, at least relative to men. Moreover, given the binary bias of patriarchal systems, the psychological development of gender non-binary or diverse individuals was often provided as an afterthought, if at all, and described in negative terms as well. Women and TGNC scholars always have been a part of scientific inquiry, though their work was often not mentioned, erased, or worse, taken away from them and credited to male colleagues (what has been called the *Matilda effect*, see Arredondo et al., 2022). Thus, it has been male scientists whose work has been consistently transmitted across generations of students, researchers, and society leaders, a legacy that remains today, in terms of who seeks education and training in many of these disciplines. It was not until the nineteenth century that egalitarian sociopolitical movements, as based on gender, race/ethnicity, religion, etc. began to take hold for many populations after global colonization. Over the past 150 years, these movements led to profound changes around the world in political and legal processes (e.g., the right to vote, discussed in the next section), education systems, and scholarly inquiry, including psychology. The next section reviews the impact of some of these sociopolitical changes in the U.S. in the last century as a key component of societal change and advocacy for women and TGNC people, leading to the description of the protests within psychology that began the chapter.

Sociopolitical Considerations of Gender

Another key aspect of understanding the psychological impact of gender within patriarchal systems is to examine the sociopolitical history surrounding gender in the context of the United States (U.S.). Although we focus primarily on U.S. history in this book, the sociopolitical histories of other nations and peoples have significant effects on the psychological impact of gender, that is, these impacts are international and global as well. Thus for any individual's gender socialization within systems that have ensured the exclusion of their participation, it is important to consider gender in terms of one's own national context, regarding both native country (the country[ies] with which one identified growing up) as well as the country(ies) in which one lives as an adult, and their respective histories (e.g., laws, policies, norms, etc) surrounding gender.

In the U.S., as in many other societies, there has been a longstanding policy of exclusion relative to gender, and involvement in the political process, including the individual right to vote. When the United States was founded nearly 250 years ago, women, as well as anybody not a "biologically-determined" male were excluded legally from access to voting. As was described earlier, this exclusion was (and still is in some countries) viewed as acceptable in light of patriarchal norms, with other forms of exclusion also being accepted (e.g., race and socioeconomic status defined as property ownership). Thus, although the founding of the U.S. in the late seventeenth century was based on a revolutionary concept, representative democracy, that was meant to reflect the "will of the people" rather than that of a monarch or single leader, many, if not most, individuals were not yet considered a legitimate part of "the people" (Umhoefer, 2015).

A relevant question for this topic is how and why a political right to vote might be relevant to studying gender in psychology, particularly the impact of presumably inherent civil rights, on one's mental health. The path toward inclusion in the sociopolitical process in this country in the US is centuries old, even as old as the U.S. But, particularly in the past 150 years, as egalitarian-based social movements became popular in the U.S. and around the world, gender based rights became critical to advocate for in order to ensure all citizens of adult age were able to participate in the democratic process (Schaeffer, 2020). Despite or perhaps because of the exclusion policy, and in line with the egalitarian values that have always been part of the U.S. throughout its history, there have been many generations of people advocating to be included in the political process. Engagement in advocacy can counteract the negative impact of *exclusion as public policy* (Boehnke & Wong, 2011; Conner et al., 2023; Klar & Kasser, 2009), the consequences of which can include: stress, anxiety, depression, isolation, loss or negative sense of identity, lack of belongingness, lack of access to care, lack of safety and sense of security. This reifies interpersonal discrimination, compounding the disempowerment of individuals, that then can lead to internalization of negative sense of self/group, and disruption or disengagement from healthy development (e.g., Abrego, 2008). Instead engagement in advocacy can lead to positive mental health effects, including developing a sense of empowerment, self-acceptance, as well as a sense of belonging to the larger social structure including one's community by experiencing commonalities; developing a sense of strength in numbers; community building through advocacy; and strengthening the importance of democratic values, principles, and practices for all people in the larger society. The construct of *resistance* (Miville, 2018) is relevant here as a source of finding strength (e.g., *psychological independence*) in one's own or one's community's power; Chap. 12 will discuss resistance strategies in greater detail.

As noted earlier, unique and separate gender expectations have been the norm around the world, however, the downside of these traditions at a political level in many countries has led to systematic exclusion for gender status as a matter of public policy. Another very important takeaway is when we look at the experiences of gender by other important differences, for example, race. Racism played an integral role in how women organized and fought against sexism, with the horrifying reality that many of the original and well-known women's rights advocates, who were White, often publicly expressed racist beliefs about not supporting the right to vote regarding Black American people. Thus, during the 1800s, as the suffrage movements were becoming stronger as based on both race and gender, there was a deep sociopolitical divide across gender (White women) and race (Black Americans) that became a bitter battle in terms of who was going to get the right to vote. In the aftermath of the Civil War, which, to this day, remains the bloodiest war ever fought within the US national borders in history, taking away more than three quarters of a million lives, African Americans were granted citizenship through the 14th Amendment, and Black men were granted the right to vote with the Fifteenth Amendment (Pruit, 2021). A part of the end of slavery was the push to expand voting rights to all U.S. citizens, however, at that time only men were recognized as being capable of voting privileges and so with the 14th amendment, voting rights were no longer denied based on race. However, within one single generation, that is, 20 years, those voting rights essentially ended for Black men, especially in the South, because of Jim Crow laws and racially based policies of exclusion (Pruitt). These voting rights would not be reinstalled until the mid 1960s with the Voting Rights Act of 1964. In contrast, women were granted the right to vote in 1920 with the 19th Amendment, though this right was essentially limited to White women, given the racist policies and practices surrounding voting (Enns, 1997). It would not be until 1964 that Black women and other women of color were able to vote without barriers throughout the U.S.

Gender and Power

Our brief historical overview clearly indicates that one important construct relevant to any discussion of gender is *power* due to differing access to important privileges and resources, which have been structured and enforced through laws and public policy in many societies, though here we will focus on the U.S. It is important to understand how power is experienced differentially, as based on gender, along with its respective psychological impact. First, it is important to ask what is meant by power, and how has power been defined and by whom? Probably the longest standing definition of power is in terms of subjugation and domination, as would be familiar in patriarchal and other hierarchical systems. *Power* has been defined as "the ability of persons or groups to command compliance from other persons or groups, even in the face of opposition. Power requires resources superior to those controlled by the compliers" (Chafetz, in Jones, 2003, p. 32). Power typically concerns the *control* of resources (Sherif, 1982), including human resources, in the important institutions that make up most larger societies. A second critical aspect of power is the effective use of *sanctions*, for example, exercising control over other people's access to power, rewards, and punishment. Public discourse or propaganda that occurs around control of resources and use of sanctions represents who has access to resources, who can make decisions about who gets what, and who has access to learn and change their and others' lives (Sherif, 1982).

Sociopolitical systems, even those based on presumably egalitarian values, have different rules and policies (e.g., exclusion by gender or race) about access to resources, including the right to vote, obtain an education, own property, and get married. Since the founding of the U.S., men uniquely have had this kind of power. For instance, regarding the legal history of marriage, the property of many generations of women, and then in some states, women themselves, legally became the property of their husbands when they married: "A married woman could not own property because she *was* property" (Paul, 2017, p. 404). These restrictions extended to other financial/economic resources, such as taking out a loan or holding a bank account; the latter of which were only removed in the U.S. in 1974, with the passage of the Equal Credit Opportunity Act (Kratz, 2023). However, from the start of the U.S. government, numerous efforts were undertaken to change property and financial rights for women, although the last of these laws were not repealed until the middle of the twentieth century. Regarding same sex/same gender marriages and marriages of people who define themselves other than as men and women, these issues have only been dealt with in the twenty-first century, and in just the last few years have been codified into law for the entire country (Salmon, 2019). Since the U.S. operates through an assumed sex binary, the power exercised over TGNC people has been codified in a slightly different way. Obtaining a credit card, for instance, as a transgender woman was never specifically outlawed, but being transgender, and particularly *expressing* gender in a trans manner was criminalized in various ways depending on the state (Brightman et al., 2023; Ftacek, 2021).

Clearly power has been most often defined through a subjugation/domination lens. However, more recent postmodern understandings of power, including in psychology, have moved beyond the sociopolitical definitions of ownership and dominant/submissive paradigms. Jones (2003) described these approaches as rejecting any single entity or discourse as being "all-powerful," instead promoting "a view of power as process, whereby competing voices, positions, or discourses attain or lose dominance or focus. From this viewpoint, power is not just the property of the center or mainstream, and marginal positions do not inevitably lack power" (p. 32). Postmodern approaches in psychology incorporate multiple influences, such as culture and center-margin dynamics, to more effectively understand the role that power plays in gender-related dynamics (as well as other marginalized group identities).

Power Analysis

An important aspect about studying gender and psychology is engaging in power analysis. As noted earlier, gender is "a system of power relations that are embedded within other power relations" (Stewart & McDermott, 2004, p. 519), including race, socioeconomic status (SES), sexual orientation, gender identity and so on. As we begin to analyze power and gender, some important terms need to be defined. For example, the construct of *privilege* refers to the unearned benefits people receive based on their social status characteristics (Leavy, 2017); another way to describe privilege is the ability to live one's life without question or harassment. McIntosh (1989, in Leavy) famously described the "invisible knapsack" of unearned advantages based on both race and gender that pervade much of American life. An example of gender privilege is how men are referred to solely as "Mr", whereas women have multiple terms (e.g., Miss, Mrs, Ms) in connection to their relationship status and TGNC people developed their own terms (e.g., Mx). As Leavy notes, "The greatest privilege of all is not recognizing how you benefit from privilege. People who benefit from unearned privileges are generally oblivious to them, as they have been socialized to be. Privilege and power are invisible to those who have it" (p. 2). Privilege remains a salient concern for people living in the U.S. and around the world. In examining who has access to important resources, even in the last five years, demographic information indicates continuing stark differences among various groups of people, as based on gender (e.g., gender wage gap, see Chap. 4) and race.

Oppression is a complementary term of privilege and refers to the experiences of those individuals who may never receive resources and other forms of power due to their social status, as based on race, gender, religion, and so on; in other words, these are individuals who may be questioned or harassed by others without much accountability by authorities (Miville & Ferguson, 2014). In Chap. 4, we will review stark gender differences in terms of access to education and salaries for people of different genders through an intersectional lens. Although the trends in education have reached parity for men and women, their salaries do not yet reflect this parity. Racial intersections also are at play, in that many women of color lag far behind everyone else (e.g., Latinas make 55% of what White men earn). These demographic trends are a major source of evidence of the continuing disparities in power and privilege that exist among people living in the U.S.

The construct of *positionalities* or social locations provide a holistic way of understanding of how both privilege and oppression can intersect, even interlock, various group experiences and identities. Positionalities "possess rank, have value, and are constructed hierarchically, particularly those that are visible and discernible" (Robinson, in Miville & Ferguson, 2014, p. 9). For example, as we just noted, women of color, particularly African Americans and Latinas, are located disproportionately in low-wage jobs that afford little upward mobility (Miville & Ferguson, 2014). This situation exists because, for many women of color, "an individual's position in society is the result of the interlocking nature of race, class, and gender dominance" (p. 9).

Another important term to understand when we look at the gender analysis of power and how the larger society is structured was described earlier in the chapter, *patriarchy*: hierarchical societies in which the power is nearly exclusively held by men (Abraham, 2019; Johnson, 2014; Pharr, 1997), primarily White/Euro-American men in the U.S. Demographic information shows the impact of these structural disparities to this day, especially in education, salary and career (see also Chaps. 4 and

8), health (Chap. 10) and social policies regarding sexual violence (Chap. 11). *Sexism*, a system of oppression that leads to negative attitudes toward women who are considered inferior, is a common attitude within patriarchies (Abraham, 2019; Szymanski & Moffitt, 2012). Patriarchies are also considered as *heteronormative* and *cis-gender*, that is, favoring men who are heterosexual and align with their male biological gender/status. Another aspect of heteronormativity is that relationships (i.e., laws, policies, resources) are assumed only to be between cis-gender men and women (Pharr, 1997). Moreover, patriarchies often are based on a fairly rigid gender binary, such that the rights, needs, or resources for TGNC individuals, as discussed earlier, typically are intentionally excluded through law, sanctions, and colonization (Johnson, 2014).

Transgender and gender nonconforming (TGNC) is an umbrella term used to describe people whose gender falls outside of the cisgender binary, meaning those who are either a cisgender woman or a cisgender man, and includes trans women and men, and non-binary people of any gender (Singh & dickey, 2017). It also includes those who identify and/or present as gender nonconforming. In this book the presumptions associated with a heteronormative cisgender patriarchy are considered to be socially constructed and potentially harmful to many people, including men, heterosexuals, and cisgender people. Another important aspect of patriarchy today is the continuing presumption, either directly stated or implied, that being a man (sexism), heterosexual (heterosexism), and cisgender (cisgenderism) are in some way superior and thus "naturally" dominant (Johnson, 2014); individuals who do not have one or more of these characteristics are considered and treated as inferior or subjugated in many critical ways. *Cisgenderism* is the presumption that all people are born with a gender that has a particular biological basis, using only the binary terms of male and female exclusively (Singh & dickey). Men and women are therefore presumed to be the ideal genders, and people who do not attach themselves to those labels are then looked at in a downward negative way. In this book we view these kinds of "isms" as powerful (dominative) in the larger society, as well as quite harmful, including people that come from more privileged identities.

Finally, in addition to adopting negative downward attitudes towards others, there are the processes of *internalizing* these attitudes, or coming to believe these "isms" as true as they apply to oneself and one's communities (Miville & Ferguson, 2014; Szymanski & Moffitt, 2012). For example, regarding sexism, women are told for much of their life that who they are, what they do, what they bring to the table is always less than what men do (e.g., girls cannot do math or science). And at some level, many girls and women come to believe this about themselves, even preverbally, that is, one may not even know or feel these internalized attitudes until they see it in themselves, and make educational and career choices that shift them away from anything math-related. This is an example of *internalized sexism*, in which a person comes to believe the negative and inferior attitudes about oneself. In sum, the negative impact of "isms" are not just negative attitudes towards others, these attitudes actually can be turned inward against oneself and one's communities.

Sources of Power

Another way of understanding power is to examine its multiple sources which are neither necessarily good nor bad, but have different consequences (Biaggio et al., 1997). For example, in examining *rewards* such as giving approval and resources, it is the access to rewards that is critical. At a psychological level, this can be represented as who has the power or right to say "yes" or "no" to any number of important issues, such as asserting "you're healthy" as a human being. Unfortunately, in the field of psychology, there is over a century's worth of negative attitudes toward women and TGNC folks. Only recently have women and TGNC people, particularly people of color, begun to create a public discourse on what "health" means from their own various community perspectives, rather than solely through a patriarchal and Euro-centric colonial platform.

Another way that power can be affirmed or ensconced in society is through *coercive* means (Biaggio et al., 1997), referring to beliefs about power relating to subjugation and domination. In addition to oft-used physical coercion and violence, another form of coercion is psychological subjugation, for example, through disapproval, devaluing, and demeaning a person or group of persons, that is, *psychological coercion*. Moreover, powers are upheld through coercion simply by saying or enacting through policies "because I said so, because I will hurt you, because I can put you in jail, because I get to do bad things to you, without any legal consequence, and I get to take away good things, like your home, your money, your family" and so on. Coercion has been a primary way that many patriarchal societies have enforced their structures, though it is critical to acknowledge that it is not the only means (Abraham, 2019).

Other sources of power emanate from people who are admired or emulated as role models, known as a *reference* power. The importance of having people who look and sound like oneself is a profoundly important source of power, especially for young people, such as students. Role models can be powerful teaching resources by showing others the power inherent in oneself, illuminating important new pathways in life. Power also arises through *information*, in terms of who gets to produce, possess, and dispense information, as well as who has access to adequate and accurate information. Given the many "isms" that have dominated U.S. society, including the field of psychology, access to adequate and accurate information for many critical issues remains a serious concern for multiple communities. An excellent example refers to what is considered "healthy," given the limited number of people who have defined what a healthy person is for any gender. Not surprisingly, for many generations, a psychologically healthy person sounded quite coincidentally, like a healthy White man. This definition in turn was applied to defining health for women, TGNC folks, people of color, who not surprisingly then were relegated to being "less than" and "never can be" fully healthy people.

A final source of power is legally oriented by contract, that is, a *legitimate* source of power. A quick example is when the terminal educational degree and the license/certificate to practice as a mental health professional provides a certain level of legitimate power per the degree and the credential that has been earned. It is notable to mention that professional psychology practice has been, and continues to be in many ways, a driving force of determining what is considered healthy or unhealthy.

Power Analysis of Gender and Psychological Research

Utilizing the analysis of power by Biaggio et al. (1997), we next review research in psychology regarding who has benefited from different sources of power. That is, how has power and privilege shaped what have become understood as facts and evidence, key constructs to the social sciences and the entire endeavor of scientific inquiry. As will be seen in the next section, there are starkly (and embarrassingly) negative examples of how women and people of color were portrayed in the psychological literature up through and including the late twentieth century.

A major benefit of the civil rights movements of the past century has not only been to open up access to voting rights, but other significant resources, including access to higher education for many people in the U.S., including women and TGNC people and multiple diverse racial-ethnic communities, including African Americans, Indigenous, Latinx, Asian Americans, and recently Muslim/Arab Americans. Not coincidentally, psychology began to change as a field as well, once women, TGNC folks, and people of color were able to access graduate study in many disciplines. As people earned degrees in psychology, the field itself began to change (e.g., definition of health). The way psychology viewed women and communities of color significantly changed as women and people of color entered into psychology and began to define problems and develop questions, to conduct research, to create and build psychological knowledge and theories, as well as begin to develop interventions to improve and support psychological health. Today is quite different in terms of how the field defines psychological health, primarily because of who is doing the research. Stanley Sue in 1999 famously challenged psychologists to seriously explore the construct of validity via the generalizability of scientific findings beyond the small subset of participants who were part of research studies in psychology (mostly White male higher SES university students). He demanded to know how and why *external validity* (applicability of findings to diverse populations) had not yet been sufficiently addressed. Sue's call for better approaches to ensure external validity represents a type of power analysis of psychological research that was critical, because it called out the lack of effort to investigate how applicable or valid study findings are for people in general or, more specifically, a particular community or person. Another example comes from Latinx-inspired liberation psychology (Comas-Díaz & Torres Rivera, 2020) which challenges the presumption in Western psychology that there is such an entity as a "universal person" who can meaningfully be decontextualized from their cultural background, gender, SES, and so on. Instead liberation psychological approaches prioritize sociopolitical liberation and systemic change as a form of healing.

Fischer and DeBord (2013) assert it is important to do an analysis of power regarding psychological research, by asking the following questions: (1) Who benefits from the research; (2) How do privilege and power shape what is seen and found ("how" instead of "whether"); (3) Who is and is not represented in the "literature" or "evidence"; (4) What are the research questions, methods, interpretations; (5) What are the motivations of the researchers; (6) How does an "individual" focus may obscure contexts and the dynamics of power. It is important to critique research, and engage in a power analysis of what was done, per the above questions, so as to truly understand what was asked and investigated in a particular study. Liberation psychologists have long criticized U.S. psychology for its decontextualized approach, stating that this ultimately obscures the impact of context and the dynamics of power (Comas-Díaz & Torres Rivera, 2020). Researchers and practitioners need to ask what and how privilege and oppression have played out in studies and interventions. And as authors, we must acknowledge how we have been socialized in this way, too, and that a Western perspective is part of this book.

Qualitative research Patty Lather has a relevant construct about power and research which is to *trouble* the data, that is, to explore research and data "that situate researchers not so much as experts 'saying what things mean' in terms of 'data,'… [but being] situated as a witness giving testimony to the lives of others (in Fotheringham, 2013, p. 1). As researchers begin to "trouble" (critique) psychological research (including their own), their methods, analyses, interpretations, and applications, uncovering presumptions and biases may help form the next set of studies and findings. Potential sources of biases include if it is written vs. handed down orally or on social media, presented in a mainstream journal, is in English (as is this book), and uses a lot of jargon and psychological jargon (Fischer & DeBord, 2013). These all may indicate unexamined Western privilege and power, and potentially inadequate and inaccurate information as a result.

Examples of Power Analysis of Gender and Psychological Research

We can delve a little bit more in depth of power analysis by critiquing two basic "facts" that are parroted regarding gender, one of which is that *women are more depressed than men*, implying perhaps that there may be something in their biology that "weakens" women. Recall the term *hysteria*, an ancient Greek term promoting deeply gendered understandings about anxiety and depression as it occurs in women (Tasca et al., 2012). Hysteria literally means "moving womb," so that women's feeling states, especially as expressed in depression, were long attributed to some kind of weakness in their biology, especially their genitalia. However, what is missing in this understanding is context, especially considering the multiple legal, financial, and education disparities women have lived with over the centuries, as well as the sheer work overload, lack of self-expression about their situation, and legal advocacy regarding domestic and sexual violence. In other words, higher levels of depression in women involves much more than looking at biology, as has occurred with more recent models of depression. Indeed, beginning with Freud, mental health professionals have identified anger and other painful emotions, such as shame, as the more likely cause, especially if one does not feel safety and security (Lamia, 2019). Given the many disparities that occur for girls and women, it is not surprising that depression is more often indicated in women. Oddly enough, many important health organizations still discuss women's propensity for depression by first highlighting biological concerns (e.g., menstruation, postpartum depression, and more recently, menopause), continuing to only emphasize biological dysfunction, rather than highlighting contextual factors as well (e.g., https://www.nimh.nih.gov/health/publications/depression-in-women). It is possible these organizations continue to emphasize biological factors as a means of destigmatizing mental health issues, but unfortunately this has the potential to reify the stereotype about women and physical/emotional weakness.

Consider another common psychological "fact", *men are more aggressive and violent than women,* reflecting something inherent in their biology regarding their "natural" dominating expression. However, is it biology only or primarily, or is it that men have been socialized and rewarded to express certain emotional states, especially those linked with anger and violence? Contextual factors to consider include the kinds of rewards to express these or other emotions (e.g., sadness, fear, affection), and social reinforcements (punishment and rewards) to express some feelings, while suppressing others. There is a much more limited range of emotions that men traditionally may express, and perhaps that might be a reason as to how men might engage in more violent and aggressive behaviors, including verbal behavior. Another consideration to examine is how gender privilege might affect the expression of emotions and behavior, especially behaviors that are more violent and aggressive (recall as well the emphasis on power and patriarchy and how men are rewarded to support these structures and punished if this structure is threatened) (See also Chap. 7).

History of Gender in Psychology

We turn next to some highlights of how gender has been studied in psychology (for more extensive reviews, please see Johnston & Johnson, 2018; Etaugh & Bridges, 2013). There are several phases that best describe the past 150 plus years of research and practice: (1) Gender (i.e., women, TGNC people) as a "problem" (i.e., deficit model); (2) gender differences and similarities; (3) feminist study of women's lives (i.e., focus primarily on cis-women's perspectives); and (4) womanist/intersectional/TGNC perspectives. The first phases in the late nineteenth and early twentieth centuries were characterized by men (predominantly White/Euro-American) nearly exclusively participating and thus dominating the field from the start. As a result, women, and by implication, TGNC people were viewed as some kind of "problem" to consider. That is, much as populations of color were considered from a *deficit* perspective in psychology during this era (Sue & Sue, 2016), so there was the persistent presumption that women and TGNC folks were somehow "lacking" in a permanent and genetic/biological way. For example, women specifically were theorized by some very well known early psychologists (Freud to Erikson) as never being able to achieve a state of psychological development and health, per their theoretical frameworks, thus the emphasis for many decades in psychology were gender differences presumed to be deficits. In line with early theories presuming the stunted development of women, women who wanted to pursue careers normally followed by men, including science training, were viewed as not adjusted to their anatomy which should be about nurturing children. There was a presumption for at least the first century of psychology that *biology was destiny psychologically*, as well as physically. One's biology (unique gender characteristics) determined one's psychology (cognitive and emotional capacities) so biologically healthy or "normal" women were considered as passive, motivated by motherhood, who always spurned achievement. An important note regarding the word "normal" is that it has been an effective tool to oppress those who do not fit particular standards in society.

To be sure, as both Johnston and Johnson (2018) and Chrisler and McHugh (2018) report, from the start of the discipline, there were numerous individual women, along with other public scholars, who "claimed space" and engaged in controversy regarding the social status of women. Famous women psychologists in the initial century included the first woman president of APA, Mary Caulkins (1896, in Johnston & Johnson), a mentee of William James at Harvard, who began the study of sex differences and also challenged the biological nature of differences in gender. Another famous early psychologist was Hollingsworth (Johnston & Johnson) who in 1914 challenged the notion that "women's biology", in this case, menstruation which is critical to childbirth, causes cognitive and physical dysfunction. Yet another highly impactful early woman psychologist was Karen Horney (Chrisler & McHugh, 2018), who had been trained as a psychoanalyst in the Freudian tradition and set about developing theories and constructs that were more representative of women's experiences and perspectives. For example, rather than emphasizing "penis envy" women suffer, leaving them psychologically dysfunctional, Horney suggested that men may instead experience *womb envy*, brought about by the inability to produce children (though it should be noted that there are men who can give birth). She also asserted that women "overvalue love" because of their gender socialization, not because of biology.

The second phase of gender research in psychology focused on sex and gender differences. Although this began with Calkin's work in the late 1800s, research expanded in the mid-twentieth century. Some of this early work demonstrated the deficit model still at work, as in the case of McClelland (1953, in Eagly, 2018) whose research method of student achievement developed with male students then was applied to women. When the same methods did not predict women's success, it was the women participants who were attributed as lacking in motivation, rather than the method itself (Chrisler & McHugh, 2018)! This has remained a challenging aspect of sex and gender difference research over the years: using methods and theoretical frameworks originally developed by and for men can lead to women being erroneously framed as "deficient and devalued" (Chrisler & McHugh, p. 74). Yet at the same time, some valuable research has been conducted over the years within the framework. For example, Deaux (1984, in Chrisler & McHugh) found that sex-differences research "has been used effectively to refute the contention that differences between women and men are universal, significant, and stable" (Chrisler & McHugh, p. 75). Another important aspect of this research is the concern of whether researchers are simply over-emphasizing differences, thereby heightening stereotypes, and diminishing any meaningful understanding of the similarities or parallels across individuals (Eagly, 2018). Another concern raised by Fausto-Sterling (1993, 2000, in Chrisler & McHugh) effectively critiqued the entrenched binary framework. Moreover, the terms *sex* and *gender* can be confusing in their usage. As Chrisler and McHugh note, "To speak of sex differences or sex roles is to strip away the context of behavior and assume instead that it has one root cause (i.e., biology), whereas both first- and second-wave feminists have argued that behavior has multiple causes and is strongly influenced by sociopolitical context" (p. 76). As was recommended by APA in 1977, the term *gender* is now the preferred term, including even for the journal *Sex Roles*.

An important offshoot of some researchers having these concerns has been to simply move forward to develop other research methods, theoretical frameworks, and interventions that emanate from the participants' own experiences, leading to the final 2 phases emphasizing feminist approaches first, and then more inclusively, womanist, intersectional, and TGNC frameworks. The third phase centralizing women's perspectives in both the research and practice of psychology were feminist models. As with the U.S. suffrage movement described at the beginning of the chapter, these feminist frameworks originally reflected White/Euro-American values, norms and customs (e.g., definition of body image) since primarily White women had the means with which to attend graduate study in large numbers. Key aspects of feminist approaches to psychology include the basic belief that the "personal is the political", that is, many of the problems women experience in life are due more to problems in living along with being sensitive to the many stressors and disparities women typically are exposed to (Enns, 1997). This involves treating symptoms as ways of communicating about problems or coping strategies (e.g., dependency as arising from inequality).

As Enns (1997) recognized in her seminal work on feminist therapy, feminist perspectives were developed early on by White scholars without much acknowledgement of the racial and cultural encapsulation of many of these works. Most recently, since the late twentieth century into the present time, began the entry of women of color (e.g., African American, Latina, Asian American, Indigenous, multiracial), in much larger numbers. These psychologists helped to expand current research, theoretical, and interventions models of women, that included both womanist/*mujerista* and intersectional approaches (i.e., considering multiple experiences, such as race and gender) within the same study or intervention (Bryant-Davis & Comas-Diaz, 2016). Perspectives of TGNC individuals also expanded in the last 20 years, as highlighted by the first ever set of practice guidelines being approved by the APA in 2015 (APA, 2015) and major publications for working with TGNC individuals (Singh & dickey, 2017). An important distinction between feminist and womanist/intersectional frameworks is that the former tends to highlight gender solely, whereas womanist/intersectional perspectives incorporate other important identities, such as race or socioeconomic status, as well as men's perspectives, especially men of color. Non-binary perspectives also typically take more intersectional approaches as well in research and practice. (Singh et al., 2017).

In addition to adding new psychological theory and research approaches, women psychologists began to advocate and become organizational leaders in psychology as well. Not coincidentally, these movements occurred around the same time that larger sociopolitical movements were happening, most significantly the voting rights initiatives of the early 1900s and again in the 1960 and 1970s during the second wave of the feminist movement, leading to the protests described at the beginning of the chapter, along with the first APA division and psychology journal to study gender and issues affecting women.

Since that time, another APA division (51) was formed in 1995 to focus on the unique gender issues facing men in psychology, calling attention to important gender concerns faced by boys and men. Non-binary and transgender issues were included in APA Division 44, originally focused solely on sexual orientation. In sum, the past 50 years have seen another phase of tremendous change and expansion of not just who and how gender is incorporated, but also how the field has been organized and led as a discipline. Indeed, the presence of women now is so predominant in psychology, the majority of people pursuing study in psychology are women. The term *feminization of psychology* was coined by Ostertag and McNamara in 1991 to note the change in sex ratio in the discipline. As noted earlier, coining the phrase represents how disciplines as they are initiated are presumed to be male-dominant, such that it becomes news for a discipline to change in this way (unlike teaching and nursing which have always been women dominated).

Diversity of Women in Psychology

Diverse women have been a part of psychology since the early 1900s, although not in large numbers, with the challenges of intersectionality always a salient factory. Early writings by both Black and Jewish women noted their experiences with the challenges of being both women and racially-ethnically diverse. The experiences for example of Rose Butler Brown, the first Black woman to earn a PhD at Harvard in psychology during the 1930s, were quite poignant. She found that her dissertation committee tried to stop her from receiving her degree, and she reflected back on this harmful episode by saying, "I never did discover whether my being a woman or a girl and African American had triggered the reaction. Most likely it was the combination" (Browne, 1969). Mamie Clark, co-author of the famous doll experiments, also described feeling constant pressure to "go back home" to teach in the South (Chrisler & McHugh, 2018).

It was not until the 1960s and 1970s that many more women of color entered the discipline, for example, in 1962 the first Latina woman Martha Bernal earned her Ph.D. as did the first Indigenous woman Marigold Linton in 1964 (Chrisler & McHugh, 2018). Asian American women psychologists became known in the 1970s, with Dr. Christina Ijima Hall being the very first woman president of the Asian American Psychological Association (AAPA), and Dr. Alice Chang forming a women's division in AAPA.

In addition to the inclusion of women, and particularly diverse women in psychology, many organizational leadership positions are now being occupied by women (e.g., most APA Presidents since 2012 have been women or diverse racially, or both). Thus, in addition to just simply having a doctorate and either practicing or engaging research, women of all backgrounds are now engaged in serious leadership and advocacy in the field as a whole. In 2012, APA had its first ever woman psychologist of color, Dr. Melba Diaz, followed a few years later by the first Black woman psychologist, Dr. Jessica Henderson Daniel; since that time, many more women of color have served as APA President than ever in its 125 plus year history.

Men in Psychology

Regarding men and psychology, the presence of men, particularly White men, has never been a concern, as the discipline of psychology was invented around the mid-1800s by men (first psychology professor was William James at Harvard University; Fancher, 2000). However, it would be more than a century later before the study of gender in psychology as this uniquely applies to boys and men would start, that is, the exploration of what it means psychologically to be a man. In 1981, *The Myth of Masculinity* referred to the construct of *gender role strain* (GRS) for men, acknowledging that a privileged social role as a man may have its own psychological impact, especially one that is potentially negative and harmful. GRS was one of the very first gender-based constructs for men that explained the impact of maleness on one's psychological makeup. The counterintuitive notion, that a privileged identity can also be a harmful identity, demonstrated the importance of studying gender not only for marginalized people, but for privileged individuals as well. The notion of GRS, which has a nearly 40-year record of published evidence, implies that the women's movement alone cannot be expected to fully explicate the complexity of men's lives. In other words, psychologists also need to understand what it means to be a man, and any mental health professional needs to understand the impact of maleness on one's mental health. A final point from Pleck on masculine mythology suggested that any society that has narrow definitions of acceptable gender behavior for any person is not conducive to optimal mental health, a significant change in view from the earlier personality theorists.

In addition to the first APA division focused on men and masculinity formed in 1995, the very first conference was organized in 2007 focused on boys and men in psychology. Today, masculinity, like femininity, is no longer viewed as an essentially biologically programmed result of evolution (Kiselica & Englar-Carlson, 2010) by many psychologists. Manhood has come to be understood as a set of complex social prescriptions that each culture attaches to the biological sex of men. This is best understood within the dual patriarchal context of oppression described earlier, such that it is not just men who oppress women, but that men who also oppress each other and themselves through rigid and restricted gender roles. Although these roles can privilege men with power, they can also lead to negative outcomes, especially regarding physical and mental health and associated risk taking behaviors.

Diversity of Men in Psychology

No discussion of gender in psychology is complete without acknowledging the many diverse men in psychology who have played a significant role in advancing research, practice, and leadership/advocacy for many communities. Diverse men in psychology have been around throughout much of the twentieth century, for example, the first Latino psychologist, George Sanchez, earned his doctorate in 1935, and was one of the first psychologists to investigate the impact of intelligence testing and the lack of external validity for Mexican children. He is considered the founder of Chicano educational psychology and was the first Latino psychology faculty member at University of Texas at Austin. In 1970, Dr. Joseph White was the first Black psychologist to call for a psychology for and about African American people in an *Ebony* magazine article. He became known as the father of Black Psychology, living a long productive life as a faculty member at University of California in Irvine, and mentoring many diverse students throughout his entire career. Also in the early 1970s, Asian American psychologist Derald Wing Sue founded the Asian American Psychological Association, and since has become the most cited scholar in the entire field of multicultural psychology. Diverse men were critical in the founding of all of the racial-ethnic psychology associations that exist today, beginning in the 1960s and 70s, and continue to provide important research and practice innovations as well as key leadership and advocacy of diverse communities to this day.

TGNC People in Psychology

Psychology's history with TGNC communities is fraught and filled with overt structural violence, epistemological confusion, and medicalization in both helpful and unhelpful ways (Drescher, 2010). From the formation of the discipline of psychology in the 1800s, psychology has often conflated any and all gender nonconformity with sexual orientation or otherwise sexual preferences (Tosh, 2014). In fact, what occupies much of the history of psychology, psychiatry, social work, and psychoanalysis is a pervasive pathologization of subverted gender norms (Drescher, 2010; Tosh, 2014). There have been many terms used to pathologize or even overtly provide diagnosis for both gender nonconformity and the transgender experience. The most common include the introduction of "gender identity disorder" into the DSM-III when it was published in 1980, along with several terms that are now considered gendered slurs (Kronk & Dexheimer, 2021; Tosh, 2014). Previous to the DSM-III, gender and sexuality were conceptualized and inexorably the same, as in to be transgender or gender nonconforming is the same as to be queer or not straight (Tosh, 2014). Currently, the DSM-V-TR includes "gender dysphoria" as a diagnostic category, which many TGNC activists fought to keep in the DSM due to fears that, if it were removed, insurance would not cover gender affirmative care (Drescher, 2010; Tosh, 2014). We will address important issues more in depth for TGNC people in Chap. 6.

Psychologists have typically viewed sex (presumed biology) and gender as "inseparable and inextricably intertwined" (Yoder & Kahn, 2003, p. 17). However, gender is "what culture makes out of the raw material of one biological sex" (Unger & Crawford, 1992, p. 18). Recent research further helps us understand that there exists no biological sex binary either, but rather a multiplicity of biological factors indicating sex. Today, when gender is discussed as being constructed, biology is recognized as playing a role. However gender also is explored by looking at the unique and collective expressions of gender, based in part on biology, but also on one's personal as well as cultural expressions of that. Moreover, how people define themselves as gendered beings now includes the possibility, the reality, even the normalcy and healthiness, of gender *not* being part of one's identity makeup. Today, gender is best understood as something that one *does*, and also as something one *is* (Johnston & Johnson, 2018). Doing gender is about displaying oneself, enacting roles, and accomplishing things as a gendered (including agender) being.

Conclusion

This chapter has summarized important historical contexts regarding gender in both the larger sociopolitical realm (including historical perspectives) and within psychology itself. We traced important trends that affected the study of gender, such as the scientification of gender and the impact that power dynamics in society and in science have played in how gender has been defined and measured. We identified critical times and people in the field who have played a significant role in advancing more nuanced, flexible, and inclusive meanings of gender.

References

Abraham, K. (2019). *Persisting patriarchy: Intersectionalities, negotiations, subversions*. Springer International Publishing. https://doi.org/10.1007/978-3-030-21488-3

Abrego, L. (2008). Legitimacy, social identity, and the mobilization of law: The effects of Assembly Bill 540 on undocumented students in California. *Law & Social Inquiry, 33*(3), 709–734.

American Psychological Association. (2015). Guidelines for psychological practice with transgender and gender nonconforming people. *American Psychologist, 70*(9), 832–864. https://doi.org/10.1037/a0039906

Anderson, A., Chilczuk, S., Nelson, K., Ruther, R., & Wall-Scheffler, C. (2023). The myth of man the hunter: Women's contribution to the hunt across ethnographic contexts. *PLoS One, 18*(6), e0287101. https://doi.org/10.1371/journal.pone.0287101

Arredondo, P., Miville, M. L., Capodilupo, C. M., & Vera, T. (2022). *Women and the challenge of STEM Professions: Thriving in a chilly climate*. Springer. https://doi.org/10.1007/978-3-030-62201-5

Biaggio, M., Paget, T. L., & Chenoweth, M. S. (1997). A model for ethical management of faculty—Student dual relationships. *Professional Psychology: Research and Practice, 28*(2), 184–189. https://doi.org/10.1037/0735-7028.28.2.184

Blackless, M., Charuvastra, A., Derryck, A., Fausto-Sterling, A., Lauzanne, K., & Lee, E. (2000). How sexually dimorphic are we? Review and synthesis. *American Journal of Human Biology: The Official Journal of the Human Biology Council, 12*(2), 151–166. https://doi.org/10.1002/(SICI)1520-6300(200003/04)12:2<151::AID-AJHB1>3.0.CO;2-F

Boehnke, K., & Wong, B. (2011). Adolescent political activism and long-term happiness: A 21-year longitudinal study on the development of micro- and macrosocial worries. *Personality & Social Psychology Bulletin, 37*(3), 435–447. https://doi.org/10.1177/0146167210397553

Brightman, S., Lenning, E., Lurie, K. J., & DeJong, C. (2023). Anti-transgender ideology, laws, and homicide: An analysis of the trifecta of violence. *Homicide Studies*, 10887679231201803. https://doi.org/10.1177/10887679231201803

Brown. (2024, January 5). *The development of agriculture*. National Geographic. https://education.nationalgeographic.org/resource/development-agriculture

Browne, R. B. (1969). *Love my children: An autobiography*. Meredith Press.

Bryant-Davis, T., & Comas-Díaz, L. (Eds.). (2016). *Womanist and mujerista psychologies: Voices of fire, acts of courage*. American Psychological Association.

Chrisler, J. C., & McHugh, M. C. (2018). Feminist critiques of psychology. In *APA handbook of the psychology of women: History, theory, and battlegrounds* (Vol. 1, pp. 71–89). American Psychological Association. https://doi.org/10.1037/0000059-004

Comas-Díaz, L., & Torres Rivera, E. (Eds.). (2020). *Liberation psychology: Theory, method, practice, and social justice* (pp. xx, 314). American Psychological Association. https://doi.org/10.1037/0000198-000

Conner, J. O., Crawford, E., & Galioto, M. (2023). The mental health effects of student activism: Persisting despite psychological costs. *Journal of Adolescent Research, 38*(1), 80–109. https://doi.org/10.1177/07435584211006789

Depression in Women: 4 Things to Know—National Institute of Mental Health (NIMH). (n.d.). National Institute of Mental Health. Retrieved April 22, 2024, from https://www.nimh.nih.gov/health/publications/depression-in-women

Dreger, A. D., & Herndon, A. M. (2009). Progress and politics in the intersex rights movement. *GLQ: A Journal of Lesbian and Gay Studies, 15*(2), 199–224. https://doi.org/10.1215/10642684-2008-134

Drescher, J. (2010). Queer diagnoses: Parallels and contrasts in the history of homosexuality, gender variance, and the diagnostic and statistical manual. *Archives of Sexual Behavior, 39*(2), 427–460. https://doi.org/10.1007/s10508-009-9531-5

Eagly, A. H. (2018). Making a difference: Feminist scholarship. In *APA handbook of the psychology of women: History, theory, and battlegrounds* (Vol. 1, pp. 91–108). American Psychological Association. https://doi.org/10.1037/0000059-005

Enns, C. Z. (1997). *Feminist theories and feminist psychotherapies: Origins, themes, and variations*. Haworth Press.
Etaugh, C., & Bridges, J. (2013). *Women's lives: A psychological perspective* (3rd Ed). Routledge.
Fausto-Sterling, A. (1993). The five sexes. *The Sciences, 33*(2), 20–24. https://doi.org/10.1002/j.2326-1951.1993.tb03081.x
Fausto-Sterling, A. (2000). *Sexing the body: Gender politics and the construction of sexuality* (1st ed.). Basic Books.
Fausto-Sterling, A. (2012). *Sex/gender: Biology in a social world*. Routledge.
Fischer, A. R., & DeBord, K. A. (2013). Critical questioning of social and feminist identity development literature: Themes, principles, and tools. In *The Oxford handbook of feminist multicultural counseling psychology* (pp. 87–111). Oxford University Press.
Fotheringham, S. (2013). Exploring the methodology of getting lost with Patti Lather. *The Qualitative Report, 18*(13), 1–4. https://doi.org/10.46743/2160-3715/2013.1541
Ftacek, J. (2021). Reflections: Egg hatching; or, letting the eighteenth century be trans. *Eighteenth-Century Fiction, 33*(4), 577–580. https://doi.org/10.3138/ecf.33.4.577
Geary, D. C. (2021). *Male, female: The evolution of human sex differences* (3rd ed.). American Psychological Association. https://doi.org/10.1037/0000181-000
Gowaty, P. A. (2018). Biological essentialism, gender, true belief, confirmation biases, and skepticism. In C. B. Travis, J. W. White, A. Rutherford, W. S. Williams, S. L. Cook, & K. F. Wyche (Eds.), *APA handbook of the psychology of women: History, theory, and battlegrounds* (pp. 145–164). American Psychological Association. https://doi.org/10.1037/0000059-008
Hyde, J. S., Bigler, R. S., Joel, D., Tate, C. C., & van Anders, S. M. (2019). The future of sex and gender in psychology: Five challenges to the gender binary. *American Psychologist, 74*(2), 171–193. https://doi.org/10.1037/amp0000307
Johnson, A. G. (2014). *The gender knot: Unraveling our patriarchal legacy* (3rd ed.). Temple University Press.
Johnston, E., & Johnson, A. (2018). Reimagining the history of the psychology of women. In C. B. Travis, J. W. White, A. Rutherford, W. S. Williams, S. L. Cook, & K. F. Wyche (Eds.), *APA handbook of the psychology of women: History, theory, and battlegrounds* (Vol. 1, pp. 3–26). American Psychological Association. https://doi.org/10.1037/0000059-001
Jones, L. S. (2003). Power and women in the counseling relationship. In M. K. Kopala & M. A. Keitel (Eds.), *Handbook of counseling women* (pp. 31–39). Sage.
Kiselica, M. S., & Englar-Carlson, M. (2010). Identifying, affirming, and building upon male strengths: The positive psychology/positive masculinity model of psychotherapy with boys and men. *Psychotherapy: Theory, Research, Practice, Training, 47*(3), 276–287. https://doi.org/10.1037/a0021159
Klar, M., & Kasser, T. (2009). Some benefits of being an activist: Measuring activism and its role in psychological well-being. *Political Psychology, 30*(5), 755–777. https://doi.org/10.1111/j.1467-9221.2009.00724.x
Kratz, J. (2023). On the basis of sex: Equal credit opportunities. *National Archives Pieces of History*. https://prologue.blogs.archives.gov/2023/03/22/on-the-basis-of-sex-equal-credit-opportunities/
Kronk, C. A., & Dexheimer, J. W. (2021). An ontology-based review of transgender literature: Revealing a history of medicalization and pathologization. *International Journal of Medical Informatics, 156*, 104601. https://doi.org/10.1016/j.ijmedinf.2021.104601
Lamia, M. C. (2019, June 29). *The perplexing notion of depression as "Anger turned inward" | Psychology Today*. Psychology Today. https://www.psychologytoday.com/us/blog/intense-emotions-and-strong-feelings/201906/the-perplexing-notion-depression-anger-turned
Laqueur, T. W. (1990). *Making sex: Body and gender from the Greeks to Freud*. Harvard University Press.
Leavy, P. (Ed.). (2017). *Privilege through the looking-glass*. Sense Publishers. https://doi.org/10.1007/978-94-6351-140-7
Lugones, M. (2007). Heterosexualism and the colonial/modern gender system. *Hypatia, 22*(1), 186–209. http://www.jstor.org/stable/4640051

Miville, M. L. (2018). No rest for the nasty: Mentoring as mobilizing for change and advocacy. *The Counseling Psychologist, 46*(1), 100–115. https://doi.org/10.1177/0011000018754323

Miville, M. L., & Ferguson, A. D. (2014). Intersections of race-ethnicity and gender on identity development and social roles. In M. L. Miville & A. D. Ferguson (Eds.), *Handbook of race-ethnicity and gender in psychology* (pp. 3–21). Springer. https://doi.org/10.1007/978-1-4614-8860-6_1

Ostertag, P. A., & McNamara, J. R. (1991). "Feminization" of psychology: The changing sex ratio and its implications for the profession. *Psychology of Women Quarterly, 15*(3), 349–369. https://doi.org/10.1111/j.1471-6402.1991.tb00413.x

Paul, K. (2017). Private/property: A discourse on gender inequality in American Law. *Minnesota Journal of Law & Inequality, 7*(3), 399.

Pharr, S. (1997). *Homophobia: A weapon of sexism*. Distributed by the Women's Project.

Pleck, J. H. (1981). *The myth of masculinity*. MIT Press.

Pruit, S. (2021). *When did African Americans actually get the right to vote*? History. https://www.history.com/news/african-american-voting-right-15th-amendment?

Salmon, M. (2019). *The legal status of women, 1776–1830*. The Gilder Lehrman Institute of American History. https://ap.gilderlehrman.org/essay/legal-status-women-1776%C3%A2%E2%82%AC%E2%80%9C1830

Schaeffer, K. (2020). *Key facts about women's suffrage around the world, a century after U.S. ratified 19th Amendment*. Pew Research Center. https://www.pewresearch.org/short-reads/2020/10/05/key-facts-about-womens-suffrage-around-the-world-a-century-after-u-s-ratified-19th-amendment/

Sherif, C. W. (1982). Needed concepts in the study of gender identity. *Psychology of Women Quarterly, 6*(4), 375–398. https://doi.org/10.1111/j.1471-6402.1982.tb01067.x

Singh, A., & Dickey, LM. (Eds.). (2017). Introduction. In *Affirmative counseling and psychological practice with transgender and gender nonconforming clients* (pp. 3–18). American Psychological Association. https://doi.org/10.1037/14957-001

Spence, J. T., & Buckner, C. E. (2000). Instrumental and expressions traits, trait stereotypes, and sexist attitudes: What do they signify? *Psychology of Women Quarterly, 24*(1), 44–62. https://doi.org/10.1111/j.1471-6402.2000.tb01021.x

Stewart, A. J., & McDermott, C. (2004). Gender in psychology. *Annual Review of Psychology, 55*, 519–544. https://doi.org/10.1146/annurev.psych.55.090902.141537

Sue, D. W., & Sue, D. (2016). *Counseling the culturally diverse: Theory and practice* (7th ed.). Wiley.

Szymanski, D. M., & Moffitt, L. B. (2012). Sexism and heterosexism. In *APA handbook of counseling psychology, Vol. 2: Practice, interventions, and applications* (pp. 361–390). American Psychological Association. https://doi.org/10.1037/13755-015

Tasca, C., Rapetti, M., Carta, M. G., & Fadda, B. (2012). Women And hysteria in the history of mental health. *Clinical Practice and Epidemiology in Mental Health: CP & EMH, 8*, 110–119. https://doi.org/10.2174/1745017901208010110

Tosh, J. (2014). *Perverse psychology: The pathologization of sexual violence and transgenderism*. Routledge.

Umhoefer, D. (2015). "When the Constitution was written, (only) 20 to 25 percent of the people in the country could vote." *Politifact*. https://www.politifact.com/factchecks/2015/apr/16/mark-pocan/mark-pocan-says-less-25-percent-population-could-v/

Unger, R. K., & Crawford, M. (1992). *Women and gender: A feminist psychology*. Temple University Press.

Wagner, S. R. (2020). *How Native American Women inspired the women's rights movement*. Women's Suffrage Centennial Commission; https://www.nps.gov/articles/000/how-native-american-women-inspired-the-women-s-rightsmovement.htm

Wiesner-Hanks, M. E. (2011). *Gender in history: Global perspectives* (2nd ed.). Wiley-Blackwell.

Yoder, J. D., & Kahn, A. S. (2003). Making gender comparisons more meaningful: A call for more attention to social context. *Psychology of Women Quarterly, 27*(4), 281–290. https://doi.org/10.1111/1471-6402.00108

Chapter 2
Cultural and Ethnic Contexts of Gender

Culture and Ethnicity

The intersections of gender with cultural background related to one's career, education, and family roles first involve distinguishing culture and ethnicity from race (which will be expanded further in Chap. 3). *Race* is a societal construct that assigns individuals an external categorization (Kaur, 2023). In the United States, the term race is used to describe a collection of individuals who share specific physical characteristics, such as skin color, texture of hair, or the shape of their eyes, which are presumed to originate from a shared lineage (Kaur, 2023). The categories for race utilized by the U.S. Census Bureau and other federal agencies are determined by the U.S. Office of Management and Budget and recognize five racial categories: American Indian or Alaska Native, Asian, Black or African American, Native Hawaiian or Other Pacific Islander, and White.

On the other hand, *culture* includes habits, ways of thinking, values, and beliefs, including religion, that is learned during childhood and is a part of one's entire life, although individuals may distance themselves, or even reject, some aspects of their culture (Bryce & Pappas, 2023; CIDA, 2000). Cultural elements and influences can come from anywhere, though each individual develops their own sense of cultural identity (Miville, 2013). *Ethnicity* denotes a collective of individuals with a common cultural background and generational heritage. While often associated with one's country of origin, ethnicity can overlap with racial identity in some contexts (McGoldrick et al., 1982, p. 4; Kaur, 2023). For instance, someone might be racially categorized as Asian while being ethnically identified as Chinese. People can also explore and embrace multiple identities by embracing various aspects like language, nationality, culture, and religion (Bryce & Pappas, 2023). For example, someone might consider themselves Latina American, British Somali, or Ashkenazi Jewish. Each identity encompasses a distinct combination of racial heritage, cultural practices, ancestral roots, and religious beliefs. These identities go beyond simple labels,

M. L. Miville et al., *Counseling and Gender*,
https://doi.org/10.1007/978-3-031-69172-0_2

representing the experiences and histories that shape a person's understanding of themselves and their place in the world.

The interpretation of ethnicity can vary significantly across different regions. In China, for instance, ethnicity is defined with greater specificity, recognizing 56 distinct ethnic groups acknowledged by the government, such as the Han, Mongols, and Uyghurs (Dede, n.d.). When it comes to identifying race, ethnicity, and gender on census surveys and various forms, the process is largely based on an individual's self-identification. However, societal perceptions often exert a significant influence on how people's racial, ethnic, and gender identities are perceived by others, which may not align with their self-perception. Therefore, in terms of understanding a person's unique heritage and value system, ethnic identity may be more informative than race (Atkinson et al., 1993; Johnson, 1990; Hays, 1996).

When considering gender and ethnic identity and culture, it is crucial to consider historically constructed gender-related issues that are a part of one's cultural and ethnic makeup, including gender roles, employment and labor division, and familial responsibilities, and the social implications these have on mental well-being related to gender. As described in Chap. 1, cultural contexts have significantly influenced how gender has been perceived and understood throughout history in different cultures, starting with psychologists originally viewing gender as "what culture makes out [of] the 'raw material' of biological sex (Unger & Crawford, 1992, p. 18) to the more recent shift where many psychologists are beginning to conceptualize gender as being more about what individuals' do" and how they present themselves (Wood & Eagly, 2015).

Socialization Practices and Individual Identity

Gender socialization is complex and can best be understood as it relates to an individual's upbringing and other dimensions of their identity based on geographic origins, parents' education, generational and socioeconomic status, religious affiliation, and status as an immigrant or non-immigrant (Agree, 2017). As gender relates to ethnic identity, it is essential to be mindful of how ethnicity can negatively and positively affect individuals (Ifekwunigwe, 2004). On the one hand, like race and gender, it has been used as a means to marginalize or oppress people, as exemplified by the Rwandan genocide in 1994 (United Nations, n.d.). On the other hand, ethnicity can also empower individuals by allowing them to control how they define their identities, as described by the scholar Gloria Anzaldúa for Latina Americans regarding "borderland" experiences (2022; Hays, 1996). Socialization practices, rooted in cultural beliefs and traditions, significantly influence how individuals understand themselves as gendered beings. From childhood, individuals are exposed to specific gender norms and expectations, shaping their behavior, values, and aspirations. These socialization practices can vary widely across ethnic communities, reinforcing stereotypes and expectations for people of all genders.

To expand upon the intricate connections between culture, ethnicity, and gender, we present various examples from various cultural origins in the U.S. The examples span a range of ethnicities and cultures, including Latina/x/e/o, Asian ethnicities, Native American, and Black/African American, investigating the influence of cultural and ethnic variables on gender roles and identity within specific communities. Although not exhaustive, we hope to provide insights into the diverse gender experiences observed across various cultural contexts. We then discuss how gender roles and expectations may appear within specific religious contexts and generationally.

Latine Multicultural Worldview

According to the U.S. Census, Latine (gender-inclusive word for people of Latin American origin or descent; Merriam-Webster, 2023) Americans make up nearly 64 million people (19%) of the U.S. population (U.S. Census Bureau, 2023). Latine Americans have approximately 30 subgroups who come from Mexico, South and Central America, as well as the Caribbean. They also are made up of multiple racial groups, each with their unique ethnic practices (e.g., White/European, African, indigenous, and multiracial), although much of Latine culture is marked by an acceptance of "mestizaje" (mixed or blended) cultural norms, practices and values (Gonzalez Barrera, 2015). The relationships of the U.S. with many of its Latin American neighbors have often been fraught with political and economic tensions, including historic border disagreements, armed conflicts, and covert actions that continue today. Negative attitudes and harmful policies have resulted that also lead to racialized experiences for many Latine people in the U.S., which will be discussed in greater detail in Chap. 4.

Latine families are characterized by a notably stronger sense of unity than their European-descendant counterparts (Halgunseth et al., 2006). The concept of *familismo* (familism) encapsulates this unique cultural expectation, emphasizing the importance of maintaining close family connections, relying on the family for both practical and emotional support, valuing loyalty to the family, and typically prioritizing family well-being above personal ambitions and desires (Nagayama Hall, 2017; Miller, 2013) This deep-rooted familial loyalty and unity play a critical role in preserving traditional values, particularly among Latine immigrants. For many first-generation immigrants in the United States, preserving the culture and traditions of their homeland is incredibly important. For example, Latine Americans may often embrace the language of their new country while maintaining their original religious practices (Valentine & Mosley, 2000, Borenstein, 2023). Limonic (2014, in Borenstein, 2023) observed that Latine Jewish individuals are in continuous negotiation of their Jewish, Latine, and for those in the U.S., American influences. This preference for integration over assimilation underscores heritage significance for first-generation Latine immigrants. Nonetheless, this attachment to origin culture may evolve with subsequent generations as they become more immersed in Western culture.

Latina women often face the challenge of navigating between two vastly different cultures, grappling with contrasting expectations related to gender that can impede their success in both spheres. As discussed by Gomez and Fassinger (1994), the way Latinas approach achievement can be significantly influenced by their degree of acculturation into Western society, which prioritizes a competitive, assertive, and power-driven methodology. Conversely, Latine cultural norms often prioritize more communal achievement styles, emphasizing the role of women as caregivers and valuing contributions to others as a measure of worth. This divergence in values leads to a situation where Latinas must adapt to Western achievement norms to succeed professionally, despite these being at odds with their cultural heritage. As individuals belonging to two marginalized groups—Latine individuals and women—there is an added pressure to conform to multiple achievement standards, attempting to validate their capacities and contributions within their ethnic and gender identities (Gomez & Fassinger, 1994; Miller, 2013).

Marianismo, for example, is a Latina gender role phenomenon based on traditional cultural norms and the values of Catholicism (Jezzini et al., 2008). Encompassing the concepts of self-sacrifice, passivity, caretaking, duty, honor, sexual morality, and the Latina's role as a mother, the implicit socialized concept of marianismo is often likened to the martyrdom of the Virgin Mary, a significant figure in the Catholic religion (Comas-Diaz, 1988; Ramirez, 1990; Ginorio et al., 1995; Gil & Vazquez, 1996; qt. in Rivera-Marano, 2000). Marianismo expects Latinas to be spiritually and morally superior to men while accepting men's authority (Gil & Vazquez, 1996). This rigid gender identity exerts pressure on individuals to conform, potentially hindering fulfillment and meaning if this conflicts with that individual's aspirations and orientations, such as for feminist women, Latine Jews and other Latines from non-Christian and non-theistic backgrounds, and LGBTQIA folx (Borenstein, 2023; Hays, 1996).

For Latinas, this rigidity lays a foundation for the *Maria Paradox*, a concept related to the roles and expectations placed on Latinas. Gil and Vazquez (1996) asserted that the process of acculturation, a social process composed of changes in cultural patterns that occur after individuals of different cultures come into continuous firsthand contact with each other (Laroche et al., 1998) poses challenges for Hispanic/Latina women primarily due to the presence of traditional gender roles that impede adaptation to life in the United States. Their book provided a psychological examination of the ideology of marianismo and how the "10 commandments of the Maria Paradox" may be limiting. These commandments include: (1)Do not forget a woman's place; (2) Do not forsake tradition.; (3)Do not be single, self-supporting, and independent-minded; (4) Do not put your own needs first; (5)Do not wish for more from life than being a housewife; (6) Do not forget that sex is for making babies—not for pleasure; (7) Do not be unhappy with your man or criticize him for infidelity, gambling, verbal and physical abuse, or alcohol or drug abuse; (8) Do not ask for help; (9) Do not discuss personal problems outside the home; (10) Do not change those things that make you unhappy that you can realistically change. Since these commandments may be limiting, this dual identity between Latine and Western culture necessitates a juggling act. Latinas must present themselves differently in professional settings compared to their personal lives, especially given the traditional Latine cultural emphasis on *respeto* (respect) and the expected roles of women as caretakers.

The struggle of balancing a Western lifestyle with traditional cultural expectations has been explored in various studies (Parra, 2007). While some find the dual identity advantageous, many must conceal their assimilation into Western norms from their families to adhere to expected roles, particularly in the eyes of first-generation immigrant parents who may view "Americanized" aspirations as incompatible with traditional homemaking duties. For example, the cultural perception within Mexican-American communities traditionally does not equate a woman's value with her participation in the workforce, framing her primary role within domestic spheres. However, economic pressures have increasingly pushed Latinas into the job market, a trend paralleled by historical shifts in the United States, such as the expansion of the women's workforce during World War II (Parrena, 2005). This shift not only challenges traditional gender roles but also places additional burdens on the daughters of these working women, who may inherit expectations to contribute financially while also fulfilling domestic responsibilities, a scenario compounded by the limited employment opportunities for their male counterparts. These layered expectations highlight the complex interplay of gender and ethnicity in shaping the experiences of Latinas, underscoring the significant impact these factors have on their lives and the multifaceted challenges they encounter in striving for success and fulfillment across cultural boundaries.

Bratini, Ampuero, and Miville (2013) in their qualitative study on gender roles among Latinas found that Latinas were socialized in many of the ways we described here. As they progressed in their lives, however, they engaged in a "continuous transformation and negotiation throughout the process of learning who they are as gendered beings which includes negotiating among a variety of roles along the way…Thus Latinas' views about themselves and their roles are constantly changing, in some cases from traditional views on gender roles (given their socialization) to more unconventional views on the roles of women in gender and of Latinas in particular" (p. 163).

Latinos (Latino men) also have cultural frameworks to navigate. The concept of *machismo* is a male-gender socialization phenomenon, encompassing the concepts of exaggerated masculinity, physical prowess, dominance, patriarchal authority, and male chauvinism (Baca Zinn & Dill, 1994). Latinos often experience strong expectations regarding fatherhood. Stereotypical images portray them as strict disciplinarians, yet many share decision-making with their wives and actively engage in their children's lives. The role of a man's father significantly influences his perception of fatherhood, both positively and negatively. The complex interplay of machismo and chivalry, or *caballerismo,* further shapes Latino gender roles (Toth & Xu, 1999). *Machismo* and *caballerismo* are bidimensional constructs within Latine cultures, in which machismo embodies negative aspects of hypermasculinity (rigid, controlling); and *caballerismo* represents the more positive attributes of masculinity (protective). These constructs contribute to the complex tapestry of gender identities and expectations within Latine communities.

In their study of Latino men and gender roles, Diaz, Miville, and Gil (2013) found their participants were openly socialized regarding machismo and caballerismo, with most participants being aware of the negative aspects of Latino masculinity (being controlling, power over others). However, "they identified with more positive notions of Latino masculinity, such as thinking of and putting the needs of others first" (p. 111). Latino participants described that, as they became adults, they developed their own sense and style of being a man, many of whom transformed some of the more negative or violent images they were raised with into fuller ways of expressing themselves. As Latino scholar Abalos (2002, in Diaz et al., 2013) suggests, "Latino men have it within their capacity to go beyond the inherited traditional stories of patriarchy and uncritical loyalty that leave them partial selves" (p. 125). Diaz et al. found with their participants who had survived some extremely difficult experiences, these "renegotiations and reconstructions of men's gender roles that both incorporate and transcend the traditional are not only possible, they are necessary" (p. 125).

Asian American Ethnicity/Cultures

Asian Americans are made up of approximately 30 subgroups in the U.S., each of which comprises unique cultural traditions, beliefs, and languages (Corpus & Miville, 2013). Over the past 200 years, Asians immigrated to the U.S. over a number of waves, beginning in the mid-1800s. The first wave consisted originally of male workers from China, Japan, the Philippines, Korea, and India, who eventually were viewed as threats by some White American workers for both jobs and marital partners. As a result, negative attitudes began to develop toward Asian Americans as well as laws restricting both immigration and interracial marriage. Another outcome, described in greater detail in Chap. 3, were gendered racial stereotypes concerning negative images of Asian men and women (Lau et al., 2013).

Like Latine ethnicities, Asian ethnicities are similarly shaped by a rich tapestry of cultural, historical, and societal influences that offer a distinct perspective on gender dynamics focused on community-oriented familial practice. Historically, the composition of Asian American families has been diverse, including arrangements such as split-household families, transnational families, extended families, nuclear families, and households comprising multiple nuclear families. Chinese split-household families were characterized as having a dual structure: men worked abroad for income generation, while the domestic sphere, encompassing childrearing and elderly care, was managed by wives and relatives back in China (Glenn, 1983). This family model was prevalent among Chinese families from 1850 to the 1920s during the initial immigration wave and underscored the cultural importance of familism, which emphasizes cooperation, collectivism, and obligation among family members (Zhou & Gatewood, 2000). These familial responsibilities are traditionally delineated to and drawn from Confucian principles of gender and age that apply to many Asian ethnic groups: from father to son, elder brother to younger, and husband to wife (Chan, 1991). Similarly, the "Three Obediences" concept for women (obedience to father, husband, and son) encompasses familial roles and societal expectations of what it means to be a good wife, mother, elder caregiver, conveyer of traditions and customs, and homemaker with a maternal closeness (Chan, 1991). Evidence for the impact of the obediences concept was described by Corpus and Miville (2013) in their qualitative study on gender among Asian American women in the core narrative of *model minority/model woman*,

> reflecting the myth or presumption that Asian American women are expected to meet idealized prescriptive standards in the United States. In other words, Asian American women are expected to fulfill both the model minority stereotype–that is, not rock the boat–while being academically ambitious, achievement oriented, and financially successful. They also felt expected to fulfill stringent culturally informed gender roles common for most Asian American women, including being subservient to men in the family, supportive of their husbands, and sacrificial of personal educational or professional attainment for the sake of their families. In short, our participants felt they were at the intersection of both stereotypes and cultural scripts regarding their gender roles. (pp. 209–10)

Asian American women often grapple with the tension between their cultural identity and dominant Western American culture, and may find themselves pressured to adhere to societal and familial expectations of being obedient, compliant, and respectful towards their family, particularly older generations (Shih et al., 2019; Shih, 2017; Shih & Pyke, 2010).

Regardless of ethnicity, Asian American women may experience a paradox in American culture as they enter educational and economic spheres. It is implied that they should, on the one hand, act in a way that is consistent with the racial stereotypes hyperfeminine, submissive, quiet, obedient, and passive qualities (Suzuki et al., 2013; Shih et al., 2019). However, there are also depictions of the fierce, powerful, and dominant women, ultimately further exoticizing and dehumanizing Asian women (Suzuki et al., 2013). Within the framework mentioned above, women's roles are characterized by passivity and a focus on nurturing the family's welfare (Hildebrand et al., 2000). With the latter, Asian American women are fetishized in popular U.S. culture as exotic, alluring sexual objects. When combined, these pictures have shaped expectations for how Asian American women see themselves and how other people see and interact with them (Shih et al., 2019).

Regarding Asian American men and gender socialization, some research indicates that Asian American men may view masculinity as complementary to femininity, not its direct opposite (Chua & Fujino, in Lau et al., 2013). Some men may take a more "yin" (submissive) role with parents and authority figures, and "yang" (masculine) concerning other relationships (spouse) or a social injustice. However, most Asian men are socialized to enact fairly rigid gender roles within their marriages and own families. As well, most Asian communities, including in the U.S., still prominently feature hierarchical, especially patriarchal, relations. Lau et al. conducted a qualitative study on gender roles among Asian American men of various ethnic backgrounds, and developed a model of gender role socialization for

Asian American men that describes how cultural values (e.g., country of origin, family, collectivism) influence the socialization process, leading to gender role construction. They noted that gender role conflict (O'Neil, in Lau et al., 2013), which they renamed simply as *tension*, was an important aspect of this process for men: "During these moments of tension and conflict, a participant has the opportunity to reject or integrate particular roles and identities" (p. 194). One area of potential conflict is cultural values, as in the case of one's ethnic values and mainstream US norms: "When cultural values are incongruent with each other, participants must process conflict goals and priorities. To the extent the United States is more individualistic and Asian cultural values are more collectivistic and family focused, an Asian American man growing up in the United States must somehow resolve what it means to be a man from these competing perspectives" (p. 194). Other sources of tension included generational differences regarding roles of women and men, racial, and public "ideal" images of masculinity. Another important process of the model involved *agency*, or the internal processes that occurred when dealing with tension and socializing forces, and the extent to which individuals "actively or consciously take part in their gender role construction versus when gender role socialization arises from external pressures or subconscious/covert influences" (p. 198).

African Diaspora and American "Black Culture"

African Americans make up 50 million Americans, according to the 2020 U.S. Census (Coritz et al., 2023). Although the ancestors of many African Americans arrived to the U.S. by human trafficking during its 400-year history of slavery, today many African Americans also identify with sub-Saharan African as well as Caribbean backgrounds. Thus, today's African American communities are marked by multiple cultural influences, norms, and values. As with Latine and Asian American communities, African Americans have been longtime targets of harmful racial attitudes and public policies.

When considering the lived gendered experiences of folks in the African diaspora within the USA, there is a complex interplay of resilience, fairness (Collins & Champion, 2011; Simons et al., 2007) and self-regulation (Baumeister et al., 2007) amidst exposure to systemic racism and adversity. In general, though, the US literature has frequently overlooked differentiating Africans and members of the African Diaspora from African Americans and Black Caribbean immigrants who have distinct experiences in their ethnicity and culture from native-born Americans who are descended from enslaved West Africans. Among Akan immigrants from Ghana, for example, boys and girls are taught specific cultural values and socialization practices through rites of passage and storytelling (Diabah & Appiah Amfo, 2015). Boys undergo rituals to prepare them for adulthood and leadership roles, emphasizing bravery and assertiveness and girls, conversely, participate in ceremonies emphasizing patience and community (Diabah & Appiah Amfo, 2015). This differentiation in cultures for many Black Americans emphasizes a dilemma that many share: a deep desire to have an identity rooted in "Black culture" (Hudley, 2016; Niemiec, 2020; Simien, 2014).

"Black culture" uniquely has been shared to evolve and adapt to new influences, contexts, and generations, avoiding monolithic standing and encompassing a wide range of elements, including history and heritage, language and vocabulary, music, dance, and art, religion and spirituality, food, fashion, community and social activism (Black, 2023). The development of Black culture in America is a result of historical and social factors, such as the legacy of slavery, segregation, and the Civil Rights Movement and has emerged as a unique and significant component of the broader American cultural fabric. However, hooks (1995) has expressed that "Black culture" has come to be defined exclusively by black men in the US with there "rarely being genuine interest in and concern for the welfare of Black women and their civil rights other than as an extension of the Black male agenda" (p. 130).

Researchers within history and psychology highlight Black familial culture by exploring the dual model of African American family structures as either patriarchal or matriarchal configurations. This structure typically highlights the father as the primary provider or the mother assuming a central role in single-parent households (Stewart, 1990, p. 12). A significant number of African American children have previously been documented to be living without their biological fathers, highlighting the historical importance yet frequent absence of father figures due to racialized systemic forces outside of the family's control (Thomas et al., 2007).

A mother's role within African American families tends to be influenced by marital status, with married mothers predominantly managing household responsibilities without gender-specific roles, unlike White families (Wilson, 1995). Wilson notes the full-time nature of these duties, in addition to external employment, impacts the family's life satisfaction. He also highlights that 94% of African American single parents are mothers, with many viewing single motherhood as a proactive choice in response to various circumstances. Extended family members play a critical supportive role in African American single-parent families, providing various forms of assistance, from childcare to financial support (Jones et al., 2006). This collective effort underscores the extended family's vital contribution to the well-being and development of children within these family structures.

hooks (1995) notes that although women may make the majority of decisions related to children's upbringing and extended family, "these decisions do not equate to a true matriarchy" (p. 144) due to various forms of male dominance via financial support or violence to exert control towards them or their children. More recent studies show that a considerable portion of African American nonresident fathers visit their children on a daily or weekly basis (Thomas et al., 2007). The role of fathers varies from spending quality time with children to providing discipline (Hamer, 2001), whereas others emphasize their role as providers and decision-makers (Thomas et al., 2007). Stewart (1990) described the aforementioned single-parent family as a social institution interconnected with others, supporting values integral to African American communities across various domains, including education and health (p. 10).

Research has highlighted how facing racism not only galvanized African Americans of multiple ethnic backgrounds towards greater political and social justice involvement (Mattis et al., 2004; Niemiec, 2020) but also fostered a deep sense of community and teamwork with the larger Black culture highlighting the importance of education as well. Outside of the United States, though, this can present with challenges. In sub-Saharan African regions, young women are over 1.5 times less likely than young men to be formally employed or undergoing education or training (Santos & Rubiano-Matulevich, 2019), with similar statistics for other African diaspora immigrants. There can be unequal access to education, early marriage, and unpaid domestic duties that contribute significantly to the gender gap in technical and vocational education and training (TVET). In the United States, Black women have been instrumental in advocating for furthering their own educational rights igniting the fight for educational equality (Rhodes, 2020). Marguerite Daisy Carr, New Jersey natives Gladys Hedgepeth and Berline Williams, and Trenton, New Jersey native Gladys Hedgepeth, for example, were the sparks that ignited the fight for educational equality within their community. They played a crucial role in advancing civil rights during the 1950s and 1960s. Figures like Ruth Batson and Ellen Jackson, hailing from Boston, Massachusetts, dedicated themselves to dismantling unjust laws and policies that denied Black students access to quality education and transportation.

This led to a subsequent advantage for Black women in educational attainment and is linked with more favorable labor market opportunities and stronger incentives for employment for educated Black women. However, Black people, particularly Black men, still lag far behind Whites in their rates of college completion with recent research revealing that about one third of the gender gap can be explained by gender differences in experiences with institutional punishments (Thompson, 2023). Though Black boys and girls have similar family backgrounds and grow up in similar neighborhoods, results suggest that Black girls have a persistent advantage in educational attainment due in part to their lower levels of exposure to exclusionary school discipline and the criminal justice system. Indeed Black men continue to face harsh realities stemming from these differences, with statistics showing that today, more Black men are incarcerated than were enslaved in 1850 (Miville & Sahadath, 2013). In addition, gender differences in early achievement, early externalizing behavioral problems, school experiences, and substance use in adolescence and early adulthood are associated with gender differences in educational attainment (Thompson, 2023). Taken together, these results illustrate the importance of punishment disparities in understanding disparate educational outcomes over the life course of Black men and women.

Redway and Miville (2013) investigated gender roles among African American women using qualitative methods. They found that participants shared narratives that were

> emotionally charged, deeply felt, and often quite painful issues…the core narrative of evolution and change of gender roles recognizes not only the central socialization processes that have so strongly affected their current constructions and experiences of race and gender, but also takes into account the many inherent contradictions, negotiations, and shifts

> that occur among Black/African American racial ethnic norms, the larger society, and within each woman as she makes sense of these multiple values, expectations, and norms in constructing gender roles. (p. 89)

For example, several participants in the study experienced contrasting notions and expectations of femininity learned from both their families and communities, as well as the larger society. Participants were socialized by their mothers, extended family members, church leaders, among others, that their role was "in support of, even subordinate to, those of men who were viewed as leaders" (p. 89). At the same time, they were expected to take on major household responsibilities, should the need arise, that often are linked with more masculine traits, such as independence and autonomy, without any clear indication from others that such traits would be considered acceptable or desirable by others. Some felt pressure to present in a more "ladylike" even Eurocentric way, whereas others were able to see themselves and other Black women through Afrocentric lenses, celebrating Black women's unique qualities and features (pp. 94–95).

Miville and Sahadath (2013) explored gender roles among Black men and found that, like their women counterparts, they "were in constant negotiation about their gender roles and what it means to be a man. These young men perceived that ongoing struggle or evolution, in essence, in becoming or 'being a man' as a process embedded within the social context and the network of relationships a man negotiates with others" (p. 25). A major theme participants identified as critical to one's sense of manhood was responsibility and being a role model or leader for others, far outstripping the more traditional roles of protector and provider usually ascribed to men. The participants, instead, focused on what to teach other people, and the "importance of becoming conscious, being mindful, of one's role as a man, and making decisions about how to act within society, particularly the consequences of one's action, is what distinguishes him from being a child" (p. 26).

The intersection of systemic racism with cultural heritage shapes distinct experiences, and the African diaspora in the US still has more complicated gender dynamics. Despite the fact that most historical accounts focus on Black men, it is essential that we not forget the special struggles and achievements of both Black women and men. Women have played a central position in shaping and experiencing Black culture as demonstrated by their role in advancing educational rights and supporting community well-being. Black men in the U.S., on the other hand, have often been denied the privilege commonly associated with being male in most societies, instead dealing with difficult harsh public policies and social practices, often at high cost to their physical and mental health (Miville & Sahadath, 2013), while at the same time taking major leadership roles in the public civil rights movements over the years. Highlighting the strength and empowerment of Black men and women enhances comprehension of the diaspora and highlights the need for specific assistance to conquer the long-lasting gaps in educational and occupational possibilities. Recognizing the diversity of Black culture and the dynamic roles that individuals play within it, this focus promotes a more inclusive and accurate portrayal of Black culture.

Native Americans

Native Americans represent indigenous people who lived in what is now known as the United States prior to the arrival of Westerners. Over 6.3 million individuals identified as Native American for the 2020 U.S. Census, with another 1.3 million who identified as Latin American indigenous (Sanchez-Rivera et al., 2023). There are 574 currently recognized tribes/nations by the U.S. governments, with over half living in 5 states: Oklahoma, Arizona, California, New Mexico, and Texas. Since the arrival of Europeans in the fifteenth and sixteenth centuries, Native Americans were targeted for particularly harsh policies and brutal military campaigns that led to only a 10% survival rate by the end of the eighteenth century (Sue & Sue, 2016). The impact of these events is still felt today by many if not most Native American people, with major disruptions to family and community functioning, as well as the loss of many cultural values, practices, and languages. A key concern has been described as the "soul wound" (Duran, 2006) regarding the chronic and intergenerational effects of historical trauma.

Cultural vs. racial identity is a complex issue for Native Americans, especially as it relates to gender. The impact of colonization on gender dynamics across tribes in the United States informs current understanding of how Native Americans' roles have been modernly shaped (Burnette, 2015a; Gurr, 2015; Liddel et al., 2021; Theobald, 2019). Historically, regarding women's roles, Native American mothers have been essential to the survival of their families and communities. Pre-colonization, Liddel, McKinely, Knipp, and Scarnato (2021) found that numerous Native American societies were organized along matrilineal lines as opposed to patriarchal structures (Murray, 1998; Shoemaker, 1995; Weaver, 2009), with more modern themes for women's roles including mothers as caregivers, mothers as the center of the family and role models, and women prioritizing family over economic and educational goals. Mothers are now more expected to care for their families' physical and emotional needs, to serve as the family's center and role model, and to be disciplinarians. However, there is still a dearth of research that has examined their roles today.

In numerous Indigenous societies with patriarchal structures, the task of imparting knowledge and skills related to agriculture, hunting, fishing, storytelling, and practical education primarily fell to men (Krech, 2002). It was the duty of elder men to prepare the younger men for roles as warriors or protectors of their communities (Densmore, 1979 p. 6). Despite the tendency of some modern Westerners to idealize Indigenous peoples as the "noble red-man" (Krech, 2002, p. 81), this lifestyle was far from easy, marked by a relentless quest for food. The notion of an idyllic existence in a First Nations' paradise is overshadowed by the harsh realities of their daily lives, which are starkly different from the comforts available in the twenty-first century (Preece, 1999).

Gender relations pre-colonization also tended to be more balanced and equitable compared to European colonization societies, with a notably lower occurrence of gender-based violence (Murray, 1998). Egalitarian gender norms played a role in fostering resilience and mitigating violence (Amin & Chandra-Mouli, 2014; Liddel et al., 2021). In many tribal communities, men and women operated in complementary and non-hierarchical manners (Shoemaker, 1995; Sullivan & Rodning, 2010). For instance, hunting activities were collaborative efforts where men captured game and women processed it (Burnette, 2015b). There was flexibility in gender roles, allowing individuals to undertake tasks beyond those traditionally associated with their gender (LaFromboise et al., 1999; Liddel et al., 2021; Shoemaker, 1995). Such roles in the tribes have been characterized as complementary, cooperative, reciprocal, and balanced, indicating a foundation of resilient and harmonious gender dynamics (Brave Heart et al., 2012; Burnette, 2015a; Guerrero, 2003; LaFromboise et al., 1999; Liddel et al., 2021).

Historical oppression (both historic and contemporary) has influenced current gender roles in Native American communities, reversing original matrilineal gender norms in favor of patriarchy. The spread and enforcement of Western religions significantly diminished the role of women in indigenous spiritual traditions, replacing them with the worship of a single male deity and thus eroding the prominence of women spiritual figures that existed previously (Burnette, 2015a; LaFromboise et al., 1999; Liddel et al., 2021; Mihesuah, 1996; Weaver, 2009). This shift towards a male-dominated religious framework had profound implications, particularly in how Western patriarchal values have since shaped the experiences of Native American men and women in more violent relationships today, serving as a continuation of colonial strategies aimed at cultural suppression, oppression, and the instillation of patriarchal and dehumanizing ideologies (Burnette, 2015a). Christianity's influence, particularly in the Deep South, has also contributed to a culture of silence around the issue of violence, discouraging women from leaving harmful or abusive situations (Burnette, 2015a).

Furthermore, the establishment of boarding schools further eroded traditional gender roles by isolating children from their communities and strictly imposing European gender norms (Brave Heart et al., 2012; LaFromboise et al., 1999; Liddel et al., 2021; Murray, 1998; Vinyeta et al., 2016; Weaver, 2009). These institutions specifically targeted Native American girls, indoctrinating them with Western notions of femininity and submissiveness, whereas boys were socialized to take on more Western notions of masculine dominance. This educational approach was strategically designed to mold the attitudes and behaviors of future generations, perpetuating a cycle of cultural and gender role transformation (Gurr, 2015; Theobald, 2019).

Tribal membership and Native American historical relations with the U.S. government are primary factors affecting issues of identity (Cornell, 1990) with "Two-Spirit" as another example. This identity transcends modern LGBTQ+ labels, offering a unique perspective on gender identity and sexuality within Native American and Alaska Native cultures (Mesa-Miles, 2018; Pruden & Gorman, 2014; Indian Health Service, n.d.). Traditionally, Two-Spirit people embodied both masculine and feminine qualities, frequently occupying a distinct gender status beyond the male-female binary, and were sometimes recognized as being a third or fourth gender, depending on the tribe's traditions (Mesa-Miles, 2018; Pruden & Gorman,

2014). These specialized roles varied by tribe, but they typically included tasks and crafts such as weaving, pottery, and spiritual and ceremonial practices. Navajo Two-Spirit males may become weavers and healers, which are traditionally gender-segregated roles, whereas Two-Spirit females may engage in hunting and leadership. Two-Spirit identity was inextricably linked to spiritual beliefs, which were frequently revealed through divine visions or dreams, granting these individuals important roles as shamans and ceremonial leaders. They also formed meaningful same-sex relationships, adding to the social and spiritual fabric of their communities (Mesa-Miles, 2018; Pruden & Gorman, 2014).

However, the advent of colonialism and its accompanying forces—missionaries, government policies, and assimilation tactics—severely disrupted Two-Spirit traditions. Many of these practices were condemned or forced underground, resulting in the near-extinction of this important aspect of Native culture. In recent decades, there has been a revival among North American LGBTQ+ Native people who are reconnecting with and celebrating Two-Spirit traditions through national and regional gatherings (Mesa-Miles, 2018; Pruden & Gorman, 2014; Indian Health Service, n.d.). This resurgence not only honors their heritage, but also challenges and expands contemporary understandings of gender and sexuality, indicating a powerful reclamation of identity and tradition within Native American communities (Mesa-Miles, 2018; Pruden & Gorman, 2014; Indian Health Service, n.d.).

Religious and Spiritual Socialization Practices

Religion and spirituality, as exemplified by Native American Two-Spirit people, have a significant impact on cultural and societal gender norms, expectations, and family roles (Bellah, 1991; Bendroth, 2002; Cott, 2002). In the United States, religious institutions frequently promote familism (Christiano, 2000; Edgell, 2006), which, shaped by religious ideology, dictates acceptable behaviors and beliefs required to maintain a healthy social structure (Bellah, 1991; Bendroth, 2002; Christiano, 2000; Cott, 2002). Mainstream religious institutions typically promote monogamous, reproductive cisgender heterosexual marriages (Sherkat & Ellison, 1999; Siordia, 2016), reflecting underlying values of androcentrism, gender polarization, and biological essentialism (Bern, 1993; Edgell & Docka, 2007). These values place an emphasis on traditional gender roles, with men in the public sphere and women in the private sphere (Bendroth, 2002; Christiano, 2000; Cott, 2002; Sherkat & Ellison, 1999), reinforcing gender inequality and supporting the idea that men and women are fundamentally different and women are subordinate. More recent research by Borenstein (2023) indicated that at least within Jewish traditions, variability exists among individuals regarding the flexibility of how these roles may be enacted.

If religious institutions reflect patriarchal values in shaping religious ideology, one could argue that such systems disproportionately benefit men at the expense of women (Norris & Inglehart, 2003, 2004; Stark & Finke, 2000; Siordia, 2016). This systemic bias influences religious beliefs, which shape attitudes toward gender roles, exacerbating gender inequality. The Hindu faith offers a thought-provoking juxtaposition through its notion of Ardhanarishvara, which represents the convergence of the divine masculine and divine feminine energies, which together form the cosmic energy (Chakravarti, 1986). This underscores the importance that Hindu practices place on gender equality and equilibrium. In contrast, certain branches of Christianity that use gendered language to describe God frequently reinforce patriarchal notions, contributing to women's oppression (Boersma, 2022). These gender relations are frequently the subject of heated debate because of their significant and immediate consequences for people of all genders.

Gender roles, particularly those of women as wives and mothers, are powerful indicators of cultural change or continuity. The political potential of such symbols is demonstrated by how religious and political movements emphasize women's roles, frequently framing resistance to Western influences as adherence to religious or cultural values (CIDA, 2000). Efforts by various women's groups to reinterpret religious texts and reaffirm traditions that promote freedom and dignity highlight the complex relationship between religious beliefs and national identity.

Religion, Spirituality, and Trans and Gender Nonconforming People

Given the importance of religious/spiritual socialization for gender roles, we next discuss the experiences of TGNC people in this area. Exploring the impact of religious and spiritual beliefs on attitudes toward transgender and gender-nonconforming (TGNC) people reveals a variety of viewpoints within religious communities. According to a Pew Research Center survey (Lipka & Tevington, 2022), religious views on gender identity vary, with a sizable proportion of White evangelical Protestants believing that societal acceptance of transgender people has gone too far, whereas those without religious affiliations tend to advocate for more acceptance (Lipka & Tevington, 2022). These attitudes extend to policy, where a majority of White evangelical Protestants support regulations that align transgender people's public lives with the gender assigned to them at birth, in contrast to less widespread support among Catholics, Black Protestants, and the religiously unaffiliated. Notably, support for policies involving transgender athletes varies significantly depending on religious affiliation (Lipka & Tevington, 2022).

Exline et al. (2021) expand on this discussion by investigating TGNC individuals' experiences with religion and spirituality. Their research discovered that rejection by religious communities (rejection from the culture that the person may have grown up with), beliefs about divine disapproval, and internalized transphobia are all significant predictors of religion/spirituality conflict, which is associated with increased stress among gender minorities. This emphasizes the importance of thoroughly investigating these conflicts in research and clinical settings in order to better understand and support TGNC individuals. Understanding the religious and spiritual dimensions of gender provides a more complete picture of how cultural beliefs and practices intersect with gender roles. This investigation provides insights into the diversity and complexities of gender dynamics in various ethnic and religious communities, emphasizing the need for nuanced approaches in both academic and clinical settings.

Generational Influences on Gender

The consistency of values and needs related to gender and work-life balance is evident across different generations, with cultural and ethnic influences adding nuanced perspectives (Turner, 2014). As an example, younger generations like Millennials (a person born between the early 1980s and the late 1990s) and Generation X-ers (a person born between 1965 and the early 1980s) in the US are more diverse and open-minded when it comes to challenging traditional gender norms compared to Baby Boomers (a person born between 1946 and 1964). According to a study, a higher percentage of Millennials (69%) and Gen Xers (67%) believe that it is beneficial for parents to encourage boys to participate in activities typically associated with girls, compared to Boomers (59%) and the Silent Generation (54%; adults born from 1928 through 1945) (Parker et al., 2017); though it is important to note that all these generations endorsed these attitudes at over 50%. This level of openness can be partially attributed to a broader understanding and appreciation of different cultures, as well as increased education on the importance of gender diversity. Generation Z, born between 1995 and 2015, signifies a significant change. Comprising 32% of the global population, they surpass all previous generations in numbers and boast a remarkable level of ethnic diversity and education. Their impact extends beyond just their generation, as it is rooted in their distinct combination of cultural, ethnic, and gender consciousness. Consequently, they have the potential to greatly influence societal norms and values in a world that is becoming more aware of the connections between ethnicity, culture, and gender.

According to a recent study by Lampert et al. (2021), Generation Z (Gen Z) is showing a distinct set of attitudes that differ significantly from those of older generations. As an illustration, Lampert et al. discovered that 62% of Gen Z respondents expressed support for flexible gender roles, which is an 11% increase since 2014, in contrast to 55% among older groups. In terms of patriarchal household dynamics, it is interesting to note that the belief that the father should be the head of the household has seen a decline among Gen Z. Only 34% of Gen Z hold this belief, which is a decrease of 6% since 2014. In comparison, older cohorts have a slightly lower percentage of 30%. This dynamic reflects a greater acceptance of diverse family and gender structures, which is likely influenced by the generation's varied cultural and ethnic backgrounds and their inclusive education (Lampert et al., 2021).

In addition, there has been a 5% increase in pessimism about the future among 46% of Gen Z individuals since 2014, compared to 37% among older generations

(Lampert et al., 2021). There may be a sense of pessimism present, which could be attributed to a heightened awareness of systemic issues that impact different ethnic and gender groups. When it comes to same-sex marriage, the majority of Gen Z, at 60%, support it, while older populations have a slightly lower percentage of 52% in favor. In addition, a majority of individuals, 52%, support the idea that individuals should have the freedom to determine their gender, regardless of their biological sex. This viewpoint is also shared by 46% of older individuals. These perspectives may shed light on Generation Z's comprehensive grasp of gender and sexuality (Lampert et al.). In addition, there is a noticeable difference in concerns about discrimination between Gen Z and older generations. Among Gen Z, 26% express worries about discrimination, while among older generations, this percentage is 17%. This heightened concern can be attributed to their increased exposure to and consciousness about discrimination based on gender and ethnicity. In general, the unique perspectives of Generation Z may be influencing a future that is more attuned to the complex issues of gender, culture, and ethnicity. These statistics provide additional evidence of the historical shifts in social attitudes that have taken place since the conclusion of World War II. Particularly noteworthy are the various civil rights movements in the mid-twentieth century that concentrated on issues of race, gender, and sexuality (Lampert et al., 2021).

Conclusion

Gender dynamics in various communities are impacted by cultural and ethnic factors. It stresses the importance of long-established religious and cultural practices in shaping gender roles and how these in turn impact people's lived experiences. Although there are similarities in the ways cultures enforce gender norms, this investigation of different ethnic groups shows that there are also significant variations in the internalization and expression of these roles. Both long-established and new social forces work to uphold and alter preexisting gender norms and expectations. This conversation lays the groundwork for a more complex view of gender as an adaptive and culturally situated phenomenon that changes and adapts in response to shifting social mores and personal struggles. Next, we will discuss race and identity in the following chapters, building on this foundational knowledge. It is important to consider the rich tapestry of cultural, ethnic, and religious influences when examining gender.

Case Study

Maria, a 26-year-old White Latina woman who identifies as cisgender and heterosexual, sought therapy for persistent social anxiety and family-related stress affecting her relationships. Employed and in a committed partnership, she navigated life at the intersection of Cuban-American and mainstream White American cultures. Maria reported longstanding difficulties in workplace relationships, attributing her struggles to form healthy boundaries to her family dynamics. She also revealed a history of anxiety and perfectionism, dating back to her childhood, which she feels exacerbates her family conflicts. Her father, although somewhat understanding of her anxiety, made it feel like a "burden," advising her as a teen to avoid becoming "like other Latinas" and to focus on her career. Around that time, she became aware of her father's alcohol issues, coinciding with her parents' plans to separate. Although her father initially supported her move to New York City, Maria severed financial ties, feeling that the money was a form of control. Maria's challenges are deeply entwined with her family's values on self-worth, productivity, and self-sufficiency. Internalized gender stigmas—such as the idea that women are burdensome—have influenced her interpersonal relationships, leading to heightened social anxiety marked by an obsessive concern with others' evaluations.

Discussion Questions

1. How do Maria's experiences reflect the intersectionality of ethnicity and gender? Consider how both Cuban-American and mainstream White American cultural norms have affected her gender identity and how she acts.
2. In what ways have Maria's family dynamics and socialization practices influenced her understanding of her gender role? Talk about how her father's ideas and expectations about gender roles affected her.
3. How do Maria's anxiety and need to be perfect affect her mental health and how do cultural expectations about work and self-worth affect her? Look into how these cultural expectations relate to stereotypes about certain genders.
4. What role might religious or spiritual beliefs play in shaping Maria's perceptions of gender and self-worth? How could these things be inferred from the way her family acts and behaves, even though they are not said directly?
5. How do the difficulties of immigrating and adapting to a new culture add to the pressures Maria already faces because of her gender? Explore the details of balancing two different cultural identities.
6. What kinds of culturally sensitive therapy might help Maria deal with her social anxiety and stress from her family? Talk about how important it is for therapy to recognize and include her cultural and ethnic background.
7. How do Maria's ethnic community's social support systems either help or hurt her mental health problems and experiences with gender-based expectations?

References

Agree, E. M. (2017). Social changes in women's roles, families, and generational ties. *Generations, 41*(2), 63–70.

Amin, A., & Chandra-Mouli, V. (2014). Empowering adolescent girls: Developing egalitarian gender norms and relations to end violence. *Reproductive Health, 11*(1), 75. https://doi.org/10.1186/1742-4755-11-75

Anzaldúa, G. (2022). *Borderlands/La frontera: The new mestiza* (5th ed.). Aunt Lute Books.

Atkinson, D. R., Morten, G., & Sue, D. W. (1993). *Counseling American minorities: A cross-cultural perspective* (4th ed., pp. ix, 387). Brown & Benchmark/Wm. C. Brown Publ.

Baca Zinn, M., & Dill, B. T. (1994). *Women of color in U.S. society*. Temple University Press.

Baumeister, R. F., Vohs, K. D., & Tice, D. M. (2007). The strength model of self-control. *Current Directions in Psychological Science, 16*(6), 351–355. https://doi.org/10.1111/j.1467-8721.2007.00534.x

Bellah, R. N. (1991). *Beyond belief: Essays on religion in a post-traditionalist world*. University of California Press.

Bendroth, M. L. (2002). *Growing up Protestant: Parents, children, and mainline churches*. Rutgers University Press.

Bern, S. L. (1993). *The lenses of gender: Transforming the debate on sexual inequality*. Yale University Press.

Black, Dope. (2023, June 14). What is Black culture all about? *Dope Black*. Retrieved from https://dopeblack.org/what-is-black-culture/

Boersma, H. (2022, August). Saving mankind. *First Things Journal*, pp. 1–5.

Borenstein, J. (2023). *Latinx Jews: Exploring the relationships of acculturation, Jewish identity, and Latinx gender role scales*. Doctoral dissertation, Columbia University. Columbia Academic Commons. https://academiccommons.columbia.edu/doi/10.7916/rrgn-2z91

Bratini, L., Ampuero, M. C., & Miville, M. L. (2013). Latina gender roles. In M. L. Miville (Ed.), *Multicultural gender roles: Applications for mental health and education* (pp. 133–168). Wiley.

Brave Heart, M. Y. H., Elkins, J., Tafoya, G., Bird, D., & Salvador, M. (2012). Wicasa Was'aka: Restoring the traditional strength of American Indian boys and men. *American Journal of Public Health, 102*(S2), S177–S183. https://doi.org/10.2105/AJPH.2011.300511

Bryce, E., & Pappas, S. (2023, February 1). What's the difference between race and ethnicity? *LiveScience*. https://www.livescience.com/race-vs-ethnicity-differences

Burnette, C. (2015a). Historical oppression and intimate partner violence experienced by Indigenous women in the United States: Understanding connections. *Social Service Review, 89*(3), 531–563. https://doi.org/10.1086/683336

Burnette, C. E. (2015b). Indigenous women's resilience and resistance to historical oppression: A case example from the United States. *Affilia, 30*(2), 253–258. https://doi.org/10.1177/0886109914555215

Chakravarti, M. (1986). *The concept of Rudra-Śiva through the ages*. Motilal Banarsidass.

Chan, S. (1991). *Asian Americans: An interpretive history* (Immigrant heritage of America Series). Twayne Publishers.

Christiano, K. (2000). Religion and family in modern American culture. In H. A. Pankhurst (Ed.), *Family, religion, and social change in diverse societies* (pp. 43–78). Oxford University Press.

CIDA. (2000). *Questions about culture, gender equality and development cooperation*. OECD. https://www.oecd.org/dac/gender-development/1850708.pdf.

Collins, J. L., & Champion, J. D. (2011). An exploration of young ethnic minority males' beliefs about romantic relationships. *Issues in Mental Health Nursing, 32*, 146–157. https://doi.org/10.3109/01612840.2010.538813

Comas-Diaz, L. (1988). Mainland Puerto Rican women: A sociocultural approach. *Journal of Community Psychology, 16*(1), 21–31.

Coritz, A., Lowe, R. H. Jr., & Peña, J. E. (2023, October 17). Over half of those who reported their race as Black or African American identified as African American, Jamaican, or Haitian.

United States Census Bureau. Retrieved from New Population Counts for 62 Detailed Black or African American Groups.

Cornell, S. (1990). Land, labour and group formation: Blacks and Indians in the United States. *Ethnic and Racial Studies, 13*, 368–388.

Corpus, M. J., & Miville, M. L. (2013). Asian American female gender roles. In M. L. Miville (Ed.), *Multicultural gender roles: Applications for mental health and education* (pp. 207–230). Wiley.

Cott, N. (2002). *Public vows: A history of marriage and the nation*. Harvard University Press.

Dede, K. (n.d.). *Ethnic minorities in China*. Asia Society. https://asiasociety.org/ethnic-minorities-china

Densmore, F. (1979). *Chippewa customs*. Minnesota Historical Society Press.

Diabah, G., & Appiah Amfo, N. A. (2015). Caring supporters or daring usurpers? Representation of women in Akan proverbs. *Discourse & Society, 26*(1), 3–28. https://doi.org/10.1177/0957926514541343

Diaz, M. A., Miville, M. L., & Gil, N. (2013). Latino male gender roles. In M. L. Miville (Ed.), *Multicultural gender roles: Applications for mental health and education* (pp. 97–132). Wiley.

Duran, E. (2006). *Healing the soul wound: Trauma-informed counseling for indigenous communities*. Teachers College Press.

Edgell, P. (2006). *Religion and family in a changing society*. Princeton University Press.

Edgell, P., & Docka, D. (2007). Beyond the nuclear family? Familism and gender ideology in diverse religious communities. *Sociological Forum, 22*(1), 26–51.

Exline, J. J., Przeworski, A., Peterson, E. K., Turnamian, M. R., Stauner, N., & Uzdavines, A. (2021). Religious and spiritual struggles among transgender and gender-nonconforming adults. *Psychology of Religion and Spirituality, 13*(3), 276–286. https://doi.org/10.1037/rel0000404

Gil, R. M., & Vazquez, C. I. (1996). *The Maria paradox: How Latinas can merge old world traditions with New World self-esteem*. G.P. Putnam's Sons.

Ginorio, A. B., Gutiérrez, L., Cauce, A. M., & Acosta, M. (1995). Psychological issues for Latinas. In *Bringing cultural diversity to feminist psychology: Theory, research, and practice* (pp. 241–263). American Psychological Association. https://doi.org/10.1037/10501-011

Glenn, E. N. (1983). Split household, small producer and dual wage earner: An analysis of Chinese-American family strategies. *Journal of Marriage and the Family, 45*(1), 35–46. https://doi.org/10.2307/351293

Gomez, M. J., & Fassinger, R. E. (1994). An initial model of Latina achievement: Acculturation, biculturalism, and achieving styles. *Journal of Counseling Psychology, 41*(2), 205–215. https://doi.org/10.1037/0022-0167.41.2.205

Gonzalez Barrera, A. (2015). 'Mestizo' and 'mulatto': Mixed-race identities among U.S. Hispanics. http://pewrsr.ch/1Hi1oRN

Guerrero, M. A. J. (2003). "Patriarchal colonialism" and indigenism: Implications for Native feminist spirituality and Native womanism. *Hypatia, 18*(2), 58–69. http://www.jstor.org/stable/3811011

Gurr, B. (2015). *Reproductive justice: The politics of health care for Native American women*. Rutgers University Press.

Halgunseth, L. C., Ispa, J. M., & Rudy, D. (2006). Parental control in Latino families: An integrated review of the literature. *Child Development, 77*(5), 1282–1297. https://doi.org/10.1111/j.1467-8624.2006.00934.x

Hall, G. C. N. (2017, April 13). Familismo. *Psychology Today*. Retrieved from https://www.psychologytoday.com/intl/blog/life-in-the-intersection/201704/familismo

Hamer, J. (2001). *What it means to be daddy*. Columbia University Press.

Hays, P. A. (1996). Addressing the complexities of culture and gender in counseling. *Journal of Counseling & Development, 74*(4), 332–338. https://doi.org/10.1002/j.1556-6676.1996.tb01876.x

Hildebrand, V. P., Phenice, L. A., Gray, M. M., & Hines, R. P. (2000). *Knowing and serving diverse families* (2nd ed.). Pearson.

hooks, b. (1995). *killing rage: Ending racism*. Owl Books.

Hudley, C. (2016). Achievement and expectations of immigrant, second generation, and non-immigrant Black students in U.S. higher education. In C. Hudley (Ed.), *Adolescent identity and schooling: Diverse perspectives* (pp. 123–137). Routledge/Taylor & Francis Group.

Ifekwunigwe, J. O. (2004). Introduction: Rethinking "mixed race" studies. In J. O. Ifekwunigwe (Ed.), *"Mixed Race" Studies* (pp. 1–29). Routledge. https://www.taylorfrancis.com/chapters/edit/10.4324/9780203643617-1/introduction-jayne-ifekwunigwe

Indian Health Service. (n.d.). *Two-Spirit.* https://www.ihs.gov/lgbt/health/twospirit/#:~:text=Traditionally%2C%20Native%20American%20two%2Dspirit,status%20as%20two%2Dspirit%20people

Jezzini, A. T., Guzmán, C. E., & Grayshield, L. (2008). Examining the gender role concept of marianismo and its relation to acculturation in Mexican-American college women. *Semanticscholar.org*.

Johnson, R. A. (1990). Measurement of Hispanic ethnicity in the U.S. census: An evaluation based on latent-class analysis. *Journal of the American Statistical Association, 85*(409), 58–65. https://doi.org/10.1080/01621459.1990.10475306

Jones, D. J., Zalot, A. A., Foster, S. E., Sterrett, E., & Chester, C. (2006). A review of childrearing in African American single mother families: The relevance of a coparenting framework. *Journal of Child and Family Studies, 16*(5), 671–683. https://doi.org/10.1007/s10826-006-9115-0

Kaur, H. (2023, May 30). *The differences between race and ethnicity—And why they're so hard to define*. CNN. https://www.cnn.com/2023/05/30/us/race-ethnicity-difference-explainer-cec/index.html

Krech, P. (2002). Envisioning a healthy future: A re-becoming of Native American men. *The Journal of Sociology & Social Welfare, 29*(1). https://doi.org/10.15453/0191-5096.2788

LaFromboise, T. D., Heyle, A. M., & Ozer, E. J. (1999). Changing and diverse roles of women in American Indian cultures. In *Gender, culture, and ethnicity: Current research about women and men* (pp. 48–61). Mayfield Publishing Co.

Lampert, Papadongonas et al. (2021). Meet Gen Z: Redefining gender roles and challenging patriarchy. *Glocalities*. https://glocalities.com/reports/meet-gen-z

Laroche, M., Kim, C., Hui, M. K., & Tomiuk, M. A. (1998). Test of a nonlinear relationship between linguistic acculturation and ethnic identification. *Journal of Cross-Cultural Psychology, 29*(3), 418–433. https://doi.org/10.1177/0022022198293003

Lau, M. Y., Chen, Y., Huang, J., & Miville, M. L. (2013). Gender roles among Asian/Asian American men. In M. L. Miville (Ed.), *Multicultural gender roles: Applications for mental health and education* (pp. 169–206). Wiley.

Liddell, J. L., McKinley, C. E., Knipp, H., & Scarnato, J. M. (2021). "She's the center of my life, the one that keeps my heart open": Roles and expectations of Native American women. *Affilia, 36*(3), 357–375. https://doi.org/10.1177/0886109920954409

Lipka, M., & Tevington, P. (2022, July 7). Attitudes about transgender issues vary widely among Christians, religious 'nones.' *Pew Research Center*. https://www.pewresearch.org/short-reads/2022/07/07/attitudes-about-transgender-issues-vary-widely-among-christians-religious-nones-in-u-s/

Mattis, J. S., Beckham, W. P., Saunders, B. A., Williams, J. E., McAllister, D., Myers, V., Knight, D., Rencher, D., & Dixon, C. (2004). Who will volunteer? Religiosity, everyday racism, and social participation among African American men. *Journal of Adult Development, 11*(4), 261–272. https://doi.org/10.1023/B:JADE.0000044529.92580.6d

McGoldrick, M., Pearce, J. W., & Giordano, J. (Eds.). (1982). *Ethnicity and family therapy*. Guilford Press.

Merriam-Webster. (2023). Latine. *Merriam-Webster Dictionary*. https://www.merriam-webster.com/dictionary/Latine

Mesa-Miles, S. (2018, September 13). Two Spirit: The trials and tribulations of gender identity in the 21st century. *IndiJ Public Media*. https://ictnews.org/archive/two-spirit-the-trials-and-tribulations-of-gender-identity-in-the-21st-century?redir=1

Mihesuah, D. A. (1996). *American Indians: Stereotypes & realities*. Clarity.

Miller, S. (2013). Living in two worlds: Torn identities and gender expectations of Latinas in the United States. *UC Merced Undergraduate Research Journal, 5*(1). https://doi.org/10.5070/M451020764

Miville, M. L. (Ed.). (2013). *Multicultural gender roles: Applications for mental health and education*. Wiley.

Miville, M. L., & Sahadath, J. (2013). Gender roles among African American men. In M. L. Miville (Ed.), *Multicultural gender roles: Applications for mental health and education* (pp. 23–63). Wiley.

Miville, M. L., Bratini, L., Corpus, M. J., Lau, M. Y., & Redway, J. A. K. (2013). Negotiating multicultural gender roles: A proposed model. In M. L. Miville (Ed.), *Multicultural gender roles: Applications for mental health and education* (pp. 231–246). Wiley.

Murray, V. H. (1998). A comparative survey of the historic civil, common, and American Indian tribal law responses to domestic violence. *Oklahoma City University Law Review, 23*(1 and 2), 433–458.

Niemiec, R. (2020). United in strengths briefing. *Strengths in the Black community, 1*(*3*). https://www.viacharacter.org/news/united-in-strengths-briefing-june-2020

Norris, P., & Inglehart, R. (2003). *Rising tide: Gender equality and cultural change around the world*. Cambridge University Press.

Norris, P., & Inglehart, R. (2004). Sacred and secular: Religion and politics worldwide. *Cambridge University Press*. https://doi.org/10.1017/CBO9780511791017

Parker, K., Horowitz, J. M., & Stepler, R. (2017, December). *Gender, generation and partisanship come into play in attitudes about raising boys and girls*. Pew Research Center. https://www.pewresearch.org/social-trends/2017/12/05/gender-generation-and-partisanship-come-into-play-in-attitudes-about-raising-boys-and-girls/

Parra, M. O. (2007). *Sociocultural, resilience, persistence and gender role expectation factors that contribute to the academic success of Hispanic females*. Kansas State University. https://krex.k-state.edu/handle/2097/353

Parreñas, R. S. (2005). *Children of global migration: Transnational families and gendered woes*. Stanford University Press.

Preece, R. (1999). *Animals and nature: Cultural myths, cultural realities*. University of British Columbia Press.

Pruden, H., & Gorman, B. (2014, February 14). *Two-Spirit people: Then and now*. Indian Health Service. https://www.ihs.gov/sites/lgbt/themes/responsive2017/display_objects/documents/lgbttwospirithistory.pdf

Ramirez, M. (1990). Mexican American children and adolescents. In J. T. Gibbs & L. N. Huang (Eds.), *Children of color*. Jossey-Bass.

Redway, J. A. K., & Miville, M. L. (2013). Gender roles among African American women. In M. L. Miville (Ed.), *Multicultural gender roles: Applications for mental health and education* (pp. 65–95). Wiley.

Rhodes, B. (2020, December). How Black women changed the face of education in America. *National Trust for Historic Preservation*. https://savingplaces.org/stories/black-women-activism-and-brown-vs-board-of-education

Rivera-Marano, M. (2000). The creation of the Latina Values Scale: An analysis of Marianismo's effects on Latina women attending college. *Dissertation Abstracts International, 5-B*.

Sánchez-Rivera, A. I.,Jacobs, P., & Spence, C. (2023). *A look at the largest American Indian and Alaska Native tribes and villages in the nation, tribal areas and states. U.S. Census*. Retrieved from https://www.census.gov/library/stories/2023/10/2020-census-dhc-a-aian-population.html.

Santos, I., & Rubiano-Matulevich, E. (2019, August). *Minding the gender gap in training in Sub-Saharan Africa: Five things to know*. World Bank Blogs. https://blogs.worldbank.org/africacan/minding-gender-gap-training-sub-saharan-africa-five-things-know

Sherkat, D. E., & Ellison, C. G. (1999). Recent developments and current controversies in the sociology of religion. *Annual Review of Sociology, 25*, 363–394. https://doi.org/10.1146/annurev.soc.25.1.363

Shih, K. Y. (2017). Addressing power and resistance with Chinese American daughters-in-law and their immigrant mothers-in-law. In K. Quek & S. Fang (Eds.), *Transition and change in collectivist family life* (pp. 11–20). Springer. https://doi.org/10.1007/978-3-319-50679-1_2

Shih, K. Y., & Pyke, K. D. (2010). Power, resistance, and emotional economies in women's relationships with mothers-in-law in Chinese immigrant families. *Journal of Family Issues, 31*, 333–357. https://doi.org/10.1177/0192513X09350875

Shih, K. Y., Chang, T.-F., & Chen, S.-Y. (2019). Impacts of the model minority myth on Asian American individuals and families: Social justice and critical race feminist perspectives. *Journal of Family Theory & Review, 11*, 412–428. https://doi.org/10.1111/jftr.12342

Shoemaker, N. (Ed.). (1995). *Negotiators of change: Historical perspectives on Native American women*. Routledge.

Simien, J. (2014, February). *5 things to know about black culture now*. CNN. https://www.cnn.com/2014/02/25/living/justin-simien-black-culture-now/index.html

Simons, T., Friedman, R., Liu, L. A., & McLean Parks, J. (2007). Racial differences in sensitivity to behavioral integrity: Attitudinal consequences, in-group effects, and "trickle down" among Black and non-Black employees. *The Journal of Applied Psychology, 92*(3), 650–665. https://doi.org/10.1037/0021-9010.92.3.650

Siordia, C. (2016). On the relationship between gender roles attitudes, religious ideology and familism in a sample of adults in the United States. *Journal of International Women's Studies, 17*(4), 229–244. Available at: http://vc.bridgew.edu/jiws/vol17/iss4/16COREMetadata, citation and similar papers at core.ac.ukProvided by Virtual Commons - Bridgewater State University

Stark, R., & Finke, R. (2000). *Acts of faith: Explaining the human side of religion*. University of California Press.

Stewart, J. B. (1990). Back to basics: The significance of Du Bois's and Frazier's contributions for contemporary research on Black families. In H. E. Cheatham & J. B. Stewart (Eds.), *Black Families: Interdisciplinary perspectives* (pp. 5–27). Routledge.

Sue, D. W., & Sue, D. (2016). *Counseling the culturally diverse: Theory and practice* (7th ed.). Wiley.

Sullivan, L. P., & Rodning, C. B. (2010). Residential burial, gender roles, and political development in late prehistoric and early Cherokee cultures of the southern Appalachians. *Archaeological Papers of the American Anthropological Association, 20*(1), 79–97. https://doi.org/10.1111/j.1551-8248.2011.01029.x

Suzuki, L. A., Ahluwalia, M. K., & Alimchandani, A. (2013). Asian American women's feminism: Sociopolitical history and clinical considerations. In C. Z. Enns & E. N. Williams (Eds.), *The Oxford handbook of feminist multicultural counseling psychology* (pp. 183–198). Oxford University Press.

Theobald, B. (2019). *Reproduction on the reservation: Pregnancy, childbirth, and colonialism in the long twentieth century*. University of North Carolina Press.

Thomas, P. A., Krampe, E. M., & Newton, R. R. (2007). Father presence, family structure, and feelings of closeness to the father among adult African American children. *Journal of Black Studies, 38*(4), 529–546. https://doi.org/10.1177/0021934705286101

Thompson, M. E. (2023). Examining the Black gender gap in educational attainment: The role of exclusionary school discipline & criminal justice contact. *Social Forces, 102*(3), 926–951. https://doi.org/10.1093/sf/soad110

Toth, J. F., & Xu, X. (1999). Ethnic and cultural diversity in fathers' involvement: A racial-ethnic comparison of African American, Hispanic, and White fathers. *Youth & Society, 31*(1), 76–99. https://doi.org/10.1177/0044118X99031001004

Turner, C. (2014, October). Gender and generational differences: The intersection. *HuffPost*. https://www.huffpost.com/entry/gender-and-generational-d_b_5974624

U.S. Census Bureau. (2023). *Hispanic heritage month: 2023*. https://www.census.gov/newsroom/facts-for-features/2023/hispanic-heritage-month.html

Unger, R. K., & Crawford, M. E. (1992). *Women and gender: A feminist psychology* (pp. xiii, 706). Temple University Press.

United Nations. (n.d.). *Outreach Programme on the Rwanda Genocide and the United Nations*. https://www.un.org/en/preventgenocide/rwanda/historical-background.shtml

Valentine, S., & Mosley, G. (2000). Acculturation and sex-role attitudes among Mexican Americans: A longitudinal analysis. *Hispanic Journal of Behavioral Sciences, 22*(1), 104–113. https://doi.org/10.1177/0739986300221006

Vinyeta, K., Powys Whyte, K., & Lynn, K. (2016). *Climate change through an intersectional lens: Gendered vulnerability and resilience in indigenous communities in the United States* (PNW-GTR-923; p. PNW-GTR-923). U.S. Department of Agriculture, Forest Service, Pacific Northwest Research Station. https://doi.org/10.2737/PNW-GTR-923

Weaver, H. N. (2009). The colonial context of violence: Reflections on violence in the lives of Native American women. *Journal of Interpersonal Violence, 24*(9), 1552–1563. https://doi.org/10.1177/0886260508323665

Wilson, M. N. (Ed.). (1995). *African American family life: Its structural and ecological aspects*. Jossey-Bass.

Wood, W., & Eagly, A. (2015). Two traditions of research on gender identity. *Sex Roles, 73*(11), 461–473. https://doi.org/10.1007/s11199-015-0480-2

Zhou, M., & Gatewood, J. V. (Eds.). (2000). *Contemporary Asian America: A multidisciplinary reader* (1st ed.). New York University Press.

Chapter 3
Racial Contexts of Gender

Introducing Race and Gender

As briefly mentioned in Chap. 2, *race* is a social construct that assigns individuals an external categorization (Kaur, 2023). When considering race and racial socialization, these terms have typically constructed how society views racialized stereotypes and the construction of gender. Racialized socialization is the transmission of messages and teachings about race and racism from parents to their children across generations (Neblett et al., 2008, 2016).

Similarly, for nearly a century, psychologists treated gender merely as a nuisance variable, primarily overlooked and constrained within a biological context (Yoder & Kahn, 2003, p. 17). However, the contemporary perspective has shifted significantly, with psychologists more likely to adopt a constructionist approach to understanding gender. Scholars have recognized racial and gendered socialization as a complex construct that includes a variety of messages, activities, and behaviors passed from parents to children, similar also to the way ethnic identities are formed (Bowman & Howard, 1985; Boykin & Toms, 1985; Hughes et al., 2006; Stevenson, 1994). Unlike ethnicity or culture, though, which people are raised with, the evolution of race is often *imposed* from external sources (Crenshaw, 1991). This chapter delves into how individuals comprehend, are socialized, and ultimately define—or choose not to define—themselves regarding race and gender. Today, the prevailing thought is that gender is not an inherent biological trait that permanently defines individuals, similar to race. Instead, it is seen as an aspect of identity that is actively constructed and performed, suggesting that gender is something we "do" rather than a fixed state of being we are irrevocably confined to (Unger & Crawford, 1992, p. 18).

M. L. Miville et al., *Counseling and Gender*,
https://doi.org/10.1007/978-3-031-69172-0_3

Street Race and Colorism

Nancy López, a sociology professor at the University of New Mexico, challenges the notion that race is determined by genetic or biological lineage as well as the idea that race, ethnicity, and cultural heritage are interchangeable terms. She outlines three dimensions of race, beginning with "street race," or how an individual believes other "Americans" perceive that individual's race at the level of the street. Someone's *street race* is a visual social status based on the social meanings assigned to a combination of physical attributes, including skin color, facial features, and hair texture (López et al., 2017). In other words, in a public setting, street race refers to what race do you believe others would assume an individual is based on the person's are based on your physical appearance. Other aspects of street race can include colorism (López et al., 2017), the "allocation of privilege and disadvantage according to the lightness or darkness of one's skin," often interlinked with gender (Burke, 2008, p. 17). Colorism beliefs and practices operate within and across racial and ethnic groups (Bonilla-Silva Ray, 2009), with practices of colorism tending to favor lighter skin over darker skin, as indicated by a person's appearance as proximal to a White phenotype (Hall, 2006; López et al., 2018). Hair texture, eye color, facial features, education, and income also affect perceptions of who is considered dark or light-skinned (Hunter, 2007). Lopez also described two other dimensions of race: (2) "ascribed race," or socially assigned race, which refers to how a person believes others usually classify that person's race in the U.S.; and (3) "self-perceived race," or how one typically self-classifies their race on questionnaires (López et al., 2018, p. 49).

Davis (1991) provided a thorough outline of how this system of racial categorization evolved in U.S. society, with both African Americans and White Americans essentially and unspokenly accepting this system of racial classification (Sandefur et al., 2004). As a result, most persons with African American ancestry have a strong socially imposed identity or "street race." If they were to choose another identity, they would likely receive little social support for that identity. A study by Waters (1991) supports these ideas. She found that although more than half of her interview respondents were aware of non-Black ancestors, none of the respondents reported that they would identify with this part of their ancestry. She concludes, "the 'one-drop rule' operates to keep non-Black ancestors from mattering to Black individuals' present-day identifications" (Waters, 1991, p. 68) within the U.S.

However, there is some evidence that this situation is changing, or at least becoming more complex, due to increased interracial marriage and references to how other countries similarly handle race-related topics. Intermarriage rates for African Americans, though still much smaller than rates for different groups (Carroll, 2007) have been increasing significantly over the past few decades (Livingston & Brown, 2017). This increase has created a sizable population of biracial (Black-White) persons. South Africa's apartheid history influence, where indigenous South African groups are considered Black and descendants of British and Dutch colonists are considered White, has an additional third option, "Coloured." The term *coloured* refers to South Africans of mixed ethnicity, often descending from interracial couplings of Black Africans and White settlers, as well as South Asians until the end of apartheid (Adhikari, 2013; Laster, 2014). These evolving dynamics underscore the need for a more nuanced understanding of race that accommodates the increasing diversity within populations, reflecting a global shift towards recognizing and valuing the complexity of racial identities.

When considering race in the United States, it is always essential to incorporate at least two questions: How do a person identify, and how does one think others see the individual's race if only one box is checked for race on the census. López et al. (2018) urges mental health professionals engaged in both research and practice to critically evaluate street race as a crucial step towards developing a deeper comprehension of the experiences of research participants and counseling clients who may belong to different street races and encounter distinct interactions in their daily lives than might be presumed upon first glance (Lopez et al.), of which might be impacted by gender as well.

Exploring Intersectionalities: Race, Gender, and Context

Self-reflection and understanding street race serves as a foundation for exploring intersectionalities between race, gender, and context that can unravel how these identifications and societal perceptions intersect with other identity dimensions, influencing experiences, opportunities, and social interactions. *Intersectionality* is a framework that recognizes the multifaceted nature of identity, highlighting how various aspects of social identity, such as race, gender, class, and sexuality, intersect and interact to shape experiences and perceptions (Crenshaw, 1991).

Kimberle Crenshaw (1989/1993) is credited for coining the term "intersectionality" in response to the "single-axis framework" dominant in anti-discrimination law, feminist theory, and anti-racism politics. This original framework typically included White women and men of color who focused exclusively on just one aspect of oppression: gender *or* race. While the importance of intersectionality in psychological research is increasingly acknowledged, there is still necessary work to be done. Researchers must consider who is included in their studies, explore the role of inequality, and recognize group differences and similarities (Cole, 2009; Miville et al., 2013). Practitioners must also follow suit with their clients, highlighting the ongoing nature of this research.

Seneca Falls Declaration

Historical milestones and enduring challenges shape the current discourse on the intersections of race and gender. The Seneca Falls Declaration, a pivotal moment in the women's rights movement in the mid-1800s, emphasized the detrimental effects of marriage on women, particularly highlighting the loss of property rights (Onion et al., 2017; Zapata et al., 2017). This moment marked a significant awakening in women's rights consciousness, highlighting a shift towards recognizing and advocating for women's autonomy and equality. However, the journey toward achieving gender equality was divisive. The women's suffrage movement, spanning from the mid-1800s to the early 1900s, was deeply segregated racially, a division poignantly reflected in the controversial stance by famed suffragist Elizabeth Cady Stanton, asserting White women's voting rights superiority over those of Black men (Davis, 1983). Stanton wrote:

> With the Black man, we have no new element in government, but with the education and elevation of women we have a power that is to develop the Saxon [White] race into a higher and nobler life and thus, by the laws of attraction, to lift all races to a more even platform than can ever be reached in the political isolation of the sexes. (in Davis, p. 72)

In stating this, she indicated this country's early history of racial versus gender divide regarding how to navigate through the public policies of exclusion from voting of entire groups of people.

Today, there is a much more nuanced understanding and awareness about the issue of racism and segregation, as it occurred in that initial push for women to get the right to vote. The right to vote, granted via the 19th Amendment in 1920, was practically more accessible to White women, mainly middle-class and wealthy women. As noted in Chap. 1, even with the voting rights movement for African Americans, it was not until the 1960s that women of color could exercise their right to vote in real or proportionate numbers (Enns, 1997). Additionally, it was also not until the 1970s that women of color, in general, began to develop disciplinary focus in psychology and the social sciences, anthropology, and so on, which started to centralize Black women and women of color's experiences (Crenshaw, 1991).

Amid these challenges, Black scholar Anna Julia Cooper called on Black men leaders to confront sexist discrimination, urging a more inclusive approach to civil rights that accounted for the intersectionality of race and gender (Belle, 2015). Her advocacy foreshadowed the emergence of a more nuanced discourse on oppression, which found a powerful voice in the Combahee River Collective's *Black feminist manifesto* in the 1970s, famously highlighting, "We find it difficult to separate race from class from sex oppression because, in our lives, they are most often experienced simultaneously" (in Eisenstein, 1978, p. 4) The manifesto articulated the intricate interplay of race, class, and gender oppressions experienced simultaneously in the lives of Black women, reinforcing the necessity of an intersectional lens in understanding and addressing the complexities of identity and inequality.

Looking today at the roles of both Latinas and indigenous women for voting rights, there has always been a racial divide among women activists, as seen in the 2016 U.S. Presidential race. Many supporters of Hillary Clinton, the first woman to run for U.S. President in a major political party, were women of color, especially Black women who voted 90+% (Davis, 2020). In contrast, White women voted by majority, 53%, for Trump, who then selected U.S. Supreme Court justices who took away reproductive health choices regarding abortion that were in place for half a century. This historical backdrop, enriched with milestones and challenges, accentuates the imperative for an intersectional approach in contemporary discourses on gender and race. Recognizing the intertwined nature of race, gender, and context is crucial in unraveling the layers of individual and collective experiences and struggles, offering a more comprehensive and empathetic understanding of the multifaceted dimensions of oppression and identity.

Power and Positionality

As we described at length in Chap. 1, *power* is a central theme in understanding how various forms of oppression operate. With U.S. history in mind, power is understood as subjugation and domination, particularly from those controlling the resources. Gender is viewed as a system of power relations embedded within other power relations (Stewart & McDermott, 2004). Another critical set of power relations centers on race (Crenshaw, 1991) and is similar to colorism. When examining the concepts of privilege and oppression, consider how they impact an individual's capacity to lead the life they desire and access vital resources. The more power dynamics exist in which a person lacks dominance, the more significant the reduction in their access to opportunities and control over their life. Consequently, as the layers of these imbalanced power relationships accumulate, the individual's experience of oppression becomes increasingly pronounced and impactful in their daily existence.

The construct of *positionalities*, or "social locations," as described in Chap. 1, is similarly related to power (Harley, Jolivette, McCormick, & Tice, 2002, in Miville & Ferguson, 2014). If the group(s) someone is from has a lot of power, that person will likely be located socially on a hierarchy with more access to resources. In other words, people in higher positionalities are more likely to classify, categorize, and construct the social values deemed important in the larger society (e.g., the U.S.). So positionalities, or one's social locations, possess rank and value and have a hierarchy that can be pretty visible (e.g., demographic trends in education and salary). In the media, one's presence or lack thereof is one example of one's social positionality.

In 2020, the election of Kamala Harris as the nation's first Black and Asian woman to Vice President marked a historic milestone, symbolizing a significant shift in the United States's traditional power dynamics. Harris's ascent to such a pivotal position in American politics challenged long-standing norms and reflected a gradual dismantling of entrenched barriers related to race and gender. This breakthrough is particularly noteworthy considering the voting trends observed in previous elections, such as in 2016, 2008, and 1984, where the majority of White women voters appeared to prioritize race and class interests over gender solidarity. In light of the recent Dobbs vs. Jackson Women's Health decision (The National Constitution Center, 2022) overturning Roe v. Wade (1973) and Planned Parenthood v. Casey (1992), it will be intriguing to observe how these dynamics evolve and influence future voting patterns among different racial groups of women, especially among White women, as the nation continues to grapple with complex issues of identity, representation, and rights.

One's positionality in society results from the interlocking nature of race, class, and gender dominance. The election of a single individual, such as Kamala Harris as Vice President, does not instantaneously alter the deep-seated positionalities within society. Instead, it signifies the beginning of a gradual transformation in the foundational structures of our societal norms. Consider the impact on both the current generations (Generation X/Millennials) and younger generations (Generation Z or Generation Alpha) who observed not only Harris' election but also the ascension of women, many of whom would be identified as women of color in the United States, to prominent leadership positions worldwide—including roles like House Speaker, President, Prime Minister, and Chancellor in regions like Asia, Africa, and Latin America. These global shifts challenge long-standing assumptions about the "natural" roles designated by race, class, and gender, questioning the historical norm that leadership is predominantly masculine and necessarily reflective of a country's dominant racial group. Over the past two decades, there has been a transformation in these perceptions, despite concurrent challenges such as racial and gender-based violence and significant legal and political decisions affecting women's rights, like the Dobbs decision.

White Racial Identity and Power

Whiteness and White racialized identity refer to the way that White people, their customs, culture, and beliefs operate as the standard by which all other groups are compared. Whiteness is also at the core of understanding race in America. Whiteness and the normalization of White racial identity throughout America's history have created a culture where non-White persons are seen as inferior or abnormal (Smithsonian, 2022; McIntosh, 1989). For White men, enduring pain silently can be linked to their societal power, where maintaining their status and privilege necessitates appearing unscathed by life's challenges. This silence reinforces systemic racism by valorizing emotional imperviousness despite the significant adversities faced by men of color in various spheres like teaching, employment, housing, healthcare, and legal systems (Liu & Wong, 2018).

Goodman and Brimhall-Vargas (2019) explore the concept of positionality and its impact on the interaction between two distinct individuals: a low-income, gay, White man and a wealthy, heterosexual Latina. These two individuals from varied backgrounds bring unique perspectives shaped by their socioeconomic status, sexual orientation, gender, and ethnicity. The man, while enjoying the societal privileges associated with being White and a man, also faces challenges due to his sexual orientation and economic status. Conversely, the woman, benefiting from her wealth and heterosexuality, encounters societal hurdles due to her Latina heritage and gender. Brimhall-Vargas reflected on this intersectional dynamic, suggesting that although their worldviews might significantly differ due to these positional factors, there is potential for common ground if they acknowledge how their positionality influences their interaction. Knowledge surrounding self-awareness about social advantages and disadvantages can lead to a mutually enlightening exchange, allowing individuals to share insights about diverse experiences. Such an understanding can enhance their perception of how individuals navigate and experience their environment, highlighting the multifaceted nature of social interaction and identity.

Gendered Racism and Double Oppression

The year 2020 stood as a pivotal moment in the United States' ongoing dialogue about racial injustices, highlighted by the harrowing murder of George Floyd and the recognition of the specific dynamics of *gendered racism* as conceptualized by Philomena Essed (1990) and Jioni Lewis (2017). This event catalyzed a broader reckoning with the systemic police brutality that disproportionately affects Black men, alongside men of Indigenous and Latine heritage. The emphasis on Black men is particularly significant, embedded in a historical context fraught with the legacies of slavery and Jim Crow laws, which underscores the imperative for the continued vigor of the #BlackLivesMatter movement.

Simultaneously, the tragic case of Breonna Taylor foregrounded the intersection of race and gender, signaling a pivotal shift in societal awareness. This shift, compared to the landscape years prior when Kimberlé Crenshaw articulated her insights on intersectionality (1991), indicates a growing recognition of the compound marginalization faced by women of color. Crenshaw's framework poignantly illustrates the systemic neglect and erasure that women of color experience, underscoring the necessity of integrating the analysis of sexism and racism to address and understand these intertwined forms of oppression fully. This juxtaposition —between the growing influence and presence of women in power and ongoing systemic disparity issues—underscores Crenshaw's original insights and highlights the persistent relevance of movements like "#SayHerName," and the considerable journey that remains in achieving true equality and dismantling entrenched biases. Intersectionality, as Crenshaw elucidates, transcends a simple binary framework of race and gender, inviting a more holistic understanding of human identity, emphasizing that individuals navigate a complex matrix of interlocking oppressions and privileges. This nuanced perspective is especially crucial for mental health professionals who are encouraged to apply an intersectional lens in their practice.

The notion that men, particularly those from diverse racial and cultural backgrounds, should remain impervious to pain has distinct impacts as it relates to how gendered racism plays out in the US through stereotypes for men as well. Stereotypes play a pernicious role in shaping societal perceptions and interactions. Historical portrayals of Black men, for instance, have evolved from images of subjugation to menacing, agile, and uniquely athletic figures, reflecting shifts in societal anxieties and attitudes in the Civil Rights Era (Welch, 2016). Collins (2004) has also shared that for Black men, "the relationship between race and gender is intensified, producing a Black gender ideology that shapes ideas about Black masculinity…" (p. 6). Black boys and men are often expected to maintain a facade of calmness ("cool pose"; Majors & Billson, 1993) or stoicism in the face of racial stress and trauma that often can affect their health (Hammond, 2012). This expectation can exacerbate shame, especially for boys and men of color, who not only endure dehumanization and violence (Quam et al., 2020) but also face the "invisibility" of their mental health struggles (Franklin, 1999).

This evolution of stereotypes is not confined to Black men. Asian men, particularly during and after World War II and then during the COVID-19 pandemic, were cast into roles that oscillated between subservient positions and perceived threats or "invaders," mirroring the broader geopolitical tensions of the times. Asian men have frequently been depicted in stereotypes as simultaneously effeminate and patriarchal (Chen, 1999). Today, Asian American men's psychological distress is often overlooked due to the "model minority" myth (Liu & Chang, 2007; Shih et al., 2019; Ruiz et al., 2023; Jin, 2021; Iwamoto et al., 2010) which portrays an inherently successful and problem-free individuals, in contrast with other communities of color, thus the term "model minority". However, the complexities surrounding Asian Americans mislead and ignore the group's diversity and individual challenges (Brand, 1987; Siu, 1992). This notion obscures the struggles of those who do not fit this stereotype, potentially leading to neglect or insufficient support for students in need. These stereotypes, whether seemingly positive or overtly negative, act as mechanisms of dehumanization, stripping individuals of their unique identities and complexities. Hyperaggressive stereotypes surrounding Latino men (i.e., machismo) also can have negative effects on many Latinos who may adapt negative behaviors, including violence and substance abuse as a means of taking control of these images and feeling empowered in difficult economic circumstances (Diaz et al., 2013; Miville & Ferguson, 2014). Studies have demonstrated that internalizing unfavorable machismo stereotypes can be harmful to Latinos and their families. Conversely, given the combination of imagery (violent, effeminate, and more recently, "geeky") present in US society, the effect of gendered racism is rather complicated for Asian American men. Liu and Concepcion (2010) emphasized the marginalization of Asian American men brought about by these images as well as the misunderstanding and tension that could arise while negotiating more positive images.

Women of color face a tapestry of unique stereotypes that are distinctly different from those encountered by their men counterparts. As mentioned in Chap. 2, Latinas and Asian women, for instance, often contend with the exoticization of their identities. For instance, while Latinas may be seen as *santas* (saints), eternally self-sacrificing mother figures, or *La Malinche,* a manipulative traitor (Arredondo, 2002), images of Asian women include "the 'good' Asian women as being 'subservient, passive, and docile'; the 'erotic or sensual woman,' a stereotype that arose in the context of anti-immigration policies toward Asians in the late 1800s (i.e., lacking morality) and still in use to promote images of Asian and Asian American women as dehumanized sex workers; the untrustworthy, manipulative 'Dragon Lady'; and the 'extremely conscientious, hardworking, sexless employee or 'busy worker bee'" (Kawahara & Fu, in Corpus & Miville, 2013, pp. 174–175). As can be seen, many of these stereotypes often conflict with each other, with violent, sexualized, and obedient images bombarding people of color daily (Miville & Ferguson, 2014). These are stark contrasts to the prevalent stereotypes affixed to Black women, among many other ethnic and racial stereotypes (Pyke & Johnson, 2003).

In the discourse on Black/African American women, post-World War II and civil rights era narratives have popularized the stereotype of the "angry Black woman." Such gendered racist stereotypes are not merely external labels but can become internalized, influencing how women of color perceive themselves and modulate their behavior in fear of fulfilling these stereotypes. Assertiveness in Black women, for instance, is often misconstrued as anger, underscoring the potency of such stereotypes.

The experiences of African women and Black women of the African Diaspora are shaped by multiple, interconnected levels of oppression, necessitating a deeper understanding of these broader dimensions (Collins, 1990). Patricia Hill Collins (1990) coined the term "matrix of domination" to describe the range of inequalities affecting the construction of gender within this community. Pamela Reid highlights the heterogeneity among Black women, emphasizing that attempts to define them as a single category or a single-axis framework (i.e., just gender or just race) fall short, as their experiences are more diverse than ever before, as historically mentioned in the Seneca Falls Declaration. The potential election of a Black woman president, for example, could significantly alter this narrative, providing an empowering reflection for Black women, as well as women from other racial backgrounds. Additionally, while Black men students face racial biases in education, their maleness may serve as a buffer against particular challenges, making it essential to recognize the unique struggles faced by Black women intellectuals (hooks, 2016; hooks & West, 1995).

The concept of intersectionality is not only a framework for understanding individual identity but also a crucial lens for examining psychological research. Elizabeth Cole's scrutiny over a decade ago into how intersectionality is integrated into psychological studies offers valuable insights (2009). Researchers are prompted to question who is included in their studies, the role inequality plays in their hypotheses, and the importance of identifying both differences and similarities among participants. Cole's framework encourages an examination of the inclusivity of research, the acknowledgment of sociohistorical contexts, and a balanced inquiry into the similarities and differences among individuals. As Milner (2007) expressed even earlier, researchers should be aware of their racialized and cultural positionality in the research process because, when not mindful, the results can be dangerous to communities and individuals of color. More recently, Ellis and his colleagues (2021) suggest that a complete restructuring of the research process is needed. This approach is vital for providing care that acknowledges and addresses the multifaceted nature of clients' experiences and challenges researchers to move beyond monolithic categorizations, considering the multifaceted nature of human identity. Unfortunately, many studies, particularly outside specialized journals, still neglect to address race, ethnicity, and even gender, undermining the depth and relevance of their findings.

In career and counseling settings, understanding intersectionality becomes profoundly personal and professional with the influx of women into the professional counseling industry. It raises questions about the influence of gender and racial-ethnic socialization on career choices. Reflecting on whether the field's leadership resonates with one's cultural and gender identity can profoundly impact one's sense of belonging and purpose in the profession. Moreover, contemplating how someone's multiple identities—such as being a woman of Asian descent or a gender-expansive individual with a White background—intersect and influence professional aspirations is vital. This introspection extends to how one's identity aligns or conflicts with one's professional identity, shaping one's approach and ethos in one's chosen field. Thus, intersectionality not only informs an understanding of societal structures but also deeply influences individual paths and professional landscapes.

To provide an example for helping professionals, when working with a Black Latina, the intersection of race and gender creates unique challenges and opportunities (Sanchez, 2021). At home, they may be embedded in cultural contexts emphasizing matriarchal values, where women hold influential roles as caretakers, decision-makers, and pillars of strength within their families. These cultural norms often reinforce the importance of collective identity, community support, and resilience. However, in the workplace, Black Latinas may encounter marginalized statuses due to race, ethnicity, and gender, which can result in discrimination, stereotype threat, and limited opportunities for advancement. For Black men, the intersection of race and gender brings forth unique challenges and opportunities. They often confront modern stereotypes that depict them as hyper-masculine or dangerous, which can result in heightened scrutiny, racial profiling, and limited avenues for emotional expression. Gendered racism encompasses the specific forms of discrimination faced by people of color that arise from the intersection of racism and sexism. These harmful biases and microaggressions contribute to a sense of double oppression, where individuals face simultaneous discrimination based on their race and gender. Understanding and addressing gendered racism is crucial for fostering a more inclusive and equitable society.

The historical and contemporary depictions of marginalized groups highlight the enduring impact of stereotypes, which are deeply entrenched in the fabric of American society. These depictions are a powerful reminder of the need to challenge and dismantle these simplistic narratives, advocating for a culture that recognizes and appreciates the rich tapestry of human diversity. As we delve deeper into the intricacies of intersectionality, we are called to foster a more inclusive, empathetic, and nuanced understanding of the myriad ways race, gender, and other identity facets converge, profoundly shaping individuals' experiences and realities.

Feminism, Womanism, and Empowerment

Feminism and womanism provide essential frameworks for understanding and challenging gender inequality and discrimination. Feminism, originating from predominantly White women's experiences, focuses on advocating for gender equality and dismantling patriarchal structures (Enns, 1997; UN Women, 2020). Womanism, on the other hand, emerged within Black communities and encompassed a broader perspective that addresses not only gender but also race, class, and other intersecting identities; it also has expanded to different ethnic groups such as Mujerismo for Latinas (Bryant-Davis & Comas-Diaz, 2016). Feminism and womanism provide valuable frameworks for understanding and challenging gender inequality and discrimination. These ideologies emphasize empowerment, inclusivity, and social justice, offering tools for women with historically marginalized identities to navigate and challenge intersecting forms of oppression.

The influence of stereotypes on women's experiences is significant. For White women, endorsing feminist beliefs was often seen as conflicting with endorsing feminine values and norms. However, for women of color, particularly Black women who have been subjected to harmful stereotypes such as the 'angry Black woman,' endorsing feminine values and norms has been positively linked with feminist beliefs (Redway & Miville, 2013). These stereotypes profoundly impact how they are perceived and how they navigate their lives (Crenshaw, 1991). Recent empowerment movements have allowed women of color to challenge and reshape these stereotypes, contributing to a more diverse and inclusive narrative.

Womanism celebrates women's cultural strengths and a commitment to social justice. It incorporates a spiritual basis and can draw from liberation psychology from Latin America (Mujerismo/mujerista) and the women's movement among Asian American women. The experience of multiple intersecting oppressions often leads women of color to cultivate unique strengths, including 'ethno gender intuition, prophetic abilities, and healing capacities' (Comas-Diaz, 2008). For instance, within communities of color, many healers are women. It is important to recognize that these women's identities as women undergo significant transformations due to their esteemed positions as healers (Comas-Diaz, 2008). According to Hoch-Smith and Spring (1978), women healers experience a process of liberation, which enables them to effectively challenge the established gender dynamics. Therefore, the cultivation of empowering abilities enhances marginalized women's status, granting them recognition, autonomy, and access to valuable resources within their respective societies (Espin, 1996).

Comas-Diaz (2008) described the heroine's journey as well. The heroine's journey represents a feminist reinterpretation of Joseph Campbell's (1949) hero's journey. This concept of the hero's journey can be understood as a framework historically associated with individuals' spiritual growth and development within Western male-dominated culture. According to Maureen Murdock's work (1990), the heroine's journey revolves around the inherent desire of women to reconcile their suppressed maternal aspect and incorporate it with a masculine element. This integration is seen as a prerequisite for women to attain a state of fulfillment. According to Murdock, it is argued that women are responsible for addressing the internal division that has led them to disregard their emotions and intuition, which are crucial aspects of their unique way of understanding the world.

Based on this particular model, the heroine's journey can be delineated into five primary stages:

1. The negation of feminine attributes
2. The alignment with masculine qualities
3. The re-establishment of a connection with feminine characteristics
4. The resolution of conflicts between mother and daughter
5. The integration of intuition and rationality

Murdock ultimately guided women in embracing their role as spiritual warriors and emphasized the importance of integrating both feminine and masculine elements within themselves.

Socio-Cultural Profiles and Contextual Challenges

When thinking critically about how one presents oneself, context matters. Clinical assessment models such as Fuentes and Adames' (2014) Sociocultural Profile (SCP) consider issues related to culture, including race, ethnicity, and gender. The SCP promotes engaging in meaningful dialogues with clients regarding different facets of their identity while encouraging practitioners to critically examine the power, privilege, and subordination dynamics that may be linked to each aspect of their identity (Fuentes & Adames). The SCP requires that clients disclose their affiliation with various sociocultural classifications, including race, ethnicity, socioeconomic status, sex/gender, gender identity, religion, sexual orientation, and ability/disability (both mental and physical). After identifying their memberships, clients are requested to identify the systemic and personal statuses linked to them, encompassing power and privilege and whether they are mixed or subordinate. The SCP also encompasses several vacant categories, which enable clients to recognize additional noteworthy sociocultural factors, such as language and appearance, that impact their sense of self and operational capabilities. This tool facilitates recognizing the dynamic, fluid, and synergistic nature of identity by clinicians and clients. Furthermore, utilizing the SCP framework allows individuals to acknowledge that identity is contingent upon the context, emphasizing that certain facets of one's identity may hold greater significance in particular settings.

For example, the challenges and rewards associated with being a Black Latina woman in different contexts have significant implications for mental and physical health outcomes. The dissonance between matriarchal values and marginalized statuses can lead to stress, role strain, and conflicts between traditional cultural expectations and workplace demands. These challenges may manifest as higher rates of anxiety, depression, and chronic health conditions. Understanding Black Latina women's specific dynamics and stressors is crucial in developing targeted interventions and support systems that address their unique health needs (Fouad & Byars-Winston, 2005; Fuentes & Adames, 2014). Understanding these context-specific challenges is vital in developing tailored interventions and support systems.

Conclusion

We delved into the nuanced interplay of race and gender, underscoring the necessity of a thorough exploration of racial identity and its implications in both personal and professional spheres. When assessing race, two pivotal questions emerge: one's self-identification and the perception of one's race by others, particularly in a reductive societal context that often demands classification into a single category. This dual perspective is crucial for mental health providers aiming to cultivate a profound understanding of their clients' racial experiences. A concept that particularly illuminates this is 'street race'—how individuals are racially perceived in daily interactions, which can significantly diverge from their self-identification. This concept, as emphasized by Lopez (2023), offers a unique lens for mental health providers, providing a deeper understanding of the complexities of racial experiences. Throughout this chapter, we navigated the intricate interrelations between race and gender, emphasizing the critical role of racial socialization in shaping gender perceptions and experiences across different racial groups. This examination sheds light on the dynamic and evolving nature of racial identity and its intersection with gender, revealing how these dimensions are molded by and responsive to varying contexts and socialization practices.

By delving into the contrasts between racial and gender experiences in various settings, from familial environments to professional domains, we unravel the complexities that individuals with multiple marginalized identities face. These complexities are influenced by factors such as matriarchal values and marginalized statuses, which play a significant role in shaping individuals' mental and physical well-being. Understanding these systemic factors is crucial for mental health providers and academics interested in the intersection of race and gender, as it can guide more effective interventions and policies. This underscores the need to consider not just individual experiences, but also the broader societal and cultural contexts that shape them.

Moreover, the exploration of feminist and womanist theories alongside the concept of gendered racism offers vital lenses through which we can understand and address the distinct challenges encountered by individuals at the intersection of race and gender. These frameworks not only provide analytical tools but also advocate for a shift towards more inclusive and affirmative spaces that recognize and celebrate the diversity of experiences and identities. Their application in mental health practice and academic research can lead to more comprehensive and effective approaches to addressing the mental health needs of individuals at the intersection of race and gender. This highlights the potential of these theories to not just understand, but also actively address, the challenges faced by individuals with marginalized identities.

In essence, this chapter champions a holistic and empathic approach to understanding the multifaceted nature of race and gender. It advocates for an inclusive dialogue that acknowledges the complexity of individual experiences. By embracing the intersectionality of race and gender, we pave the way for more nuanced understandings and interventions that honor the full spectrum of human diversity, fostering environments where every individual can thrive unencumbered by the constraints of stereotypical categorizations. This approach is not just a suggestion but a call to action for all mental health providers and academics interested in the intersection of race and gender.

Case Study

Liz is a 19 year old Black American cisgender woman who grew up in New York, NY and is currently living in Athens, OH attending her first year of college. She has lived exclusively with other Black people throughout her life and has lived within predominantly African American neighborhoods for as long as she can remember, making her experience in the predominantly White town of Athens notably different. She relays knowing the intricacies of racial dynamics and "knew what [she] was signing up for" when she accepted her admission to the university. She works as a research assistant in the sociology department at her school alongside two Black men and their research director who is a White woman. Despite having a secure racial identity that she has thought about significantly, she has felt uncomfortable being one of the few Black women she sees on a daily basis. Liz has felt silenced in research meetings, distrusted in classes, and undervalued as a student and community member since starting the program. She shared struggling to understand the interpersonal dynamics that happen, especially from her research team who all study race, and has had a difficult time attributing the reactions she receives from them as racially coded. She is considering transferring schools to be closer to home but feels that is her "giving up too quickly".

Discussion Questions

1. How do Liz's experiences show how race and gender are both present in a mostly White academic setting? Think about how her identity as a Black woman affects how she interacts with others and how they see her.
2. How might Liz's upbringing in mostly Black neighborhoods have affected how she sees and responds to racial issues in a mostly White college town? Discuss what it might be like for her to go from being in a racially familiar place to one where she is unknown and treated as a minority.
3. Consider the times Liz felt ignored, doubted, and unimportant. What aspects of gendered racism can be seen in the places she has worked and the people she has studied with?
4. What are some ways that feminist or womanist views might help Liz understand her experiences and maybe even face them? What do you think these points of view can add to the conversation about how to empower people?

5. How does Liz's secure racial identity help her or make it harder for her to get along in new school and social settings? Talk about how racial identity affects how you deal with interactions that are based on race.
6. Liz considers transferring schools as possibly "giving up too quickly." Thinking about what this choice means for you and for society is important. What does this say about the problems that minority students in schools with mostly White students face?
7. Since Liz works with a team that studies race, how can her coworkers, especially the head of the research team, be allies? What do allies need to do to recognize and deal with racial and gender issues in these situations?

References

Adhikari, M. (Ed.). (2013). *Burdened by race: Coloured identities in southern Africa*. UCT Press.

Arredondo, P. (2002). Mujeres latinas: Santas y marquesas. *Cultural Diversity and Ethnic Minority Psychology, 8*(4), 308–319. https://doi-org.ezproxy.cul.columbia.edu/10.1037/1099-9809.8.4.308

Belle, K. S. (2015). Anna Julia Cooper. *The Stanford encyclopedia of philosophy*. https://plato.stanford.edu/entries/anna-julia-cooper/

Bonilla-Silva, E., & Ray, V. (2009). When Whites love a Black leader: Race matters in Obamerica. *Journal of African American Studies, 13*, 176–183.

Bowman, P. J., & Howard, C. (1985). Race-related socialization, motivation, and academic achievement: A study of Black youths in three-generation families. *Journal of the American Academy of Child Psychiatry, 24*(2), 134–141. https://doi.org/10.1016/S0002-7138(09)60438-6

Boykin, A. W., & Toms, F. D. (1985). Black child socialization: A conceptual framework. In H. P. McAdoo & J. L. McAdoo (Eds.), *Black children: Social, educational, and parental environments* (pp. 33–51). Sage.

Brand, D. (1987, August 31). The new whiz kids: Why Asian Americans are doing so well, and what it costs them. *Time*. https://time.com/archive/6710164/education-the-new-whiz-kids/

Bryant-Davis, T., & Comas-Díaz, L. (2016). Introduction: Womanist and mujerista psychologies. In T. Bryant-Davis & L. Comas-Díaz (Eds.), *Womanist and mujerista psychologies: Voices of fire, acts of courage* (pp. 3–25). American Psychological Association. https://doi.org/10.1037/14937-001

Burke, M. (2008). Colorism. In W. Darity (Ed.), *International encyclopedia of the social sciences* (Vol. 2, pp. 17–18). Thomson Gale.

Campbell, J. (1949). *The hero with a thousand faces*. Pantheon Books.

Carroll, J. (2007). *Most Americans approve of interracial marriages*. Gallup News Service. https://news.gallup.com/poll/28417/most-americans-approve-interracial-marriages.aspx

Chen, A. S. (1999). Lives at the center of the periphery, lives at the periphery of the center: Chinese American masculinities and bargaining with hegemony. *Gender and Society, 13*(5), 584–607.

Cole, E. R. (2009). Intersectionality and research in psychology. *American Psychologist, 64*(3), 170–180. https://doi.org/10.1037/a0014564

Collins, P. H. (1990). *Black feminist thought: Knowledge, consciousness, and the politics of empowerment* (1st ed.). Routledge.

Collins, P. H. (2004). *Black sexual politics: African Americans, gender, and the new racism*. Routledge. https://doi.org/10.4324/9780203309506

Comas-Diaz, L. (2008). Spirita: Reclaiming womanist sacredness into feminism. *Psychology of Women Quarterly, 32*(1), 13–21. https://doi.org/10.1111/j.1471-6402.2007.00403.x

Corpus, M. J., & Miville, M. L. (2013). Asian American female gender roles. In M. L. Miville (Ed.), *Multicultural gender roles: Applications for mental health and education* (pp. 207–230). Wiley.

Crenshaw, K. (1991). Mapping the margins: Intersectionality, identity politics, and violence against women of color. *Stanford Law Review, 43*(6), 1241–1299. https://doi.org/10.2307/1229039

Davis, A. Y. (1983). *Women, race, and class.* Vintage.

Davis, F. J. (1991). *Who is black? One nation's definition.* Pennsylvania State University.

Davis, R. (2020). Polling results estimate 94 percent of Black women voters chose Hillary Clinton. *Essence.* https://www.essence.com/news/politics/most-black-women-voted-for-hillary-clinton/

Diaz, M. A., Miville, M. L., & Gil, N. (2013). Latino male gender roles. In M. L. Miville (Ed.), *Multicultural gender roles: Applications for mental health and education* (pp. 97–132). Wiley.

Eisenstein, Z. (1978). *The Combahee River Collective Statement.* https://americanstudies.yale.edu/sites/default/files/files/Keyword%20Coalition_Readings.pdf

Ellis, C., Jacobs, M., & Kendall, D. (2021). The impact of racism, power, privilege, and positionality on communication sciences and disorders research: Time to reconceptualize and seek a pathway to equity. *American Journal of Speech-Language Pathology, 30*(5), 2032–2039. https://doi.org/10.1044/2021_AJSLP-20-00346

Enns, C. Z. (1997). *Feminist theories and feminist psychotherapies: Origins, themes, and variations.* Haworth Press.

Espin, O. M. (1996). Leaving the nation and joining the tribe: Lesbian immigrants crossing geographical and identity borders. *Women & Therapy, 19*(4), 99–107. http://ezproxy.cul.columbia.edu/login?url=https://www.proquest.com/scholarly-journals/leaving-nation-joining-tribe-lesbian-immigrants/docview/61376919/se-2

Essed, P. (1990). *Everyday racism: Reports from women of two cultures.* Hunter House.

Fouad, N. A., & Byars-Winston, A. M. (2005). Cultural context of career choice: Meta-analysis of race/ethnicity differences. *Journal of Career Development, 53*(3), 223–233. https://doi.org/10.1002/j.2161-0045.2005.tb00992.x

Franklin, A. J. (1999). Invisibility syndrome and racial identity development in psychotherapy and counseling African American men. *The Counseling Psychologist, 27*, 761–793. https://doi.org/10.1177/0011000099276002

Fuentes, M. A., & Adames, H. Y. (2014). Theories, models, and practices for understanding gender, race, and ethnicity in clinical assessment. In M. Miville & A. Ferguson (Eds.), *Handbook of race-ethnicity and gender in psychology.* Springer. https://doi.org/10.1007/978-1-4614-8860-6_14

Goodman, L., & Brimhall-Vargas, M. (2019, October). What are intersectionality, privilege and positionality? *Brandeis Now.* Retrieved from https://www.brandeis.edu/now/2019/october/intersectionality-privilege-thetake.html

Hall, R. E. (2006). The bleaching syndrome among people of color: implications of skin color for human behavior in the social environment. *Journal of Human Behavior in the Social Environment, 13*, 19–31.

Hammond, W. P. (2012). Taking it like a man: Masculine role norms as moderators of the racial discrimination-depressive symptoms association among African American men. *American Journal of Public Health, 102*(Suppl 2), S232–S241. https://doi.org/10.2105/AJPH.2011.300485

Hoch-Smith, J., & Spring, A. (1978). *Women in ritual and symbolic roles.* Plenum.

hooks, b., & West, C. (1995). *Killing rage: Ending racism.* Owl Books.

hooks, b. (2016). The Future of Feminist Activism and the Quandary of Gender. *Thinking Woman: A Philosophical Approach to the Quandary of Gender*, 158.

Hughes, D., Rodriguez, J., Smith, E. P., Johnson, D. J., Stevenson, H. C., & Spicer, P. (2006). Parents' ethnic-racial socialization practices: A review of research and directions for future study. *Developmental Psychology, 42*(5), 747–770. https://doi.org/10.1037/0012-1649.42.5.747

Hunter, M. (2007). The persistent problem of colorism: Skin tone, status, and inequality. *Sociology Compass, 1*, 237–254. https://doi.org/10.1111/j.1751-9020.2007.00006.x

Iwamoto, D. K., Liao, L., & Liu, W. M. (2010). Masculine norms, avoidant coping, Asian values, and depression among Asian American men. *Psychology of Men & Masculinity, 11*(1), 15–24. https://doi-org.ezproxy.cul.columbia.edu/10.1037/a0017874

Jin, C. H. (2021, May 25). 6 charts that dismantle the trope of Asian Americans as a model minority. *NPR*. https://www.npr.org/2021/05/25/1000092069/6-charts-that-dismantle-the-trope-of-asian-americans-as-a-model-minority

Kaur, H. (2023, May 30). *The differences between race and ethnicity – and why they're so hard to define*. CNN. https://www.cnn.com/2023/05/30/us/race-ethnicity-difference-explainer-cec/index.html

Laster, W. N. (2014). *Racial limbo: A systematic study of the history of coloured South Africans and their contemporary attitudes, perceptions of deprivation, and racial identifications*. Doctoral dissertation, Vanderbilt University. https://ir.vanderbilt.edu/bitstream/handle/1803/14118/Laster.pdf?sequence=1&isAllowed=y

Lewis, J. A., Williams, M. G., Peppers, E. J., & Gadson, C. A. (2017). Applying intersectionality to explore the relations between gendered racism and health among Black women. *Journal of Counseling Psychology, 64*(5), 475–486. https://doi.org/10.1037/cou0000231

Liu, W. M., & Chang, T. (2007). Asian American Masculinities. In F. T. L. Leong, A. Ebreo, L. Kinoshita, A. G. Inman, L. H. Yang, & M. Fu (Eds.), *Handbook of Asian American psychology* (2nd ed., pp. 197–211). Sage.

Liu, W. M., & Concepcion, W. R. (2010). Redefining Asian American identity and masculinity. In W. M. Liu, D. K. Iwamoto, & M. H. Chae (Eds.), *Culturally responsive counseling with Asian American men* (pp. 127–144). New York, NY: Routledge.

Liu, T., & Wong, Y. J. (2018). The intersection of race and gender: Asian American men's experience of discrimination. *Psychology of Men & Masculinity, 19*(1).

Livingston, G. & Brown, A. (2017). *Intermarriage in the U.S. 50 years after Loving v. Virginia*. Pew Research Center. https://www.pewresearch.org/social-trends/2017/05/18/1-trends-and-patterns-in-intermarriage/.

López, N., Edward, V., Melina, J., Lisa, C.-S., & Sonia, B. (2017). What's Your "Street Race"? Leveraging Multidimensional Measures of Race and Intersectionality for Examining Physical and Mental Health Status among Latinxs. *Sociology of Race and Ethnicity 4*: 49–66. [Google Scholar] [CrossRef] [GreenVersion].

López, N., Vargas, E. D., Juarez, M., Cacari-Stone, L., & Bettez, S. (2018). What's your "street race"? Leveraging multidimensional measures of race and intersectionality for examining physical and mental health status among Latinxs. *Sociology of Race and Ethnicity, 4*(1), 49–66. https://doi.org/10.1177/2332649217708798

López, N., Erwin, C., Binder, M., & Chavez, M. J. (2023). *Making the invisible visible: Advancing quantitative methods in higher education using critical race theory and intersectionality*. In QuantCrit (pp. 32–59). Routledge.

Majors, R., & Billson, J. M. (1993). *Cool pose: The dilemmas of black manhood in America*. Touchstone Books/Simon & Schuster.

Mcintosh, P. (1989). *White privilege: Unpacking the invisible knapsack*. Wellesley Centers for Women. https://www.nationalseedproject.org/images/documents/Knapsack_plus_Notes-Peggy_McIntosh.pdf

Milner, H. R. (2007). Race, culture, and researcher positionality: Working through dangers seen, unseen, and unforeseen. *Educational Researcher, 36*(7), 388–400. http://www.jstor.org/stable/30136070

Miville, M. L., & Ferguson, A. D. (2014). Intersections of race-ethnicity and gender on identity development and social roles. In M. L. Miville & A. D. Ferguson (Eds.), *Handbook of race-ethnicity and gender in psychology* (pp. 3–21). Springer. https://doi-org.ezproxy.cul.columbia.edu/10.1007/978-1-4614-8860-6_1

Miville, M. L., Bratini, L., Corpus, M. J., Lau, M. Y., & Redway, J. A. K. (2013). Negotiating multicultural gender roles: A proposed model. In M. L. Miville (Ed.), *Multicultural gender roles: Applications for mental health and education* (pp. 231–246). Wiley.

Murdock, M. (1990). *Heroine's journey: Woman's quest for wholeness*. Shambhala Publications.

National Constitution Center. (2022). *Dobbs v. Jackson Women's Health Organization*. https://constitutioncenter.org/the-constitution/supreme-court-case-library/dobbs-v-jackson-womens-health-organization#:~:text=In%20a%20divided%20opinion%2C%20the,regulation%20to%20the%20elected%20branches

Neblett, E. W., White, R. L., Ford, K. R., Philip, C. L., Nguyên, H. X., & Sellers, R. M. (2008). Patterns of racial socialization and psychological adjustment: Can parental communications about race reduce the impact of racial discrimination? *Journal of Research on Adolescence, 18*(3), 477–515. https://doi.org/10.1111/j.1532-7795.2008.00568.x

Neblett, E. W., Sosoo, E. E., Willis, H. A., Bernard, D. L., Bae, J., & Billingsley, J. T. (2016). Racism, racial resilience, and African American youth development: Person-centered analysis as a tool to promote equity and justice. In S. S. Horn, M. D. Ruck, & L. S. Liben (Eds.), *Advances in child development and behavior* (Vol. 51, pp. 43–79).

Onion, A, Sullivan, M., Mullen, M., & Zapata, C. (2017). Seneca Falls. *History.* https://www.history.com/topics/womens-history/seneca-falls-convention

Pyke, K. D., & Johnson, D. L. (2003). Asian American women and racialized femininities: 'Doing' gender across cultural worlds. *Gender & Society, 17*(1), 33–53. https://doi-org.ezproxy.cul.columbia.edu/10.1177/0891243202238977

Quam, S., VanHook, C., Szoko, N., Passarello, A., Miller, E., & Culyba, A. J. (2020). Racial identity, masculinities, and violence exposure: Perspectives from male adolescents in marginalized neighborhoods. *The Journal of Adolescent Health, 67*(5), 638–644. https://doi.org/10.1016/j.jadohealth.2020.08.003

Redway, J. A. K., & Miville, M. L. (2013). Gender roles among African American women. In M. L. Miville (Ed.), *Multicultural gender roles: Applications for mental health and education* (pp. 65–95). Wiley.

Ruiz, N. G., et al. (2023, November 30). *Asian Americans and the 'model minority' stereotype.* Pew Research Center. https://www.pewresearch.org/2023/11/30/asian-americans-and-the-model-minority-stereotype/

Sanchez, D. (2021). Introduction to special issue on AfroLatinidad: Theory, research, and practice. *Journal of Latina/o Psychology, 9*(1), 1–7. https://doi.org/10.1037/lat0000186

Sandefur, G. D., Campbell, M. E., & Eggerling-Boeck, J. (2004). Racial and ethnic identification, official classifications, and health disparities. In N. B. Anderson, R. A. Bulatao, & B. Cohen (Eds.), *Critical perspectives on racial and ethnic differences in late life*. National Academies Press (US).

Shih, K. Y., Chang, T. F., & Chen, S. Y. (2019). Impacts of the model minority myth on Asian American individuals and families: Social justice and critical race feminist perspectives. *Journal of Family Theory & Review.* https://doi.org/10.1111/jftr.12342

Siu, S.-F. (1992). How do family and community characteristics affect children's educational achievement? The Chinese-American experience. *Equity and Choice, 8*(2), 46–49. EJ 443 932.

Smithsonian. (2022). *Whiteness.* National Museum of African American History and Culture. https://nmaahc.si.edu/learn/talking-about-race/topics/whiteness

Stevenson, H. C. (1994). Racial socialization in African American families: The art of balancing intolerance and survival. *The Family Journal, 2*(3), 190–198. https://doi.org/10.1177/1066480794023002

Stewart, A. J., & McDermott, C. (2004). Gender in psychology. *Annual Review of Psychology, 55*(1), 519–544. https://doi.org/10.1146/annurev.psych.55.090902.141537

UN Women. (2020, July 1). *Intersectional feminism: What it means and why it matters right now.* https://www.unwomen.org/en/news/stories/2020/6/explainer-intersectional-feminism-what-it-means-and-why-it-matters

Unger, R. K., & Crawford, M. E. (1992). *Women and gender: A feminist psychology*. Temple University Press.

Waters, M. C. (1991). The role of lineage in identity formation among black Americans. *Qualitative Sociology, 14*, 57–76. https://doi.org/10.1007/BF00989534

Welch, K. (2016). Black criminal stereotypes and racial profiling. *Journal of Contemporary Criminal Justice, 23*(3), 276–288. https://doi.org/10.1177/1043986207306870

Yoder, J. D., & Kahn, A. S. (2003). Making gender comparisons more meaningful: A call for more attention to social context. *Psychology of Women Quarterly, 27*(4), 17. https://doi.org/10.1111/1471-6402.00108

Zapata, C., Onion, A., Sullivan, M., & Mullen, M. (2017, November 10). *Seneca Falls convention.* History. https://www.history.com/topics/womens-history/seneca-falls-convention

Chapter 4
Socioeconomic Contexts of Gender

Social Class, Socioeconomic Status, and Classism

In Chap. 1, we described several key structural disparities associated with patriarchal/traditional gender attitudes and behaviors, along with relevant historical and social policy considerations. This chapter explores these disparities regarding their impacts on socioeconomic status (SES). In the first section, we present a general overview of SES, followed by an in-depth exploration of demographic information relevant to education and income.

Socioeconomic status in the U.S. is signified by an uneven distribution of resources across major categories of people, most commonly indicated by gender and race. Lott (in Smith, 2005) described the consequences of "class privilege (i.e., unearned advantage and conferred dominance) and power" (p. 688) as *classism*, which Smith in turn identified as a form of social oppression: "prejudice plus power: It is an interlocking system that involves domination and control of social ideology, institutions, and resources, resulting in a condition of privilege for one group relative to the disenfranchisement of another" (p. 688). In other words, although anyone can possess attitudes regarding wealth and poverty, Smith suggested that the term "classism" refer to a set of negative attitudes directed toward poor people who often lack the institutional or cultural power to enforce their attitudes (Smith, 2005). In contrast, Liu, Colbow, and Rice (2016) offered a more expanded definition of classism:"the marginalization or derision of an individual or group based on the belief that all members of that group possess characteristics or abilities specific to that group," (p. 414), asserting that it is critical to understand the psychological impact of wealth and affluence as well (e.g., pressure to achieve, anxiety, isolation and detachment from others). Liu et al. (2016) distinguished between the the terms *social class* and SES: "SES speaks to gradients and permeable and porous barriers, whereas social class focuses on distinct social class positions and groupings" as well as "a subjective or individual experience rather than a predetermined definition

M. L. Miville et al., *Counseling and Gender*,
https://doi.org/10.1007/978-3-031-69172-0_4

according to objective indicators" (p. 414). Liu et al. acknowledged the terms have been used interchangeably in the literature; in this chapter, we use "SES" as a shorthand reference to the multiple nuances relevant to this topic.

Smith, Romero, and Baranowski (2014) described potential intersections between gender and SES, first beginning with a typology of social class in the U.S. drawn from the work of Leondar-Wright (2005, in Smith et al.) and Zweig (2000, in Smith et al.): (1) *Poverty*, working class people who for various reasons (health, unemployment) do not have enough income to support their basic needs; (2) *Working class*, people with little power or control over their jobs, lower income, net worth, and education; (3) *Middle class*, people who are managers or small business owners; they likely have college education, but rely on their earnings/savings to support themselves and their families; and (4) *Owning class*, people who own enough wealth and property, they do not need to work; they also own and control resources of other people and have significant types of power, including economic, social, cultural, and political. As can be seen, individuals differ in the types of privileges they have access to, as based on the typology, for example those living in poverty versus those in the owning class. Smith et al. (2014) note that individuals with fewer economic resources, particularly those living in poverty, have "elevated rates of threatening and uncontrollable life events, noxious life conditions, marital dissolution, infant mortality, many diseases, violent crime, homicide, accidents, and deaths from all causes" (Belle et al., 2000, p. 115). A primary mechanism by which these rates persist is that those living in poverty are "placed at risk by a deficit of 'health-promoting' resources, differences in access to high-quality treatment, and differences in attitudes and beliefs held by health care workers'" (Lott, 2002, in Smith et al., p. 115). Moreover, as with negative gender and racial attitudes, classist attitudes toward people experiencing poverty can be internalized to the detriment of the individual (Liu et al.), as poignantly described by the famous White Southern author, Dorothy Allison,

> The inescapable impact of being born in a condition of poverty that this society finds shameful, contemptible, and somehow deserved, has had dominion over me to such an extent that I have spent my life trying to overcome or deny it…We were not noble, not grateful, or even hopeful. We knew ourselves despised. (1994, in Smith et al., p. 115)

SES is best understood within contextual and situational factors (Liu et al., 2016). For example, racial and ethnic disparities are quite evident in the wage earnings and poverty rates in the U.S., such that people of color (Black, Asian, Latine, Indigenous) own less than a dime of every White dollar and that when White people live in poverty, they tend to live there for a relatively shorter period and with less deprivation (Smith et al., 2014). Another issue reinforcing these disparities is the general economic wage stagnation that has affected income earners in the U.S., particularly for working class employees, over many decades (Kochhar, 2023). Gender plays a significant role in poverty, with women being 40% more likely to live in poverty than men, particularly at the more extreme ends; in other words, "sexism, patriarchal values, and the subordinate position assigned to women across ethnicities and races seem to be at work" (Smith et al., p. 117). As we will show in this chapter, the persistence of the gender wage gap continues in the U.S., despite major gains in the completion of higher education degrees. Finally, as we discuss in greater depth in Chap. 11, issues of gender-based violence, particularly domestic violence, can force women into homelessness and unemployment. In short, poverty has become "feminized" in the U.S. (Smith et al., 2013), and "the burden of coping with poverty falls most heavily on women" (Lott & Bullock, 2007, in Smith et al., 2013, p. 159). We also provide clear evidence that another gender minoritized population, TGNC people, similarly is overrepresented as living in poverty, particularly transwomen.

This chapter reviews demographic data that demonstrate how disparities regarding gender, race, ethnicity, and SES continue to be intertwined phenomena in the U.S. We highlight the wage gap and experiences of living in poverty for both women and TGNC people, along with important events that have occurred in the past several decades, including the economic impact of the recent global pandemic. Finally, we highlight SES considerations for men, particularly the impact of living in poverty.

Seeking and Education and Career: The Wage Gap and Covid-19

Over the past 50 years, there has been a great increase of all individuals seeking educational opportunities in the U.S., for example, the completion of higher education degrees. According to the Pew Research Center, today more women than men earn higher education degrees, especially among younger generations (Millenial and later) (Parker, 2021). This increase in college attainment, particularly for women, has occurred across all racial ethnic groups, despite other ongoing racial-ethnic disparities. These disparities are present here in that White, non-Hispanic women earn the most higher education degrees, followed by African Americans, Latina, and Asian American women. Significant SES barriers remain for many individuals seeking higher education degrees, especially for Black and Latine individuals, for example, the lack of financial resources as well as the need to work in order to support their family.

In light of increased numbers of women earning university degrees, another gendered SES issue to consider is how this increase in learning, skills and career preparation are reflected in what they actually earn financially. That is, what do salaries look like relative to the increased rates of educational degrees and professional skills? Unfortunately demographic information demonstrates that, despite the higher rates of education, there still is a persistent *wage gap* in terms of earnings; women on average today are making about 80% of what men make in the U.S. This wage gap is quite well-spread; for example, Hsu (2020) reported the men outpace earnings of women at every educational level, from high school to graduate school, with the gap widening at each level of education. McElrath and Hernandez (2023) report that the gender wage gap is so entrenched, even when women and men hold the same exact degree in the same field, men still make more money for their work. For instance, in the field of electrical engineering, the highest earning field on record, men earned a median salary of $123,000 in 2022, whereas women made 15% less at $105,000. In elementary education, a field overrepresented by women, men still made more than women in 2022, by $10,000 ($64,380 vs. $54,070)! McElrath and Hernandez further note that fields that are predominantly male vs. female (at least 60%) displayed wage gaps with male-dominated fields (e.g., engineering, computer science) earning on average more than female-dominated fields (e.g., nursing, social work). Interestingly, the wage gap has closed somewhat more for women who do not have college degrees (Kochhar, 2023), with the gap closing from 62% in 1982 to 83% in 2022, as compared with college graduates (69% to 79%). Key reasons cited by Kochhar are the wage stagnation of working class men during this time period, along with the rise of pay for all women across positions; men with college degrees were the *only* earners to see a positive wage growth during this time period.

Another concerning trend about the wage gap is that the gap expands with age; as women age, they earn even less than men of their same-age cohort (Kochhar & Bennett, 2021). In 2022, young women (25–34) earned 92% of men earners, but for those aged 35 and older, the gap widened to 83%, stubbornly remaining as such for the next 2 decades, after which the gap widened further to 79%. Kochhar attributed parenthood as a key factor in the widening of the wage gap. Many women, as a result of having children, may either work fewer hours or leave the workplace altogether, at least for a period of time, leading to less income earned, per a phenomenon known as the *motherhood wage penalty*. Parenting has the opposite effect on men to the extent that demographers have identified a *fatherhood wage premium* for this group (Kochhar). That is, men with children earn the highest wages, relative to women with or without children, and men without children (though this last group still earns relatively more than both groups of women).

Claudia Goldin who won the Nobel Prize for Economics in 2023 offers another perspective on the wage gap (Miller, 2014, 2023). First, she highlights the "quiet revolution" that occurred throughout the twentieth century that continues today regarding the increased presence of women in the workplace (Goldin, 2006)--a "revolutionary" achievement that she refers to as "the most significant change in labor markets during the past century" (p. 1). For example, women today occupy far more jobs in higher earning positions, as might be found in STEM fields, business and finance, and the law, relative to 4 decades ago (40% in 2022 vs 26% in 1982) (Kochhar & Bennett, 2021). Goldin suggests the primary concern for women in the workplace is the long inflexible hours that employees are expected to devote to their jobs. Goldin provides evidence that the wage gap is actually larger within rather than between occupations, and largest in the highest earning fields which generally require the highest levels of formal education. Goldin contends that if workers were equally productive and paid an hourly wage, rather than paid a salary and be on constant call, the gap would disappear (2014). She suggests that for most couples, particularly for heterosexuals, one partner typically is available for work responsibilities (husband), whereas the other partner is more available for home obligations (wife). Goldin wryly observes that it is not so much that women step back from work because they have rich husbands, but rather that their husbands become rich because women step back from work (Miller, 2019).

Another wage gap can be seen in overall household incomes. Not surprisingly, households that have more than one adult who can bring home wages make significantly more money than single headed households. However, when women head the household, as might be seen in a single mother home, the pay gap widens tremendously. Single male headed households, which make up just 20% of single parent homes, earn considerably less than dual headed homes. However, because women make almost $20,000 less than men do in single headed homes, it is single woman households that struggle the most with lower incomes (Guzman & Kollar, 2023). In the next section we discuss racial-ethnic SES disparities, and the impact of the wage gap on communities of color.

Racial-Ethnic Impact on Gender and SES Differences

As we described at the beginning of the chapter, racial-ethnic disparities exist across household incomes in the U.S. According to the U.S. Census (Guzman & Kollar, 2023), Asian households typically display the highest levels of household incomes ($109,000), perhaps due to the fact that many Asian households typically are multigenerational, so that there are more than two people bringing home pay. Other households are more likely to be one or two headed households. According to recent U.S. Census data (Guzman & Kollar), the median income for White American households was approximately $81,000 in 2022, whereas Black and Latine households were below the median, at $53,000 and $63,000, respectively. These are quite significant racialized SES differences, especially when one considers what $55–65,000 vs. $80,000 or more can afford in the current age.

Salary comparisons between women and men within their own racial-ethnic groups illuminate important gendered SES considerations as well. For example, White, non-Hispanic women make about 80% of what their male counterparts make. Over the past 40 years, White women's wage earnings have seen a substantial increase, to the point where they are now among the highest earners of any racial-ethnic group in the U.S. (Patten, 2016). This change reflects larger societal progress on structural sexism for some women with the existing lack of similar progress on structural racism for other women. As a result, these data significantly contrast with both Black and Latine households in which women make only somewhat less than their male counterparts. When comparing earnings to White men, stark race by gender disparities are apparent in the wage gap of Black, Latina, and Indigenous women. Recent data demonstrate that Black women make just 64% and Latinas and Indigenous women make 57% of what White men earn in the United States. A key reason suggested for this is *occupational segregation*; that is, women of color historically have worked in jobs involving service, care, and domestic work, which usually have low pay, little advancement, and less flexibility (Bleiweiss et al., 2021; Miller, 2023). On the other hand, Asian women make 85% as much as White men, signifying a somewhat different SES positionality for Asian American women in the U.S. However, Bleiweiss et al. note that earnings disparities are problematic for women across Asian ethnicities, with wage gaps ranging from lows in the 50s (Burmese and Nepalese women) to the 90s and beyond (Taiwanese, Indian, Malaysian, Chinese, and Japanese women) (Kochhar & Cilluffo, 2018). Bleiweiss et al. state, "Simply put, there has never been a time in this country when there has not been a wage gap that exists along intersecting gender and racial lines."

Wage gaps for men of color in comparison with White men also have been an historical trend that remains stubbornly in place today, particularly for Black and Latino men. For example, in 1980, Black men made 73% and Latinos 71% of White men's earnings, changing very little over the next four decades (73% and 69%, respectively) (Patten, 2016). These disparities invoke the concept of *racial capitalism* (Robinson, 1983). Racial capitalism theory outlines how the structure of capitalism and *class* develop mutually, in a matrix alongside *race* and racism (Robinson, 1983). In contrast, Asian men now earn at least as much as 117% as much as White men (Patten). However, as with Asian women, there are considerable disparities among Asian ethnic groups, with Asians as a whole identified as having the greatest in-group income inequality in the U.S. (Kochhar & Cilluffo, 2018).

LGB and TGNC Populations and the Gender Gap

According to a report by the Human Rights Campaign (HRC, 2021), LGBT people as a whole have been found to have a wage gap of 90% compared with the wages of the "typical worker," defined as "the median wage for all workers in the United States." As we just noted in the previous section, exploring racial-ethnic intersections are relevant for this population as well. White LGBT workers (all genders) have a wage gap of just 97%, and Asian populations are at 100%, whereas Latine workers' gap is 90%, Black workers are at 80%, and Native Americans have the largest gap at 70%. The gender gap relative to men and women is also present within the LGBT community, as men earn 96% of the typical U.S. worker, and women earn 87%. Regarding race by gender statistics, HRC found that LGBT Black, Latine, and Indigenous women have the largest wage gaps. White and Asian women earned 96% and 100%, respectively, of the typical earner, whereas Black, Native American, and Latina women all earned significantly less (85%, 75%, and 72%, respectively). However, it is TGNC populations who are most dramatically affected by the wage gap as gender minoritized individuals. As a whole, TGNC people earn 70% of the typical earner, transmen earn 70%, and transwomen have among the largest gaps of any U.S. subpopulation at 60% (HRC). Ralph (O'Dwyer & Ralph, 2021) asserts that:

> struggles for trans liberation are the same as broader working-class struggles…[Although] some of this is explained by the unique oppression that trans people face (and, of course, trans people's experience of these issues can vary wildly based on gender, race, work, dis-

ability and other things). But clearly trans people are impacted by the same structures that oppress the working class.

In Chap. 8, we will discuss the potential psychological impact of the wage gaps and SES disparities relative to educational and career aspirations. Suffice to say that many workers of color as well as TGNC individuals who experience wage disparities also report experiences of being treated less fairly in the workplace, including hiring, pay, and promotion opportunities, as well as the overall sense that their race and their gender make it harder for them to succeed (Bleiweiss et al., HRC, 2021).

The Covid-19 Pandemic

In 2020–2021, most people around the world were greatly impacted by the Covid pandemic; during the affected years gender played a major role in how the pandemic affected individuals and families. Although many people were financially affected, women, relative to men, took a major hit regarding their salaries, the stability of their jobs, and what their actual daily lives became (Gogoi, 2020). TGNC individuals also were significantly affected (File & Marshall, 2021). The significant overall loss of jobs became a major economic issue for many families. As well, people were sequestered at home to a far greater level, along with masking and social distancing, and there still were far less people working outside the home. In December 2020 alone, the Board of Labor Statistics reported 140,000 jobs were lost (Gogoi). However, for men, they actually had a gain of 16,000 jobs during the time period. Essentially 140,000 people who lost their jobs were *all* women. Although Martin-Caughey (2023) reports that ultimately men lost more jobs than women (4.1% vs. 3.4%) during the entire Covid era (2019–2021), they continued to outnumber women in the workforce.

The economic impact of the Covid-19 epidemic for women was so dramatic, the situation was reminiscent of 1988 (Gogoi, 2020). That is, during the pandemic times, only 57% of women were in the paid labor force. Thus, the financial status of women rose significantly for 40 years, and then crashed in a single year. Why did this occur for women in particular? Gogoi suggests that women may have left the workplace because of *push out* pressures in the workforce as well as pressures to stay home, particularly for women with young children. That is, women lost their jobs because they disproportionately worked in sectors that were more strongly affected by the pandemic (e.g., hospitality jobs, education, social services). In addition, women still had much unpaid labor to do at home, historically distributed unevenly in most two-headed (heterosexual) households (Krishnan, 2020). Other concerns may have been the lack of flexibility of work hours, feeling the need to always be available for work, anxiety about how home responsibilities might be viewed by employers, difficulties sharing with their work supervisors the difficulties they were facing, feeling surprised constantly by ever changing circumstances, and the inability to be their whole selves at work (McKinsey Quarterly, n.d.). Some recent good news, however, indicates that despite the labor and financial crash that many women experienced during the pandemic, since February 2023, women are at an all-time high regarding their participation in the labor force, at rate of 77% (Bureau of Labor Statistics, 2023).

According to the HRC (Whittington et al., 2020), LGBT individuals (which included TGNC individuals) also were impacted by the pandemic, since nearly 5 million of the estimated 14 million LBTQ adults and 2 million youth worked in jobs affected by the pandemic (e.g., food services, health care, and retail). Dawson, Kirzinger, and Kates (2021) reported that a larger share of these individuals (56% vs. 44%) either experienced a job loss or knew someone who did. Another concern for this population was that many were unable to take paid leave to care for their families (Whittington et al.). Finally, food insecurity was identified by the U.S. Census Bureau as another concern, with 13.1% of LGBT adults living in a household that experienced food insecurity, in comparison with 7.2% of non-LGBT adults (File & Marshall, 2021). The next section will highlight another significant impact of the intersections of SES and gender, living in poverty.

Gender and Poverty

At the beginning of the chapter, we described one definition of classism as negative attitudes regarding those living in poverty. As we just described, U.S. workers' earnings demonstrate great disparities attributed to gender, race, and ethnicity. We turn now to exploring how gender intersects with SES for those living in poverty. The U.S. Census defines poverty in the following way:

> Poverty status is determined by comparing annual income to a set of dollar values (poverty thresholds) that vary by family size, number of children, and the age of the householder. If a family's before-tax income is less than the dollar value of their threshold, that family and every individual in it are in poverty. For people not living in families, poverty status is determined by comparing the individual's income to their poverty threshold. (Benson, 2023)

For example, in 2022, the poverty threshold was approximately $30,000 for a family of four, and $15,000 for an individual (Olya, 2024); in 2022, the national poverty rate was 12.6% (Benson).

Today gender minoritized communities, that is, women and TGNC people, are at a higher risk of living in poverty in the United States, relative to men (Sun, 2023; Badgett, 2020). One in 9 women (12%) lived in poverty in 2021, nearly half of whom lived in extreme poverty (i.e., income at or below 50% of the federal poverty guidelines in 2021) (Sun); men's rates were at 9%. Women of color are at a particular risk, especially Black (19%), Latina (17%), and Indigenous women (21%), all of whom have heightened levels of poverty. Asian American women (10%) also had heightened levels of poverty, especially those from some ethnic backgrounds (e.g., Burma and Nepal) (Bleiweiss et al.; Sun).

SES and Single Mothers

Unfortunately, until recently the field of psychology's treatment of women living in poverty has been marked by an overemphasis on deficiencies, rather than strength and resilience (Smith, 2005). In this section, we delve deeper into looking at a specific group of women who are particularly affected by SES, classism, and conditions of poverty, single mother (SM) families, per the scholarly work of Naomi Torres-Mackie (2020). Torres-Mackie cites bell hooks in her reasoning as to why SMs must be better centered in research on gender and SES: "The most profound betrayal of feminist issues has been the lack of mass-based feminist protest challenging the government's assault on single mothers " (p. 3).

Who are single mother (SM) families? Over the past 60 plus years, there has been a tremendous social change in who raises children. In 1960, only 9% of kids were being raised by single parents, whereas in this century, a *quarter* of all children are raised by single parent households (Torres-Mackie). Nearly 70% of all children today will spend some portion of their childhood in a single parent household. As noted earlier, 80% of all children raised in single parent households are raised by a single mother. These changes in the likelihood of being raised in SM families reflect larger societal changes in the mid-twentieth century regarding the rights of women to maintain a family independently, including the right to open bank and credit accounts (see Chap. 1).

According to Torres-Mackie (2020), society views single mothers quite differently than single fathers, though to be sure, single fathers do have their own challenges, including the lack of adequate information for this group of parents. There are many different reasons why people become single parents, especially women, including becoming widowed or divorced, or, in some way separated from their spouse. In the twenty-first century, increased numbers of women have chosen to have children without marriage (31% in 1994 vs. 55% in 2014); the majority of women in 2014 in their 40s who never married have had a baby (Livingston, 2018). Racial-ethnic differences are apparent in the decision to have a child as a single woman, in that the rates for Black women and Latinas were 75% and 68%, respectively, as compared with White women (37%).

Single women with children have often been viewed as somehow destructive to the larger society (Torres-Mackie, 2020). Negative, blaming attitudes exist in many areas of the larger society towards single mothers and their children regarding their overall impact on society. Today strong attitudes are still expressed about SM families: "any family that does not include a man can be faulted as deficient, defective, disrupted, broken" (Sidel, 2006, from Torres-Mackie, personal communication, February 15, 2017). There also are heterosexist core beliefs, and the notion that two headed households as man and woman are considered the only kind of acceptable way to have a family (discussed further in Chaps. 5 and 9). Cultural beliefs and expectations influence social beliefs about how and why a family should be composed (heterosexual, married, etc). Children of single mothers (COSMs) similarly have been viewed negatively, not just by society but within the social sciences as well. The sheer lack of studies that Torres-Mackie found in her research focused on the strengths of COSMs point to this difficult reality. Furthermore, there are still presumptions among mental health professionals that there is something about a single parent's gender that is more important than what the actual facts have to say about single children of single parents.

For many SM families, economic stressors are a main source of strain. For example, the official poverty rate for SM families in 2022 was 32%, twice the rate of single-father families (Sun, 2023); these rates are higher for Black, Latina, and Indigenous SM families, and relatively lower for Asian and White SM families. Unfortunately economic stress itself can lead to other difficulties, especially mental health concerns of anxiety, depression, social isolation, feelings of incompetence and even poor performance, both at school and at work. There also are social stressors that arise, in that many single mothers feel they have little time and energy for themselves (Torres-Mackie, 2020). A helpful framework to understand these strains is as a *poverty of time*, another outcome of the intersections of SES, race and gender disparities for SMs. When one person is individually responsible for children, they must work, and subsequently experience this poverty of time that may lead to a number of mental health concerns.

Another primary source of stress are the additive impacts of negative sexist, racist, and classist attitudes that other people may still feel towards single moms, what has been called *single-mother stigma* (Torres-Mackie, 2020). Historically, single mothers have been viewed as a socially deviant threat to society, at times being isolated and ostracized (recall *The Scarlet Letter* by Nathanial Hawthorne), further leading to mental health impacts. On the positive side, supportive networks, as now exist online and in live settings, can help single mothers in terms of their mental and emotional well being. A related source of stress is discrimination in the workplace where they may be perceived as bad workers, lazy, unmotivated, uncommitted, distracted, and simply not available (Torres-Mackie, 2020), leading to further concerns about their financial situation. There have been court cases involving SMs who were fired from their jobs due to their single status as mothers, being viewed as "bad role models" for adolescents. The lack of public assistance for childcare further compounds this area of stress, again leading to experiences of poverty of time. Unfortunately, SM discrimination can become generational (lower paying jobs lead to a lack of higher education for the children, creating the cycle of poverty).

A final note from the innovative research of Torres-Mackie is her critique of the available literature on single mothers regarding its limited focus on only the risks of single motherhood. Instead, Torres-Mackie urges an empirical focus on the many strengths of individuals from single parent households, which is strikingly missing in the extant literature. Some strengths include being strong, self reliant, a positive role model for their children, hard working resilience, and so on. We will discuss children of single mothers (COSMs) in greater detail in Chap. 9.

Ability and Age

Intersections with other identities are crucial to consider regarding the impact on gender and SES. For example, disabled women are at high risk (27%) of living in poverty, as are disabled men (23%). Another important intersection is age. A woman who enters the labor force later in life or who steps away for a period may be engaged in positions that do not pay as much or have as many benefits. That is why older women are more likely to live in poverty than older men, representing 61% of people over 65 living in poverty (Sun, 2023). Older women of color are disproportionately represented among women (about 18% for Black, Latina, and Indigenous women; Sun). White non-Hispanic women are the least likely of all women in the United States to live in poverty at 9%, demonstrating that race and ethnicity more than gender affects those living in poverty.

LGB and TGNC Populations

LGB and TGNC populations are at significantly higher risk of living in poverty (Badgett et al., 2019). Badgett et al. found that poverty rates were nearly double for this diverse group (21.6%), with TGNC individuals showing the highest levels of poverty at 29.4%. Cis-gender differences among women and men also were found, with lesbian women having higher poverty rates than gay men (18% vs. 12%), although lesbian women as a whole were not found to have different rates from heterosexual women. Surprisingly, bisexual women were found to have quite high poverty rates by Badgett et al., matching rates found for TGNC people (29.45). Racial-ethnic differences showed that LGBT people of color showed heightened levels of poverty (e.g., 38% for Latines, 31% for Black LGBT people, 27% for Indigenous people, and 23% for Asian Americans).

Economist Lee Badgett (2020; Badgett et al., 2019) has written extensively about the multiple impacts of economic disparities on the lives of LGB and TGNC individuals. She highlights that, despite tremendous advances in legislation, social policies, and the health sciences over the past 50 years, negative attitudes toward LGBT individuals, *homophobia*, predominate throughout much of the world, including many parts of the U.S. (witness the number of anti-TGNC laws attempted and/or passed in the U.S. in recent years; see https://translegislation.com). Badgett asserts that the situation is so dire that "*every* country is a 'developing country' when it comes to enacting rights for LGBT people and in taking action to make LGBT people's lives better," including the U.S. (p. 7). In her interviews with 57 LGBT people who had left their places of origin to live in New York City, Badgett wrote that "they spoke of the pain and necessity of leaving home to escape the violence of homophobia; they spoke in anguish about lost family and community ties" (p. 5). Badgett expressed strong concerns about the health impacts of these experiences, what she calls "the hidden effects of exclusion" (p. 12) that can lead to a potential downward cycle toward poverty: "Poorer health makes it harder to get and keep a job, adding to the economic consequences of homophobia and transphobia" (p. 12).

Regarding specific economic impacts, Badgett (2020) stated that interviewees lost educational opportunities because of violence and discrimination: "the costs are clear: countries lose people. And those people lose education, time, social support, energy, and possibly much more. From an economic perspective, it adds up" (p. 5). Badgett offered hope in her observation of a major positive outcome: "encouraging the creation of a community based on LGBT identities and a social movement to change the harsh realities," (p. 5), highlighting the resilience and advocacy of this diverse and much maligned population. And as a number of scholars have emphasized for communities of color, single mothers, and others, Badgett contended that "it's *inequality* that threatens our economic capacity…[and] poses political and productive threats" (p. 10). She acknowledged the potential loss to society without the contributions of well known LGBT individuals (e.g., Turing, Woolf, Copland, Elton John, etc.), yet observes that:

> It's that every LGBT person contributes something, whether they are teachers, cashiers, nurses, custodians, in the beauty industry, unpaid caregivers, and truck drivers, or whether they are in the underground or informal economy. Their individual human losses from being unfairly targeted turn into our collective social losses as we miss out on the full benefit of their skills, experience, and creativity. (p. 10)

Badgett urged that improving gender equality and dismantling economic disparities for LGBT people through increased access to resources, education, housing, better paying jobs, and so on will "provide new ideas and new participants in nations' economies" (p. 10) that benefits the whole nation.

SES and Men

> I am convinced that the truest act of courage, the strongest act of manliness is to sacrifice ourselves for others in a totally non-violent struggle for justice. To be a man is to suffer for others. God help us to be men. (César Chávez, hunger strike of 1968 (Jensen & Hamerback, 2002, in Ojeda & Organista, 2016, p. 299)

In this section, we focus on SES impacts on men. Although both women and TGNC people are disproportionately affected by SES disparities, gender and SES intersect in important ways for men as well. For most men, masculinity is closely connected with what it means to be a man in terms of SES and becoming economically viable (Liu et al., 2016). Being the "breadwinner" as well as becoming self-sufficient is a primary theme for most men's gender identity development, so that one's sense of masculinity may be deeply connected with one's ability to be productive, to earn money, and to support one's family. Liu et al. explored SES differences among men, including the different stereotypes across SES categories. When considering working class men, there are a number of strong negative stereotypes (e.g., being/appearing tough, willing to take risks, being biased toward others per race, gender/gender identity, and sexual orientation). Liu et al.'s (2016) work contradicts many of these presumed beliefs. For example, their research has revealed that people from the working class tend to be more compassionate than their wealthier counterparts, a finding that seems reasonable given that compassion is linked with a working life (i.e., most people know what this feels like). As a result, many working class men may have a sense of generosity and compassion for others who may fall on hard times. Working class families may be better tuned to other people's distress because of their own personal experience with instability or precariousness in the workplace, especially its impact on their young children. As a result, they may be more generous, trusting or even helpful to others in financial distress.

The sense of *precarity* that many working class people may experience is an important contextual variable to understand men's attitudes toward themselves and others (e.g., Blustein et al., 2022). Precarity refers to "uncertainty, loss, disruption, and anxiety which differentially impacts people across contexts" (p. 565). The construct of precarity enables a better understanding of how people "cope with the overwhelming sense of vulnerability" as might have occurred during pandemic times or in jobs with little security or benefits; it is "best understood as a subjective experience that is inherently relational" (p. 566). Precarity also has been associated with masculinity, referred to as *precarious manhood* (Vandello et al., 2023), "the belief that manhood is an achieved social status that must be earned and constantly defended, because it can be lost or taken away" (p. 2); Vandello et al. noted that a parallel process for women is rarely observed. When men feel their gender status is threatened, they may become motivated to defend themselves by "broadcasting masculine competence to others…[and] enacting aggressive or risky behaviors that demonstrate toughness and courage" (p. 2). These behaviors may lead to the more negative health outcomes predominantly associated with many men throughout their lives (Vandello et al; also see Chap. 10).

Returning to SES contexts' influence on men, Liu et al. (2016) note that men in the upper middle to upper income brackets are socialized throughout their lifespan to exude qualities of fierceness, competitiveness, and dominance, reflecting the traditional understanding of power we described in Chap. 1. Dominance, and what is assumed to be strength, are actually reflections of classist ideas of what is understood as a strong person: somebody who is competitive, dominant, and tough. In contrast, for many working class men, although they too are pressured to exert at least the appearance of strength, there is at the same time an emphasis on compassion, since one has to be tough minded to be compassionate for somebody else. Many men, especially wealthy men, are raised in social contexts where they are fostered to be fiercely competitive (i.e., to "go for the jugular"). As a result, more feminine qualities for men of wealth tend to be suppressed early in life; qualities such as nurturing, caring, and kindness are seen as a weakness ("girly"). This socially dominative framework has been linked with anti-egalitarian attitudes toward women among wealthy men (Liu et al.), although men from all SES backgrounds have consistently been found to have higher levels of anti-egalitarian attitudes, relative to women. Moreover, across many contexts and SES classes, but especially upper class settings, *not* taking on a fierce competitive presentation, can lead to harassment, aggression, both verbal and physical, of boys and men (Liu et al., 2016).

Breadwinner Role

Many men see themselves and their role in the large society and the larger economy as the breadwinners, the primary income earners for their families (recall the fatherhood wage premium in the wage gap). Closely identifying with this role is often associated with positive mental health outcomes of positive self esteem and a sense of power and purpose (Kroska, 2009; Zuo & Tang, 2000, in Liu et al., 2016). Men are socialized to see themselves as the person who will go out and earn the money. Thus the presumption for many if not most men is an expectation of doing little to no work at home, since money is often equated with power. Therefore, boys and men of many racial-ethnic backgrounds have fairly negative attitudes about work at home, since housework is not "their" work as it is considered "menial" work not deserving of their time and attention. These negative stereotypes about contributing to household maintenance are socialized from a very young age. When boys and men do contribute to housework, it is usually tasks that are considered too rough or taxing for women, as modeled by older male relatives, for instance, working in the yard, cleaning gutters, or appliance repair. Usually in the American sphere, outside work is "male" (e.g., outside cooking is acceptable, even extending to specifically-male territory in the US), and inside work is "female" (Donner, 2020). This division of labor harks back to the traditional gender roles of women being at home, in the private world, and whereas men are out in the external world, including their own backyards. Even when this menial housework is completed, the larger cultural frame typically is that men are "helping" women when doing this, as opposed to tending to their own home.

Since the 1960s, some data show that men have doubled their share of housework, changing from 5% to 10%, as compared with women's share shrinking from nearly 30% to 15%(Parker & Wan, 2013). One area of significant change is childcare, since spending time with children has become a valued experience for both parents (Donner, 2020). An interesting portrait of men's attitudes toward women has emerged, in which men, especially younger men, are more likely to endorse gender equality in the workplace, but are more reluctant to do so at home, at least in terms of sharing real tasks.

Given the critical importance of the breadwinner role, when it comes to experiences with unemployment, the loss of a job has far greater psychological meaning for men than money, since the loss may be felt as personal in terms of power in the home, both financially and as the presumed leader of the home (Liu et al., 2016). SES matters, so the impact of where or how one has been socialized to understand one's social class, affects how one views the loss of a job which in turn is affected by how an individual views oneself in the larger economy. When men cannot fulfill the traditional breadwinner role, they may experience a sense of inadequacy and feel like a failure because they cannot fulfill their prime family role. As a result, some men may struggle to feel they know what their role is in the family, lose their sense of purpose and control in their lives, and as a result, feel guilty about the inability to contribute, and feel badly about themselves (Liu et al.).

Not surprisingly, there are mental health symptoms that can arise as a part of the loss of the traditional role of breadwinner (Liu et al., 2016). There can be an overreaction to being out of work, as might be understood in psychoanalytic terms. For example, some men may take on a super-authoritarian stance with their family, and become even more controlling of their spouses and their children. This actually can lead to cascading effects, such as risky health behaviors, including substance abuse, depression, and marital discord. Some men may start arguing with their partners, especially about who is bringing home the money, who is spending money, whose right is it to spend the money, because the loss of control as the primary breadwinner role has been upended. Worse, some men may begin to engage or become more engaged in domestic violence and, worse, sexual violence (Liu et al.).

Racial-Ethnic Considerations for Men and SES

As we noted in Chap. 2, there are cultural and societal expectations of being a provider, and sometimes in low-income and/or heterosexual families, when a man (husband) loses his job, there is an upending of the traditionally understood gender roles. For heterosexual couples, the spouse (wife), can experience a sense of being a reluctant provider, in that she becomes the provider of the family, but does not experience much of a sense of empowerment. Or there may be covert feelings by the woman spouse about having empowerment and how they may come to view their male spouse. And as a result, this can lead to marital strain, even dissolution, as in the case of families with few other resources (e.g., Parker & Stepler, 2017).

One of the most common issues that we see in U.S. society in regards to race, men, and class is the *school to prison pipeline*, "a term used to describe the connection between exclusionary punishments like suspensions and expulsions and involvements in the criminal system" (Bacher-Hicks et al., 2021, p. 52); zero-tolerance policies stemming from the war on drugs greatly increased mass incarceration of young men of color in the 1980s and 1990s, an issue still reflected in today's prison populations. As Bacher-Hicks et al. report, Black and Latino students "are far more likely than White students to be suspended or expelled, and Black and Hispanic Americans are disproportionately represented in the nation's prisons" (p. 52). Although this group of students made up just 8% of male high school students in 2015, they made up an astounding 25% of out-of-school suspensions and over half of all law enforcement referrals and arrests (see american.edu/blog/school-to-prison-pipeline/). Such statistics indicate the continuing criminalization of young men of color as special targets of police interventions on school campuses. As a result, today there are still disproportionately large numbers of incarcerated men of color. Yet another impact of these higher rates of punishment for boys of color is they may drop out of school entirely, increasing the risk of future incarceration as well as the prospects of obtaining low-wage jobs. This situation heightens the risk of boys and men of color and their families of becoming caught in a cycle of poverty. As Powell (2008) poignantly observes regarding the situation for Black boys and men, "In essence, these violent institutions are leaving African American men stranded in a society that dehumanizes and economically devalues them, leaving them with low self-worth and the feeling that they have little control over their lives" (p. 318).

Latine families are characterized by fairly strong traditional gender roles that are socialized from birth (Bratini et al., 2013). In a heterosexual family, the husband is generally presumed to be the authority and decision maker of that family, often per religious beliefs and norms. However many Latine families actually engage in more cooperative and collaborative decision making privately, but then what gets expressed publicly is typically through the man as being the presumed speaker. As we described in Chap. 2, most Latinos and Latinas each follow their respective traditional gender roles, breadwinner and protector for men, and caregiver for women. That is where the notion of machismo emanates. Machismo is not the hyper masculine stereotype depicted in the media; machismo is actually about being a provider and protector of one's family (Diaz et al., 2013). In line with their Indigenous roots, many Latine families view gender roles as different but not necessarily unequal, as each is considered valuable. However, it is very critical to understand that partners, husbands and wives in particular, are not meant to compete with each other. However, for many families who have immigrated, women can become the primary earner, especially if they get a job first, or make a larger amount of money. As a result, tensions can arise, and some navigation about these role differences is important for couples to do, relative to their socialized gender roles and then in comparison to who's making what, in terms of money.

We next turn to explore SES and gender among *White Americans*, including those living in poverty. Recall the demographic information of White men being among the top earners across all SES classes and educational levels of attainment. Until recently, White men earned the most money in the United States, although wages for all working class men have been stubbornly stagnant for several decades. What happens in situations of White men and their families living in poverty? Historically, the U.S. always has had a large population of White people living in poverty; numerically speaking, Whites today make up the majority of people living in poverty. Isenberg (2016) in her book *White Trash* documents how this began in the 1700s, when England viewed the emerging U.S. as a place to dispose of their poorest citizens. Isenberg contends this is the "central, if disturbing, thread in our national narrative" (p. 320). She suggests the term "waste people" to describe the brutish way many White individuals were brought to the U.S. as indentured servants who worked without pay for years in the poorest conditions, ultimately leading to a similar fate in the U.S., locked into a cycle of poverty across many generations. Throughout U.S. history, Isenberg details the many slurs used to describe White Americans living in poverty, including terms like offscourings (fecal matter), useless lubbers, crackers, scalawags, and trailer trash. She highlights how the wealthy elite in the U.S. target them to this day, variously as workers in low-paying, dangerous jobs, subjects of medical experiments and sterilizations, consumers of unhealthy, even addictive, products (e.g., fast food, tobacco, pain pills), and even as presumably easily influenced voters and spiritual believers. To be sure, the U.S. has celebrated its share of White working class heroes, from Abraham Lincoln to Bruce Sprinsteen. However, recent research demonstrates that negative attitudes toward poor White people remain fairly entrenched among many Americans, including those who label themselves as "liberal" (Cooley et al., 2019). It is understandable that there is anger and a sense of loss about what this underserved group of American men has experienced, especially in the past 50 years, as the number of well-paying union jobs dissipated, and wages stagnated, as compared with what their fathers and grandfathers might have earned.

As is common among White Americans, many poor Whites typically do not attribute their difficulties in life to their race (only 5% do so; Pew Research Center, 2016) or SES. Instead what is observed is these individuals seeking to blame other low-income people, most often people of color, whom they have been socialized to believe have taken resources that are rightfully theirs. As a number of scholars have described, wealthy Whites throughout U.S. history have played a game of harmful manipulation (e.g., Merritt, 2017), starting with slave owners in the South who feared potential uprisings from poor Whites' underclass existence as a result of slavery. Programs were developed that enforced illiteracy, the banning of books that might incite dissent, and even poll taxes to keep White low-income individuals from voting. Ultimately wealthy White elites are attributed as instrumental in invoking race-baiting and notions of White supremacy as a means of instilling fear and loathing in White Americans living in poverty toward other Americans who were similarly shut out from many opportunities (Merritt). These beliefs became so entrenched that many low income White men and their families today continue to support political candidates and public policies that are detrimental to themselves, out of socialized fear and hatred, for the sake of preserving a false sense of racial superiority.

Conclusion

In this chapter, we reviewed multiple ways of how gender and SES together influence the economic opportunities and disparities for people of all genders and SES circumstances. We presented demographic data as evidence to highlight key issues and constructs that emerged from our review of these concerns. Taking a more nuanced approach of intersections among multiple group experiences, per gender, gender identity, race, ethnicity, and SES facilitates a more accurate understanding of how and why these variables together influence the financial realities and psychological impact of SES for many individuals in the U.S.

Case Study

John, a 47-year-old White American cisgender man living in Mahwah, NJ, recently lost his $11-an-hour job: He was driving a forklift at his company's plant when he accidentally crashed into a ladder. No one was hurt and nothing was damaged—but he was an at-will worker at a company with no union, and he was fired. Shortly afterward, his wife, who was making $8 an hour at a cleaning company, decided to leave him. The stress of failing to find a job and being alone made him too depressed to eat. He recently came to the free health clinic where you are working as a counselor, complaining of chest pains. After passing a physical check up, John is referred to you for career assistance and support. He begins the session complaining about "those [expletive about Latine people] taking up all the jobs," despairing of ever finding good-paying work again. He also says he is angry at his wife for leaving him, saying he constantly thinks about "following her to see if she is seeing someone else." John notes that the only "good times" he has these days is being with his friends at a local sports bar, drinking and betting on weekend football games. This time away from home keeps John from worrying about eviction.

Discussion Questions

1. To what extent do gender norms in society, such as the expectation that men should provide for their families financially, exacerbate the mental health problems that people like John face?
2. Discuss how at-will employment and the absence of union protections can make workers feel even more stressed and insecure. What advocacy measures could be taken to lessen the impact of these issues?
3. Consider how John's preconceived notions about race affected his life and emotional well-being. While offering support and direction, how can counselors successfully confront such biases?
4. How do you think the chapter's highlighted demographic trends—such as low-income single mothers and women of color—could interact differently for men and women in comparable socioeconomic situations?
5. Determine the impact of John's social support systems on his present situation. What kinds of social and community resources could help someone like John?
6. John's coping methods are going to a sports bar, drinking, and betting. Discuss how these actions could affect his mental health and his financial situation in the future. How can he be influenced towards more constructive means of dealing with stress?
7. How would things change for John if he were from a different SES, a person of color, or a single parent? Describe how SES, gender, and race affect people's experiences of poverty and joblessness.

References

Bacher-Hicks, A., Billings, S., & Deming, D. (2021). Proving the school-to-prison pipeline: Stricter middle schools raise the risk of adult arrest. *Education Next, 21*(4), 52–57.

Badgett, L. (2020). *The economic case for LGBT equality: Why fair and equal treatment benefits us all*. Beacon.

Badgett, M. V. L., Choi, S. K., & Wilson, B. D. M., (2019, October). *LGBT poverty in the United States: A study of differences between sexual orientation and gender identity groups*. The Williams Institute. https://williamsinstitute.law.ucla.edu/wp-content/uploads/National-LGBT-Poverty-Oct-2019.pdf

Belle, D., Doucet, J., Harris, J., Miller, J., & Tan, E. (2000). Who is rich? Who is happy? *American Psychologist, 55*(10), 1160–1161. https://doi.org/10.1037/0003-066X.55.10.1160

Benson, C. (2023, December). *Poverty in states and metropolitan areas: 2022*. U.S. Census American Community Survey Briefs. https://www.census.gov/content/dam/Census/library/publications/2023/acs/acsbr-016.pdf

Bleiweiss, R., Frye, J., & Khattr, R. (2021, November). *Women of color and the wage gap*. Center for American Progress. Retrieved from https://www.americanprogress.org/article/women-of-color-and-the-wage-gap/.

Blustein, D. L., Smith, C. M., Wu, X., Guarino, P. A., Joyner, E., Milo, L., & Bilodeau, D. C. (2022). "Like a tsunami coming in fast": A critical qualitative study of precarity and resistance during the pandemic. *Journal of Counseling Psychology, 69*(5), 565–577. https://doi.org/10.1037/cou0000615

Bratini, L., Ampuero, M. C., & Miville, M. L. (2013). Latina gender roles. In M. L. Miville (Ed.), *Multicultural gender roles: Applications for mental health and education* (pp. 133–168). Wiley.

Bureau of Labor Statistics, U.S. Department of Labor, The Economics Daily. (2023). Labor force participation rate for people ages 25 to 54 in May 2023 highest since January 2007 at https://www.bls.gov/opub/ted/2023/labor-force-participation-rate-for-people-ages-25-to-54-in-may-2023-highest-since-january-2007.htm

Cooley, E., Brown-Iannuzzi, J. L., Lei, R. F., & Cipolli, W. I. I. I. (2019). Complex intersections of race and class: Among social liberals, learning about White privilege reduces sympathy, increases blame, and decreases external attributions for White people struggling with poverty. *Journal of Experimental Psychology: General, 148*(12), 2218–2228. https://doi.org/10.1037/xge0000605

Dawson, L., Kirzinger, A., & Kates, J. (2021, August). *The impact of the COVID-19 pandemic on LGBT people*. KFF. https://www.kff.org/coronavirus-covid-19/poll-finding/the-impact-of-the-covid-19-pandemic-on-lgbt-people/

Diaz, M. A., Miville, M. L., & Gil, N. (2013). Latino male gender roles. In M. L. Miville (Ed.), *Multicultural gender roles: Applications for mental health and education* (pp. 97–132). Wiley.

Donner, F. (2020, February). The household work men and women do, and why. *New York Times*. https://www.nytimes.com/2020/02/12/us/the-household-work-men-and-women-do-and-why.html

File, T., & Marshall, J. (2021, August). *Household pulse survey shows LGBT adults ore likely to report living in households with food and economic insecurity than non-LGBT respondents*. U.S. Census Bureau. https://www.census.gov/library/stories/2021/08/lgbt-community-harder-hit-by-economic-impact-of-pandemic.html

Gogoi, P. (2020, October). *Stuck-at-home moms: The pandemic's devastating toll on women*. National Public Radio. https://www.npr.org/2020/10/28/928253674/stuck-at-home-moms-the-pandemics-devastating-toll-on-women

Goldin, C. (2006). The quiet revolution that transformed women's employment, education, and family. *American Economic Review, 96*(2), 1–21. https://doi.org/10.1257/000282806777212350

Goldin, C. (2014). A grand gender convergence: Its last chapter. *American Economic Review, 104*(4), 1091–1119.

Guzman, G., & Kollar, M. (2023, September). *Income in the United States: 2022* (Current Population Reports No. P60-279). U.S. Government Publishing Office, Washington, DC.

Hsu, A. (2020, October). *Even the most successful women pay a big price*. National Public Radio. https://www.npr.org/2020/10/20/924566058/even-the-most-successful-women-are-sidelining-careers-for-family-in-pandemic?ft=nprml&f=928323746

Human Rights Campaign. (2021). *The wage gap among LGBTQ+ workers in the United States*. https://www.hrc.org/resources/the-wage-gap-among-lgbtq-workers-in-the-united-states

Isenberg, N. (2016). *White trash: The 400 year untold history of class in America*. Viking Press.

Kochhar, R. (2023, March). *The enduring grip of the gender pay gap*. Pew Research Center. https://www.pewresearch.org/social-trends/2023/03/01/the-enduring-grip-of-the-gender-pay-gap/

Kochhar, R., & Bennett, J. (2021, September). *Despite the pandemic, wage growth held firm for most U.S. workers, with little effect on inequality*. Pew Research Center. https://www.pewresearch.org/short-reads/2021/09/07/despite-the-pandemic-wage-growth-held-firm-for-most-u-s-workers-with-little-effect-on-inequality/

Kochhar, R., & Cilluffo, A. (2018, November). *Income inequality in the U.S. is rising most rapidly among Asians*. Pew Research Center. https://www.pewresearch.org/social-trends/2018/07/12/income-inequality-in-the-u-s-is-rising-most-rapidly-among-asians/

Krishnan, M. (2020, April). *The COVID-19 challenge to gender equality*. McKinsey & Company. https://www.mckinsey.com/id/our-insights/the-covid-19-challenge-to-gender-equality

Liu, W. M., Colbow, A. J., & Rice, A. J. (2016). Social class and masculinity. In Y. J. Wong & S. R. Wester (Eds.), *APA handbook of men and masculinities* (pp. 413–432). American Psychological Association. https://doi.org/10.1037/14594-019

Livingston, G. (2018, January). *They're waiting longer, but U.S. women today more likely to have children than a decade ago*. Pew Center Research. https://www.pewresearch.org/wp-content/uploads/sites/20/2018/01/Pew-Motherhood-report-FINAL.pdf

Martin-Caughey, A. (2023, March). *Men continued to outnumber and outearn women among full-time, year-round workers in 2021*. U.S. Census Bureau. https://www.census.gov/library/stories/2023/03/women-and-men-occupation-changes-during-covid-19.html

McElrath, K., & Hernandez, E. L. (2023, December 13). *Education does not resolve gender wage gap*. U. S. Census Bureau. https://www.census.gov/library/stories/2023/12/education-does-not-resolve-gender-wage-gap.html

McKinsey Quarterly. (n.d.). T*he pandemic's gender effect*. McKinsey & Company. https://www.mckinsey.com/featured-insights/diversity-and-inclusion/five-fifty-the-pandemics-gender-effect

Merritt, K. L. (2017). *Masterless men: Poor Whites and slavery in the antebellum south*. Cambridge Press.

Miller, C. C. (2014, April). The pay gap is because of gender, not jobs. *The New York Times*. https://www.nytimes.com/2014/04/24/upshot/the-pay-gap-is-because-of-gender-not-jobs.html

Miller, C. C. (2019, April). Women did everything right. Then work got 'greedy.' *The New York Times*. https://www.nytimes.com/2019/04/26/upshot/women-long-hours-greedy-professions.html

Miller, C. C. (2023, October). Claudia Goldin's Nobel-winning research shows 'why women won'. *The New York Times*. https://www.nytimes.com/2023/10/11/upshot/claudia-goldin-nobel-prize.html

O'Dwyer, F., & Ralph, N. (2021, August). *Why trans liberation is a class issue*. New Economics Foundation. https://neweconomics.org/2021/08/why-trans-liberation-is-a-class-issue

Ojeda, L., & Organista, K. C. (2016). Latino American men. In Y. J. Wong & S. R. Wester (Eds.), *APA handbook of men and masculinities* (pp. 299–318). American Psychological Association. https://doi.org/10.1037/14594-014

Olya, G. (2024, March). *What income is considered poverty level in 2024?* NASDAQ. https://www.nasdaq.com/articles/what-income-is-considered-poverty-level-in-2024

Parker, K. (2021, November). *What's behind the growing gap between men and women in college completion?* Pew Research Center. https://www.pewresearch.org/short-reads/2021/11/08/whats-behind-the-growing-gap-between-men-and-women-in-college-completion/

Parker, K., & Stepler, R. (2017, September). *Americans see men as the financial providers, even as women's contributions grow*. Pew Research Center. https://www.pewresearch.org/short-reads/2017/09/20/americans-see-men-as-the-financial-providers-even-as-womens-contributions-grow/

Parker, K., & Wan, W. (2013, March). *Modern parenthood: Roles of moms and dads converge as they balance work and family*. Pew Research Center. https://www.pewresearch.org/wp-content/uploads/sites/20/2013/03/FINAL_modern_parenthood_03-2013.pdf

Patten, E. (2016, July). *Racial, gender wage gaps persist in U.S. despite some progress*. Pew Research Center. https://www.pewresearch.org/short-reads/2016/07/01/racial-gender-wage-gaps-persist-in-u-s-despite-some-progress/

Pew Research Center. (2016, June). *On views of race and inequality, Blacks and Whites are worlds apart*. https://www.pewresearch.org/social-trends/2016/06/27/on-views-of-race-and-inequality-blacks-and-whites-are-worlds-apart/

Powell, K. (2008). *The Black male handbook: A blueprint for life*. Simon and Schuster.

Robinson, C. J. (1983). *Black marxism: The making of the Black radical tradition*. University of North Carolina Press.

Smith, L. (2005). Psychotherapy, classism, and the poor: Conspicuous by their absence. *American Psychologist, 60*(7), 687–696. https://doi.org/10.1037/0003-066X.60.7.687

Smith, L., Appio, L., & Chang, J. (2013). Feminist multicultural counseling psychology and poverty. In C. Z. Enns & E. N. Williams (Eds.), *The Oxford handbook of feminist multucultural counseling psychology* (pp. 155–168).

Smith, L., Romero, L., & Baranowski, K. (2014). Poverty at the intersections: Implications for socially just community-based practice. In M. L. Miville & A. D. Ferguson (Eds.), *Handbook of race-ethnicity and gender in psychology* (pp. 111–130). Springer. https://doi.org/10.1007/978-1-4614-8860-6_6

Sun, S. (2023, January). *Poverty among women & families*. National Women's Law Center Fact Sheet. https://nwlc.org/wp-content/uploads/2023/02/2023_nwlc_PovertySnapshot-converted.pdf

Torres-Mackie, N. (2020). *Cultivating capacities: How children of single mothers manage stigma and endure strain*. Doctoral dissertation, Columbia University. Columbia Academic Commons. https://academiccommons.columbia.edu/doi/10.7916/d8-10ya-je80

Vandello, J. A., Wilkerson, M., Bosson, J. K., Wiernik, B. M., & Kosakowska-Berezecka, N. (2023). Precarious manhood and men's physical health around the world. *Psychology of Men & Masculinities, 24*(1), 1–15. https://doi.org/10.1037/men0000407V

Whittington, C., Hadfield, K., & Calderón, C. (2020, March). *The lives and livelihoods of many in the LGBTQ community are at risk amidst COVID-19 crisis*. Human Rights Campaign. https://hrc-prod-requests.s3-us-west-2.amazonaws.com/files/assets/resources/COVID19-IssueBrief-032020-FINAL.pdf

Chapter 5
Sexual Orientation and Gender

Note on Language

We begin our chapter with a note on language, since with this subject in particular, it is especially important to note that language is changing constantly. We recognize that even while writing this, the terminology used to describe sexual orientation and gender, and specifically their intersection continues to undergo radical changes. It is our hope that we capture the current zeitgeist, though a goal of our book is to demonstrate the importance of embracing change and nuance to help build a better understanding of the unique lived experiences of people.

History and Sexual Orientation

In this chapter, we discuss the intersection of sexual orientation and gender while subsequently applying these considerations to the field of counseling. To do so, we must first introduce and operationalize "sexual orientation" in a historical, sociopolitical, and cultural context. Defining sexual orientation does not come without its challenges; it is deeply contextual and dependent upon complex cultural matrices (i.e. interacting systems/institutions) of a given place. Being that the focus of this volume is working with gender and counseling within the United States, the majority of the chapter will engage with the cultural matrices found within the U.S., though included is also brief histories and considerations for other contexts. Sexual orientation "refers to the sex, [gender, and/or expression] of those to whom one is sexually and[/or] romantically attracted" (adapted from: American Psychological Association, 2012). As Fausto-Sterling (2019) aptly points out, defining sexual orientation within a scientific context often lacks complexity and focuses on differences between groups of people to build the definition. Inherent problems in this

M. L. Miville et al., *Counseling and Gender*,
https://doi.org/10.1007/978-3-031-69172-0_5

approach involve lacking complexity and fluidity in how these identities are embodied and experienced materially (Fausto-Sterling, 2019). Attuning to this complexity involves situating the term within a historical understanding, which will be included throughout the chapter. The chapter concludes with a case example detailing the complexity in intersection between gender and sexual orientation, while also building upon context from earlier chapters on race, ethnicity, and social class.

Developing a timeline of sexual orientation would involve outlining all of human history, however providing a brief description of sexual orientation as a recognized social identity in the current era is more manageable. Pre-colonial and ancient terminology for sexual orientation has a history as rich as any other subject with numerous understandings of human sexuality proliferating across the world with expansive fluidity and multiplicity, much like with gender (as discussed in Chaps. 1 and 6). Many terms used to describe human sexuality outside of current understanding can be found in other languages, though their use today is often construed through the lens of Western definitions of sexuality, particularly "sexual orientation". Though the attribution of the origin of the term "sexual orientation" is unclear, the term gained traction in the 1860s and 1870s in Western academic settings. Similar terms to describe sexual orientation, such as "homosexuality" and "heterosexuality" were in use in the late 1800s as well, thus creating a dichotomy between "normative" sexuality and "non-normative" sexuality (Foucault, 1978). This Western understanding of sexual orientation became commonplace in areas impacted by colonialism—in other words, throughout most of the world.

What this also points to is the concurrent effects of racism, sexism, ableism, classism, and heterosexism. These effects can be seen throughout the world, particularly in areas where colonialism has remained a bastion for Western thought. In the United States, as we described in Chap. 2 and elsewhere, racism and heterosexism are so influential in their intersections that they should be identified in the first part of this chapter. Racism and heterosexism influence and complement one another through various social movements throughout history. This intersection in the United States has often manifested as waves of social progress, eventually cut off with socially conservative backlash (Elledge, 2018). For instance, the early 1900s were wellsprings of gender and sexuality fluidity, particularly in urban areas, which then was followed by negative reactions through legal, social, and cultural means in the 1940s and 50s (Elledge, 2018). Examples of the epistemological and material pushback against fluidity are included throughout the remainder of this section.

The nineteenth into the twentieth century started a trend of attempting to *scientify*, or empirically define and measure, gender, race, and sexual orientation (see Chap. 1). Eugenic "science" in this era categorized people as unbefitting to participate in society due to inherent, supposedly biologically-based, characteristics. Not being White and not being heterosexual (that is, the vast majority of the world's population) were seen as "threats to the future of White society" in the U.S., which meant that queer and transgender people of color were specifically targeted for acts of sterilization, violence, murder, psychiatric hold, and social isolation (McWhorter, 2009). Moreover, people were encouraged to consider eugenic viability when choosing partners, which inherently excluded people of color, LGBTQ+ people, disabled people, and anyone with non-reproductive sexual interests (McWhorter, 2009).

Despite having a strongly supported historical basis in now radically disproven theories, there are many unfortunate eugenic holdovers that remain through societal expectations, biases, and attitudes held by people. This can be felt especially poignantly by members of LGBTQ+ communities who are still very much under scrutiny within the U.S. In fact there is still significant public discourse on whether people holding LGBTQ+ identities are "real" and if they remain disruptors of civilization (McWhorter, 2009). These holdovers are necessary considerations when engaging with counseling and gender/sexual orientation.

Within the United States particularly, sexuality has been aggressively policed both materially and metaphorically (Ritchie & Jones-Brown, 2017). A historical manifestation of this policing within the United States includes what is often referred to as "the Lavender Scare" during the mid-twentieth century. People who identified or were thought to be queer were determined to be morally corrupt and capable of corrupting others, which resulted in tangible, systemic consequences for any departure from heteronormativity and cisnormativity (Johnson, 2004). These consequences included being formally investigated and fired from jobs, not being hired, blackmail and extortion, violence by fellow citizens, by the police state, and by carceral psychiatric intervention (Cervini, 2020; Johnson, 2004).

Another salient example of both metaphoric and material policing of sexual orientation and gender is found in the U.S. in the early twentieth century when gay men were considered a particular class of "moral criminals" and consequently could be jailed for various laws relating to supposed solicitation or degeneracy, which also forced many gay men to then police their sexual and gendered expression to appear conventionally masculine and thus "fit in" (Polchin, 2019). Lesbians were similarly targeted, but these cases were often hidden from the public, since authorities did not want to influence "respectable" women (Derry, 2021). In these examples, both sexual orientation and gender are targeted simultaneously. Social rules posited, and still do in many cases, that gender as a gay man or a lesbian was/is distinguished solidly from being heterosexual. In this way, gender was different for gay/lesbian people than it was for heterosexuals. Taking an intersectional approach to counseling, gender is indeed a necessary construct through these examples alone, though layers of complexity are added when considering that these same sets of laws also were used against people of color, particularly Black women and men in the U.S., and that the majority of arrests through these means occurred with gay/lesbian women and men of color. We will present other examples of gendered heterosexist laws throughout the world later in the chapter. When considering sexual orientation and its intersections with gender in the counseling setting, it is imperative that we consider the many histories of sexual orientation as they relate to specific cultural, national, ethnic, racial, and gendered groups.

Sexual orientation and gender are often viewed as distinct social constructs that possess interplay but are ultimately separate. However, sexual orientation and gender are dependent upon one another as context to serve as accurate descriptors. A lesson learned from radical LGBTQ+ movements throughout time is that gender and sexual orientation are aspects of one another, each lending reciprocal and specific information about the other in a continuous dynamic. In other words, it means something specific that a lesbian woman is both a woman and attracted to other women; being either attracted to women or being a woman would not alone constitute the lived experience, material reality, or self-identity as a lesbian woman. This lesson becomes crucial as psychological science often attempts to extricate interdependent socio-political identities from one another in order to operationalize these terms in a more manageable way (Bullough & Bullough, 1997). While this creates a more easily legible science, it unfortunately also creates a less accurate science as this style of operationalization forgoes context for brevity.

Terminology

Terminology used to describe those within LGBTQ+ communities has changed significantly throughout time, which strengthens the need for a historical framework. Even terms that are commonly used now have rich histories that often go undiscussed. The term "queer" for instance, often used today as an umbrella term for people who are not straight, first came into popular use in the English language in the sixteeenth and seventeenth centuries to mean "strange" or "weird" (Sayers, 2005). By the 1920s and 30s, it became commonly associated with being queer, although even then there were complexities. In the early 1900s, before it's popular understanding as gay, queer was used as an intentional wedge by middle-and-upper-class gay White men to differentiate themselves from more effeminate, working class, people of color who were less acceptable to the hegemonic norm (Heaney, 2017). Similarly, the word "heterosexual" in English was first published by a medical doctor in 1892 outlining it as a form of sexual perversion where an individual seeks sexual intercourse for pleasure (Katz, 2007). The meaning of heterosexual changed in the 1930s in the United States to refer to someone who is cisgender and attracted sexually to someone who is of the "opposite sex", which then was taken as a tool of normalization where those who were White, middle-class-and-above, and U.S. citizens were subsumed into normalcy (Katz, 2007). The term heterosexual, like queer, possesses a history as a tool of heteronormativity, racism, and classism. Normalization in this sense is the act of creating a system of what is "normal" that is then distinguished from what is "abnormal" and is a fundamental aspect of heteronormativity. As demonstrated throughout this volume, all systems of oppression work in tandem to develop distinctions between normalcy and abnormalcy as social means of control and violence.

With this nuance in mind, and the former note that language is constantly shifting, below are some relevant terms in use today that are being utilized throughout the chapter. The descriptions below are not holistic and are not meant to be exhaustive, but may offer ease in understanding through the chapter.

- *Aromantic*- a person who does not experience romantic attraction, but may experience platonic or sexual attraction.
- *Asexual*- an individual who does not feel any (or feels little) sexual attraction. This does not mean that they necessarily do not engage in sexual behaviors or align with sexuality.
- *Bisexual*- the attraction to people of two or more genders.
- *"Coming out" or "out"*- the philosophy that an individual has to announce their being non-heterosexual in any form (based in heterosexism).
- *Femme*- people who align with conceptions of femininity, either by expression, philosophy, behavior, or lived experience.
- *Gay*- an individual that is attracted to someone of the same gender, though gay men as a subgroup of gay people are often most associated with the term.
- *Heteronormativity/heterosexism*- the cultural norm and sociopolitical system of assuming, valuing, and privileging heterosexuality above all other sexualities.
- *Identity*- an individual's self-described in-group.
- *Lesbian*- historically, women who are attracted to women, though recent cultural shifts have also included femme people who are attracted to other femme people.
- *Masc*- people who align with conceptions of masculinity, either by expression, philosophy, behavior, or lived experience.
- *Monosexual*- the attraction to only one gender of person. This can include gay men, gay/lesbian women, and straight people, but can also include TGNC people who are only attracted to one gender.
- *Pansexual*- someone who is attracted, or has the potential for attraction, to people of all genders.
- *Sexuality*- an umbrella term for the capacity and desire for things sexual in nature.
- *Straight*- someone who is attracted to those of genders that are different from theirs, exclusively. This term is gender-specific: men who are attracted to women or women who are attracted to men, and does not apply to non-binary people who are only attracted to men or only attracted to women.
- *Queer*- an intentionally ambiguous label that can describe sexuality, sexual orientation, gender, or philosophy.

Differentiation of Behavior, Identity, and Materiality

Categorically, *identity* is not sufficient to explain the complexities of the sexual orientation/gender matrix. We include in our analysis elements of behavior and materiality, respectively, that can elucidate more clearly the aspects of sexual orientation and gender that make them distinct as sociopolitical and consequently psychological realities. Counseling as a field has historically viewed sexual orientation as primarily a set of behaviors that were either "homosexual" or "heterosexual", particularly drawing upon Western binary thought that denied internal realities in service of observable behavior. This also led to the field's involvement in "sexual orientation change efforts" or, as it is better known, conversion therapy (Moleiro & Pinto, 2015). With the addition of identity as a psychological consideration, the field made progress in witnessing the fullness of sexual orientation (American Psychological Association, 2012). A common framing within the field of counseling, however, is that sexual orientation is an "invisible identity", one that is entirely concealable. Adopting a systemic and cultural analysis, we suggest that there exists a set of interlocking materialities of sexual orientation that the "invisible identity" framework does not account for. Materiality here refers to the theory that humans, the social world, and our identities hold tangible, organic, and physical aspects (Holt, 2014). To put it simply: identities are not just in our minds, we can also observe them, behave them, and experience them in physical and social ways.

In modern society, where gendered sexual orientation is made hypervisible, aspects of physicality are often labeled through the lens of sexual orientation as *gendered*. In colloquial terms, this is often referred to as "gaydar": the ability to "tell" if someone is a part of LGBTQ+ communities from limited information and without disclosure. To arrive at this conclusion, people cite behavioral departures from gendered heteronormativity, somatic quirks that strike them as *queer*, and inflections of voice that are expected to belong to someone not straight, or not cisgender. To state directly: this type of conclusion is not scientifically or even phenomenologically appropriate or possible because people of all sexual orientations can possess typically queer-coded inflections, mannerisms, or interests. That is not to say, however, that materiality of gendered sexual orientation does not exist within our social worlds. In fact, this example can be seen as a challenge to the invisible identity model. Moving towards specificity, there exists no consistent phenotypes, behavioral traits, or physicalities of queerness, instead, the materiality of queerness is contextualized through its subversion of heteronormativity. In other words, what appears to be queer is such because it does not appear to be straight, or appears to be in opposition to straightness. A popular quote from bell hooks in a conversation at The New School in 2014 exemplifies this point:

> …queer not as being about who you're having sex with – that can be a dimension of it – but queer as being about the self that is at odds with everything around it and it has to invent and create and find a place to speak and to thrive and to live…. (hooks, 2014)

This portrays a material life, one that centers both around *being* and *doing* in opposition to a structure that is tangibly integrated into society. As argued throughout this chapter thus far, it is also necessary to understand the ways in which gender and sexual orientation are inextricably intertwined. To punctuate this point further, queerness in any form is in opposition to straightness because the systems of heteronormativity and cisnormativity work in tandem to demand that opposition.

Gender and Heteronormativity

As discussed, the relationship between sexual orientation and gender is reciprocally influential, and they inform each other significantly. The context of sexual orientation and gender is such that heterosexism as a social system, enforced by numerous institutions, sets forth guidelines for inclusion/exclusion called heteronormativity, dictates behavior, identity, and access to normalcy through oppressing people at the intersection of sexual orientation and gender. Heterosexism, sexism, and cissexism act together to influence culture and systems on individual, group, institutional, cultural, and systemic levels. Within the system of heterosexism, heterosexuality and cis-ness are seen as rational and natural, while all other forms of relationship to gender and sexual orientation are seen as "different", "new", or "transgressive" (Heaney, 2017). Some examples of heterosexism are the beliefs that queer people are disgusting and unnatural, queer identified family friends, or colleagues are rejected, housing, workplace, or educational discrimination is accepted. Systemic manifestations also may occur, such as the restriction of access to federal rights (Szymanski et al., 2008).

Gender and heteronormativity considerations are plentiful, ranging from a client's internalization of gendered sexual orientation policing (i.e., surveilling with intent to control or demean), the policing of others' expression of gendered sexual orientation, expressing negative attitudes about sexual orientation groups and/or perpetrating or victimizing through violence (Szymanski & Moffitt, in Fouad et al., 2012). For example, Boldt (1996) explicated the ways in which gendered sexual orientation policing manifested in her elementary school classroom. Boldt begins by building a narrative around how an "effeminate" boy, who was often presumed to be gay, was policed by his classmates through instruction about how he should act, talk, move, and behave socially. Similar research has detailed the ways in which policing gender through the use of heterosexist harassment appears at work, specifically that those who deviate from heteronormativity are often subject to punishment either socially or institutionally, even if they are straight (Konik & Cortina, 2008). In a recent study, 76.9% of LGBQ+ people reported experiencing gender harassment at work as opposed to 30% of the straight people surveyed (Konik & Cortina, 2008).

The forms and effects of heteronormativity on gender are multifold, encompassing many different experiences within the matrices of gender and sexual orientation. The remainder of this chapter will be utilized to discuss specific sexually orientated groups and notable intersections between other socio-political identities and gender.

Sexual Orientation and Gender Considerations

The ensuing section of this chapter focuses on potential considerations for specific groups within LGBQ+ communities. The groups portrayed are common within the U.S. and these considerations presented are drawn largely from research within the field of psychology. As such, they should be applied as potentialities, ones that apply to those that are represented in the research drawn upon. This section is non-exhaustive but represents important cultural groups within the U.S. and the ways in which they *may* experience gendered sexual orientation. The data presented for each group are meant to serve as a list of potential issues that may affect individuals and subpopulations within LGBTQ+ communities. It is notable to mention that each consideration can be traced to heterosexism, cissexism, and sexism. To analyze most accurately each of these groups is to also inherently consider the ways in which intersectionality is fundamental to identity, particularly the concurrent effects of culture, race, ability, social class, and ethnicity/religion, which significantly inform the specific ways that sexual orientation and gender interact.

Lesbians

In lesbian communities, which for the majority of history have consisted of primarily cisgender women, there exists a rich history of gender categorization and gender play (Hiestand & Levitt 2005a; Schwartz, 1998). Open expression of same-sex/same-gender relations among cisgender women in the U.S. began during the twentieth century (Faderman, 1991), particularly as women as a whole gained political rights, educational opportunities, and greater independence to live their own self-defined lives. During the 1970s and 1980s, lesbian psychologists began to develop important research and practice interventions for this diverse population (e.g., Boston Lesbian Psychologies Collective, 1987), identifying key concerns and challenges, including experiences of homophobia, as well as its intersections with sexism, racism, and classism; overt and covert discrimination; and pervasive experiences of invisibility in the larger society (e.g., www.lesbianvisibilityweekusa.com).

Transgender women can also identify as lesbians but have often been excluded from lesbian discourse. The situation has changed greatly, however, in how cis-lesbians view trans-lesbians and TGNC people in general. Ashenden (2023) reported that cis-lesbians hold more positive views of TGNC people than other LGBT people (96% vs 89% for all LGBT people), and much more so than non-LGBT populations (69%). Similarly, there is a growing cultural movement to include self-identified lesbians who are not women, as evidenced in the theme of a recent global set of events focused on lesbians, *United not Uniform* (e.g., www.lesbianvisibilityweek-usa.com). This exemplifies the argument throughout this book that labels are fluid and evolutionary in nature. Part of this tradition stems from the intense compulsory heterosexuality forced upon women due to the patriarchal need for women to subsume the role of "other" in relationships with cisgender men (Rich, 1980). Compulsory heterosexuality refers to the intense socialization that many individuals experience through various institutions in the larger society in order to maintain traditional gender roles and the larger patriarchal norms present throughout much of Western and other societies. Due to the strength of compulsory heterosexuality in lesbians' gendered lives, existing as a lesbian in and of itself is a form of resistance (Schwartz, 1998). Relatedly, "lesbian" has historically been used as a social moniker to describe women who resist against traditional gender norms despite their sexual orientation (Schwartz, 1998); indeed this resistance has been a main driver in lesbian political advocacy in the larger society and in psychology (Enns, 1997). Resistance to traditional straight women's gender norms is a cornerstone of lesbianism, particularly when accounting for the labels "butch" and "femme", which are distinct, unique gender experiences for lesbians (Hiestand & Levitt, 2005b). Lesbian gendered experiences can include constant conflict navigation in finding authenticity with one's internal sense of gender, while accounting for safety, gender role expectations, the invisibility of all queer women and femmes' sexual orientation, and interpersonal connection (Hiestand & Levitt, 2005a). Safety remains a particular concern for lesbian women as violence may be used as a tool to instill fear and submission.

Gender expression, and the resistance to gender norms, is particularly important to Black lesbians (Wilson, 2009), rurally-based lesbians (Kazyak, 2012), and butch lesbians (Hiestand & Levitt, 2005b). Despite cultural attempts at erasing lesbian identity, materiality of identity remains a consideration when lesbians forgo traditional gender norms in service of what feels authentic and consonant with their identities. Being perceivable or even suspected as a lesbian can cause people to act violently towards lesbians. In the case of lesbian cisgender women, sexual orientation-based violence is nearly always also sexist violence (Szymanski & Moffitt, in Fouad et al., 2012). Considering multiple marginalizations for lesbians is necessary in the counseling setting. For example, Wilson (2009) delineated how being Black, being a lesbian, being a woman, and being femme/butch/androgynous/genderqueer all contributed to body image, romantic relationships, sexual dynamics, and gender expression.

Gay Men

The term "gay men" encompasses all people who identify as a man and all people who also identify as gay concurrently. Unlike with queer women, who are often made invisible or erased, gay (and queer) men are often experienced as hypervisible. The perceived and assumed *effeminacy* of gay men is a fear response based in heterosexism, and may be internalized by gay men themselves (Taywaditep, 2001). This response arises from the departure that gay men are presumed to make from traditionally masculine roles. In reality, just because a man is gay does not mean he will appear more feminine than a man who is straight; however because masculinity is so heavily policed, even a small departure is often hypervisible to others–this underlines the materiality of the gay male identity. This gay materiality is unique by intersections of race, gender, ethnicity, social class, and disability—for example, Black gay men face increased policing both structurally and of their masculinity (Bowleg, 2013). Much like with lesbian communities, gay men are also open to resistance, particularly when rejecting masculine gender norms in service of subversive masculinities or other expressions of gender (Connell, 1992).

Due to the pressure that men face to adhere to the role of enforcer for patriarchy, violent means may be used when a man resists traditional gender norms–this can be seen as a modeling of sorts, where gay men are victimized by violence in part to show them how to enact violence against others. Regarding violence, the data show that gay men are most likely to experience gendered sexual orientation-based violence in comparison to those in other sexual orientation categories (Herek, 2008; Szymanski & Moffitt, in Fouad et al., 2012). This is especially true for Black, Brown, and Indigenous gay men (Ritchie & Jones-Brown, 2017).

As detailed throughout the book thus far, intersectionality is a necessary construct to contextualize the lived experiences (Crenshaw, 1989). To engage with the specific experiences of intersectionality for gay and bisexual Black men, Lisa Bowleg (2013) conducted in-depth qualitative interviews which focused on gathering how they perceived their intersecting identities. Bowleg gathered that for gay and bisexual Black men, it is impossible to separate out their experiences being men, being Black, and being gay/bi:

> Well it's hard for me to separate [my identities]. When I'm thinking of me, I'm think of all of them as me. Like once you've blended the cake, you can't take the parts back to the main ingredients. (Bowleg, 2013)

These identities are intertwined and all contribute to lived experience conjointly (i.e. material reality) (Bowleg, 2013). Within the study, participants endorsed positive aspects of this specific intersection, citing that to live in the world as a Black gay/bi man has made [them] a better person and connected them more intentionally with community and themselves (Bowleg, 2013).

Bisexual

People of any gender can be bisexual and bisexual people can be attracted to people of any gender as well, despite the commonly held myth that bisexual people are only attracted to cisgender women and cisgender men. Bisexual people face pervasive erasure from both the queer community and the larger heteronormative culture (Brewster & Moradi, 2010; Morgenroth et al., 2022). This manifests as the cultural insistence that bisexuality is not its own distinct sexual orientation, but instead as a waypoint towards being monosexual, typically gay (Brewster & Moradi, 2010; Burleson, 2005). For bisexual men, the belief is often that they are "actually" gay men, whereas for bisexual women, the belief is that they are "truly" straight women

(Yost & Thomas, 2012). In both cases, the expectation is that people are attracted most and exclusively to cisgender men, which reflects larger themes of sexism and the politics of desirability of cisgender men. Another macro-level cultural myth of bisexuality is that bisexual people are sexually "greedy" or "promiscuous" (Rust, 2002; Yost & Thomas, 2012). These stereotypes may even compound on racial, ethnic, gender, or class-bound stereotypes to increase the intensity or specific messaging of antibisexual attitudes (Bowleg, 2013; McConnell et al., 2018). A thought process underlying this myth is that to be attracted to multiple genders means that one must, categorically, be having sex with both, consistently, to be considered "actively" bisexual.

Bisexual people experience stigma from "both sides", indicating that heteronormativity and monosexuality as cultural systems interact uniquely at the intersection of people who are not straight and are also not gay. Navigating this dynamic can be challenging, though bisexual people may find that they are able to access psychological resources such as bicultural self-efficacy and cognitive flexibility to assist in this navigation (Brewster et al., 2013). In not successfully navigating experiences of antibisexual attitudes and discrimination, bisexual people may face higher levels of internalized antibisexual attitudes, body surveillance, and body-related shame (Brewster et al., 2014; Polihronakis et al., 2021). In fact, much research on bisexual populations indicates that bisexual people view antibisexual attitudes/discrimination and internalized biphobia as central to their mental health status (Brewster et al., 2014; Flanders et al., 2015; Polihronakis et al., 2021). With these data in mind, it is important to note that most of the research about bisexual people comes from predominantly White participants (Ghabrial & Ross, 2018). While Whiteness pervades all of psychological research, and specifically sexual orientation research, it is notable that bisexual identity research is particularly White (Ghabrial & Ross, 2018), which ossifies intersectionality as a necessary counseling framework, especially with bisexual people.

Queer/Pansexual

As the LGBT political movements expanded during the early twenty-first century, fluidity of labels and identities became far more centralized in the public discourse and in psychological research and practice. Queer and pansexual are two such distinct sexual orientations that encompass a wide range of sexual, romantic, and behavioral patterns, and may also overlap at points (Galupo et al., 2017). With these overlaps, as well as the intentional ambiguity and flexibility of the identities, much of psychological research groups them with other LGBTQ+ identities, or with each other specifically. Epistemologically and in practice, there are countless differences between people who identify as queer and/or pansexual, which is reflective of the philosophical push for specificity and difference. This being said, there are also similarities connecting queer and pansexual people (often along with bisexual and sexually fluid people) in that self-hood may transcend identity, that there are numerous forms of attraction that are accepted, and an embrace of the constantly-shifting landscape of sexuality (Galupo et al., 2017). In a recent article, Morandini and colleagues (2017) surveyed queer and pansexual people and found that on established sexuality indices, most participants who were pansexual fell in the "bisexual range" whereas most people who were queer fell in the "homosexual range". This finding, though dated, demonstrates the flexibility of these identities.

As discussed throughout this chapter, "queer" is a label that encompasses many possibilities for sexual, romantic, and relational behavior; in this way it is different from monosexual identities such as gay or straight. People who identify as queer may intentionally choose this label *because* it is vague and open-ended (Kolker et al., 2020). Queer people may also resonate with this label because it can describe their gender identity as well as their sexual orientation (Kolker et al., 2020). Where the label of queer is often seen as an "umbrella", pansexual may be viewed as a "fringe identity", or a hyper-specific identity that only a few people belong to (Hayfield & Křížová, 2021). Pansexuality is often relegated to a different form of bisexuality, or as an opposition to the perceived (but not actual) binary of bisexuality (Hayfield & Křížová, 2021). Both queer and pansexual identity categories embrace movement, fluidity, and context specific attraction.

Asexual

There exists a misnomer about asexuality: that asexual people are completely void of sexual attraction to others and do not even engage in sexual activities. The truth is that asexuality is a spectrum; many asexual people engage in sexual activity and can develop sexual attraction (Jones et al., 2017). Asexual people can be oriented towards people of the same or different genders–in other words, they can be "straight and asexual" or "gay and asexual" or any other sexual orientation. This fact alone can make coming to the identity of asexuality difficult for many people; to want aspects of relationships but not others that are often seen as essential can create confusion and insecurity for the individual as well as others they may date or partner (Winer et al., 2024). Heteronormativity, in all its pervasiveness, can play a role in the negative psychological consequences of navigating the development of an asexual identity (Kelleher et al., 2023).

Identity formation for asexual people is often non-linear; many asexual people will identify as one or more other sexual orientations at some point before working their way "into" an asexual identity (Robbins et al., 2016; Winer et al., 2024). The "coming out" process for asexual people can also be complicated. Some asexual people report not needing to come out due to the applicability of the concept to them, whereas other asexual people express that they are not accepted and/or met with skepticism and even hostility (Robbins et al., 2016). There are a number of reasons someone may identify as asexual, and not having interest in sexual activities is only one of them (Jones et al., 2017). Anecdotally, asexual people express themselves in a variety of ways: they may want to decentralize the perceived-to-be-implicit importance of sexual relationships to a healthy relational dynamic, they may want to engage with establishing a non-sexual relationship with people due to political or philosophical reasons, or they may simply have no interest in sexual activities. These reasons range on spectrums and are often seen in combination with one another (Gressgård, 2015; Jones et al., 2017). This is also not an exhaustive list. It is important to engage asexual people in the counseling setting as one would with any sexual orientation: with curiosity and an open mind.

Straight

Straightness has been discussed throughout this book, and particularly in this chapter, as a sexual orientation that is often expected, even demanded, of people; moreover heterosexual people often benefit from the systems of cissexism and heteronormativity. There is an attitude and a culture to straightness that stems from heteronormativity (Silva, 2019) which we suggest harms straight people as well as LGBTQI+ communities, similar to the way rigid masculinity may be harmful to cisgender men (see Chap. 10). Taking this into account, there are many assumptions about straightness and straight people that must be negated if societies are to move forward past privileging heteronormativity.

One enduring belief about straight people is that one realizes they are straight and then never has to navigate or develop their sexual orientation like "non-straight" people do (Morgan, 2012). To arrive at an identity of straightness is not always so obvious for people and it is perfectly typical to explore, navigate, develop, and change before identifying as straight (Morgan, 2012). Exploration of the gender roles one may play as a straight person may be an important part of this process of exploration, especially since research has shown that taking an unexamined and rigid approach to identifying, for example, as a straight cisgender man, may lead to several unhealthy mental and physical outcomes (Mahalik, et al., 2007). Altogether, heteronormativity is harmful to everyone and should be explored and unpacked within counseling settings, including with straight clients. An unfortunate clinical trend in counseling fields is seen in the attention that is given to sexual orientation with LGBTQI+ clients, but not with straight clients; this trend represents a major area of growth for the field of counseling.

Conclusion

The intersection of sexual orientation and gender is historically and epistemologically rich. For much of human history, and the history of psychology, gender and sexual orientation have been conceptualized as inextricably intertwined, or even one in the same. The separation of the two sociopolitical positionalities in the U.S. occurred, in part, due to the influence of mainstream psychology developing alongside a growing understanding of sexual orientation in the 1970s and 1980s. Contemporaneously, many community members and scholars are increasingly contextualizing the two as dependent upon one another. For this way of knowing, people make sense of their gender through sexual orientation and make sense of their sexual orientation through gender–they are not distinct categories.

Case Study

Kevin, a 28 year old Korean-American pansexual cisgender man living in Houston, TX, entered therapy presenting as frustrated and anxious about his inability to find a romantic partner. He has been publicly "out" since he was 15 and, as an only child to his mother and father, he enjoyed a warm reception from his parents. He is sexually and romantically interested in people of all genders, but prefers dating men. Over the past few years Kevin has had one romantic relationship that lasted a few months, but struggles to consistently find people that "see him for who he is." Similarly, he shares that "the gay guys I date all expect me to be submissive," which does not match with his masculine identity and expression. He feels it is difficult for him to be an Asian pansexual man and still feel like others respect his "manhood." Trying to date more women or nonbinary people may be the only way to have this respect, he posits. He also notes that he does not have many friends and that most of them are heterosexual men from college. He reports that the loneliness he feels as a result of this long-term dynamic has felt especially difficult to manage.

Discussion Questions

1. Analyze Kevin's experiences and interactions within the LGBT community and society at large through the lens of heteronormative and gender standards. How do these standards influence his emotional well-being and the dynamics of his relationships?
2. In what ways does Kevin's journey as an Asian pansexual man mirror the chapter's description of the LGB community's complicated processes of identification and labeling?
3. Because of his sexual orientation and ethnic origin, Kevin thinks that his masculinity is not recognized. Discuss how those who do not fit the mold of traditional masculinity, like Kevin, are impacted by society's norms regarding masculinity.
4. Kevin vents his anger at the fact that the possible romantic partners in his life do not "see him for who he is." What part do societal expectations of gender and sexuality play in his difficulty in establishing and sustaining relationships? Consider how the societal expectation to be partnered as well as his sexual orientation and dating preferences may interact.

5. What are the points of stress presented in this case? How could these factors contribute to his presenting concern and to what extent could traditional gender and sexuality norms figure into his stress?
6. Kevin mentions that he is lonely and does not have many friends who share his current identity. How could his sexual orientation and the unique dynamics of his friendships affect his feelings of belonging or loneliness?
7. Kevin and others like him face unique obstacles to exposure, forming relationships, and gaining social acceptance; what mental health practices could help them overcome these obstacles?

References

American Psychological Association. (2012). Guidelines for psychological practice with lesbian, gay, and bisexual clients. *American Psychology., 67*, 10–42. https://doi.org/10.1037/a0024659

Ashenden, A. (2023, March). Lesbians being anti-trans is a lesbophobic trope. *Gay Times*. Retrieved from https://www.gaytimes.com/originals/lesbians-are-not-anti-trans/

Boldt, G. (1996). Sexist and heterosexist response to gender bending in an elementary classroom. *Curriculum Inquiry, 26*(2), 113–132.

Boston Lesbian Psychologies Collective. (1987). *Lesbian psychologies: Explorations and challenges*. University of Illinois Press.

Bowleg, L. (2013). "Once you've blended the cake, you can't take the parts back to the main ingredients": Black gay and bisexual men's descriptions and experiences of intersectionality. *Sex Roles, 68*, 754–767.

Brewster, M. E., & Moradi, B. (2010). Perceived experiences of anti-bisexual prejudice: Instrument development and evaluation. *Journal of Counseling Psychology, 57*(4), 451–468. https://doi.org/10.1037/a0021116

Brewster, M. E., Moradi, B., DeBlaere, C., & Velez, B. L. (2013). Navigating the borderlands: The roles of minority stressors, bicultural self-efficacy, and cognitive flexibility in the mental health of bisexual individuals. *Journal of Counseling Psychology, 60*(4), 543–556. https://doi.org/10.1037/a0033224

Brewster, M. E., Velez, B. L., Esposito, J., Wong, S., Geiger, E., & Keum, B. T. (2014). Moving beyond the binary with disordered eating research: A test and extension of objectification theory with bisexual women. *Journal of Counseling Psychology, 61*(1), 50–62. https://doi.org/10.1037/a0034748

Bullough, B., & Bullough, V. (1997). Are transvestites necessarily heterosexual? *Archives of Sexual Behavior, 26*(1), 1–12. https://doi.org/10.1023/a:1024589618410

Burleson, W. E. (2005). *Bi America: Myths, truths, and struggles of an invisible community*. Harrington Park Press.

Cervini, E. (2020). *The deviant's war: The homosexual vs. the United States of America* (1st ed.). Farrar, Straus and Giroux.

Connell, R. W. (1992). A very straight gay: Masculinity, homosexual experience, and the dynamics of gender. *American Sociological Review, 57*(6), 735–751. https://doi.org/10.2307/2096120

Crenshaw, K. (1989). Demarginalizing the intersection of race and sex: A Black feminist critique of antidiscrimination doctrine, feminist theory and antiracist politics. *University of Chicago Legal Forum, 1989(1)*, Article 8. http://chicagounbound.uchicago.edu/uclf/vol1989/iss1/8

Derry, C. (2021). *Lesbianism and the criminal law of England and Wales*. Open Learning. https://www.open.edu/openlearn/society-politics-law/law/lesbianism-and-the-criminal-law-england-and-wales

Elledge, J. (2018). *The boys of fairy town: Sodomites, female impersonators, third-sexers, pansies, queers, and sex morons in Chicago's first century*. Chicago Review Press.

Enns, C. Z. (1997). *Feminist theories and feminist psychotherapies: Origins, themes, and variations*. Haworth Press.

Faderman, L. (1991). *Odd girls and twilight lovers: A history of lesbian life in twentieth-century America*. Columbia University.

Fausto-Sterling, A. (2019). Gender/sex, sexual orientation, and identity are in the body: How did they get there? *The Journal of Sex Research, 56*(4–5), 529–555.

Flanders, C. E., Dobinson, C., & Logie, C. (2015). "I'm never really my full self": Young bisexual women's perceptions of their mental health. *Journal of Bisexuality, 15*(4), 454–480.

Fouad, N. A., Carter, J. A., & Subich, L. M. (Eds.). (2012). *APA handbook of counseling psychology, Vol. 1. Theories, research, and methods* (pp. 423–451). American Psychological Association. https://doi-org.ezproxy.cul.columbia.edu/10.1037/13754-016

Foucault, M. (1978). *The history of sexuality: An introduction* (Vol. 1). Random House.

Galupo, M. P., Ramirez, J. L., & Pulice-Farrow, L. (2017). "Regardless of their gender": Descriptions of sexual identity among bisexual, pansexual, and queer identified individuals. *Journal of Bisexuality, 17*(1), 108–124. https://doi.org/10.1080/15299716.2016.1228491

Ghabrial, M. A., & Ross, L. E. (2018). Representation and erasure of bisexual people of color: A content analysis of quantitative bisexual mental health research. *Psychology of Sexual Orientation and Gender Diversity, 5*(2), 132–142. https://doi.org/10.1037/sgd0000286

Gressgård, R. (2015). Asexuality: From pathology to identity and beyond. In M. Carrigan, K. Gupta, & T. Morrison (Eds.), *Asexuality and sexual normativity* (pp. 68–81). Routledge.

Hayfield, N., & Křížová, K. (2021). It's like bisexuality, but it isn't: Pansexual and panromantic people's understandings of their identities and experiences of becoming educated about gender and sexuality. *Journal of Bisexuality, 21*(2), 167–193.

Heaney, E. (2017). *The new woman: Literary modernism, queer theory, and the trans feminine allegory*. Northwestern University Press.

Hiestand, K. R., & Levitt, H. M. (2005a). Gender within lesbian sexuality: Butch and femme perspectives. *Journal of Constructivist Psychology, 18*(1), 39–51. https://doi-org.ezproxy.cul.columbia.edu/10.1080/10720530590523062

Hiestand, K. R., & Levitt, H. M. (2005b). Butch identity development: The formation of an authentic gender. *Feminism & Psychology, 15*(1), 61–85. https://doi.org/10.1177/0959353505049709

Holt, J. P. (2014). *The social thought of Karl Marx*. Sage.

hooks, B. (2014). *Are you still a slave? Liberating the Black female body [Lecture]*. Eugene Lang College.

Johnson, D. K. (2004). *The lavender scare: The Cold War persecution of gays and lesbians in the federal government*. University of Chicago Press.

Jones, C., Hayter, M., & Jomeen, J. (2017). Understanding asexual identity as a means to facilitate culturally competent care: A systematic literature review. *Journal of Clinical Nursing, 26*(23–24), 3811–3831.

Katz, J. N. (2007). The invention of heterosexuality: The debut of the heterosexual. In K. E. Lovaas & M. M. Jenkins (Eds.), *Sexualities & communication in everyday life: A reader* (pp. 21–40). Sage.

Kazyak, E. (2012). Midwest or lesbian? Gender, rurality, and sexuality. *Gender & Society, 26*(6), 825–848. https://doi.org/10.1177/0891243212458361

Kelleher, S., Murphy, M., & Su, X. (2023). Asexual identity development and internalisation: A scoping review of quantitative and qualitative evidence. *Psychology & Sexuality, 14*(1), 45–72.

Kolker, Z. M., Taylor, P. C., & Galupo, M. P. (2020). "As a sort of blanket term": Qualitative analysis of queer sexual identity marking. *Sexuality & Culture: An Interdisciplinary Quarterly, 24*(5), 1337–1357. https://doi.org/10.1007/s12119-019-09686-4

Konik, J., & Cortina, L. M. (2008). Policing gender at work: Intersections of harassment based on sex and sexuality. *Social Justice Research, 21*(3), 1313–1337. https://doi.org/10.1007/s11211-008-0074-z

Mahalik, J. R., Burns, S. M., & Syzdek, M. (2007). Masculinity and perceived normative health behaviors as predictors of men's health behaviors. *Social science & medicine, 64(*11), 2201–2209.

McConnell, E. A., Janulis, P., Phillips, G., II, Truong, R., & Birkett, M. (2018). Multiple minority stress and LGBT community resilience among sexual minority men. *Psychology of Sexual Orientation and Gender Diversity, 5*(1), 1.

McWhorter, L. (2009). *Racism and sexual oppression in Anglo-America: A genealogy*. Indiana University Press.

Moleiro, C., & Pinto, N. (2015). Sexual orientation and gender identity: Review of concepts, controversies and their relation to psychopathology classification systems. *Frontiers in Psychology, 6,* Article 1511. https://doi-org.ezproxy.cul.columbia.edu/10.3389/fpsyg.2015.01511

Morandini, J. S., Blaszczynski, A., & Dar-Nimrod, I. (2017). Who adopts queer and pansexual sexual identities? *The Journal of Sex Research, 54*(7), 911–922.

Morgan, E. M. (2012). Not always a straight path: College students' narratives of heterosexual identity development. *Sex Roles, 66*, 79–93.

Morgenroth, T., Kirby, T. A., Cuthbert, M. J., Evje, J., & Anderson, A. E. (2022). Bisexual erasure: Perceived attraction patterns of bisexual women and men. *European Journal of Social Psychology, 52*(2), 249–259. https://doi.org/10.1002/ejsp.2773

Polchin, J. (2019). *Indecent advances: A hidden history of true crime and prejudice before Stonewall*. Counterpoint.

Polihronakis, C. J., Velez, B. L., & Brewster, M. E. (2021). Bisexual men's sexual health: A test of minority stress theory. *Psychology of Men & Masculinities, 22*(1), 201–215. https://doi.org/10.1037/men0000304

Rich, A. (1980). Compulsory heterosexuality and lesbian existence. *Signs: Journal of Women in Culture and Society, 5*(4), 631–660. https://doi.org/10.1353/jowh.2003.0079

Ritchie, A. J., & Jones-Brown, D. (2017). Policing race, gender, and sex: A review of law enforcement policies. *Women and Criminal Justice, 27*(1), 21–50. https://doi.org/10.1080/08974454.2016.1259599

Robbins, N. K., Low, K. G., & Query, A. N. (2016). A qualitative exploration of the "coming out" process for asexual individuals. *Archives of Sexual Behavior, 45*, 751–760.

Rust, P. C. (2002). Bisexuality: The state of the union. *Annual Review of Sex Research, 13*, 180–240.

Sayers. (2005). The etymology of queer. *ANQ: A Quarterly Journal of Short Articles, Notes and Reviews, 18*(2), 17–19. https://doi.org/10.3200/ANQQ.18.2.17-19

Schwartz, A. E. (1998). *Sexual subjects: Lesbians, gender, and psychoanalysis*. Psychology Press.

Silva, T. J. (2019). Straight identity and same-sex desire: Conservatism, homophobia, and straight culture. *Social Forces, 97*(3), 1067–1094.

Szymanski, D. M., Kashubeck-West, S., & Meyer, J. (2008). Internalized heterosexism: A historical and theoretical overview. *The Counseling Psychologist, 36*(4), 510–524. https://doi.org/10.1177/0011000007309488

Taywaditep, K. J. (2001). Marginalization among the marginalized: Gay men's anti-effeminacy attitudes. *Journal of Homosexuality, 42*(1), 1–28. https://doi.org/10.1300/J082v42n01_01

Wilson, B. D. M. (2009). Black lesbian gender and sexual culture: Celebration and resistance. *Culture, Health & Sexuality, 11*(3), 297–313. https://doi.org/10.1080/13691050802676876

Winer, C., Carroll, M., Yang, Y., Linder, K., & Miles, B. (2024). "I didn't know ace was a thing": Bisexuality and pansexuality as identity pathways in asexual identity formation. *Sexualities, 27*(1–2), 267–289.

Yost, M. R., & Thomas, G. D. (2012). Gender and binegativity: Men's and women's attitudes toward male and female bisexuals. *Archives of Sexual Behavior, 41*, 691–702. https://doi.org/10.1007/s10508-011-9767-8

Chapter 6
Transgender and Gender Nonconforming Contexts of Gender

Introduction of Gender Expansiveness

Gender expansiveness, the multiplicity or plurality of gender, has existed since time immemorial. The language we use to describe gender and provide context to difference has evolved throughout the history of humanity to include strict definitions of gender along a binary (McNabb, 2017). The binary in question consists of who are now understood to be cisgender women and cisgender men, on opposite sides of a spectrum (as referenced in Chap. 1). As also discussed in Chap. 1, this spectrum is a construct of colonialism, capitalism, and scientification (Lugones, 2007; Russett, 1991; Wiesner-Hanks, 2011). Non-binary gender terminology has existed since gender as a conceptualization of difference arose and includes numerous categorizations of people which would each require a separate volume to honor appropriately (McNabb, 2017). Instead, this chapter will focus on current manifestations of gender that is trans, including gender that is non-binary. The term "transgender" is typically used as a social positionality, an umbrella term, and a social identifier, all to describe someone whose gender is different than the one they were assigned at birth (Bockting et al., 2020).

It is important to note that this chapter leans heavily on the scaffolding of Chap. 1, particularly in that it extends the concepts of biological essentialism, the false scientification of gender, and the coloniality of gender to modern transgender communities. Some terms that are common in the U.S. currently as identifiers are: non-binary, transgender, trans, agender, genderfluid, gender queer, demigender, and bigender. In the U.S. it is also imperative to recognize that there exist precolonial terms to describe gender that is outside of the Western and colonially-constructed "man/woman", namely Two-Spirit. Two-Spirit people may not necessarily identify as transgender as their gender categorization developed before the term of transgender and to inherently place Two-Spirit communities into the "transgender" box would be an exercise of colonial power. Also notable in this chapter is the

M. L. Miville et al., *Counseling and Gender*,
https://doi.org/10.1007/978-3-031-69172-0_6

engagement with change. Language is constantly developing, changing, evolving, and expanding; this book is written in a particular historical context and we recognize that it will require revision as transgender communities progress. By design, the contents in this chapter are subject to change.

Another significant topic to introduce when considering TGNC communities is the use of pronouns. Pronouns are a regular part of language that are used to identify the person or thing being mentioned in a sentence. Common pronouns in English include: I, me, we, she, he, it, you, they. There are also what are known as neopronouns—the crafting of new language to describe shifting understanding of gender—which can take any form, but may commonly include ze, xe, fae. For TGNC people, pronouns may shift over their lifespan. For example, someone who was assigned male at birth but later comes to the realization that she is a woman would go part of her life using he/him/his pronouns before transitioning to she/her/hers pronouns to more accurately reflect her gender. Because TGNC people are subject to intense scrutiny about their gendered appearance (as rooted in cissexism and heteronormativity), people may not view them as their identified gender and consequently use the incorrect pronouns. Identifying people by their correct pronouns is a simple way to engage TGNC people effectively through honoring their lived experience; it can also have profound positive effects on mental health (Sevelius et al., 2020). The problem, however, is that pronouns have become a central topic of debate, inquiry, and ire from the larger society, yielding a narrow focus on the much larger issue of people not viewing transness as a valid construct of gender like they do with cisness. Pronouns are in fact important, but to treat pronoun usage as the epistemic end of transgender care is a disservice (McNabb, 2017; Sevelius et al., 2020).

Gender Construction and Context

To understand fully the inception of transness (of being transgender), one must grapple with several fundamental concepts, including: the history of gender (Chap. 1), the scientification of gender (Chaps. 1 and 7), the coloniality of gender (Chaps. 1, 2, and 3), and the gender binary. Psychology and counseling as significant fields of study investigating human behavior have built most of their foundations of theory and practice on assumptions of the gender binary and biological essentialism (Yoder & Kahn, 2003). This means that much of the education people have received in these fields in particular is skewed.

The phrase "gender is a construct" has recently circulated throughout the world, especially in LGBTQI+ communities. This phrase is often used to affirm transgender people in their right to identify, though it also applies to cisgender people and today the psychological study of gender. To be cisgender is a construction, one that was built to create and maintain power differentials within the larger societal structure (Lugones, 2007). This does not mean that being cisgender is wrong, much like being transgender is not wrong, but instead that cisness (of being cisgender) was created to establish systems of power along observable differences to phenotype and biological characteristics. Observable differences and the impact they have on peoples' tangible circumstances in life, as noted in the previous chapter, can be framed as "materiality".

To work towards an understanding of TGNC communities that goes beyond pronoun usage and respects the materiality of their experiences, one should seek to understand two systems of privilege and oppression that uniquely impact TGNC folks: cissexism and cisnormativity. *Cissexism* can be defined as the system of power that privileges those who identify with the gender they were assigned at birth and marginalizes those who identify with a gender different than what they were assigned at birth (Hibbs, 2014). Cissexism is a part of the larger system of sexism that relies specifically on biological essentialism to enforce the gender binary. As a result of cissexism, TGNC people may face a variety of different negative experiences including gender microaggressions, misgendering, increased body vigilance, physical violence, political oppression, and social rejection (Puckett et al., 2023). *Cisnormativity* is a structural attitude that stems from cissexism where cisgender is seen as "normal" and all other gender identities are seen as departures; this attitude is inherently linked to colonialism, racism, and sexism (Marshall et al., 2024).

Similarly, we discussed *gender expression* in Chap. 1, though TGNC folks have unique experiences with gender expression that deserve to be discussed. As a review, gender expression refers to how a person chooses to express their internal sense of gender, as well as how their gender is viewed by the world around them. In this way, gender identity, gender expression, and the materiality of gender in the world could all be different for TGNC people. For example, if someone was assigned as a woman at birth, identifies as non-binary, and has medically and aesthetically transitioned and now appears to be a man from passers-by, their gender expression is that of a man. This does not refute their non-binary identity in the slightest, but instead adds to the complexity of their gendered experience as a trans-masc non-binary person who *passes* as a man. Within TGNC communities, the colloquial term for being able to be perceived as one's gender identity by others is called *passing*, which we discuss later in this chapter after the necessary context has been established. This complexity is precisely why it is always important to be specific with those that clinicians work with in the counseling setting.

As mentioned before, part of how transness, transgender identity, and gender expansiveness were formed in the global context historically was as a reaction to the absolute and extreme regime of cisness as a necessary arm of colonialism (Lugones, 2007; McNabb, 2017; Russett, 1991). Cissexism, cisnormativity, and the politics surrounding "passing" and material gender are derivatives of colonialism, racism, sexism, and heterosexism.

The Coloniality of Gender

A crucial facet of gender that warrants dedicated attention is the impact of colonial forces on it as a construct. Scholars from various disciplines, both within and outside academia, have posited the profound effects of colonization on gender and the global perception of difference (Fanon, 1968; Lugones, 2007; Oyěwùmí, 1997; Russett, 1991). Lugones (2007) is credited with coining the term "coloniality of gender" which she defines through a series of considerations, including: colonization as a major changing event in Indigenous gender systems (especially with the enforcement of a European gender binary), the introduction of racialized definitions/parameters of gender, the introduction of colonial patriarchal systems of control (e.g. policing, paternalism, men as superior), and the racialization of gender. Through colonization, all people were labeled as "man" or "woman", then degrees of attaining these polar ideals were granted onto groups of people in no small part using the colonial and White supremacist tools of colorism, featurism, texturism, racism, and a newly minted *cissexism* (Lugones, 2007; Oyěwùmí, 1997). Specifically, when Europeans colonized Africa, the Americas, and Asia, they saw people that did not look like them and whose appearance, behavior, and social systems were new to them; to the mind of the colonizer, this warranted the need to control what they did not know, which established the gender binary (Russett, 1991; Oyěwùmí, 1997). The colonial advent of the gender binary and the construction of "woman" and "man" sought specifically to afford people the privilege of being "womanly" or "manly", which can be understood as standards that are altogether cissexist, sexist, and racist (Lugones, 2007; Oyěwùmí, 1997; Russett, 1991).

Despite calls from scholars as far back in the field as Frantz Fanon (1968) and Martín-Baró (1994) to confront coloniality in psychology, progress has been slow. Some efforts, such as Stephens and Boonzaier's (2020) study on Black lesbian women in South Africa, offer a psychological lens on citizenship, introducing nuance and a decolonial critique of gender. Likewise, research on psychological wellness and liberation for Afro-Latine women embraces a decolonial framework of the intersection of gender, race, and ethnicity (Comas-Diaz, 2021). Similarly, Fernandez and Gutierrez (2020) contribute a study from an East Cuban, decolonial, gendered standpoint, including a critique of colonial thought. Additionally, a South African critique of current framings of gender-based violence, centered on the coloniality of gender, appears in the social psychological literature (Segalo & Fine, 2020). Although decolonial critiques of gender have proliferated recently in the fields of counseling and psychology, there is a dearth of research focusing on TGNC populations within a colonial context.

Consequently, engaging with the concept of transness involves not only grappling with difference but also recognizing it as a product of Western hegemonic colonization efforts. Gender is inseparable from race, sexuality, and colonialism (Lugones, 2008; Mendoza, 2015; Oyěwùmí, 1997), which means that to address the application of counseling to TGNC communities at all necessitates a decolonial approach that centers intersectionality.

Failure to adopt the perspective that gender has been fundamentally shaped by colonization results in a psychological discourse that overlooks the experiences of the majority of the world (Fanon, 1968; McNabb, 2017; Snorton, 2017). An inclusive psychology that incorporates coloniality as a central concept acknowledges the pursuit of control, power, and exploitation by hegemonic colonial powers, contrasting sharply with the experiences of historically colonized individuals, who endure brutalization and dehumanization (Cariño & Montelongo González, 2022; Fanon, 1968; Lugones, 2008). An application of this theory comes from Snorton's 2017 text "Black on Both Sides: A Racial History of Trans Identity" where Snorton describes how enslaved African communities were subjected to extreme forms of racial and gendered regulations. To be policed in this context was not simply about gender or race, but the unique confluence of both and more. Historically speaking, cisness was a system imposed upon enslaved African people in the Americas *because* of colonization (Oyěwùmí, 1997; Snorton, 2017). Contemporaneously, Black TGNC people face disproportionate violence that is rooted in the coloniality of gender (Sherman et al., 2020). This is seen particularly with the over-policing of Black men and the school-to-prison pipeline (Chaps. 4 and 8). With Black women, this manifests through the history of gynecology and the current issue of Black maternal health disparities (Chap. 10). With Black TGNC people, we see disproportionate levels of gender-based violence and increased levels of poverty (Sherman et al., 2020; Snorton, 2017). Applying our analysis to this fact includes an understanding of cisgender gender standards being set-up intentionally to control BIPOC TGNC communities (Snorton, 2017).

Transgender Identity

Having established the importance of fluidity in language and the colonial onset of the gender binary, we turn now to the current understanding of being transgender. *Gender identity* is a term that came into use in the 1970s in Western academic spheres after being coined in 1960s (Money, 1973). It can be defined as someone's internal sense of their gender (Meyerowitz, 2004). Currently, gender identity is a generally accepted component of gender for TGNC communities, though it is notable to add that everyone has a gender identity; cisgender people simply identify with the gender they were assigned at birth. In research literature, an unfortunate trend is that the term gender identity is often only used about TGNC people, similar to how "gender" as a term was predominantly used in the study of women in the 1970s and 1980s (Scott, 1986; Stewart & McDermott, 2004). Burgeoning terminology faces social and institutional marginalization as a means to suppress the naming of phenomena that are dangerous to the system.

Transgender identity encapsulates all of these experiences: gender identity, gender assigned at birth, gender expression, the coloniality of gender, and fluidity. *Transgender identity* can be defined as the identification of being transgender and the subsequent belief that this identity is important to someone's self-concept; in other words, how they see themselves (Barr et al., 2016). Psychological literature has gone quite a way to operationalize the terms introduced thus far in this chapter. This is a feat because to research such complex forms of selfhood is quite difficult without oversimplifying or missing the mark. Despite this, however, research about TGNC people has significantly increased in the last decade (Delli & Livas, 2021). Correlations between transgender identity and areas of particular note have been well established in that meta-analyses about the following topics are available: intimate partner violence (Peitzmeier et al., 2020), depression and suicide prevelance (Pellicane & Ciesla, 2022; Surace et al., 2021), HIV prevelance (Stutterheim et al., 2021), and substance use (Cotaina et al., 2022), to name a few. Similarly, the fields of psychology and medicine have focused much of the research and many of the interventions for TGNC people on the body (Canner et al., 2018; Lopez et al., 2017; Ziegler et al., 2018). This is most likely due to the rampant societal cissexism and cisnormativity that have proliferated out of colonialism. Plainly: if someone is different from the hegemonic norm, institutions want to study why they are different, what makes them different, and what can be done about it. One positive outcome is that this has increased the knowledge and breadth of medical intervention strategies for TGNC people, yielding many safe and effective medical interventions which will be discussed later in this chapter.

Like any sociopolitical identity, transgender identity is multifaceted and involves several different dimensions that respectively explain different parts of the lived experience of TGNC people (Hinton et al., 2022). In addition to how sociopolitical identity shapes class and other tangible, material experiences in the world politically, it also invokes an intra-and-inter-psychological phenomenon. This means that people can better understand how they move through the world socially using different psychological processes. One psychological process that is particularly important to consider with TGNC folks is identity centrality.

Identity centrality is the importance of a certain identity to someone's sense of self (Hinton et al., 2022; see also Chap. 7). The salience of which being a particular social identity is a significant psychological component of identity and can inform how connected someone feels to community with other transgender people and subsequently can promote psychological well-being (Cruwys et al., 2013; Hinton et al., 2022). A TGNC person with high levels of identity centrality may benefit from greater social engagement, a strong sense of self, and more mental and emotional resources (Cruwys et al., 2013; Greenaway et al., 2017; Jetten et al., 2017). This is tempered, however, by the fact that social structures (such as cissexism and cisnormativity) can inhibit the benefits gained from high identity centrality (DeMarco & Newheiser, 2019; Hinton et al., 2022). The inhibition of benefits from identity centrality can also change based on intersectionality; much of the research about identity centrality consists of White participants (Hinton et al., 2022). Identity centrality is only one psychological process, which is also dependent upon other constructs, including: "outness", visibility, disclosure practices, material circumstances, and gender expression.

Visibility for TGNC People

Visibility is a fraught and non-encompassing solution for marginalization (Berberick, 2018; Foucault, 1978). To be a TGNC person in the U.S. is to be hypervisible, meaning that their social positionality is so politicized that it creates a dynamic of otherness. Anyone who is observed as departing from the cisgender norm is seen as a threat to the binary and therefore made hypervisible. The perceived ambiguity of gender threatens the system of cissexism and hetero/cisnormativity, as well as racism and colonization (Butler, 2007). As discussed above, Whiteness and European standards of gender dominate the gender binary and therefore the threshold for gendered otherness is lower for BIPOC people, which manifests through gendered racism, particularly for TGNC people and women. This conceptualization is strengthened when considering that TGNC people outside of the U.S. are subject to unique colonial dynamics (Sherif, 2020). Globally, transgender existence is often criminalized and subject to either hypervisibilization or invisiblization (Butler, 2007; Sherif, 2020). To engage in visibility as a topic is to engage with the larger politics of safety, hypervisibility, and representation. One critical aspect of visibility within TGNC communities in particular is the ability to move through the world with safety.

Navigating safety is an important part of daily life for TGNC people. Whether it be navigating what it means to be safe, attempting to conceal or perform particular gendered expressions, or determining what would be least threatening to others, safety is a significant concern (Colliver & Silvestri, 2022). This navigation is especially important for trans people of color who often experience intersectional elements of visibility (Hennekam & Dumazert, 2023). One example of this is from a qualitative study by Hennekam and Dumazert where a participant explicated their decisions to express their gender a particular way as a person of color:

> I'm already very visible, so I'm trying to make it less visible by playing it cool, by downplaying the way I express myself. I'm appearing like a typical man so I don't draw attention to myself. (p. 1595)

This speaks to the fear of retribution and fear of violence. Victimization in hate crimes and in violence generally often contain elements of visibility, hypervisibility, and invisibility in that those who have been victimized conceptualize their degree of visibility as important markers of why they were targeted (Colliver & Silvestri, 2022). This initiates a discussion on the politics of "passing". *Passing* can refer to a few different concepts which are both interrelated and highly contested within both the academic literature and colloquially in-community (Colliver & Silvestri, 2022). Passing has been taken to mean the authenticity to which someone lives and expresses their gender (Sellberg, 2012), or that someone is conforming to gendered expectations of society (i.e. cisnormativity) (Roen, 2002). Recent critiques highlight the importance of deconstructing the dichotomy between "passing" and"not passing" (Colliver & Silvestri, 2022; Serano, 2007). The importance of passing as a concept is that it mirrors our discussion of *materiality*; there is something unique and important about the ability to move through the world without being perceived as TGNC. More information about exposure to violence and the statistics of violence will be discussed in Chap. 11: Gender and Violence.

Passing is ultimately the material navigation of visibility (Hennekam & Dumazert, 2023; Roen, 2002). Often, passing invokes conversations around privilege (Roen, 2002). If we adopt the definition of passing about how to "pass" as meaning to appear cisgender, then passing, in this respect, would certainly be a privilege because the material, observable experience of that person would be influenced by their ability to avoid some degree of overt cissexist behavior from others. This is complicated, however, by the fact that *concealment* of trans identity is a compensatory pattern of behaviors that stem from the need to keep oneself safe. As the above example from Colliver and Silvestri's (2022) study introduces, sometimes it is necessary to conceal trans identity in particular contexts. This of course speaks to the fact that transgender identity is possible to conceal in some ways, however this possibility should be tempered by the context outlined in this chapter thus far. Colonization, racism, classism, and sexism all influence that ability and decision for some people to conceal their gender identity, which is necessary context for why it occurs. The epistemic and social harm that arises from media representations of TGNC people is also a hindering factor.

When talking about marginalization, representational politics often arise as accurate and non-oppressive media portrayal of marginalized groups is scarce. This is true of TGNC communities as well. Koch-Rein and colleagues (2020) detail how TGNC representation in media has been particularly problematic in that it often represented TGNC people within tropes. These tropes include someone feeling they are "in the wrong body", reduced to their genitalia, or even overtly as mentally unwell or violent (Koch-Rein et al., 2020). Within this history, the trans people who are represented typically fall within certain parameters such as being White, being transgender in a binary way, such as transgender women or transgender men, and the majority of their character development focusing on their relationship to their bodies (Berberick, 2018; Koch-Rein et al., 2020). These depictions create a false narrative surrounding TGNC people which perpetuates hegemonic beliefs of the community. One notable belief is that, to be transgender especially, medicalization is required.

Medicalization and the TGNC Body

Medicalization is the process in which a group of people are subject to intense scrutiny about their bodies and subsequently made to be medical phenomena. TGNC people are medicalized intensely, to the point where much of the academic focus on trans people has been on trans bodies, surgeries, and other medical interventions (see: Canner et al., 2018; Lopez et al., 2018; Ziegler et al., 2018). Studies such as these are critical to improving the medical practices in the field of gender affirming care, however the majority of psychological research on TGNC people is also reflective of this trend of medicalization (Dewey & Gesbeck, 2017; Kronk & Dexheimer, 2021). Medicalization for TGNC people is a complicated topic in that many in the community want treatments that are medical in nature to affirm their identity and align their expression to their internal sense of gender (Johnson, 2015). To medicalize someone, however, is to necessitate a medical intervention to consider them effectively transgender (Davis et al., 2016; Johnson, 2015).

In this way, to medicalize oneself has become an expectation of transgender people. Anecdotally, many TGNC people are asked about what surgeries they have received or plan to receive, which is reflective of this "medical gaze" (Davis et al., 2016). The dynamic that this sets up is the privileging of passing as cisgender and the projected desire to change one's body as the ultimate form of affirmation. The manifestation of TGNC medicalization presents as very little agential control over one's body as a TGNC person (Davis et al., 2016). In the field of counseling, counselors of all types often serve as gatekeepers to medical interventions for trans patients (Johnson, 2015). To serve as a gatekeeper in this context means that psychological providers (usually cisgender) are privileged with the "responsibility" to determine if someone they are seeing indeed shows enough evidence to be diagnosed with Gender Dysphoria (in the DSM) and therefore qualify for gender affirming medical care (Davis et al., 2016; Johnson, 2015). This comes in the form of providers having to write letters of support for their TGNC clients for insurance companies to cover the treatments or for hospitals or clinics to schedule a consultation for surgery.

Regarding power: medicalization establishes a tangible, material power dynamic between TGNC clients and their mental health providers. Dynamically, this can create complications such as TGNC people needing to perform certain levels of distress surrounding their body; they are charged with displaying that their bodies disturb them enough to *need* to change them medically. Gatekeeping is a form of social control, which for TGNC people involves a particularly heinous degree of bodily control as well (Dewey & Gesbeck, 2017). To control the opportunities TGNC people have to modify their bodies as they see fit, especially in adulthood, is relatively unparalleled in the field of medical and psychological care (Dewey & Gesbeck, 2017; Johnson, 2015).

Consider an example of someone whose primary concern in therapy is processing their family dynamics. They may spend the vast majority of their sessions talking about the intricacies of their family's behavior and their reactions to it, but spend little time discussing their relationship to their body. Then, one session they mention needing a letter to undergo gender-affirming chest surgery. In practice, providers are required to gather sufficient evidence from this client that they have been considering this intervention for a certain amount of time, and demonstrate that they ruled out the potential for psychological causes for this request. The sessions must then focus on establishing this body of knowledge, which could distract from the important work they have been engaging in for months. This example is common in the field, though no research exists at this time that studies this particular phenomenon in counseling. Important take-aways from this brief example are that counselors are often positioned as authorities over TGNC people's bodies, which limits autonomy and causes power differentials in the counseling relationship (Johnson, 2015). Gatekeeping is a particularly insidious manifestation of colonialism and reflective of societal paternalism/patriarchal practices of health care.

Important to mention also is the recent trend within the U.S. of states passing cissexist bills that limit or ban the amount of services that both medical and mental health providers are able to give to their TGNC clients. The impact that this has on TGNC people includes increased anxiety, depression, and suicidal ideation/suicide attempts (Barbee et al., 2022; Cunningham et al., 2022; Horne et al., 2022). The recent influx of anti-transgender legislation increases stigma, prevents access to care, and ultimately prevents TGNC people from having autonomy over their bodies (Cunningham et al., 2022). This is a significant problem in politically conservative states and in rural areas where ease of access to health care has a different baseline than in urban areas with supportive infrastructure. Due to the fact that this is a systemic and large scale political problem, interventions for TGNC people must address the systemic level of injustice (Lemerand & Duran, 2024). Ultimately, when discussing medicalization of TGNC people, it is important to remember the political and legislative context of the particular area/state/country one is counseling in.

Transgender and Gender Nonconforming Counseling Considerations

The following section of this chapter focuses on considerations or topics that may arise when working with TGNC people in the counseling setting. The groups outlined are those that are common in the U.S. and do not represent the fullness of possible TGNC experiences, and in fact only represent a small portion of experiences. The context for these considerations are the extant systems of power that form the hegemonic norm: cissexism, cisnormativity, colonialism, racism, classism, and sexism. This means that intersectionality is critically important in all considerations for TGNC people. Another important note is that there are different forms of transition, including social transitioning and medical transitioning (Carvalho et al., 2024). We have discussed medical transitioning, which could involve surgeries, hormone treatment, or vocal therapy. Social transitioning can include the decisions to be "out", visible, and "open" about one's transness (Carvalho et al., 2024). This may involve telling some members of one's social support network, but not others, or it can mean that someone may widely talk about their transness and desire for people to regularly use their pronouns and refer to them as the correct gender. Contextually, little research exists that adequately separates out different gendered categories of transgender, gender non-conforming, and gender fluid individuals. Instead, much of the literature chooses to group all transgender people together, creating a vast and often unhelpful amalgamation of experiences.

Transgender Women

Transgender women are people who identify as women who were not assigned "female" at birth. Trans women may undergo gender affirmative surgeries to attain a particular ideal of gender expression, or to move towards an expression of gender that, at times, feels comfortable for them, though this is not necessary for them to be considered trans women (Kozee et al., 2012). There is an expectation of trans women to express hyperfemininity; for a trans woman to be considered a woman by others (Ching & Persing, 2022). Epistemologically, this represents a societal requirement for trans women to "make-up for" not being assigned female at birth, as seen through the continuation of cissexism, sexism, and cisnormativity. Additionally, trans women in media and popular culture are often hypersexualized (Ching & Persing, 2022; Koch-Rein et al., 2020). This leads to assumptions that trans women often perform sex work, or are otherwise sexually promiscuous.

Trans women may experience elements of shame, self-objectification, and social anxiety due to the intensity of gender expression policing they face (Carvalho et al., 2024). As we have discussed throughout this book thus far, femininity is policed at disproportionate levels due to sexism, racism, heteronormativity, and cissexism. These dynamics cannot be understated in how they influence transgender women's lived experiences. As a result of marginalization, trans women may face increased levels of suicidal ideation, traumatic experiences of violence or rejection, self-harm, and substance use issues (Pinna et al., 2022; Yang et al., 2015). Body dissatisfaction and self-objectification are significant elements of disordered eating for transgender women (Brewster et al., 2019). Trans women of color in particular are subject to high levels of fetishization, objectification, and gender expression policing (Anzani et al., 2021). The intersections of gender and race are especially strong for trans women of color due to the unique confluence of the coloniality of gender and cissexism.

Health barriers are a significant obstacle for transgender women due to the rampant cissexism, fetishism, and policing of femininity within the U.S. Trans women of color may face disproportionate levels of healthcare discrimination, especially in conservative and rural parts of the country (Smart et al., 2022). This exemplifies the argument earlier discussed that health barriers are contextual to the region where someone lives. Lastly, trans women face disproportionate levels of violence, which has been discussed in various forms throughout the book. Specifically, transgender women and especially BIPOC transgender women are likely to be victims of physical, relational, and discriminatory violence (Wirtz et al., 2020). These considerations are non-exhaustive but represent some of the major areas of exploration while working with trans women. Because of the vast diversity in experiences amongst trans women by race, class, sexuality, and gender expression, it is important to focus on inquiry as opposed to leading with assumptions based on cissexist narratives of trans women.

Transgender Men

Transgender men as a category includes anyone that identifies as a man and was not assigned "male" at birth. Trans men, like trans women, may possess a binary identity or a non-binary identity while identifying ultimately as a transgender man. In the research literature, trans men display higher levels of non-suicidal self injury than many other gender groups (Mcdowell et al., 2019). Gender dysphoria, body dysmorphia, and cissexism interact in unique ways for trans men, particularly in goals around exercise and body monitoring (Milano et al., 2020; Velez et al., 2016). Body monitoring in particular is strong for transgender men, increasing with anti-trans discrimination exposure (Velez et al., 2016). As discussed in Chap. 5, masculinity is policed as a form of violence towards men to maintain hegemony and power societally. This is true for trans men as well, which can lead to disproportionate focus on one's body.

Additionally, transgender men experience heightened levels of depression, anxiety, and substance use issues (Pinna et al., 2022). Trans men of color report more significant mental health distress in these areas than White trans men (Lefevor et al., 2019). It is theorized that much of these disparities arise from experiences of discrimination, gender policing from others, and consequent internalization of cissexism (Hendricks & Testa, 2012). This speaks to our analysis of otherness, perceived normalcy, and cisnormativity as driving factors in TGNC gender development and identity. These differences are not accounted for between gender groups within the TGNC umbrella. Trans men may experience a level of invisibility and hyperfocus on their level of perceived masculinity due to these experiences. Loneliness and specifically romantic loneliness may contribute to the significance of disparities in mental health concerns with trans men (Fernandez-Rouco et al., 2019).

Health barriers and social isolation are of particular importance to consider when working with trans men. The intersections of race, ethnicity, class, and region are paramount to this phenomena (Abelson, 2016; Lefevor et al., 2019). In rural areas of the U.S., trans men are subject to high levels of discrimination, limited access to healthcare, and social discrimination due to their identity (Abelson, 2016; Lefevor et al., 2019). One important health factor that is often ignored for transgender men is pregnancy. Trans men can and do become pregnant and often do so without disruption to their identity as a man (Obedin-Maliver & Makadon, 2016). A consideration that stems from this is intentional exploration about gender identity, healthcare access, and medical maltreatment surrounding obstetrics and gynecology.

Nonbinary People

The last group that we will be discussing are nonbinary people. Nonbinary is both an umbrella term and a specific gender identity that can represent a variety of different gendered experiences. To be nonbinary requires an acknowledgement of a gender binary and a subsequent rejection of the importance and imposition of that binary on someone. In psychological science, nonbinary people are regularly grouped together with other transgender people, resulting in data that is hard to parse and not specific to the complexity of nonbinary gender identity (Breslow et al., 2021). This complexity is difficult to capture in traditional academic, qualitative, empirical research, however it is not impossible. The intersectional experiences of nonbinary people of color, for instance, have been captured in great depth in qualitative research.

When considering the implications of the coloniality of gender, there is no group that is impacted more than nonbinary people, who seek to deconstruct the Eurocentric, colonial binary with their very existence. In Hsu et al.'s (2024) edited collection, "My Race is My Gender: Portraits of Nonbinary People of Color," the authors and editors paint a vivid picture of intersectionality in action. One of the authors, Ignacio G Hutía Xeiti Rivera (2024), narrates how their gender is inherently connected to their Black, Taino, Boricua heritage and how themes of the ocean, water, and fluidity of the natural world mirrors the movement and fluidity of their gender identity. Narratives like this can provide a much more accurate and effective understanding of the intersections of identity and positionality discussed throughout this chapter.

With this, there are considerable uses to quantitative, empirical research; they can help inform policy, add to the breadth of knowledge, and privilege the lived experiences of people in quantifiable ways. As found in studies about other groups of transgender people, nonbinary people experience significant levels of increased anxiety, depression, eating disorders, non-suicidal self injury, and suicidal ideation (Pinna et al., 2022; Price-Feeney et al., 2020; Tebbe & Budge, 2022). Notably, nonbinary people report lower mental health concerns than binary transgender people in some studies (Jones et al., 2020) and higher levels of anxiety and depression than binary trans people in other studies (Thorne et al., 2019). For nonbinary people, some of this may stem from complexities surrounding the lack of archetypal representation of nonbinary experiences. There is a significant lack of examples of nonbinary existence both in history and in the media and popular culture, resulting in potentially fewer expectations about what nonbinary people "should look like", but it can also create feelings of confusion about how to present or act. Invalidation of identity and confusion of nonbinary gender identity by others may contribute to increased mental health distress (Johnson et al., 2023).

Ultimately, nonbinary people make a deliberate choice to forgo the binary in a way that opens them up to intense forms of discrimination and engages them with difficult decisions about gender expression, gendered behavior, and relationships (Johnson et al., 2023). To be in constant odds with a system that is so deeply entrenched throughout the world can take a mental toll as well as providing opportunities for freedom, happiness, and authenticity. A foundational take-away from the lived experiences of nonbinary people, especially those who are multiply marginalized and embody their gender in particular ways, is that these odds are a choice that lead to a multiplicity of consequences. For example, Nicolazzo (2016) collected stories from two Black, non-binary trans people and summatively found that both participants saw living at these odds to be liberatory, limiting, difficult, and inspiring. This complexity is reflected throughout the community and points to the importance of authenticity, resilience, and liberation through struggle.

Euphoria, Resistance, and Liberation

As demonstrated here, TGNC people experience significant hardship because of the intersecting systems of cissexism, racism, colonialism, classism, ableism, and heterosexism. However, we have also discussed a few examples of people in these communities finding inspiration in their material realities, their heritage/inheritance, and their community. This is far from uncommon and is often referred to as "resilience" though we propose that the more liberatory and newer term "resistance" be used as an alternative. *Resilience* is a complicated subject as the material circumstances and discrimination many marginalized communities experience are often silenced or minimized because they are seen as "resilient" and not in need of support or tangible change. In other words, they are dismissed by the complacency of others out of the fact that they can survive. Resilience in psychological literature has been critiqued as individualistic and trait-oriented (Puckett et al., 2023). *Resistance*, however, frames the struggles of TGNC people (and others) as a radical act of healing and freeing oneself from the effects of oppression (Puckett et al., 2023).

Community connection is a strong strategy used by TGNC people to engage in resistance. Studies show that TGNC people tap into the wealth of community resources in intersectional ways, connecting to those who share similar identities and can engage in meaningful ways because of that (Kia et al., 2023). Utilizing peer support, especially in the face of multiple marginalizing institutions and in navigating healthcare, is also a critical resource in resisting the effects of oppression (Kia et al., 2023). To engage with community–specifically those that possess similarly intersecting identities–is to work towards liberation by resisting the systems that intentionally seek to exhaust and degrade TGNC communities.

Conclusion

The current understanding of transgender, gender nonconforming, and nonbinary identity is driven by significant historical and political events. When discussing the TGNC contexts of gender, it is imperative to not only discuss specific groups within TGNC communities, but also historical contexts. Specifically, current TGNC positionality hinges on the contemporaneous gender binary, which was established in the U.S. as a consequence of European colonization. The systems of sexism (of which cissexism and heterosexism are a part of), racism (which also includes colorism, texturism, and featurism), class, and (dis)ability all influence the parameters of this binary. Those who challenge the binary are often targeted by violence, discrimination, and silencing, and, as a result experience mental health challenges. To subvert this, TGNC communities find restoration through collective liberation, resistance to systems, and community building.

Case Study

Aarti is a 34 year old transgender Indian, Gujarati, lesbian woman currently living in New York, NY. She has been consistently utilizing therapeutic services since high school. She reports recently feeling intensely angry, which is "unlike" her. She notably decided to undergo vaginoplasty surgery a month ago. Her wife, parents, and community members are all supportive of her decision. She has been actively engaged with trans affirmative care, Hormone-Replacement Therapy, and completed breast augmentation surgery and facial feminization surgery five years ago. She is less engaged with her wife and has been experiencing a sudden increase in gender dysphoria. Aarti relayed struggling with her recent gender dysphoria as she has not experienced negative feelings about her gender for several years. The stress in this has caused a flare-up in lupus symptoms, which adds to her general sense of feeling overwhelmed. To cope, she has been spending time with new friends, developing pseudo-sexual relationships with men, and drinking more than usual. She expresses her need to "figure out" her gender dysphoria before her surgery date.

Discussion Questions

1. Given Aarti's journey, how do pronouns and other terminology specific to TGNC individuals play a role in affirming her gender identity? Discuss the importance of these elements in therapeutic settings.
2. Aarti has decided to undergo vaginoplasty surgery and has a history of other gender-affirming surgeries. How might such surgeries impact the mental health of TGNC individuals both pre- and post-operation?
3. Despite having support from her wife, parents, and community, Aarti experiences an increase in gender dysphoria. Even in a nurturing setting, why can these emotions come back? How can assistance programs better meet the complicated emotional requirements of those in need?
4. Aarti's coping techniques include increasing her alcohol use and developing pseudo-sexual relationships. Evaluate the pros and cons of these actions concerning her dysphoria management and general mental health.
5. Determine whether Aarti's current emotional distress and rage are influenced by societal expectations that are cisnormative and binary. Even in settings that seem to be helpful, how do these pressures show up?

6. How does Aarti's cultural background as a lesbian woman of Indian and Gujarati descent impact her encounters with gender dysphoria and acceptance within her ethnicity and the larger New York community?
7. During this time of heightened gender dysphoria, Aarti has been less involved with her marriage. Think about how significant life changes, like getting gender-affirming surgery, can affect close relationships and how you might deal with the fallout.

References

Abelson, M. J. (2016). 'You aren't from around here': Race, masculinity, and rural transgender men. *Gender, Place & Culture, 23*(11), 1535–1546. https://doi.org/10.1080/0966369X.2016.1219324

Anzani, A., Lindley, L., Tognasso, G., Galupo, M. P., & Prunas, A. (2021). "Being talked to like I was a sex toy, like being transgender was simply for the enjoyment of someone else": Fetishization and sexualization of transgender and nonbinary individuals. *Archives of Sexual Behavior, 50*(3), 897–911.

Barbee, H., Deal, C., & Gonzales, G. (2022). Anti-transgender legislation—A public health concern for transgender youth. *JAMA Pediatrics, 176*(2), 125–126.

Barr, S. M., Budge, S. L., & Adelson, J. L. (2016). Transgender community belongingness as a mediator between strength of transgender identity and well-being. *Journal of Counseling Psychology, 63*(1), 87–97. https://doi.org/10.1037/cou0000127

Berberick, S. N. (2018). The paradox of trans visibility: Interrogating the "Year of trans visibility". *Journal of Media Critiques, 4*(13), 123–144.

Bockting, W., Barucco, R., LeBlanc, A., Singh, A., Mellman, W., Dolezal, C., & Ehrhardt, A. (2020). Sociopolitical change and transgender people's perceptions of vulnerability and resilience. *Sexuality Research and Social Policy, 17*, 162–174.

Breslow, A. S., Wojcik, H., Cox, R., Jr., Tran, N. M., & Brewster, M. E. (2021). Toward nonbinary nuance in research and care: Mapping differences in gender affirmation and transgender congruence in an online national U.S. survey. *Transgender Health, 6*(3), 156–163. https://doi.org/10.1089/trgh.2020.0038

Brewster, M. E., Velez, B. L., Breslow, A. S., & Geiger, E. F. (2019). Unpacking body image concerns and disordered eating for transgender women: The roles of sexual objectification and minority stress. *Journal of Counseling Psychology, 66*(2), 131–142. https://doi.org/10.1037/cou0000333

Butler, J. (2007). *Gender trouble: Feminism and the subversion of identity*. Routledge.

Canner, J. K., Harfouch, O., Kodadek, L. M., Pelaez, D., Coon, D., Offodile, A. C., 2nd, Haider, A. H., & Lau, B. D. (2018). Temporal trends in gender-affirming surgery among transgender patients in the United States. *JAMA Surgery, 153*(7), 609–616. https://doi.org/10.1001/jamasurg.2017.6231

Cariño, C., & Montelongo González, A. (2022). Coloniality of power and coloniality of gender: Sentipensar the struggles of indigenous women in Abya Yala from worlds in relation. *Hypatia, 37*(3), 544–558. https://doi.org/10.1017/hyp.2022.30

Carvalho, S. A., Carvalho, F., Fonseca, L., Santos, G., & Castilho, P. (2024). Beyond the centrality of shame: How self-concealment and fear of receiving compassion from others impact psychological suffering in transgender adults. *Journal of Homosexuality, 71*(6), 1373–1391.

Ching, A. H., & Persing, J. A. (2022). Objectification of transgender female patients in surgical goals of facial feminization surgery. *Plastic and Reconstructive Surgery, 149*(2), 358e–360e.

Colliver, B., & Silvestri, M. (2022). The role of (in) visibility in hate crime targeting transgender people. *Criminology & Criminal Justice, 22*(2), 235–253.

Comas-Díaz, L. (2021). Afro-Latinxs: Decolonization, healing, and liberation. *Journal of Latinx Psychology, 9*(1), 65–75. https://doi.org/10.1037/lat0000164

Cotaina, M., Peraire, M., Boscá, M., Echeverria, I., Benito, A., & Haro, G. (2022). Substance use in the transgender population: A meta-analysis. *Brain Sciences, 12*(3), 366. https://doi.org/10.3390/brainsci12030366

Cruwys, T., Dingle, G. A., Haslam, C., Haslam, S. A., Jetten, J., & Morton, T. A. (2013). Social group memberships alleviate depression symptoms, prevent depression relapse, and protect against future depression. *Social Science & Medicine, 98*, 179–186.

Cunningham, G. B., Watanabe, N. M., & Buzuvis, E. (2022). Anti-transgender rights legislation and internet searches pertaining to depression and suicide. *PLoS One, 17*(12), e0279420.

Davis, G., Dewey, J. M., & Murphy, E. L. (2016). Giving sex: Deconstructing intersex and trans medicalization practices. *Gender & Society, 30*(3), 490–514.

Delli, K., & Livas, C. (2021). Tracking trends of transgender health research online: Are researchers and the public on the same page? *Culture, Health & Sexuality, 23*(6), 854–865. https://doi.org/10.1080/13691058.2020.1730973

DeMarco, T. C., & Newheiser, A.-K. (2019). When groups do not cure: Group esteem moderates the social cure effect. *European Journal of Social Psychology, 49*(7), 1421–1438. https://doi-org.ezproxy.cul.columbia.edu/10.1002/ejsp.2594

Dewey, J. M., & Gesbeck, M. M. (2017). (Dys) functional diagnosing: Mental health diagnosis, medicalization, and the making of transgender patients. *Humanity and Society, 41*(1), 37–72.

Fanon, F. (1968). *The wretched of the earth* (R. Philcox, Trans.). Grove Press.

Fernández, A., & Calcerrada Gutierrez, M. (2020). Colonialism, gender and mental health in psychology: A view from Eastern Cuba. *International Review of Psychiatry (Abingdon, England), 32*(4), 340–347. https://doi.org/10.1080/09540261.2020.1733941

Fernández-Rouco, N., Carcedo, R. J., López, F., & Orgaz, M. B. (2019). Mental health and proximal stressors in transgender men and women. *Journal of Clinical Medicine, 8*(3), 413.

Foucault, M. (1978). *The history of sexuality: Volume 1, An introduction*. Random House.

Greenaway, K., Amiot, C., Louis, W., & Bentley, S. (2017). The role of psychological need satisfaction in promoting student identification. In L. R. R. van Zomeren, S. A. M. R. Leach, & B. A. P. Pemberton (Eds.), *Social identity and intergroup relations: From theory to practice* (pp. 209–226). Routledge. https://doi.org/10.4324/9781315746913-ch10

Hendricks, M. L., & Testa, R. J. (2012). A conceptual framework for clinical work with transgender and gender nonconforming clients: An adaptation of the Minority Stress Model. *Professional Psychology: Research and Practice, 43*(5), 460–467. https://doi.org/10.1037/a0029597

Hennekam, S., & Dumazert, J.-P. (2023). Intersectional (in)visibility of transgender individuals with an ethnic minority background throughout a gender transition: Four longitudinal case studies. *Gender, Work and Organization, 30*(5), 1585–1610. https://doi.org/10.1111/gwao.12992

Hibbs, C. (2014). Cissexism. In T. Teo (Ed.), *Encyclopedia of critical psychology* (pp. 235–237). Springer.

Hinton, J. D. X., de la Piedad Garcia, X., Kaufmann, L. M., Koc, Y., & Anderson, J. R. (2022). A systematic and meta-analytic review of identity centrality among LGBTQ Groups: An assessment of psychosocial correlates. *Journal of Sex Research, 59*(5), 568–586. https://doi.org/10.1080/00224499.2021.1967849

Horne, S. G., McGinley, M., Yel, N., & Maroney, M. R. (2022). The stench of bathroom bills and anti-transgender legislation: Anxiety and depression among transgender, nonbinary, and cisgender LGBQ people during a state referendum. *Journal of Counseling Psychology, 69*(1), 1.

Hsu, S., Tse, K.-M., Clark, S. L., & St. Juste, J., Hutía Xeiti Rivera, I. G., & Solomon, A. (Eds.). (2024). *My race is my gender: Portraits of nonbinary people of color*. Rutgers University Press.

Jetten, J., Haslam, S. A., Cruwys, T., Greenaway, K. H., Haslam, C., & Steffens, N. K. (2017). Advancing the social identity approach to health and well-being: Progressing the social cure research agenda. *European Journal of Social Psychology, 47*, 789–802. https://doi.org/10.1002/ejsp.2333

Johnson, A. H. (2015). Normative accountability: How the medical model influences transgender identities and experiences. *Sociology Compass, 9*(9), 803–813.

Johnson, K. C., LeBlanc, A. J., Dolezal, C., Singh, A. A., & Bockting, W. O. (2023). Invalidation and mental health among nonbinary individuals. *Psychology of Sexual Orientation and Gender Diversity.* https://doi.org/10.1037/sgd0000621

Jones, B. A., Bouman, W. P., Haycraft, E., & Arcelus, J. (2020). Mental health and quality of life in non-binary transgender adults: A case control study. In *Non-binary and genderqueer genders* (pp. 133–144). Routledge.

Kia, H., Kenney, K., MacKinnon, K. R., Abramovich, A., Salway, T., Ferlatte, O., Knight, R., Charles, G., & Marshall, S. K. (2023). "It saves lives": Peer support and resilience in transgender and gender diverse communities. *SSM – Qualitative Research in Health, 3*, 100264. https://doi.org/10.1016/j.ssmqr.2023.100264

Koch-Rein, A., Haschemi Yekani, E., & Verlinden, J. J. (2020). Representing trans: Visibility and its discontents. *European Journal of English Studies, 24*(1), 1–12. https://doi-org.ezproxy.cul.columbia.edu/10.1080/13825577.2020.1730040

Kozee, H. B., Tylka, T. L., & Bauerband, L. A. (2012). Measuring transgender individuals' comfort with gender identity and appearance: Development and validation of the transgender congruence scale. *Psychology of Women Quarterly, 36*(2), 179–196. https://doi.org/10.1177/0361684312442161

Kronk, C. A., & Dexheimer, J. W. (2021). An ontology-based review of transgender literature: Revealing a history of medicalization and pathologization. *International Journal of Medical Informatics, 156*, 104601. https://doi.org/10.1016/j.ijmedinf.2021.104601

Lefevor, G. T., Janis, R. A., Franklin, A., & Stone, W. M. (2019). Distress and therapeutic outcomes among transgender and gender nonconforming people of color. *The Counseling Psychologist, 47*(1), 34–58.

Lemerand, S., & Duran, A. (2024). Supporting queer and trans students amidst a rise in anti queer and trans legislation and policies. In V. G. Couture & N. M. Bang (Eds.), *LGBTQIA Students in Higher Education: Approaches to Student Identity and Policy* (pp. 226–240). IGI Global.

Lopez, X., Marinkovic, M., Eimicke, T., Rosenthal, S. M., Olshan, J. S., & Pediatric Endocrine Society Transgender Health Special Interest Group. (2017). Statement on gender-affirmative approach to care from the pediatric endocrine society special interest group on transgender health. *Current Opinion in Pediatrics, 29*(4), 475–480. https://doi.org/10.1097/MOP.0000000000000516

Lopez, C. M., Solomon, D., Boulware, S. D., & Christison-Lagay, E. R. (2018). Trends in the use of puberty blockers among transgender children in the United States. *Journal of Pediatric Endocrinology & Metabolism: JPEM, 31*(6), 665–670. https://doi.org/10.1515/jpem-2018-0048

Lugones, M. (2007). Heterosexualism and the colonial/modern gender system. *Hypatia, 22*(1), 186–209. http://www.jstor.org/stable/4640051

Lugones, M. (2008). The coloniality of gender. *Worlds & Knowledges Otherwise, 2*(Spring), 1–17.

Marshall, K., Martin, W., Walker, R. L., & Vandenberg, H. (2024). Exploring the impacts of heteronormative and cisnormative ideologies on fertility intentions and family planning experiences within the 2SLGBTQ Community: A qualitative case study. *Journal of Holistic Nursing: Official Journal of the American Holistic Nurses' Association, 42*(2), 156–167. https://doi.org/10.1177/08980101231189653

Martín-Baró, I. (1994). In A. Aron & S. Corne (Eds.), *Writings for a liberation psychology*. Harvard University Press.

McDowell, M. J., Hughto, J. M., & Reisner, S. L. (2019). Risk and protective factors for mental health morbidity in a community sample of female-to-male trans-masculine adults. *BMC Psychiatry, 19*(1), 1–12.

McNabb, C. (2017). *Nonbinary gender identities: History, culture, resources*. Rowman & Littlefield.

Mendoza, B. (2015). Coloniality of gender and power: From postcoloniality to decoloniality. In L. Disch & M. Hawkesworth (Eds.), *The Oxford handbook of feminist theory*. Oxford Handbooks. https://doi.org/10.1093/oxfordhb/9780199328581.013.6

Meyerowitz, J. (2004). *How sex changed: A history of transsexuality in the United States*. Harvard University Press.

Milano, W., Ambrosio, P., Carizzone, F., De Biasio, V., Foggia, G., & Capasso, A. (2020). Gender dysphoria, eating disorders and body image: An overview. *Endocrine, Metabolic & Immune Disorders-Drug Targets (Formerly Current Drug Targets-Immune, Endocrine & Metabolic Disorders), 20*(4), 518–524.

Money, J. (1973). Gender role, gender identity, core gender identity: Usage and definition of terms. *Journal of the American Academy of Psychoanalysis, 1*(4), 397–402.

Nicolazzo, Z. (2016). "Just go in looking good": The resilience, resistance, and kinship-building of trans* college students. *Journal of College Student Development, 57*(5), 538–556. https://doi-org.ezproxy.cul.columbia.edu/10.1353/csd.2016.0057

Obedin-Maliver, J., & Makadon, H. J. (2016). Transgender men and pregnancy. *Obstetric Medicine, 9*(1), 4–8.

Oyěwùmí, O. (1997). *The invention of women: Making an African sense of Western gender discourses*. University of Minnesota Press.

Peitzmeier, S. M., Malik, M., Kattari, S. K., Marrow, E., Stephenson, R., Agénor, M., & Reisner, S. L. (2020). Intimate partner violence in transgender populations: Systematic review and meta-analysis of prevalence and correlates. *American Journal of Public Health, 110*(9), e1–e14. https://doi.org/10.2105/AJPH.2020.305774

Pellicane, M. J., & Ciesla, J. A. (2022). Associations between minority stress, depression, and suicidal ideation and attempts in transgender and gender diverse (TGD) individuals: Systematic review and meta-analysis. *Clinical Psychology Review, 91*, 1–11. https://doi.org/10.1016/j.cpr.2021.102113

Pinna, F., Paribello, P., Somaini, G., Corona, A., Ventriglio, A., Corrias, C., … & Italian Working Group on LGBTQI Mental Health. (2022). Mental health in transgender individuals: A systematic review. *International Review of Psychiatry, 34*(3–4), 292–359.

Price-Feeney, M., Green, A. E., & Dorison, S. (2020). Understanding the mental health of transgender and nonbinary youth. *Journal of Adolescent Health, 66*(6), 684–690.

Puckett, J. A., Wiklund, L. O., Louis, C., Gallik, C., Brown-Wren, L., Chu, H., Rodriguez, J., Langeni, N. S., & Strong, E. (2023). Clinical practice with transgender and gender diverse clients: Setting up an inclusive practice and training considerations. *Practice Innovations, 8*(4), 265–276. https://doi-org.ezproxy.cul.columbia.edu/10.1037/pri0000209

Roen, K. (2002). 'Either/or' and 'both/neither': Discursive tensions in transgender politics. *Signs, 27*(2), 501–522.

Russett, C. (1991). *Sexual science: The Victorian construction of womanhood.* Harvard University Press.

Scott, J. W. (1986). Gender: A useful category of historical analysis. *The American Historical Review, 91*(5), 1053–1075.

Segalo, P., & Fine, M. (2020). Underlying conditions of gender-based violence—Decolonial feminism meets epistemic ignorance: Critical transnational conversations. *Critical Perspectives on International Business, 16*(5), 498–513. https://doi.org/10.1111/spc3.12568

Sellberg, K. (2012). Transgender identity and passing authentically. In D. Cooley & K. Harrison (Eds.), *Pro-passing, transgender identity and literature: (Post-)transsexual politics and poetics of passing* (pp. 211–219). Ashgate.

Serano, J. (2007). *Whipping girl: A transsexual woman on sexism and the scapegoating of femininity*. Seal Press.

Sevelius, J. M., Chakravarty, D., Dilworth, S. E., Rebchook, G., & Neilands, T. B. (2020). Gender affirmation through correct pronoun usage: Development and validation of the Transgender Women's Importance of Pronouns (TW-IP) Scale. *International Journal of Environmental Research and Public Health, 17*(24), 9525. https://doi.org/10.3390/ijerph17249525

Sherif, S. (2020). Transgender visibility/invisibility: Navigating cisnormative structures and discourses. *Kohl: A Journal for Body and Gender Research, 6*(3).

Sherman, A. D. F., Poteat, T. C., Budhathoki, C., Kelly, U. A., Clark, K. D., & Campbell, J. C. (2020). Association of depression and post-traumatic stress with polyvictimization and emotional transgender and gender diverse community connection among Black and Latinx transgender women. *LGBT Health, 7*(7), 358–366.

Smart, B. D., Mann-Jackson, L., Alonzo, J., Tanner, A. E., Garcia, M., Refugio Aviles, L., & Rhodes, S. D. (2022). Transgender women of color in the US South: A qualitative study of social determinants of health and healthcare perspectives. *International Journal of Transgender Health, 23*(1–2), 164–177.

Snorton, C. R. (2017). *Black on both sides: A racial history of trans identity*. University of Minnesota Press. https://doi.org/10.5749/j.ctt1pwt7dz

Stephens, A., & Boonzaier, F. (2020). Black lesbian women in South Africa: Citizenship and the coloniality of power. *Feminism & Psychology, 30*(3), 324–342. https://doi.org/10.1177/0959353520912969

Stewart, A. J., & McDermott, C. (2004). Gender in psychology. *Annual Review of Psychology, 55*(1), 519–544. https://doi.org/10.1146/annurev.psych.55.090902.141537

Stutterheim, S. E., van Dijk, M., Wang, H., & Jonas, K. J. (2021). The worldwide burden of HIV in transgender individuals: An updated systematic review and meta-analysis. *PLoS One, 16*(12), e0260063. https://doi.org/10.1371/journal.pone.0260063

Surace, T., Fusar-Poli, L., Vozza, L., Cavone, V., Arcidiacono, C., Mammano, R., Basile, L., Rodolico, A., Bisicchia, P., Caponnetto, P., Signorelli, M. S., & Aguglia, E. (2021). Lifetime prevalence of suicidal ideation and suicidal behaviors in gender non-conforming youths: A meta-analysis. *European Child & Adolescent Psychiatry, 30*(8), 1147–1161. https://doi.org/10.1007/s00787-020-01508-5

Tebbe, E. A., & Budge, S. L. (2022). Factors that drive mental health disparities and promote well-being in transgender and nonbinary people. *Nature Reviews Psychology, 1*(12), 694–707.

Thorne, N., Witcomb, G. L., Nieder, T., Nixon, E., Yip, A., & Arcelus, J. (2019). A comparison of mental health symptomatology and levels of social support in young treatment seeking transgender individuals who identify as binary and non-binary. *International Journal of Transgenderism, 20*(2–3), 241–250.

Velez, B. L., Breslow, A. S., Brewster, M. E., Cox, R., Jr., & Foster, A. B. (2016). Building a pantheoretical model of dehumanization with transgender men: Integrating objectification and minority stress theories. *Journal of Counseling Psychology, 63*(5), 497–508. https://doi.org/10.1037/cou0000136

Wiesner-Hanks, M. E. (2011). *Gender in history: Global perspectives* (2nd ed.). Wiley-Blackwell.

Wirtz, A. L., Poteat, T. C., Malik, M., & Glass, N. (2020). Gender-based violence against transgender people in the United States: A call for research and programming. *Trauma, Violence, & Abuse, 21*(2), 227–241.

Yang, M. F., Manning, D., van den Berg, J. J., & Operario, D. (2015). Stigmatization and mental health in a diverse sample of transgender women. *LGBT Health, 2*(4), 306–312.

Yoder, J. D., & Kahn, A. S. (2003). Making gender comparisons more meaningful: A call for more attention to social context. *Psychology of Women Quarterly, 27*(4), 281–290. https://doi.org/10.1111/1471-6402.00108

Ziegler, A., Henke, T., Wiedrick, J., & Helou, L. B. (2018). Effectiveness of testosterone therapy for masculinizing voice in transgender patients: A meta-analytic review. *International Journal of Transgenderism, 19*(1), 25–45. https://doi.org/10.1080/15532739.2017.1411857

Chapter 7
Gender and Identity Development

Psychology and the Measurement of Gender Roles and Identity

This chapter describes how gender has been studied in psychology across the years with a particular emphasis on gender identity. In Chap. 1, we discussed the history of gender, tracing how gender has been defined, how it has been codified into public policy, and even how science has been pulled into what became both a cultural and politicized approach to understanding gender. The original way psychologists constructed gender has had two distinctions. The first, lasting until about 1970, examined sex differences through the prism of biological bases of gender. As described in Chap. 1, this was in line with how many cultural groups globally had understood gender for centuries, if not longer. It should be noted, however, that many other cultural groups had different approaches to understanding gender throughout history.

As a result of the Eurocentricity of early psychology, the main way of studying identity research in gender in psychology was to investigate the impact of biology, including gender identity. The very first scale that explored gender identity in psychology was developed between Terman and Miles in 1936 in which they set about differentiating men and women through their scale. That is, the primary means of examining gender/gender identity in this era was to measure and establish differences between men and women, using a single bipolar continuum of masculinity and femininity. Within this framework, masculinity and femininity were considered opposite ends of one single construct. Thus, if somebody was assessed as more masculine, then logically by this continuum, that person would necessarily be less feminine. As evidence of their scale's validity, Terman and Miles included information about "passive male homosexuals" endorsing more feminine traits, in comparison with women college athletes (presumably who would endorse more masculine traits). Today these findings are difficult to seriously consider, given the sexist and

M. L. Miville et al., *Counseling and Gender*,
https://doi.org/10.1007/978-3-031-69172-0_7

heterosexist lenses used to interpret these data. Indeed, in a comprehensive review of masculinity-femininity, Constantinople (1973) declared this construction of gender as among the "muddiest concepts in psychology," calling into question the evidence gathered using the framework. Despite the impactful critique offered by Constantinople, much of psychological science since 1973 remained tied to the bipolar understanding of "male/female". This is often referred to as *biological essentialism* (De Cecco & Elia, 1993), in which biological sex traits are presumed to determine an individual's gender and their traits, which are gendered through the same lens.

Masculinity-Femininity Research

Utilizing a single dimension to measure gender identity became a very difficult, even impossible, way of understanding, let alone measuring gender/gender identity in terms of simply sex and the biological basis of gender. By the 1970s, as reported by Constaninople (1973), there was very little evidence to support a single continuum of gender, and presumably gender typed traits such as masculinity and femininity. As many more women entered into psychology, gender research, particularly gender identity research, entered an exciting, highly productive phase, with at least two groups of psychologists who began to study gender identity from a somewhat different approach, leading to the development of two measurements that remain in use today. Although this approach still dichotomized gender and associated traits as masculine and feminine, researchers began to explore how individuals selected any of gender identity items, rather than presume per one's gender how someone "should" score on these scales.

BSRI and PAQ. Bem in 1974, and then Spence and Helmreich in 1978/1981, each began to create lists of traits drawn from cultural stereotypes of what was understood to be masculinity as well as femininity. Unlike previous researchers, these were conceptualized as unique and separate or orthogonal continua. That is, a person could be as masculine as they wanted to be as well as feminine; these two sets of traits were not thought to be opposing or interrelated ways of being. This way of understanding and constructing gender in the 1970s gave birth to the concept of androgyny which reflected a combination of both masculine and feminine traits. In fact, psychologists in the 1970s, as well as the field as a whole, embraced the concept of androgyny to the extent that it came to be viewed at that time as the "ideal way" or the most healthy type of gender identity that there can be. The new approach made some logical sense in that the combination of the best of two kinds of different worlds perhaps created a much stronger, wiser, more open, and therefore healthier human being. The notion of androgyny also seemed to support and foster feminist beliefs, the sense that women can do and be, exhibit traits, as well as engage with things behaviorally that were traditionally associated as masculine, that is, with men, appealed to feminist ideals of the second wave.

These researchers further assumed that boys and men could adopt feminine traits with healthy outcomes. The social context obviously must be considered as well, given how valued or not valued feminine and masculine traits (or both within one person) are within a community or society. Ultimately, then, how the integration of gender-related traits manifested and how that integration was valued was dependent upon how society valued or did not value things that are feminine or masculine, or both. Examples of what these early gender identity traits looked like as proposed by "gender trait" psychologists in the 1970s, using items from the Bem Sex-Role Inventory (BSRI, Bem, 1974a) which used the traditional terms of "masculinity" and "femininity" include independent, forceful, and strong personality (masculinity) as well as affectionate, sympathetic, and sensitive to the needs of others (femininity). The Personal Attributes Questionnaire (PAQ, Helmreich et al., 1981) utilized different terms, which essentially referred to the same constructs: instrumentality and expressiveness, in place of masculinity and femininity, respectively. The researchers believed that using different terms might help to avoid reifying the constructs as participants completed the instrument.

As noted earlier, although both sets of research on the BEM and the PAQ relied quite heavily on long held cultural beliefs about masculinity and femininity, what was different with the research done in the 1970s was that anyone could complete these scales and identify any trait without being negatively typecast. Scoring for the instruments was relatively simple. For example, the instructions for completing the Bem scale involve adding up all the traits per masculinity and femininity, and coming up with a raw score. There also are instructions on how to create an androgyny score. The PAQ was quite similar, but, as noted earlier, Helmreich et al. (1981) wanted to get away from the culturally familiar terms of masculinity and femininity, and instead, reconstructed them with presumably non-gendered terms, that they called instrumentality and expressiveness. As importantly, Helmreich et al. included negative aspects of each of these dimensions, so that one set of traits was not considered as necessarily better, or healthier, than another set of traits. Thus, the psychologists in the 1970s truly began to be much more engaged as scientists, rather than cultural expressionists, in their study of gender.

Regarding the psychometric properties of the PAQ, there is excellent support for the existence of both dimensions that they are indeed commonly responded to, and that they stand apart from each other. For example, Spence and Buckner (2000) reported that men significantly scored higher on the instrumentality scale, and lower on expressiveness, than women. They also reported that over the years, scores had remained the same for generations of women and men, with the important exception that women tended to score more highly on the instrumentality scale as the years proceeded; no such trend has been found for men and expressiveness scores (Twenge, 1997, in Spence & Buckner). They also found that most participants adhered to either one set or another of traits, for the most part, reflecting the traditional definitions of masculinity and femininity. However, Spence and Buckner speculated that each individual develops their own unique set of traits, which then leads to a generalized understanding of their gender identity. For cis-gender men and women, this typically meant adopting the identity of "male" or "female." As discussed in Chap. 1, "identity" is an important factor in the development of socialized norms that are gendered. Identification with a particular gender influences the internal assignment of traits as either feminine or masculine, respectively. Other research during this era investigated gender traits and their relations with career interests as a reflection of gender diagnosticity. In other words, comparing the scores of men and women with each other was done to identify gender typical interests.

As might be apparent, much of the twentieth century gender identity research presumed only a binary approach, such that nonbinary individuals, that is, transgender and nonconforming (TGNC) people, were not generally represented. The research of the 1970s focusing on gender identity, rather than two distinct sets of traits, opened the door to explore non-binary aspects of gender identity as well, leading to current constructions of gender today as being potentially more open and fluid than previously thought. Further, more recent writings of many of these researchers today acknowledge some flexibility in terms of the number of genders that are there (e.g., Spence & Buckner, 2000). It would not be until the twenty-first century that non-binary and transgender folks would have their own theoretical models and instruments.

Aspects of Gender Identity

Part of defining gender identity is distilling important aspects that help further differentiate identity across individuals. For example, an important aspect of understanding identity is its *salience* (Palomares, 2004; Bigler & Liben, 2006). Salience in this context refers to how much one's gender operates cognitively as a categorizing dimension in making decisions, and engaging with other people. Still another important component to understand about gender identity is *context*, and more specifically, discrimination. Experiencing gender-based discrimination can affect how one sees themselves as an individual, particularly one's position within society, and then one's views of society and people regarding gender (Miville & Ferguson, 2014). A third important construct related to gender identity is its importance, or, *centrality*. Centrality is a slightly different construct than salience, which is how gender comes to mind in making decisions. Centrality, as differentiated from salience, refers to how important gender is to one's self-concept (Hinton et al., 2022), and relates to critical important outcomes such as health, positive identity experiences, and homophobia. In clinical work with clients, it is common to observe that the things that are held deeply or essentially are not always the first things that come up or are expressed. That does not mean these are not important or central issues.

One example of the psychological centrality of gender is how one sees themselves as part of a gender group, for example, aspects of identity reflecting dyadic or relational and societal/collective. In addition to how one sees oneself as an individual, it also is critical to understand how one sees oneself in relation to other individuals, and then societally, collectively, how one sees oneself in the larger group of society, whether it is one's cultural group or the larger society, especially as a member of one's gender group. One way collective-level thinking can manifest for gender identity is through *collective self-esteem* (Luhtanen & Crocker, 1992). Collective self esteem refers to the feelings about a group of which one is a member. Often, when thinking about self-esteem, we think of our feelings about ourselves, but when adopting a community-oriented lens, the collective self-esteem can be characterized by how one feels about others within one's group, or one's group at large.

When it comes to the decades of research that has been conducted on gender identity, it has been observed that, regardless of who is completing the scale, the traditional trait of masculinity, is often related to positive mental health and well-being, and positive self esteem in small and moderate ways (Kiselica et al., 2016). Femininity is less strongly related to these outcomes, although it is also important to note that it is positively related as well (Lefkowitz & Zeldow, 2006). And despite all the hope and hoopla that was made of androgyny in the 1970s, it was later soundly critiqued as not being supported by available evidence (Taylor & Hall, 1982, in Lefkowitz & Zeldow) to have any added advantage to one's overall mental health and functioning; instead masculinity was the more impactful variable for both men and women. Androgyny was such an exciting and novel idea that psychologists came up with in context of profound societal changes that were happening in the mid twentieth century surrounding gender. However, the fate of this construct demonstrates how critical empirical research is in psychology, since androgyny did not have much of a unique impact on mental health, per these studies. Recently, new research conducted by Lefkowitz and Zeldow directly investigated whether androgyny, defined as high levels of both masculinity *and* femininity, affected optimal mental health. They found that both qualities were each and together impactful, raising once more the question about the balance of multiple traits traditionally associated with gender and their collective impact on mental health. The latest findings might be interpreted within the context of the twenty-first century, given the increasing levels of fluidity that many people have regarding their gender identity, and how women and men in general may have far more flexible ways of seeing themselves. In sum, gender trait research, as well as gender identity and gender salience, appear to explain small parts of gendered experiences, but none of these are quite as all-encompassing as psychological science attempted to demonstrate with them, respectively.

Gender Identity Models

The study of gender in the late twentieth century occurred with an increased study of other collective identities, that is how people think and feel about being a member of a particular group. As we described in Chap. 2, membership in racial groups has their own unique impact on identity development and mental health. *Racial identity* refers to an aspect of identity regarding how one thinks and feels about oneself as a racial being. That is, in addition to developing a gender identity, individuals also develop a racial identity, a sense of themselves as racial beings, moving from a naivete about the impact of race, to having some kind of encounter with observing that racism exists, to then starting to think more deeply and broadly about race of themselves and others (Helms, 1995). Thus, people can transform their sense of self as a racial being because of these experiences with racism and discrimination. It is critical to one's mental health to deal with discomfort at times in facing the harsh realities that have come about regarding race and individuals' sense of themselves as racial beings.

In the 1980s, as some psychologists began to study gender, other psychologists focused on racial identity. As with gender, a key issue was the distinct experience of being a person or color (or BIPOC), the focus of which originated with Black or African Americans in psychology, and then expanding to all people from non-Western backgrounds (e.g., Indigenous, Latine, Asian, etc). Being a White person, that is, a person born with racial privilege, also is important to examine, so that having privilege or not having privilege each has a distinct impact on mental well being (Helms, 1995). Psychologists in this era began to observe and investigate how social privilege (i.e., positionality, see Chap. 1) was related to identity development and overall mental health and well being.

In the mid-to-late twentieth century, psychologists also began to consider multiple kinds of identities that may be important to understand and measure, as based on gender, race, socioeconomic status (SES), abilities, sexuality, and so on. Even now, it can be mind boggling to consider how deeply complex and nuanced identity development is. A single individual can have a number of privileged identities (e.g., gender, race) as well as marginalized identities (e.g., SES). Coming up with identity models that can address all of these processes is quite challenging. However, during this time, psychologists were still thinking they could create identity models that could capture at least some of the complexity and tensions that people resolve as they think about being either a racial being or a gendered being.

Women's Identities

In 1985, Downing and Roush published a model of feminist identity development (FID) primarily aimed for women. They looked at the quality of identity, the thoughts and feelings that people have about being a woman, and they also projected a narrative development that was quite similar to the racial identity models that were beginning to be proposed in this era as well by William Cross (1991) and Janet Helms (1995). One of the key aspects about these collective identity models, whether it is based on gender, race or sexual orientation (Cass, 1979) is that they focus on one identity at a time, and presume a singular evolution of those identities, regardless of other factors, context, and so on. This is a way of thinking about identity that today does not seem realistic or adequate, if one considers our discussion of intersectionality from Chap. 1 as well as each subsequent chapter focusing on a specific intersection with gender. However, at that time, it already was an advancement to consider race or gender as psychologically central or salident, compared with what scholars were thinking just 20 years earlier, where there was almost no focus on gender except to confirm differences as biological and unidirectional in impact (i.e., women and people of color are always considered inferior). There clearly had been an evolution, but now we see where we needed to go from there.

During this era, identity development was presumed to occur through a set of stages believed to be uniform and invariant for anyone who went through it. However, later evidence showed quickly that there really was no single way to evolve a sense of identity (e.g., Cokley, 2007). It also was presumed that social justice activism was critical to developing the healthiest or most sophisticated understanding of oneself as a gendered or racial being, though little evidence was found to support this notion.

In their seminal article presenting the FID, Downing and Roush provided a comparison of their model with the Cross racial identity model, identifying both specific stages of development and several important parallels. In both models, people move from a passive acceptance of what is learned, for example, that traditional sex roles are always and only the advantageous roles to adopt. There is the notion that there is a dichotomy characterized by inferior and superior ways of being, with men being considered superior. And then there's an *encounter* (as used in racial identity models) or what Downing and Roush refer to as a *revelation*, a series of crises that results in much questioning of oneself and roles. For example, if a woman who is married with two children learns that her husband is having an affair, she may begin to deeply question what their marriage is about, as well as her role as the traditional housekeeper. It can be a very intense time, with much anger, anxiety, and guilt. Men may be perceived in rigidly negative ways. This person ideally will not stay stuck in the revelation stage or in anger for too long. In terms of talking with others, perhaps a therapist, they may begin to move beyond the anger, and ask themselves, what would a new identity for me as a woman look like? Who are other important people in my life, particularly who I can learn from, and who can learn from me? There begins to be an understanding that each person contributes different things in a relationship or the larger society based on their gender. And then there is a reopening of feelings and even behaviors when it comes to interacting with men, including as romantic partners, other women, and oneself.

Through searching and communicating, a woman might begin to develop a more authentic and positive sense of themselves, identifying particularly as a feminist. This last part reflects a presumption in the FID that the healthy way of identifying oneself as a woman necessarily is feminist, along with the belief that sex roles need to be transcended altogether (Downing & Roush). Women experiencing FID come into a more peaceful way of being, what was called "a flexible truth with the world." Ideally women begin to see men simply as individuals, and they begin to understand the world and people in more nuanced ways that include both positive and negative perspectives (Downing & Roush). Another aspect of FID is a "final" stage, called *active commitment*, which presumes that social activism is necessary. Thus, to consolidate a positive feminist identity necessarily involved transforming the world to be non-sexist, and once actions become more personalized, rather than just reactionary, as well as rational, men were viewed as equal, but certainly not the same, as women. This is only one example of a feminist identity scale, though there were a couple of feminist identity scales that were developed based on FID by other researchers, each somewhat different, but still with some important overlap. Gender identity in the 1980s and 1990s was a topic of great interest, overlapping with the full swing of second-wave feminism, and there were several groups of scientists developing scales, ways of measuring these identity models by participants responding to items that presumably reflected one's belief system as based on different FED stages.

Items measuring feminist identity, specifically an example of passive acceptance from the FIS scale by Rickard (1989) is "I like being a traditional female." From another scale, Feminist Identity Development Scale (FIDS; Bargad & Hyde, 1991), a sample item of how passive acceptance is measured is "most women will feel most fulfilled by being a wife and mother." A sample revelation item from FIS is "Regretfully, I can see ways in which I have perpetuated sexist attitudes in the past." A sample item for next stage embeddedness is, "I am very interested in women musicians," reflecting an interest in looking to connect with other women who may share important qualities and interests like music. An example of a synthesis is, "I am proud to be a competent woman" as a way of expressing transcendence of one's insecurity and bad feelings about being a woman to feeling instead pride and ownership in one's development/evolution. A final item from active commitment (FIDS), "I want to work to improve women's status," reflects a commitment to social activism.

In the early 1990s, Janet Helms and her colleagues developed the Womanist Identity Development (WID) model (Osanna et al., 1992). Womanism is a culturally contextualized understanding of feminism, drawing from the work of Alice Walker's *In search of our mothers' gardens* (1983). Walker used this term, as distinct from feminism "to emphasize love, wisdom, strength, and creativity," especially regarding the experiences of Black women. The WID (Ossana et al., 1992) model utilizes similar terms and processes as described in the racial identity model developed by Cross (1991) and Helms (1995), including the pre-encounter, encounter, immersion, and internalization constructs. The WID model begins with the negative, naive, and inferior attitudes about women to interpret gender specific information, and goes on to a more conscious awareness of gender issues, encounter or dissonance, often regarding an experience with gender discrimination, and the development of reflective criticism about gender and gender roles. This is followed by immersion, a blend of idealization of women and strong rejection of male superior views. There is then a search for positive definitions of womanhood and strong affiliations with women, leading finally to internalization, in which a woman becomes capable of conceptualizing herself and others through positive definitions of womanhood based on personal attributes, personally relevant information abstracted from her shared experiences with other women. The WID model also was used to develop an instrument that was used during the 1990s and early 2000s in numerous studies (Ossana et al.).

Men's Identities

Janet Helms also developed a men's identity development (MID) model, parallel with the White identity model that she had developed for White Americans (Miville et al., 2005). The MID model is about coming to terms regarding one's gender privilege as a man. The process begins with contact, a general naivete, or even worse, obliviousness to gender issues and being uncritical and automatic in terms of how one identifies as a man. This is followed by disintegration, becoming aware of one's privileges and their impact on others (e.g., a husband who is having an affair comes to see the impact on his stay at-home spouse). This is followed by reintegration, an idealization of the stereotypic male role or masculinity, and then followed by disintegration, in which a man may simply return to what is known, embracing traditional masculinity. Individuals may maintain these attitudes for the rest of their lives, or they can continue expanding on their thoughts and feelings about gender, perhaps eventually internalizing a more realistic image of what being a man is like as well as an intellectual understanding of what it means to be a woman. Ideally, as individuals continue to work on themselves and understand gender, autonomy might happen, which is a deliberate integration of positive psychological aspects of gender roles for both men and women. And again, it is important to point out that these models represent an exclusively binary understanding of gender, at least in their original conception.

Around this time other psychologists became focused on the gender identity of men. That is, in addition to the FID for women, there were men psychologists who began to question what it means to be a man. Pleck (1981) made a powerful statement that gender roles are socially constructed, affirming that gender roles are not about biology, but socially constructed within a larger cultural and societal context. He also noted that gender roles can be contradictory and inconsistent, and that the number of people who violate gender roles is quite high. He suggested these violations occur despite the social condemnation that may result for all involved, potentially leading to negative psychological consequences. If a person is shamed often, especially as a young boy, this can lead to internalizing these negative experiences such that individuals may come to believe these negative things about themselves (e.g., they are weak and should feel ashamed). Sometimes, as a result, people start to overconform to gender roles.

Pleck suggested that role violations have more severe consequences for men than for women, likely related to loss of privileges. Although the current authors do not ascribe to the "more harmful" perspective, it was quite revolutionary for Pleck to note that men can be harmed psychologically and physically by these longtime rigid, binary beliefs about gender. Pleck further stated that certain prescribed gender role traits like male aggression can actually be dysfunctional and harmful to people, and that people of all genders experience some kind of strain, what he called *gender role strain (GRS),* in the work and family worlds. Finally, Pleck noted the impact of context, especially historical changes, that can cause gender strain. In other words, GRS is not a process that simply happens, there also can be political pressures and decisions that lead to general, even generational strain, within families and communities.

Gender role strain is an important construct in psychology because of the acknowledgment of power differences in society as having psychological impact on boys and men in particular. In addition to the identity models we just reviewed, GRS was one of the first psychological constructs to acknowledge the power differences among genders, and that gender roles arise from and serve to protect the patriarchal social and economic order. This is quite a sophisticated understanding of gender that goes beyond the way empirical (Western) psychology was traditionally conceived, i.e., not attached to any context. GRS thus is an example of psychologists beginning to define contextual variables as affecting mental health functioning: patriarchal beliefs drive gender roles which drive mental well being.

Pleck also discussed gender as a performance, an enactment, that is independent of sex. That is, individuals can perform any combination or permutation of gender role behaviors, traits, and so on. With Pleck and gender scholars in the 1980s and 1990s, the evolution of considering only biological bases of gender and subsequent rigid and binary notions of roles was transformed to the more flexible and nonbinary understandings that took hold in the field in the twenty-first century.

Another scholar who focused on men and gender was James O'Neill (2008) who studied a related construct, *gender role conflict* (GRC), referring to the detrimental impact the traditional male gender role socialization has on many boys and men, including: "(a) restrictive emotionality; (b) health care problems; (c) obsession with achievement and success; (d) restrictive sexual and affectionate behavior; (e) socialized control, power, and competition issues; and (f) homophobia" (2008, p. 361). O'Neill in 2008 wrote a paper summarizing 25 years of research that provided clear evidence about the reality and impact of GRC for many populations, including boys and men of color.

Yet another important construct is called *masculinity ideology* which entailed psychologists identifying key aspects of the social context that drive gender roles and gender identity. Gilmore (1990) observed that there was something almost generic, repetitive even, about the criteria of playing the role of a man. An analogous term from today's world is "mansplaining" (i.e., where a man describes a phenomenon to a woman in condescending and sometimes inaccurate ways), that is, underlying the surface variations in emphasis or form are certain convergences and concepts, symbolizations and exhortations of masculinity in many societies. This is again yet another way of observing the social and cultural contexts to identify an ideology that promotes a certain, even uniform, ideology about masculinity. Many societies, if not most, today presume the following common roles for men: procreator (father), provider (worker), and protector (soldier). However, the contemporaneous existence of virtually androgynous cultures continues to raise questions about the reality of masculinity and male gender development (Gilmore, p. 201). In fact these cultures suggest that cultural values may outweigh nature in the masculinity puzzle.

A final comment regarding theory and research on men's gender roles and socialization is from the work of Kiselica and colleagues (Kiselica et al., 2016) who critiqued the primary emphasis on a deficit approach, paralleling critiques of gender research on women and TGNC people:

> extensive research findings have indicated that (a) most boys and men have secure attachments (Kiselica, 2001; Kiselica & O'Brien, 2001); (b) most boys and men are well- adjusted human beings (Kiselica, 2006a, 2006b; Kiselica & O'Brien, 2001); (c) the ability of most boys and men to recognize, experience, and express emotions is within the normal range (Kiselica & O'Brien, 2001; Wester, Vogel, Pressly, & Heesacker, 2002); (d) boys and men have long traditions of acting in a prosocial manner (Kiselica & Englar-Carlson, 2010; Kiselica et al., 2008); and (e) decent boys and men model noble notions of masculinity and pass them on from one generation of men to the next (Kiselica & Englar-Carlson, 2010; Kiselica et al., 2008; Pleban & Dietz, 2007; Snarey, 1993; Thomas, 1994). In short, there is a strong, positive counterpart to the negative male socialization experiences and the deficit model of male development that has been emphasized.... (p. 125)

We revisit these critiques in Chap. 12 when we describe counseling interventions for male clients framed on notions of positive masculinity.

Transgender/Gender Nonconforming Identities

We next turn to transgender/gender nonconforming (TGNC) identities. At the same time scholars were deconstructing cis-gender identities and roles, Butler (1990) was deconstructing concepts relative to LGBT concerns. Butler is credited with associating the concept of *performativity* with gender. In a recent interview, Butler summarized this framework:

> people are, consciously or not, citing conventions of gender when they claim to be expressing their own interior reality or even when they say they are creating themselves anew. It seemed to me that none of us totally escape cultural norms. At the same time, none of us are totally determined by cultural norms. Gender then becomes a negotiation, a struggle, a way of dealing with historical constraints and making new realities. When we are "girled", we are entered into a realm of girldom that has been built up over a long time—a series of conventions, sometimes conflicting, that establish girlness within society. We don't *just* choose it. And it is not *just* imposed on us. But that social reality can, and does, change. (Gleeson, 2021)

Notions of flexibility, fluidity, and nonbinary, key constructs in current ideations about gender and gender identity draw from the work of Butler's work in this arena.

Gender identity has been thought to precede sexual orientation, as the first occurs during childhood, and the second more clearly crystallizes in adolescence (Fausto-Sterling, 2019). That is, gender is something that people become aware of prior to thinking about whom they may be attracted to, especially if they develop a sense of awareness that they may not resonate or fit with what they are being taught is their presumed gender. For TGNC people, the ascribed category of man or woman may not resonate with who/how they think and feel they are. Many TGNC people may develop a gender identity when young, but their gendered sense of self likely occurs later (for many to most), such as in adolescence and adulthood. Unless a person is raised in a genuinely gender affirmative home regarding being TGNC, they likely will be exposed to many rigid binary notions, even in today's social context (more so now than 5 years ago, given the number of anti-TGNC laws that have been passed in the U.S. during 2023 alone; Dickey et al., 2017).

Another key issue is that nearly all gender identity models developed in psychology were originally created with an binary, invariant stage process (later revised as cognitive strategies) that do not account for fluid, nonbinary, and more complex identifications. Today's more inclusive constructs allow for variations at many levels, including gender identity, gender expression, and anatomical sex (particularly with regard to intersex characteristics). It is no longer assumed that jobs, hobbies, or traits necessarily predict how one wants to express their gender, although it still may be the case that such aspects of self may actually inspire or reflect one's gender expression.

The *gender unicorn* (transstudent.org, n.d.) is an excellent way to understand the related but distinct constructs when it comes to gender and gender identity. For example, in addition to gender expression, there is one's actual physical being that relates to one's body, hair, hips, voice, and pitch. *Gender expression* refers to a set of choices and behaviors that are typically visible to others that invoke a particular gendered experience, whereas sex assignment is usually done at birth rigidly and is an externally assigned label. Who a person is physically attracted to, and who one is emotionally attracted to are considered distinct, though often related to each other (transstudent.org). An excellent example of how and why these distinctions are important to make can be seen in the following example of gender expression regarding the colors pink and blue (Cahn, 2022). Consider Barbie–pink everywhere, as depicted in the recent Hollywood film by Greta Gerwig. But in fact, during the Victorian era up to the early 1900s, pink was considered more appropriate for boys whereas blue was used for girls. The reason was that pink, being a more decidedly stronger color, was considered more suitable for a boy, and blue, seen as more delicate and dainty, was considered prettier for girls. So here we see how color and gender is driven as much by the sociocultural context as anything else.

Regarding TGNC identity models, in 2004, Devor published one of the first models of "transsexual" (sic) identity formation. Although the term is outdated and presently considered a gendered slur, this was one of the first affirmative transgender identity models developed. Devor observed that each person has a deep need to see themselves mirrored in others' eyes as they see themselves internally. There are two clinically relevant types of processes here, the first is *being witnessed*, which leaves a feeling of having been accurately seen by others. This is in and of itself is a powerful reinforcer, especially for boosting mental health and a sense of well-being. This is particularly important for TGNC folx who more often than not have fewer of these experiences in the larger society. The second process that Devor discussed is *being mirrored* which leaves a feeling that one is recognized and accepted by others, and that one is not alone. So, in addition to being accurately seen by someone, it is also important to be recognized and accepted by others. This is a way of providing absolutely invaluable support for a client to not feel alone.

Multicultural Gender Role Model

In light of the multiple concerns about gender roles and gender identity models previously described, Miville and her colleagues (Miville, 2013) set out to develop a theoretical framework to understand how individuals, particularly those from diverse racial-ethnic backgrounds (Black, Latine, and Asian/Asian American), construct meanings about their lived experiences as gendered beings of color (only cis-gender individuals were included for the study), rather than identify a priori what these might be. Miville and her team engaged in interviews of over 60 individuals, using a qualitative data analytic approach, yielding the Multicultural Gender Role Model (MGRM) (Miville et al., 2013; see Figure 1, p. 236). The model suggests that there may be up to 8 kinds of important processes that are critical for each individual person to undergo.

The MGRM is buttressed by four very common experiences: cultural values, expectations, and norms; the stereotypes that one encounters, gender-wise, racially and so on; socializing agents and institutions, including parents, siblings, peers, schools, religious organizations, government policies, etc.; and the historic notions of masculine and femininity, culturally infused, depending on one's ethnic and racial backgrounds (see Chaps. 2 and 3). Within the context of these 4 pillars, we found that individuals continuously undergo a variety of processes in which they navigate and negotiate their gender role. In other words, the MGRM is an identity model that does not presume a particular "development" or "endpoint." Rather the model identifies important tensions that are part of negotiating one's gender roles, including resolving conflicting social messages, navigating one's privilege and oppression, understanding how one affects others, as in the example of a man coming to understand his more privileged position relative to his wife; transforming one's own self perception, perhaps resulting from an encounter with discrimination as a Black woman, for example (Fig. 7.1).

Another important tension is navigating multiple identities at once, which is newer to current understandings of gender identity in psychology. That is, as one navigates their gender identity, they also are navigating their racial as well as their sexual orientation and SES identities. Not surprisingly, this involves navigating some very difficult and challenging emotions, and ideally is associated with constructing one's own gender style and expression, which can be traditional, or one's own unique style and expression. The MGRM model does not presume the same outcome for all. Instead the model describes the kinds of tensions people may

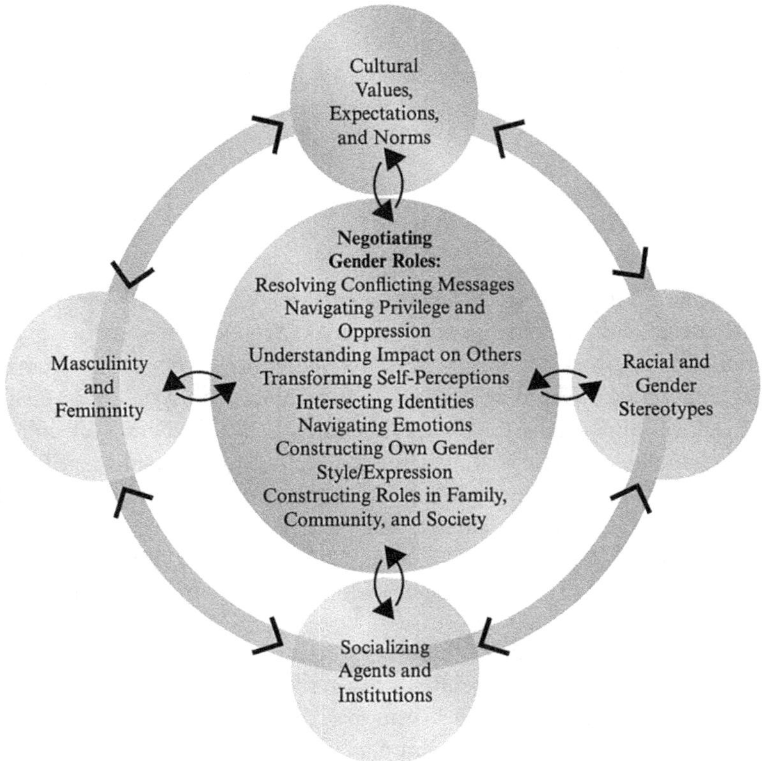

Fig. 7.1 Emergent Multicultural Gender Role Model

struggle with, as based on the responses participants provided during the study. And then, as one figures out their own expression, they also may begin to construct their own roles in their families, communities, and the larger society. Several instruments have since been developed that assess various aspects of this model for different populations, including Black women (Buque, 2019); Asian/Asian American women (Rooney, 2019), and men of color (Awad, 2019).

Conclusion

This chapter has summarized over half a century of psychological theory and research on gender identity. Over time, the field has moved from presumably biologically driven and rigid approaches to understanding gender identity, to more open and flexible approaches that do not presume a single outcome or set of processes for all. Clearly more research has been conducted on cisgender women and cisgender men, and far more evidence is needed to better understand the challenges that gender diverse individuals experience throughout their lifetime. Identity struggles remain an important area of both research as well as practice; Chap. 12 describes some of the more recent and innovative approaches to assisting clients who may be navigating their identities.

Case Study

Michelle is a 32-year-old biracial (Japanese and Black American) heterosexual cisgender woman. She recently gave birth to a baby and reports feeling exhausted by caring for her and her baby's needs. In the first session, Michelle describes experiencing significant support and affirmation from friends and family on both sides throughout the pregnancy and felt culturally valued from her father's side as a Japanese woman and from her mother's side as a Black Southern woman. A few months after the birth, however, she noticed many people were checking in on her less, and she had little energy to reach out to her social support. She has started to resent both her newborn and the fact that she is a woman, often saying, "I wish I wasn't a woman; we get no respect," along with similar expressions of hurt and detachment from her gender. Previously, she felt great pride being a woman, wife, and mother-to-be, especially because her husband, Alex, is supportive. She is financially able to stay home with her newborn and wishes to reconnect with her sense of pride in womanhood but does not know where to start.

Discussion Questions

1. Delve into Michelle's gender identity evolution, shaped by shifts in social support postpartum. Unpack her Black Southern heritage and Japanese cultural norms, which contribute to her current emotional weariness.
2. In what ways can we make sense of Michelle's anger towards her gender role in light of femininity, masculinity, and androgyny literature? Determine whether social expectations of gender features impact her postpartum mental health.
3. In the context of Michelle's transition to motherhood, how does her circumstance demonstrate the concepts of gender role tension and conflict? Consider the role these stresses may play in her apathy and bitterness.
4. Discuss the potential of feminist and womanist theories in guiding Michelle toward rediscovering her pride in being a woman. As a mixed-race woman, consider which aspects of these models may resonate.
5. How do you think the political and social settings Michelle finds herself in, as a person of different races, impact her gendered sense of self? Explore whether these factors changed as she went from being pregnant to a mother.
6. Considering the support she experienced initially and her present feelings of loneliness, what can Michelle do to reawaken her gender identity pride? Please suggest some valuable methods or materials for her during this time.

7. Take stock of the pre-and post-pregnancy support networks that Michelle benefited from. What can be done to ensure that new moms continue to receive support after giving birth, and how do gender expectations impact this support?

References

Awad, M. (2019). *The development and evaluation of the Multicultural Gender Roles Scale—Male Version*. Doctoral dissertation, Columbia University. Columbia Academic Commons. Retrieved from https://academiccommons.columbia.edu/doi/10.7916/d8-h8fj-2959

Bargad, A., & Hyde, J. S. (1991). Women's studies: A study of feminist identity development in women. *Psychology of Women Quarterly, 15*(2), 181–201. https://doi-org.ezproxy.cul.columbia.edu/10.1111/j.1471-6402.1991.tb00791.x

Bem, S. L. (1974a). *Bem sex role inventory* [Database record]. APA PsycTests.

Bem, S. L. (1974b). The measurement of psychological androgyny. *Journal of Consulting and Clinical Psychology, 42*(2), 155–162. https://doi.org/10.1037/h0036215

Bigler, R. S., & Liben, L. S. (2006). A developmental intergroup theory of social stereotypes and prejudice. In L. S. Liben & R. S. Bigler (Eds.), *Advances in child development and behavior: The role of gender in educational contexts and outcomes* (pp. 39–89). Academic. https://doi.org/10.1016/S0065-2407(06)80004-2

Buque, M. (2019). *Development and initial validation of the Multicultural Gender Roles Scale—Black women (MGRS—BW)*. Doctoral dissertation, Columbia University. Columbia Academic Commons. Retrieved from https://academiccommons.columbia.edu/doi/10.7916/d8-qz2r-9q09

Butler, J. (1990). *Gender trouble: Feminism and the subversion of identity*. Routledge.

Cahn, L. (2022, November). *How pink and blue became the "girl" and "boy" baby colors. Reader's Digest*. Retrieved from https://www.rd.com/article/pink-for-boys/

Cass, V. (1979). Homosexual identity formation: A theoretical model. *Journal of Homosexuality, 4*(3), 219–235.

Cokley, K. (2007). Critical issues in the measurement of ethnic and racial identity: A referendum on the state of the field. *Journal of Counseling Psychology, 54*(3), 224–234. https://doi.org/10.1037/0022-0167.54.3.224

Constantinople, A. (1973). Masculinity-femininity: An exception to a famous dictum? *Psychological Bulletin, 80*(5), 389–407. https://doi-org.ezproxy.cul.columbia.edu/10.1037/h0035334

Cross, W. E. (1991). *Shades of Black: Diversity in African-American identity*. Temple University Press.

De Cecco, J. P., & Elia, J. P. (1993). A critique and synthesis of biological essentialism and social constructionist views of sexuality and gender. *Journal of Homosexuality, 24*(3–4), 1–26. https://doi.org/10.1300/J082v24n03_01

Devor, H. (2004). Witnessing and mirroring: A fourteen-stage model of transsexual identity formation. *Journal of Gay and Lesbian Psychiatry, 8*(1/2), 41–67.

Dickey, L. M., Singh, A. A., Chang, S. C., & Rehrig, M. (2017). Advocacy and social justice: The next generation of counseling and psychological practice with transgender and gender-nonconforming clients. In A. Singh & L. M. Dickey (Eds.), *Affirmative counseling and psychological practice with transgender and gender nonconforming clients* (pp. 247–262). American Psychological Association. https://doi-org.ezproxy.cul.columbia.edu/10.1037/14957-013

Downing, N. E., & Roush, K. L. (1985). From passive acceptance to active commitment: A model of feminist identity development for women. *The Counseling Psychologist, 13*(4), 695–709. https://doi.org/10.1177/0011000085134013

Fausto-Sterling, A. (2019). Gender/sex, sexual orientation, and identity are in the body: How did they get there? *The Journal of Sex Research, 56*(4–5), 529–555. https://doi.org/10.1080/00224499.2019.1581883

Gilmore, D. D. (1990). *Manhood in the making: Cultural concepts of masculinity*. Yale University Press.

Gleeson, J. (2021, September). Judith Butler: 'We need to rethink the category of woman'. *The Guardian*. Retrieved from https://www.theguardian.com/lifeandstyle/2021/sep/07/judith-butler-interview-gender

Helmreich, R. L., Spence, J. T., & Wilhelm, J. A. (1981). A psychometric analysis of the Personal Attributes Questionnaire. *Sex Roles, 7*(11), 1097–1108. https://doi.org/10.1007/BF00287587

Helms, J. E. (1995). An update of Helm's White and people of color racial identity models. In J. G. Ponterotto, J. M. Casas, L. A. Suzuki, & C. M. Alexander (Eds.), *Handbook of multicultural counseling* (pp. 181–198). Sage.

Hinton, J. D. X., de la Piedad Garcia, X., Kaufmann, L. M., Koc, Y., & Anderson, J. R. (2022). A systematic and meta-analytic review of identity centrality among LGBTQ groups: An assessment of psychosocial correlates. *Journal of Sex Research, 59*(5), 568–586. https://doi.org/10.1080/00224499.2021.1967849

Kiselica, M. S., Benton-Wright, S., & Englar-Carlson, M. (2016). Accentuating positive masculinity: A new foundation for the psychology of boys, men, and masculinity. In Y. J. Wong & S. R. Wester (Eds.), *APA handbook of men and masculinities* (pp. 123–143). American Psychological Association. https://doi.org/10.1037/14594-006

Lefkowitz, E. S., & Zeldow, P. B. (2006). Masculinity and femininity predict optimal mental health: A belated test of the androgyny hypothesis. *Journal of Personality Assessment, 87*(1), 95–101. https://doi.org/10.1207/s15327752jpa8701_08

Luhtanen, R., & Crocker, J. (1992). A collective self-esteem scale: Self-evaluation of one's social identity. *Personality and Social Psychology Bulletin, 18*(3), 302–318. https://doi-org.ezproxy.cul.columbia.edu/10.1177/0146167292183006

Miville, M. L. (Ed.). (2013). *Multicultural gender roles: Applications for mental health and education*. Wiley.

Miville, M. L., & Ferguson, A. D. (2014). Intersections of race-ethnicity and gender on identity development and social roles. In M. L. Miville & A. D. Ferguson (Eds.), *Handbook of race-ethnicity and gender in psychology* (pp. 3–21). Springer. https://doi.org/10.1007/978-1-4614-8860-6_1

Miville, M. L., Darlington, P., Whitlock, B., & Mulligan, T. (2005). Integrating identities: The relationships of racial, gender, and ego identity among White college students. *Journal of College Student Development, 46*(2), 157–175.

Miville, M. L., Bratini, L., Corpus, M. J., Lau, M. Y., & Redway, J. A. K. (2013). Negotiating multicultural gender roles: A proposed model. In M. L. Miville (Ed.), *Multicultural gender roles* (pp. 231–246). Wiley.

O'Neil, J. M. (2008). Summarizing 25 years of research on men's gender role conflict using the Gender Role Conflict Scale: New research paradigms and clinical implications. *The Counseling Psychologist, 36*(3), 358–445. https://doi.org/10.1177/0011000008317057

Ossana, S. M., Helms, J. E., & Leonard, M. M. (1992). Do "womanist" identity attitudes influence college women's self-esteem and perceptions of environmental bias? *Journal of Counseling & Development, 70*(3), 402–408. https://doi-org.ezproxy.cul.columbia.edu/10.1002/j.1556-6676.1992.tb01624.x

Palomares, N. (2004). Gender schematicity, gender identity salience, and gender-linked language use. *Human Communication Research, 30*(4), 556–588. https://doi.org/10.1111/j.1468-2958.2004.tb00745.x

Pleck, J. H. (1981). *The myth of masculinity*. MIT Press.

Rickard, K. M. (1989). The relationship of self-monitored dating behaviors to level of feminist identity on the Feminist Identity Scale. *Sex Roles: A Journal of Research, 20*(3–4), 213–226. https://doi.org/10.1007/BF00287993

Rooney, J. (2019). *Development of the Multicultural Gender Role Scale for Asian American women* (MGRS-AAW). Doctoral dissertation, Columbia University. Columbia Academic Commons. Retrieved from https://academiccommons.columbia.edu/doi/10.7916/d8-4jxv-sh68

Spence, J. T., & Buckner, C. E. (2000). Instrumental and expressive traits, trait stereotypes, and sexist attitudes: What do they signify? *Psychology of Women Quarterly, 24*, 44–62.

Terman, L. M., & Miles, C. C. (1936). *Sex and personality: Studies in masculinity and femininity*. McGraw-Hill Book Company. https://doi-org.ezproxy.cul.columbia.edu/10.1037/13514-000

Trans Student Educational Resources. (n.d.). Retrieved March 19, 2024, from https://transstudent.org/

Twenge, J. M. (1997). Changes in masculine and feminine scores across time: A meta-analysis. *Sex Roles, 36*, 305–325.

Walker, A. (1983). *In search of our mothers' gardens: Womanist prose*. Harcourt Brace Jovanovich.

Chapter 8
Education and Career Development

Hwang Wol-geum, 70, left corner, attending a school trip in South Korea with other grandmothers and her grandchildren. (Credit… Chang W. Lee/The New York Times)

Introduction

In this chapter, we discuss education and career, and how gender can impact in the pursuit of one's education and career. The picture above captures the central controversy when it comes to gender and education, that is, people, because of their gender, being denied the right to pursue an education, to become literate, to be able to

M. L. Miville et al., *Counseling and Gender*,
https://doi.org/10.1007/978-3-031-69172-0_8

learn basic math skills, and then after that to pursue higher learning to pursue professional degrees and ultimately seek a job or career. For generations, it has been a source of tension that only some people could pursue an education, while others could not. The above picture is of five grandmothers, women in a small rural town in South Korea (Sang-Hun, 2019). The town was losing families to the city, birth rates were plummeting, and the local school was very concerned about being able to survive. So, they decided to extend basic schooling to anybody who wanted to pursue an education. As has been the practice worldwide, some children attended school while others did not. In many communities, this was often decided by gender, such that boys went to school, and girls stayed home and helped around the house. And so, these women, in their elder years, decided to go back to school and learn to read. One of the women was so inspired by her journey that she ran for a local political office.

Gender and Education

As the story above indicates, the link between gender and education has been and remains controversial; there has been an ongoing argument about whether girls and women should go to school, and if so, for what purpose (witness the recent controversy regarding graduation remarks of a football player regarding women's education in the U.S.; Cacciola & Hoffman, 2024). From ancient times, access to education has often been monitored in many societies, with entire groups of people being allowed access, whereas other groups were not (Carlton, 2023). Significant variables for access have included gender, race, and socioeconomic status (SES; e.g., wealthy families wanting to separate their children from others). Regarding gender-based access, arguments against formal education for girls were generally based on their not having the cognitive capacity to learn academic subjects and that such learning might negatively affect their reproductive capacities (literally!) (Gershon, 2020).

In the late 1700s, twice as many men were literate as women in the U.S. (Gershon, 2020). However, as the U.S. moved toward opening public schools, many families sent all their children, including girls, to school. Thus, instead of an open call or civil protest regarding the inclusion of girls, they were simply brought to school, a practice U.S. Secretary of Education Horace Mann referred to as "smuggling in the girls" (Mann, 1853, in Tyack & Hansot, 1988, p. 33). During the 1800s, girls overtook boys in their academic performance to the point that several prominent individuals began to criticize coeducational practices, though to no avail. The criticism focused on girls' incapacities (e.g., ill effects on their being feminine and ready for homemaking roles), as well as the "feminization" of boys who were in the presence of so many women teachers (Tyack & Hansot, p. 33). At the higher education level, criticisms of women attending higher education institutions, particularly Ivy League schools, continued into the mid-twentieth century, for example, with "keep the damned women out" and "better dead and co-ed" being some public reactions as recently as 1970 (Carlton, 2023). The federal law known as Title IX initially passed in the early 1970s, went a long way toward achieving gender parity throughout many educational institutions. The year 1982 was the first year women earned more bachelor's degrees than men, and by 2019, women made up most of the U.S. college-educated workforce (Carlton, 2023).

Access to education remains controversial around the world. For example, girls and women still lack educational access in several countries around the world. In 2014 Malala Yousafzai famously won the Nobel Peace Prize at the age of 17 after being critically wounded for her public advocacy of girls' rights to education in her native country of Pakistan. According to her website (https://malala.org), 130 million girls still do not have access to formal education. Gender controversies also exist for transgender and gender nonconforming students, for example, having access to public restrooms as well as the right to play in organized sports. Indeed, educational access for TGNC students is now deeply mired in controversy and discriminatory laws around the U.S. However, states have passed affirming laws that support TGNC students' educational rights (e.g., New York State Education Department). This history and current situation provide an essential context for understanding relevant psychological processes that affect people regarding their navigation of gender in education and careers.

Education and Career: Women

When working with women regarding their education, career choices and development, and the unique challenges they may face as women, there are several concerns to attend to. The key issue is identifying the kinds of resources women have in reaching out and networking, the types of actions and resources that can support women as they pursue their various educational and career choices. As noted in the chapter introduction, it is vital to consider clients in terms of their context. As one might imagine, educational settings are quite different from one's home. So it is critical to help women when discussing a difficulty at work or school, and to have them describe the context, that is, to paint a fuller picture of what their school or work life might be like. It is also important to discuss how they balance work and school with their family life, including responsibilities and resources. For example, for children and adolescents, it is important to assess their family functioning and gender role expectations. For adults, it is important to evaluate whether they have a spouse and/or children, and childcare responsibilities.

Another consideration is to identify important barriers in their settings, including *distal*, referring to background context that affects the development of self-efficacy early on (e.g., types of role models, experiences of support or discouragement), and *proximal* variables when engaging in career decisions, for example, experiences of discrimination and quality of professional networks (Lent et al., 2000). A sense of *self-efficacy* refers to how one sees themselves in terms of capacities and ability to realistically assess those capacities. The unique impact of gender and its intersections with other marginalized identities can come into play in developing positive self-efficacy and one's gender role socialization. Consider a person who is socialized to see themselves as being acceptable to pursue a job or a career, even to pursue a vision for oneself outside of the home, versus a person who has been socialized to adhere closely to traditional gender roles, given its centrality to a sense of self as well as family and community. In both cases, navigating one's family role and outside work role may be quite complex and even difficult to manage or assess their conflicting impacts, for example, for women clients, as they struggle to figure themselves out in the world of work and their families.

Stereotype threat (Steele, 1997; Steele & Aronson, 1995) is another psychological process that is critical to understand when working with women, TGNC people, and people of color. When a student from a marginalized background is in a situation of being unique, even the "only one," for example, in a class of students taking a science or algebra test, and they are somehow reminded that they are a woman or a person for which there are negative stereotypes about doing well in that situation; being reminded of that stereotype can actually harm performance. Although the rates of degree completion, including higher education, are at their historic height in the U.S. (Parker, 2021), many students still experience marginalization or questioning of their competence in some school subjects, a sense of "I don't belong, and so, therefore, I don't have the capacity," that is what stereotype threat is. Self-doubt can impact actual performance because the threat leads a person to doubt their self-efficacy, the sense of being able to do a task, in this case, a science or math test. Stereotype threat interferes with judgment because there is almost an automatic response of fear, affirming that one cannot engage in a task or performance. The good news is that stereotype threats are treatable and can be overcome with simple, basic, direct, and, most importantly, accurate messaging about a person's abilities, for example, that one's gender, gender identity, or race or gender identity has nothing to do with capacity (Steele, 1997).

A related syndrome is *imposter syndrome* (IP; Clance & Imes, 1978) and was initially presented as a construct related to many women's socialization. Despite multiple accomplishments, a woman may somehow feel a "fake," and that despite their success, they do not experience this success internally, see themselves as intelligent and worthy of praise, and instead attribute their achievements to qualities outside themselves, such as luck or circumstance. Many who experience imposter syndrome (e.g., a newly admitted graduate student) may fear being "found out" as imposters and not deserving to hold their position. Racial-cultural identity may provide some protection against this syndrome; for example, an Afrocentric worldview that emphasizes mutual relationships and respect for internal growth may lead to lower levels of IP (Ewing et al., 1996, in Lin, 2008). A good strategy to combat IP is per a saying by famous politician/activitist Shirley Chisholm, who stated that "if there is no place at the table, bring a folding chair;" in other words, make a place for oneself if none is available.

A recent study exploring the experiences of women in academic settings in the fields of science, technology, engineering, and mathematics (STEM) found women devised a number of strategies to effectively blunt the impact of both stereotype threat and imposter syndrome (Arredondo et al., 2022). For example, successful women learned to build their own supportive communities in settings. Other important strategies involve the setting itself, where transparency regarding norms and expectations greatly assisted women in successfully navigating hostile environments. Finally, learning to become one's own advocate (as one participant noted, "Be strong!") is key to finding a space that is supportive of women and learning how to resist structural barriers and microaggressions. Such strategies are critical for improving the disparity for women entering STEM fields. Although the same number of girls and boys finished high school with an interest in STEM, only 20% of college degrees in these areas are actually earned by women (Steele, 1997).

Moreover, experiences with harassment and bullying by women in higher education and beyond also continue to be a concern, likely exasperating experiences of both stereotype threat and imposter syndrome. A less overt but more common experience of alienation at work involves experiencing a *null* environment in which there is no open support, orientation, or even welcome to a new woman employee (Betz, 1989). The study on women in STEM (Arredondo et al., 2022) described a poignant example in which a new woman faculty member was not even given a key to the main office area nor any kind of orientation and thus missed the first department meeting. Instead of an overly negative or hostile response, it was more of a "we're going to ignore you," potentially leading to feelings of alienation, anxiety, isolation, and ultimately, less success or feelings of satisfaction about one's success in the workplace.

With the appearance of younger generations since the last cycle of the women's movement (and post #MeToo movement regarding women's experiences of sexual violence in the workplace), what do these younger generations believe regarding gender roles and work vs. home settings? Most Americans, men (2/3) and women (3/4) millennials, say that they think that men and women should be equal in both the public sphere of work and the private sphere (Miller, 2018). But what is the reality? As we described in Chap. 4, women shoulder far more of the work associated with the home than men do, including childcare, elder care, cooking, cleaning, transporting family members, and, of course, for no pay at all. A recent Gallup poll (Rodriguez, 2020) further found that among heterosexual couples, disparities among household duties increases with age; one interpretation of these data is so that the longer a couple is together, the less work husbands contribute to these duties. What are the consequences of this? Unfortunately, women are twice as likely to suffer from severe stress and anxiety and consistently report higher stress levels (Medaris, 2023). So, having a job at work and then having another full-time job at home has a cost, and when it is shouldered by a person of one gender over another, that is how gender disparity is expressed at home.

Regarding younger men who are already fathers, 53% say it is better for mothers and fathers to take on traditional roles, so that is a majority of young dads who think they should have traditional roles (Wong, 2021). Among younger men who do not have children, only 24% expected to shoulder most of the childcare responsibilities, and of those with children, only 8% felt they would shoulder most of the childcare responsibilities. The numbers indicate that newer generations continue to retain more traditional views of gender roles.

Education and Career: Women of Color

In reviewing education and career issues for women of color, discussing the unique barriers they may face is important. For example, *downward mobility* (Cohen, 2022) refers to the positions that women of color may likely find themselves in, with lower pay, fewer promotions, and wage shrinkage, even earning minimum wage to support their children. Discrimination is also a concern, including the intersectional impact of race and gender, called *gendered racism,* as a woman of color (Lewis, 2023) is also a significant issue for many in education, but especially in the workplace (Battle & Carty, 2022). Isolation and loneliness can appear, similar to stereotype threat and imposter syndrome. When one feels alone in a setting, especially one that is highly competitive, people can feel isolated and lonely, so finding forms of connection is critical to this process. For example, Villaseñor, Reyes, and Muñoz (2013) described a mentoring model specifically designed for Latinas according to a culturally framed approach, *mujerismo* (i.e., Latina feminism/womanism), based on the work of Latina scholar Gloria Anzaldua's notions of mestiza consciousness (i.e., navigating the borderlands of one's own versus dominant perspectives, in Vllaseñor et al.). Villaseñor et al. define mujerista mentoring as:

> a collectivist, assets-based model that values the lived experiences and multiple ways of knowing of Chicanas/Latinas, focused on the building of communities and reciprocal mentoring relationships, and challenging models of mentoring that re-inscribe hierarchies between mentors and protégés. Moreover, where traditional mentoring focuses on assimilation by the protégé into the dominant culture of an institution of higher education, mujerista mentoring takes a more holistic approach, bridging the academic, professional, and the personal in order to create more meaningful and enduring mentoring relationships. (p. 50)

This kind of approach is quite helpful to women of color in racially and ethnically distinct settings from oneself, especially where one's social location is unique by race-ethnicity and by gender. Without such support, some individuals may find themselves altering who they are, even disidentifying from their original cultural socialization (Steele, 1997) as a means of survival. Unfortunately, many women of color can feel invisible and never fully themselves in that workplace, leading potentially to negative psychological effects. So another challenge is figuring out a way of integrating oneself into a workplace that conflicts with one's cultural values.

Another challenge, more covertly, is the communications that one may receive about needing to fit in better. A poignant topic, particularly for Black women, can be about hairstyles and the requirement to have a "neat hairstyle," (Berkemeyer, 2020), a reflection of covert racism that implies that neat hair can only look a certain way. Colorism, described in Chap. 3, is also a pervasive and widespread prejudice that significantly affects the lives and careers of women with darker skin. The term encompasses not only the favoritism towards individuals with lighter skin among various racial and ethnic groups, but also within those groups themselves (Tulshyan, 2023). Colorism is a persistent remnant of colonialism and the global dominance of White people, which unfairly affects women of color to a greater extent. Inclusive leaders have the responsibility to proactively address and mitigate colorism in the workplace, ensuring the retention of this group of workers. Professional behavior and demeanor can serve as a barrier, for example, in education, for many people from racial-ethnic groups where being vocal is a common, normal way of self-expression. School settings communicate and punish youth for being "too loud" so as to be more in line with accepted Western White norms (Caraballo, 2019). This is one example of students being "molded" into acting or not acting in certain ways to get along at school and in the workplace.

Importantly, besides barriers, it is also critical to consider important supports. For example, spirituality for many women of color is a key aspect of maintaining a sense of self, a sense of soul, and, for many, is an aspect of life that supports one's worth as a human being (Bryant-Davis & Comas-Diaz, 2016). Given the multiple barriers women face in school and at the workplace, especially regarding bullying and harassment, spirituality can be an important lifesaver and mind saver at those times. One's family also can be a source of strength, especially if one considers the extended family who can provide critical support in various ways.

The choice of coping (or resistance) strategies has been well-researched, especially the types of strategies employed (Shorter-Gooden, 2004). For example, avoidance can sometimes be a common strategy women use when facing a challenging work situation. Although this strategy works for a while, eventually, overuse of this strategy can lead to isolation, anxiety, and depression. In contrast, as mentioned earlier, seeking support from others (e.g., mentors, peers) is an active and often highly effective means of coping with challenges. Reframing a problem, perhaps even as an opportunity, is another helpful example of a coping strategy. That is, exploring ways of perceiving a challenging situation and finding some aspect that, if not positive, is at least resolvable is critical, especially at work.

Research has also found that active resistance (e.g., engaging in social justice advocacy, such as protests for undocumented students) is critical to significantly changing the social context, and is associated with positive mental health markers (e.g., Hernandez, 2018). One example is becoming involved with a network of similar people, perhaps in one's discipline, in psychologically meaningful ways that include being supportive, honest, and transparent. These networks can be crucial to building self-efficacy about skills and professional competence, that is, being able to trust those in one's networks to assess the accuracy of self-judgments. In addition to face-to-face interactions, social media networks have become a primary way to meet others and find support (Ayoola, 2022). In counseling setting, mental health providers can assist a client or student in terms of seeing how they may be either judging themselves too shortly or too negatively or not seeing an "ism" that may be right in front of their faces. As importantly, having a vision for pursuing an important goal (project, degree, career) is an important driver, and professionals can assist their clients in revisiting their visions throughout the lifespan, especially when important milestones occur (e.g., promotions, major award).

Some final strategies for all women in terms of their career are figuring out strategies for dealing with change or changing one's life, as well as enhancing physical and mental wellness, which is so critical (Pappas, 2021). Self-care and taking time and resources to care for oneself (nutrition, exercise, sleep) are important in preparing oneself for challenges and success. Knowing oneself, especially those triggers or events that can lead to depression or anxiety, is also another aspect of taking care of oneself and seeking validation. To have a social network that can provide that important sense of validation remains a key strategy for most people.

Education and Career: Boys and Men

Around 1980, several male psychologists began to seriously question the impact of gender on the psychological development and make-up of boys and men, beginning the research, theory, and intervention area that focused on gender role socialization, identity, unique career paths, and so on for boys and men (Pleck, 1981; O'Neil, 2008). Now, 40 years later, a tremendous number of studies have been generated in this topic area, including a division in the American Psychological Association (APA) Division 51 devoted to the psychological study of men and boys (e.g., O'Neil & Denke, 2016). Interest in this area has risen to such an extent that in 2018, the very first set of practice guidelines solely focused on boys and men was published by APA (see Chap. 12). This set of guidelines was the target of some public criticism, given that the guidelines did not state that masculinity is necessarily "inborn" but instead initially constructed during youth and adolescence, continuing into adulthood. Before this era, there was minimal discussion about males as being men (i.e., a gendered being), and there was very little research on boys and men in and of themselves. The focus when it was male participants was not that they were men but that they were simply considered the so-called "normal" or "universal" person. It was not until around 1980, after about a decade in which women and people of color in psychology began engaging more extensively in research and the psychological literature, as well as the practice of therapy with girls and women, that more gender-oriented approaches for boys and men began.

There are two strands of constructs and literature on gender role socialization. One was developed by James O'Neil, a counseling psychologist who focused on *gender role conflict (GRC),* a psychological state in which socialized gender roles have negative consequences for oneself and others (2015). O'Neil argued that the main source of GRC was rigid sexist or restrictive gender roles that can actually lead to negative psychological impacts. For many cisgender boys and men, GRC can lead to personal restrictions, a devaluation of self or others, as well as a violation of self or others that comes from that negative state. Unfortunately, there is a serious loss of human potential because ironically, as with ciswomen as well as TGNC folx, cis men are not seen by themselves and others as full human beings.

The bottom line of this work on cisgender boys and men is that *gender privilege* in and of itself can be a source of psychological and physical harm to self and others because of the false beliefs about superiority/inferiority regarding oneself and others and the emotional and behavioral consequences of such false beliefs or needing to "act" a certain way as a boy/man–risk-taking, disallowing strong feelings, such as sadness, other than anger or sex.

A second construct focused on boys and men is *gender role strain* (GRS) (Levant & Powell, 2017). Gender role strain is linked with gender role conflict, but there are important distinctions. Levant and Powell described the traditional male roles and socialization with a focus on encouraging and constraining boys and men to conform, comply with, or obey the traditional male role norms. This may occur by adopting what one is supposed to do, including how one is supposed to act, what one should wear, and how one behaves on a date, for example, as well as avoiding other behaviors such as not walking, dressing, or talking like "a girl."

Levant and Power highlight three types of general strain that arise from internalizing these norms, for example, *discrepancy* comes from failing to live up to how one thinks one is supposed to behave, think, and act as a man. This reflects the potential psychological impact of not conforming to these expectations per traditional male norms. There may be relevant cultural pressures because boys and men are socialized as well as to who they should act within their own communities; although there are some parallels, there are also unique roles and values within cultural communities.

The second type of gender role strain is *dysfunction,* where the requirements of being a man actually have adverse side effects on men, a topic in which GRS overlaps with GRC. The dysfunctional role strain is what has been called "the dark side of masculinity" (Levant & Powell, 2017, p. 37). Instead of failing to live up to male norms, Levant and Powell contend that actually engaging in some masculine behaviors, especially those that are more exaggerated or rigid, such as physical violence and high-risk behaviors, can have negative consequences for oneself and others.

The third type of gender role strain is *trauma*, that is, being part of a targeted group, for example, men of color, gay men, transgender people, or intersex individuals, has their own type of strain as a male-identified person which can have a traumatic impact. Being socialized as a cisgender boy or man can lead to a traumatic impact for TGNC individuals, since they do not feel that is who they truly are, leading to significant consequences if it is not observed early and supported for their true gender identity by the loved ones in that person's life.

As we begin to think about gender socialization and its impact on boys and men and their education and careers, it will not surprise you that there are very few studies that even investigate cis boys and men. As recently as 2016, a digital scan of the literature revealed there were less than 30 studies, quite a dearth! The other concern is that for many boys and men, as there is for girls and women, there is this phenomenon of *occupational segregation* (Zhavoronkova et al., 2022). When considering strain or conflict, consider a boy who wants to be a nurse, a teacher, or a traditionally women-led occupation. One can appreciate how gender socialization might lead to concerns, worry, anxiety, and even trauma when it comes to the choice of an occupation that seemingly contradicts the idealized male role. Alternatively one may choose an occupation that is high risk just because it seems to kind of promote a "bad boy" image in line with masculine ideology.

Other matters to think about in terms of cismen and their careers are wage *advantages* for White men. As we described in depth in Chap. 4, even though more women are in the workforce, even though educational attainment has increased for all women and men of color, there is still a distinctive wage advantage for men, particularly White men. When cisgender men choose non-traditional lower-paying careers, there are a number of implications and outcomes of this decision. For example, conflict and strain may exist about being in a predominantly women-led occupation. However, on a more positive note for men is the notion of a *glass escalator* (Brandford & Brandford-Stevenson, 2021; Williams, 1992) as one of the few men in a work settings, for example, psychology and the mental health fields. As a man applies to a mental health field work site or an internship, there are much fewer men now that these individuals are usually in-demand applicants, given the great need.

Education and Career: Men of Color

When it comes to looking specifically at men of color, it is not surprising there are similar parallels with career challenges relative to women of color. Regarding critical intersections, being both male and a person of color, there may be some conflict regarding privilege as a primary wage earner or the provider. There also can be conflicts that arise regarding oppressive experiences that happen at the workplace due to racism, including gendered racism for men (Banks, 2022). For most men of color, they are typically perceived and rewarded for taking on leadership roles in their families and communities. This is often in contrast to when they are in a workplace where, according to Banks, for example, Black men make up less than 2% of senior management versus White men who occupy nearly 60% of these occupations. Similarly, as with women, there can be a clash of cultural values at the workplace, where one may feel the need to conform, leave, or be fired. *Acculturation and language* differences can be both a strength and a source of strain for men of color, for example, if these do not match what is practiced at the workplace.

Additionally, men of color must deal with multiple *barriers*, including negative stereotypes, another aspect of gendered racism (Miville & Ferguson, 2014). Moreover, these stereotypes may become internalized, resulting in experiences with stereotype threat and the imposter syndrome described earlier. *Discrimination*, particularly based on gendered racism, can affect many men in the workplace, leading simply to a lack of opportunity because of stereotypes, discrimination, and so on. Some men of color also may deal with negative or unrealistic self-beliefs so they may disidentify from positions in which they do not see themselves as a part. At the same time, some boys and men can adopt unrealistic self-beliefs regarding how "easy" it may be to pursue some occupations they may identify with or how to navigate a workplace (Stiles et al., 1999).

The *school-to-prison pipeline* described in Chap. 4 refers to a phenomenon of the tremendous disparities between boys and men of color being moved quickly from the school system to incarceration within the prison system. According to Banks (2022), "Black men are, on average, 30 times more likely to be 'locked-up' than 'looked-up to' as senior-level employees. This ratio—the Ratio of Incarceration to Senior-level Employment (RISE)—is one major component of" gendered racism and what Banks calls "the American Nightmare" for many Black men. These statistics are in direct contrast with those of White men who occupy far more senior employee positions than are incarcerated. For many men of color, the *glass ceiling* remains a serious phenomenon in the workplace, in sometimes subtle ways. For example, according to Adamovic and Leibbrandt (2023), a recent review of over 12,000 job applications for leadership and non-leadership positions clearly showed positive responses for Western names (26% and 21%, respectively) vs. non-Western names (11.3% and 11.6%, respectively).

Education and Career Interventions for Men

We have discussed several challenges facing boys and men pursuing education and careers. In this section, we describe some positive *ways to intervene* with these concerns. First, *assess the gender role socialization* of clients, for example, by including available instruments for measuring gender role conflict and strain (e.g., O'Neil, 2015; Levant & Powell, 2017). Clients can complete these, discuss their responses to some of the items, and explore how their responses line up according to available norms. A client may present with concerns about coming from a family that pressures them to pursue a STEM discipline major in college, but they instead want to pursue social work, poetry, or dance. Assessing how both gender role strain and conflict are at play with this conflict may be relevant since the client may be indecisive because they feel that strain or conflict. For example, a classic scenario is a client who comes from a family that emphasizes engineering or other STEM disciplines as one of the only acceptable careers. But that young man might want to study dance, and so his indecision may come from an expectation that he is "supposed to go this way, " especially as a breadwinner, he might think, "what am I really going to do with a dance education degree?" It may be helpful for clients who are men to delve into their self-understanding about what it means to be a man, what it means to be in a particular gender role, and how they define their gender identity. This focus can occur in tandem with the traditional components of career counseling, such as providing clients with accurate information about careers (e.g., training requirements, typical work hours, and potential salaries), as this may further increase the value of career counseling and decrease the stigma for asking for help. In line with many men's hesitancy about seeking help, it is useful to explain the career counseling process and what clients can expect to get out of it to further destigmatize the experience and heighten optimism for finding a resolution.

According to Fouad et al. (2016), it will be important for mental health professionals to become aware of their biases about the role of career and work in men's lives in general. It is also important to identify one's expectations about the role of education and work. Another aspect of effective career counseling is *helping clients examine their options*, including those that go beyond the traditional male role options. Fouad et al. suggest that clients might be challenged to *not* conform, in a way, since the counseling situation is a safe place for clients to dare to think beyond what assumes one must be, as in dare to be a dancer or a pastry chef. Another critical intervention is helping clients *figure out barriers* so these can be identified, such as discrimination, conflict, and strain. Definitions and examples can be provided, after which clients might be asked how these issues apply to them. They also might be asked if they know somebody experiencing something similar to their concern (even a public example) because sometimes it can feel safer to think about somebody else struggling and then bring it back to themselves. Similarly, clients can be guided to identify key *family expectations and cultural values,* and assumptions about gender roles and the importance of work influencing their choices (Fouad et al).

Suppose clients are considering career or work options that are counter to what they know their expectations are. In that case, it may be helpful to talk with clients, especially adolescents and young men, about their family expectations, how they have dealt with these so far, and how they might want to deal with them differently. It is also important to identify potential options that they may have foreclosed on because of those family expectations as well as their own internalized "isms," for example, gendered racism, as these also may be affecting their education and work-related choices. Finally, helping clients identify supportive people who can assist them in making choices, especially by being supportive of those choices, will help clients take their concerns beyond the counseling situation. For example, a good activity is for clients to meet with people in disciplines or jobs they are considering, or even fantasizing about, and find out what the experiences have been and how these individuals overcame challenges.

Finally, there are several excellent suggestions about looking at community approaches, leveraging family and community strengths, especially among lower-income and communities of color. That is, it is in the power of togetherness that poverty can be overcome, even perceiving social protest movements as a form of community advocacy intervention (e.g., Calle, 2021). A key issue is helping individuals become more mindful about whom and what they are directing their anger at and identifying what strategies are going to work, what is fact based and what is it that actually can be effective.As mental health professionals, it is about imagining first and then collaborating with others, especially with community members, as well as integrating the expertise of community members into mental health work. Community consultation and advocacy also can focus on the power of the community to overcome poverty. In considering men in their breadwinner roles, exciting possibilities for programs can come to fruition that assist men to regain their sense of strength, power, and authority in terms of their own independence and self sufficiency and their ability to assist their families.

Education and Career: Transgender and Gender Non-Conforming People

Similar to the dearth of literature on education and career for men, available research and literature are relatively nascent for TGNC populations, although the literature has expanded considerably in the past two decades. A number of concerns have been raised for TGNC that likely impact their educational and career prospects. For example, TGNC people face rampant *transphobia and discrimination,* and there is much public discourse and discriminatory laws that recently were passed in many states across the U.S., including issues such as physical threats and violence, termination, demotion, harassment, and stereotypes (e.g., Dispenza et al., 2012; Goldberg, 2018; Goldberg et al., 2021). Equitable access to facilities (e.g., bathrooms and sports activities) remains a significant concern for many TGNC students in schools and some workplaces. These experiences also can have mental health impacts, such as social isolation, depression, and suicidal ideation. Transphobia can be internalized, leading to elevated levels of depression, anxiety, and potentially suicide. This can become a vicious cycle. However, for many TGNC people living in certain regions, such as large urban areas, the social situation is more accepting, especially among younger people (Paris & Miller, 2023). However, in smaller cities and towns, it is still a difficult context for young TGNC people to navigate.

Specific concerns that TGNC folx may be dealing with are the *transition process*, how to transition, whether to transition and how to handle that, for example, as a student in a school system with no and negative policies concerning their status. For example, Schmidt and Nilsson (2006, in Scott et al., 2011), described a *bottleneck hypothesis*, indicating that young TGNC people may delay common tasks related to career development as they are more focused on matters relevant to being transgender. For example, if a TGNC person is in the process of transitioning, their employment history may be subsumed under a different name. Scott et al. suggest this may lead to a "double-bind" for TGNC people, since they may not be eligible for employment if their history is not available, and if they should reveal this history, they may then face hostility and discrimination. Appearance is another area in which TGNC may face challenges, in terms of developing identity congruent choices for professional wear.

As there are consequences to any decision, helping clients think and feel through some of their choices is key to providing support and a path forward. When one transitions, there can be *losses* to consider, jobs as well as educational experiences. Changing one's name is an important step forward for a TGNC person's development, although this also has challenges, such as ensuring legal documents and records follow them. As someone transitions, it is very important to help spell out what that is like for them; for example problem-solving adequate access to needed facilities at school and work may be a concern and can be used as a source of harassment and bullying for some clients (Motulsky & Frank, 2018).

Other concerns TGNC people may face in education and careers include the decision to self-disclose at school or work and possible isolation at work, though it also is important to identify supportive and similar individuals in one's network (Goldberg et al., 2021). There may be an entire discussion about *passing* regarding one's gender identity, similar to a parallel issue about race some years ago, and the different consequences for each set of choices. Being open about oneself is ideal but not always possible, so helping people think that through and identify possible role models for doing so is important (Goldberg et al., Motulsky & Frank, 2018). Motulski and Frank also described *double discrimination* that can come from various aspects of one's identity conflicting with each other, so, for example, a transgender woman who transitions later in life may have to then deal with sexism as a woman at the workplace for the first time in their lives.

Motulsky and Frank (2018) and Goldberg (2018) provide several suggestions for interventions with TGNC clients regarding their education and career aspirations:

1. *Language:* It is important to carefully consider the language that is used, such as learning correct names and pronouns and being mindful about the pronouns used, whether it's about a specific client or people in general.
2. *Empathy:* Another key way to be supportive is by affirming the client's identity and learning about affirmative approaches, strengths, and empowerment. At the same time, it is important not to *ignore and minimize the challenges* and difficulties clients are experiencing or have experienced or to focus solely on gender identity as the cause of stress and mental health concerns.
3. *Trust* is key when considering the harsh discrimination that some clients may be dealing with. Trust what clients say rather than questioning them skeptically. Basic counseling skills that assist clients in telling their stories go a long way to helping them tell their stories and begin to establish trust and working relationships. It is also important to pay attention to one's vocal tone, and the questions asked to ensure trust rather than mistrust is engendered from the start.

Beyond basic skills to establish a relationship with clients, Motulsky and Frank (2018) and Goldberg (2018) described other important elements, including attending to the reliability and validity of various career instruments for TGNC people. It is also important to be aware of ongoing *legal and policy decisions* that may affect the educational and career paths of TGNC people. Helping clients find and become involved in *inclusive organizations* that can connect them to a larger community and provide social support helps alleviate experiences of isolation and social media sites that may lead to even larger communities and movements (Goldberg, 2018).

As we have been discussing throughout this book, mental health providers also can attend to the *intersectionalities* of identities in their TGNC clients, in addition to gender identity, race, SES, and other key aspects of their identities. (Motulsky & Frank, 2018) A TGNC client may have yet to articulate how intersectionality has impacted their educational and career goals. An important goal may be to help clients understand discrete aspects of identity that may be critical to them and how these are converging or not converging, even conflicting, with each other. Another practical concern refers to creating *allyship*: making sure that one's office or space is welcoming and inclusive of all clients, including wall hangings, window decals, and books to read in a waiting room, can create a sense of safe space for clients. Motulsky and Frank (2018) provide practical suggestions for TGNC clients as well, such as the basic nuts and bolts of how to get a job (resume/interview strategies, attire, job search), as well as to assess whether or not clients know about these more practical aspects. Finally, as for all clients, *advocacy* is particularly important for TGNC folks, helping beyond the counseling situation to make changes in society that are more welcome, and open, to TGNC clients.

Conclusion

In this chapter, we reviewed how gender intersects with many aspects of seeking an education and career for TGNC people, women, and men. The chapter highlighted other important intersections, primarily race-ethnicity, that are critical to consider as well. As we have discussed throughout this volume, contextual variables are key to identifying and understanding the many nuances of the intersections of gender and career, in order to develop research that accurately describes the struggles and strengths relevant among multiple individuals and to provide effective interventions for these unique communities.

Case Study

Eleni, a 23-year-old Romani-Greek cisgender woman currently living in Boston, MA, recently sought therapy due to pervasive anxiety. She immigrated to the United States from Greece with her mother, father, sister, brother, and maternal aunt a year before intake. She has found it particularly difficult to find consistent work, especially since she and her sister had not graduated from high school. Her mother, father, and brother work outside the house, though the financial burden on the family remains high. She is considering returning to school but feels anxious about people's perceptions of her, with English being her third language, as well as her ability to care for her family. In the first session, she describes wanting tools to reduce anxiety so she can focus on getting a job. She says she is "only coming to therapy as a last resort" and would prefer to keep the exploration of her past brief. Notably, she talks at length about her perceived inability to succeed in school and her anger towards her brother for his success in this area, as he received admittance to three colleges in the area and will be leaving the family home to attend. She admits that being the oldest daughter creates expectations that might be different from what she wants for herself.

Discussion Questions

1. How do the career-related theories discussed in the chapter apply to Eleni's situation? Consider how gender norms may be affecting her goals for her education and career.
2. How might stereotype risk impact Eleni's academic and professional aspirations? Compare Eleni's experiences to the potential effects of gender role strain on her brother.
3. As a Romani-Greek immigrant woman, Eleni must overcome several obstacles. Describe how intersectionality—her gender, ethnicity, and immigration status—contributes to particular barriers in her path to work and education. As the chapter covers, how do these relate to the broader obstacles women encounter?
4. Examine how hostile or null environments might affect Eleni's professional growth and psychological health. What part might these settings play in her generalized fear and reluctance to return to school?
5. How might Eleni use coping or resilience techniques to overcome her school and work obstacles? Discuss the function of networking/mentoring, good coping mechanisms, and spirituality for Eleni.
6. How does Eleni balance her goals for employment and school with the expectations connected to her responsibilities at home? Look into how these many responsibilities affect her decision-making and mental health.
7. Given the mention of little literature on men's career issues, how does Eleni's brother's experience highlight gender-specific expectations and challenges in education and work? potential gender role conflicts or job segregation.

References

Adamovic, M., & Leibbrandt, A. (2023). Is there a glass ceiling for ethnic minorities to enter leadership positions? Evidence from a field experiment with over 12,000 job applications. *The Leadership Quarterly, 34*(2), 101655. https://doi.org/10.1016/j.leaqua.2022.101655

Arredondo, P., Miville, M. L., Capodilupo, C. M., & Vera, T. (2022). *Women and the challenge of STEM professions: Thriving in a chilly climate*. Springer Nature Switzerland AG. https://doi.org/10.1007/978-3-030-62201-5

Ayoola, E. (2022, March). 10 Instagram accounts and Facebook groups to follow that create safe spaces for Black women. *Essence Magazine*. https://www.essence.com/lifestyle/social-media-accounts-for-black-women/

Banks, D. (2022, October). In his own words: Gendered racism through the lens of a Black man | Blogs | CDC. *Conversations in Equity*. https://blogs.cdc.gov/healthequity/2022/10/06/in-his-own-words-gendered-racism-through-the-lens-of-a-black-man/

Battle, S., & Carty, D. (2022, October). Gendered racism among women of color | Blogs. *Conversations in Equity*. https://blogs.cdc.gov/healthequity/2022/10/06/gendered-racism-among-women-of-color/

Berkemeyer, C. (2020). New growth: Afro-textured hair, mental health, and the professional workplace student notes. *Journal of the Legal Profession, 44*(2), 279–292.

Betz, N. E. (1989). Implications of the null environment hypothesis for women's career development and for counseling psychology. *The Counseling Psychologist, 17*(1), 136–144. https://doi.org/10.1177/0011000089171008

Brandford, A., & Brandford-Stevenson, A. (2021). Going up!: Exploring the phenomenon of the glass escalator in nursing. *Nursing Administration Quarterly, 45*(4), 295–301. https://doi.org/10.1097/NAQ.0000000000000489

Bryant-Davis, T., & Comas-Díaz, L. (2016). Introduction: Womanist and mujerista psychologies. In T. Bryant-Davis & L. Comas-Díaz (Eds.), *Womanist and mujerista psychologies: Voices of fire, acts of courage* (pp. 3–25). American Psychological Association. https://doi.org/10.1037/14937-001

Cacciola, S., & Hoffman, B. (2024, May). N.F.L. player draws rebukes (and trolling) for graduation speech. *New York Times*. Retrieved from https://www.nytimes.com/2024/05/16/style/harrison-butker-commencement-speech.html

Calle, C. Z. (2021). *Ni de aquí, ni de allá: Sense of belonging among Latinx DACA recipient university students.* Doctoral dissertation, Columbia University. Columbia Academic Commons. Retrieved from https://academiccommons.columbia.edu/doi/10.7916/d8-z3dh-yj94

Caraballo, L. (2019). Being "loud": Identities-in-practice in a figured world of achievement. *American Educational Research Journal, 56*(4), 1281–1317. https://doi.org/10.3102/0002831218816059

Carlton, G. (2023, March). A history of women in higher education. *Best Colleges*. https://www.bestcolleges.com/news/analysis/2021/03/21/history-women-higher-education/

Clance, P. R., & Imes, S. A. (1978). The impostor phenomenon in high achieving women: Dynamics and therapeutic intervention. *Psychotherapy: Theory, Research & Practice, 15*(3), 241–247. https://doi.org/10.1037/h0086006

Cohen, R. (2022, August). The ballad of downward mobility. *The Atlantic*. https://www.theatlantic.com/ideas/archive/2022/08/downward-economic-mobility-boomer-generation-x-debt/671260/

Dispenza, F., Watson, L. B., Chung, Y. B., & Brack, G. (2012). Experience of career-related discrimination for female-to-male transgender persons: A qualitative study. *The Career Development Quarterly, 60*(1), 65–81. https://doi-org.ezproxy.cul.columbia.edu/10.1002/j.2161-0045.2012.00006.x.

Fouad, N. A., Whiston, S. C., & Feldwisch, R. (2016). Men and men's careers. In *APA handbook of men and masculinities* (pp. 503–524). American Psychological Association. https://doi.org/10.1037/14594-023

Gershon, L. (2020, January). *This was the struggle for female education in the U.S. World Economic Forum*. https://www.weforum.org/agenda/2020/01/girls-gender-equality-education-history/

Goldberg, A. (2018). *Transgender students in higher education* [Report]. UCLA School of Law: The Williams Institute. https://williamsinstitute.law.ucla.edu/wp-content/uploads/Trans-Higher-Ed-Aug-2018.pdf.

Goldberg, A. E., Matsuno, E., & Beemyn, G. (2021). "I want to be safe…and I also want a job": Career considerations and decision-making among transgender graduate students. *The Counseling Psychologist, 49*(8), 1147–1187. https://doi.org/10.1177/00110000211037671

Hernandez, E. (2018). *Undocumented, unafraid, an unapologetic: Exploring the role of activism in DACAmented Latinas/os/xs' thwarted transition into adulthood.* Doctoral dissertation, Columbia University]. Columbia Academic Commons. https://academiccommons.columbia.edu/doi/10.7916/D8C55326

Lent, R. W., Brown, S. D., & Hackett, G. (2000). Contextual supports and barriers to career choice: A social cognitive analysis. *Journal of Counseling Psychology, 47*(1), 36–49. https://doi.org/10.1037/0022-0167.47.1.36

Levant, R. F., & Powell, W. A. (2017). The gender role strain paradigm. In R. F. Levant & Y. J. Wong (Eds.), *The psychology of men and masculinities* (pp. 15–43). American Psychological Association. https://doi.org/10.1037/0000023-002

Lewis, J. A. (2023). Contributions of Black psychology scholars to models of racism and health: Applying intersectionality to center Black women. *American Psychologist, 78*(4), 576–588. https://doi.org/10.1037/amp0001141

Lin, S. A. (2008). The imposter phenomenon among high-achieving women of color: Are worldview, collective self-esteem and multigroup ethnic identity protective? *ETD Collection for Fordham University*, 1–119.

Medaris, A. (2023, November). *Women say they're stressed, misunderstood, and alone*. American Psychological Association. https://www.apa.org/topics/stress/women-stress

Miller, C. C. (2018, December). Americans value equality at work more than equality at home. *The New York Times*. https://www.nytimes.com/2018/12/03/upshot/americans-value-equality-at-work-more-than-equality-at-home.html

Miville, M. L., & Ferguson, A. D. (2014). Intersections of race-ethnicity and gender on identity development and social roles. In M. L. Miville & A. D. Ferguson (Eds.), *Handbook of race-ethnicity and gender in psychology* (pp. 3–21). Springer Science + Business Media. https://doi.org/10.1007/978-1-4614-8860-6_1

Motulsky, S., & Frank, E. (2018, April). *Creating positive spaces for career counseling with transgender clients*. National Career Development Association. https://www.ncda.org/aws/NCDA/pt/sd/news_article/159199/_PARENT/CC_layout_details/false

O'Neil, J. M. (2008). Summarizing 25 Years of research on men's gender role conflict using the Gender Role Conflict Scale: New research paradigms and clinical implications. *The Counseling Psychologist, 36*(3), 358–445. https://doi-org.ezproxy.cul.columbia.edu/10.1177/0011000008317057

O'Neil, J. M. (2015). *Men's gender role conflict: Psychological costs, consequences, and an agenda for change*. American Psychological Association. https://doi.org/10.1037/14501-000

O'Neil, J. M., & Denke, R. (2016). An empirical review of gender role conflict research: New conceptual models and research paradigms. In Y. J. Wong & S. R. Wester (Eds.), *APA handbook of men and masculinities* (p. 51). https://doi.org/10.1037/14594-003

Pappas, S. (2021, November). Effective therapy with Black women. *APA Monitor, 52*(8), 38. Retrieved from https://www.apa.org/monitor/2021/11/ce-therapy-black-women

Paris, F., & Miller, C. C. (2023, June). What it's like to be a queer teenager in America today. *The New York Times*. https://www.nytimes.com/interactive/2023/06/03/upshot/up-lgbtq-teens.html

Pleck, J. H. (1981). *The myth of masculinity*. MIT Press.

Rodriguez, A. (2020, February). Millennial men are more accepting than ever, but they still won't do laundry. *USA Today*. Retrieved from https://www.usatoday.com/story/news/nation/2020/02/14/gender-equality-millennial-men-still-dont-do-laundry-house-cleaning/4748860002/

Sang-Hun, C. (2019, May). Attending school with a South Korean 70-Year-Old. *The New York Times*. https://www.nytimes.com/2019/05/01/reader-center/south-korean-illiterate-grandmothers.html

Scott, D. A., Belke, S. L., & Barfield, H. G. (2011). Career development with transgender college students: Implications for career and employment counselors. *Journal of Employment Counseling, 48*(3), 105–113. https://doi.org/10.1002/j.2161-1920.2011.tb01116.x

Shorter-Gooden, K. (2004). Multiple resistance strategies: How African American women cope with racism and sexism. *Journal of Black Psychology, 30*(3), 406–425. https://doi.org/10.1177/0095798404266050

Steele, C. M. (1997). A threat in the air: How stereotypes shape intellectual identity and performance. *American Psychologist, 52*(6), 613–629. https://doi.org/10.1037/0003-066X.52.6.613

Steele, C. M., & Aronson, J. (1995). Stereotype threat and the intellectual test performance of African Americans. *Journal of Personality and Social Psychology, 69*(5), 797–811. https://doi.org/10.1037/0022-3514.69.5.797

Stiles, D. A., Gibbons, J. L., Sebben, D. J., & Wiley, D. C. (1999, June). Why adolescent boys dream of becoming professional athletes. *Psychological Reports, 84*(3 Pt 2), 1075–1085. https://doi.org/10.2466/pr0.1999.84.3c.1075

Tulshyan, R. (2023, April 7). How colorism affects women at work. *Harvard Business Review*. https://hbr.org/2023/04/how-colorism-affects-women-at-work

Tyack, D., & Hansot, E. (1988). Silence and policy talk: Historical puzzles about gender and education. *Educational Researcher, 17*(3), 33–41. https://doi.org/10.2307/1174831

Villaseñor, M. J., Reyes, M. E., & Muñoz, I. (2013). Mujerista mentoring for Chicanas/Latinas in higher education. *Journal of College Student Retention: Research, Theory and Practice, 15*(1), 49–64. https://doi.org/10.2190/CS.15.1.d

Williams, C. L. (1992). The glass escalator: Hidden advantages for men in the "female" professions. *Social Problems, 39*(3), 253–267. https://doi.org/10.2307/3096961

Wong, B. (2021, February). Millennial men are all for gender equality, but don't ask about housework. *HuffPost*. https://www.huffpost.com/entry/couples-housework-study_l_5e50037fc5b6a4525dbaa1bf

Zhavoronkova, M., Khattar, R., & Brady, M. (2022, March). Occupational segregation in America. *American Progress*. https://www.americanprogress.org/article/occupational-segregation-in-america/

Chapter 9
Families and Relationships

Relationships are a hallmark aspect of psychological functioning and play a significant role in mental health throughout the lifespan. Issues such as attachment, intimacy and satisfaction are some examples of how relationships are defined and assessed within psychology. Gender plays an important role in forming and maintaining relationships, and in this chapter we describe how gender may impact individuals in the critical realm of functioning.

Women's Relationships

Not surprisingly, over the years, relationships, specifically friendships, among women were not considered all that important to understand, let alone to study (Castañeda & Burns-Glover, 2008). Instead, it was more men's relationships and the qualities that defined these that were the focus of scholars, particularly before the twentieth century. These relationships emphasize bravery, duty, honor, loyalty, and even feelings that are expressed under conditions of extreme danger or death, such as on the battlefield. For the most part, before the start of the twentieth century, all people were allowed some degree of freedom of expression regarding their sense of intimacy with another person. During the twentieth century, people in Western societies became more aware of or focused on rules and possible boundaries not to cross, particularly regarding sexual identity and expression (Castañeda & Burns-Glover, 2008). For the most part, historically, the primary relationships that marked most women's lives have been with their spouse/husband, their children, and then other members of their family, such as siblings, cousins, and so on.

For much of Western history, women were not considered to be generally capable of true friendships with other women, primarily because women were socialized to view each other as competitors for the most important relationship that would be part of their lives, that is, with the men who would become their husbands. About

M. L. Miville et al., *Counseling and Gender*,
https://doi.org/10.1007/978-3-031-69172-0_9

the turn of the twentieth century, especially after 1920, there had been very successful political advocacy regarding women's suffrage. As a result, the whole sociopolitical context changed for women. There was much more freedom in going beyond the private realm and even movement towards political advocacy, with advocacy serving as a basis for important friendships. Around this time, women's friendships became focused more on emotion management with a de-emphasis on the Victorian era's intense and very fervent self-disclosure (Castañeda & Burns-Glover, 2008), which can be seen in the literature written by women during this period. Instead the focus of relationships became companionship, particularly within the realm of heterosexual marriage. At the same time, there were many more opportunities for women to meet each other outside the home, including going to school, as women were pursuing higher education. Others were working outside the home, particularly with the onset of WWII and the women's movement in the 1960s. Women had many more opportunities to leave the home and develop close relationships with other people. Thus, friendships and the context and focus of friendships began to change, with an increased emphasis on how friends can help one develop a sense of self, intimacy, and who one is as an individual in relationship to others. Relationships since have become such a hallmark for women's development that there are entire therapy models based on identity, well-being, and health as being centralized in the nature of relationships one has developed for oneself (Castañeda & Burns-Glover, 2008).

One key component for many friendships in today's modern world is that friendships are presumed to happen naturally, without necessarily articulated rules unless somebody in that relationship has crossed a boundary. For example, becoming competitive with somebody else can push what seems to be a relationship without rules to having unspoken rules or norms become articulated. There also are sociocultural differences that can play a role in women's relationships outside the home; for example, many Latinas or working-class individuals may be more likely to see family members as social friends, including siblings, cousins, or maybe a younger aunt who is closer in age can sometimes be a very important source for these friendships. Relationships can also range from being very durable and strong, lasting decades even, to those that are easily disintegrated, especially if they have more of a context-bound or competitive edge, for example, a friend from work or school (Castañeda & Burns-Glover, 2008).

Some common themes that can arise in women's relationships include intimacy, self-disclosure, and sharing about oneself and one's family. A very important aspect of women's relationships is ego support, much more than might be observed between men. That is, during the twentieth century, and continuing today, women have become critical sources of positive feedback and encouragement, something along the lines of a "you can do it!" attitude. At the same time, competition can also be a part of women's friendships, and this can be an aspect of relationships that can create discomfort. However, for newer generations, as competition simply becomes a norm, one might speculate that women will learn to live with or get used to that. However, for the most part, today, many girls and young women are socialized so as not to be overtly competitive regarding jobs or performance. Another aspect of relationships can be where there is power and recognition, and even some differential of power between 2 or more people, as might be found in supervisory and mentoring relationships, or a traditional work setting. For most people, however, symmetry and power are fundamental in determining the quality or the satisfaction of that relationship. This is not to say that people do not have relationships where there is inequality of power, as might occur at work or school, as these are fairly normative. However, most individuals may feel more satisfied when there is lesser power asymmetry (Castañeda & Burns-Glover, 2008).

Another area of relationships in which women are engaged are online networks and social media. There are all kinds of friendships now that are formed in connections that are formed online through many types of apps, for example, in terms of developing research projects, creating a network of similar others in one's profession or even by gender and race-ethnicity, and so on. This area still requires a great deal of future research, but online relationships in the twenty-first century have become quite an important way of socializing (Ayoola, 2021).

Finally, relationships can be created surrounding advocacy in the public sphere. One example is the #MeToo movement regarding women coming together to combat gender-based violence and harassment, discussed more in Chap. 11. Relationships in the public sphere have become all the more common and present for girls and women, primarily starting as acts of resistance or in response to political advocacy, such as the right to vote. Then, the focus of relationships became the quality of life, and the right to have an education and good paying jobs, so that by coming together in a public sphere, women have come to redefine and empower themselves as well as each other (Castañeda & Burns-Glover, 2008). At the same time, they form important bonds and build relationships and both personal and professional networks. Beyond relationships, networks have become quite important in many women's lives in this century and the last.

Girls and Young Women

When thinking about relationships for young adult women, adolescence and comparing and contrasting young adulthood with adolescence are important to consider. A major aspect of this is managing personal intimacy as well as one's career. As one moves from adolescence into young adulthood, it becomes a time of seeking many things that are important in life, primarily, the kind of career or job one may want to do that becomes very pressing. At the same time, seeking personal intimacy could mean building a network of friends. Another type of relationship that becomes important at this time period is finding romantic partners or even a significant partner who will be a part of one's life for the long term, as in the case of marriage. There are also issues of family of origin as well as peer and societal pressures and expectations regarding marriage, birth, and children.

Related to finding a longer term relationship (though not necessarily) are timing pressures, as in the notion of biological clock, that is, a finite period of time for women who may want to birth children in order to create a family (Mills et al., 2011). There are multiple ways of creating families today that include adoption and in vitro fertilization, so that these time pressures have been somewhat relieved, with greater numbers of women postponing childbirth that in previous generations. Another very important aspect related to marriage and to having children is the impact on one's career when having children. There remain quite significant differences in the impact of children for men and for women in heterosexual relationships, though same gender couples also need to navigate how to share household and child care responsibilities. Once children enter the situation, individual lives significantly shift, and the kinds of friendships that a person may have in their lives may become more reflective of their families who have children; those relationships will change with the needs of parents.

Romantic Relationships

As we have noted throughout this book, power imbalances mark the roles the individuals may take on, including in personal romantic relationships. This may be the case particularly for heterosexual relationships in which girls and women become involved. Given the longstanding traditions of men being presumed to take on a more powerful role, per cultural and religious traditions, women may still feel the need to submit to these prescriptive roles. Although today 61% of women, especially young women (Gen Z, 68%), identify as feminist (Barroso, 2020), many communities still retain strong expectations concerning the need to maintain traditional gender roles. A recent study, for example, found that both women and men in couples who engaged in role reversals of traditional activities (Vink et al., 2022) faced social penalties, that is, women were viewed as less likable and men were viewed as weak. Another concerning statistic is that on the whole, being married may benefit the mental and physical health of men significantly more than it does women (Kiecolt-Glaser & Newton, in Grieger, 2017). Key factors for these differences include the disproportionate distribution of household work, as well as emotional labor (i.e., placing another's wishes and feelings before oneself, Hackman, 2023), the lack of emotional support for women in a relationship, and most poignantly, experiences of painful, even humiliating events, such as infidelity or worse, violence. Grieger summarizes that state of relationships today in the U.S.:

> however deeply the image of a life lived blissfully two-by-two is embedded in our collective psyche, the reality of the enduring, joyful, mutually enhancing intimate relationship often remains elusive" for many women and their partners in the U.S. (p. 352)

On a more positive note, Knudson-Martin and Mahoney (2009) describe successful ways that counselors can assist in creating equality within relationships for the benefit of both partners.

Clinical Issues

Some clinical issues to consider in terms of relationships for girls and women include challenges in establishing intimacy and experiencing relationship satisfaction; evidence shows that navigating these challenges successfully are linked with positive physical health outcomes (Gallo et al., 2003), and lower rates of anxiety and depression (Grieger, 2017). Greiger further noted the impact that social media may play in heightening experiences with shame and humiliation (e.g., unwanted sexting, internet affairs) in romantic relationships, leading some women to feel pressured to "fit in" with social norms that seem to reward these behaviors. Gender differences in heterosexual relationships also may affect intimacy and relationship satisfaction since women may attempt to establish emotional intimacy through conversation, while their male partners may focus more on solution-finding (Grieger, 2017). Moreover, there also may be issues of positive body image and satisfaction, that is, how one feels about themselves, and how this links with one's interest and openness to becoming intimate with other people.

Another clinical issue that may arise relates to the impact of self objectification (see Chap. 10), which is the process of internalizing others' perceptions regarding one's physical self as an object to be surveilled. Self-consciousness, including body image concerns, along with anxiety and depression, can evolve that are linked with the regular monitoring of one's outward appearances. There also can be some racial cultural differences in how this is experienced, as in the case of dealing with gender racist images of others regarding one's own body image and satisfaction (e.g., Mendez, 2021).

Other clinical issues that may arise in therapy in working with girls and women is the tension that can arise between intimacy and isolation. As people age, they sometimes may feel less satisfied with themselves or others, especially their long-term partner. A recent meta-analysis (Bühler et al., 2021) in a diverse sample of over 165,000 individuals, found that relationship satisfaction was linked with age and duration of relationship. Satisfaction decreased from age 20 until 40, increased until 65, and then decreased once more; for those involved in long-term relationships, satisfaction decreased during the first 10 years, reaching a low point, increased until 20 years, and then decreased again. Having children significantly predicted a somewhat lower rate of satisfaction (Bühler et al).

Gallo et al. (2003) suggested several facets of declining satisfaction, including communication, intimacy, sexuality (e.g., satisfaction about this aspect of the relationship), passion, need fulfillment, and ideals and realistic expectations about the course of a relationship. Life transitions also may impact relationship satisfaction, for example, becoming parents and caregivers, along with simultaneous career changes. Another important stressor on relationships is if an individual or both people in a couple experience minority stress (Frost et al., 2017), the more oppressive or marginalized experiences that often accompany being a woman, an LGBTQIA person, a person from a low-income background, current circumstances, and so on.

All of these experiences are sources of minority stress that can also lead to anxiety, depression, isolation, and possibly withdrawal from human relationships.

Men's Relationships

In this section we focus on relationships among boys and men. We intentionally highlight the period of childhood and adolescence, particularly adolescence, as the time in which friendships begin to shift away from proximity and activities, including trust and emotional sharing, and romances may begin (Smiler & Heasley, 2016). *Gender intensification*, defined as:

> greater adherence to gender roles associated with entry into adolescence, marks a period of renewed influence of masculinity in the areas of friendship and sexuality that involves a renewed influence of masculinity that occurs around the same time that physical changes begin to happen. (Smiler & Heasley, p. 569)

Boys begin to wrestle with what it means to be a man. Much has been made about the unique developmental approach that happens for boys relative to their parents, particularly with their mothers, because a major aspect of becoming masculine and becoming a man is for a boy to think about his independence and separation and differentiation from his parents as well as what is considered feminine. The key theme for boys, especially within a heteronormative context, is to somehow distinguish themselves from *not* being a girl. Staying away from traits or behaviors that would mark them as a girl or as feminine, for example, crying or wearing makeup, becomes a major social pressure. As importantly, especially for straight boys, is the notion of being viewed as *not* gay, that is, presumed and even stereotypical qualities or attributes associated with gayness; even wanting to be close with another boy in a more physical way, is something that adolescent boys and young adult men really focus on not being. So, "not girl" and "not gay" are distinctive themes of what it means for many young male adolescents of various cultural backgrounds to move from a boy to a man.

There are also the attachment styles of individual boys that affect how well they will develop their male identity (Smiler & Heasley, 2016). For example, being avoidant of others will have one kind of set of consequences versus boys who may be comfortable approaching others to develop friendships and other kinds of relationships. As we noted earlier, the themes for boys' and men's friendships are often marked by issues of bravery, duty, honor, loyalty, and the expression of deep feelings only under duress, as might be imagined in a battlefield or sports event. The whole process of defining masculinity is about "proving oneself," proving that one is capable, physically competent, as well as academically or intellectually competent. Competitiveness is another characteristic that begins to define relationships among boys and men.

One of the costs of a traditional masculinity identity as a young boy is the tremendous pressure to conform to what the masculine script is. In the U.S., for example, there are some quite distinct spheres of social networks for boys and girls, respectively. That is, boys and girls typically will, as adolescents, interact in separate groups and get to know each other as boy to boy and girl to girl. As we noted earlier, boys likely will work hard to shed any feminine qualities in order to become and be seen as competitive and independent. There is also a real pressure about conforming to a "boy code" (Pollack, 1998, in Smiler & Heasley, 2016) about which many societies and most parents are still rather tolerant, that is, the "boys will be boys" approach, to objectify girls as sexual partners rather than as simply friends. The boy code is rewarded by many parents, extended family, significant others, teachers, and especially in the media. At the same time, emotional intimacy remains important for health development, so there is a real need to help boys and young men create safe spaces for their emotional development. Unfortunately, the boy code can negatively impact girls in their social world, who may be shamed or humiliated in some way, often through social media, as a means of boosting a boy's social standing (Grieger, 2017).

A vital issue for relationships between boys and men is the notion that, especially in adolescence and young adulthood, they essentially live in "guyland" (Kimmel, 2008), a heteronormative world where masculinity is performed to meet peer expectations as well as to gain social capital at a loss for many of social consciousness and even emotional intimacy. To live in guyland, there are rigid rules for relationships, for example a guy code, in which boys prefer their boy friends over girls. Regarding relationships with women, these are often determined by how attractive girls and women are evaluated as sexual objects to other men (recall reports that the origins of the social media outlet Meta, formerly known as Facebook, as a means to rank college women's attractiveness, e.g., Berrin, 2020). For interactions with other boys, however, it is the opposite situation, with very strict rules about not touching or displaying acts of tenderness so the guy is not confused as a girl or gay person.

As noted earlier, one major consequence of this kind of male socialization is the potential loss of intimacy. Regarding masculinity and its intersections with romantic relationships, research has shown that having strong masculinity attitudes is linked with greater engagement in sexual behaviors, although this does not necessarily reflect on increasing emotionally intimate attitudes or behaviors (Smiler & Heasley, 2016); these attitudes are often accompanied with the view of women as sexual objects, but not necessarily as reproductive individuals. That is, physical components, such as breasts, may be viewed by young men as something that contributes to their pleasure, or to the overall objective beauty of a woman, but they may not be appreciated for their original biological purpose which is to feed the young.

In considering much of the research conducted on boys and men, masculinity, and relationships, several characteristics are very important to consider in both research and counseling, including trust, care, and intimacy as well as impact of social and cultural forces that may detract from boys' and men's experiences with intimate relationships. As Smiler and Heasley (2016) astutely observed, it is important to understand that *boys and men do no necessarily lack a capacity for intimacy, but rather a context within which such relationships can be formed and rewarded.* The impact of older role models, such as one' father, cannot be overstated, since as one's father or one's male role model goes, so will a young boy. Men who are comfortable with emotional intimacy or friendships can really inspire their sons and other young men with the potential of that as a reward. However, the social reality of living in guyland is that the consequences of not meeting these rules can be quite severe, such as violence, risk, depression, and even suicide.

LGBT Relationships

There are a number of issues to consider for LGBT individuals concerning relationship building, including the impact of their identity development regarding their sexuality and gender. At the same time, these individuals will likely feel similar pressures about finding a job and meaningful work of their interest, and then they will balance that with a person who might be a significant other in their lives. In light of advancing social policies for this population, including legal marriage, queer couples today may feel pressure to marry to a single partner, and commit to each other from themselves, family, and friends (University of British Columbia, 2016). One of the key issues in terms of relationship formation is focusing on profound changes that come from both physical and psychological/social transitions. Becoming aware of oneself, either as gay, non-binary, or trans, affects many aspects of psychological well-being, including body image, interest, intimacy, and so on. So, if someone is still figuring out who they are, that significantly affects how they relate with other people.

Part of the "coming out" process involves the renegotiation of many aspects of one's life, including identities and orientations, one's relationships, and even the type of relationships one might be interested in developing, including long-term, romantic, sexual, and asexual. There can be a real openness in terms of what kinds of relationships might be formed for some individuals, though others may struggle to feel comfortable violating heteronormative expectations (e.g., Doyle et al., 2015). Finally, family commitments may be affected, especially if one is shifting from a more heteronormative life into one that emphasizes LGBT pathways and networks. One's partner or family will have their own reactions to the transitions, and in some cases, there could be a formal change, perhaps to the point of termination, of not having that person in their life anymore. Clinical issues relate to topics such as stigma, safety, and isolation (Hammack et al., 2019). There may even be a time of "re-closeting," when a person is in a new context, such as a new job or work situation (teaching in a state with anti-LGBT laws, Just Like Us, 2023), where they may be concerned that they may be discriminated against. Thus, individuals are forced to hide themselves based on their LGBT identity.

On a positive note, there are strengths in these new identities and relationships. For example, there is a deeply felt appreciation for the spectrum of gender. Learning about oneself in the process of learning new ways of identifying and establishing intimacy with other people is another benefit. To be sure, this aspect of development, as with any young person, can be both scary and absolutely exciting, bringing about the meaning of life and love that may have been missing or misdirected up to this point.

New models have been proposed to assist with more inclusive frameworks in understanding these relations. For example, (Thomeer et al., 2020) proposed a "*gender-as-relational*" (GAR) framework emphasizing three components: own gender, partner's gender, and the gendered relational context. This feminist intersectional approach presumes that fluidity and diversity are the norm of relationships, and that conceptions of gender, rather than adhering to cisgender, heteronormative expectations, instead are best understood in the context of "queer relationship dynamics" (p. 5). Hammack et al. (2019) similarly offered a new paradigm for understanding "queer intimacies" and relationship diversity in the twenty-first century involving 7 axioms, such as, relationships featuring any combination of cisgender, transgender, or nonbinary identities; multiple gender identities across the life course; multiple relationships at once; and consensual asymmetry, power exchange, or role-play. These new paradigms, rather than emphasize reductive frameworks and "normal" relations, instead urge the "embrace of diversity, fluidity, and possibility" (Hammack et al., p. 1).

Relationships Within Families of Origin

Families are sources of strength and stress. In addition to relationships with friends, family relationships are a hallmark of how relationships are formed, and have tremendous impact on issues of trust, intimacy, and self-esteem, beginning with families of origin. Dobbins, Beale, Thornton, and Porter et al. (2014) described several waves of parenting and family studies over the course of history. They first emphasized family relationships prior to the existence of psychological and family sciences literature. In this era, practices like the "funds of knowledge" (Vélez-Ibáñez & Greenberg, 1992) included following traditions that arose in a particular society or community, as reflected by sayings such as "spare the rod and spoil a child." These reflect the kinds of observations and norms that many cultures around the world developed per their own traditions.

Then, in the twentieth century, the fields of family sciences and child development evolved by examining family content, with a particular focus on traditional parenting roles in heterosexual families, centering on the mother as a major influencer of all children's development. However, in the early years of these fields, little to no attention was paid to culture and the historical context. More recently, Dobbins et al., working in the early twenty-first century, began to emphasize the importance of understanding the family context as well as the role of power, privilege, and oppression, including within the family, as well as how one navigates oppression, both within and beyond the family system. For example, for issues of race and racism, one can imagine how racial oppression affects individuals beyond the family system. However, racism also occurs within a family, as in the case of *colorism*, where children within the family may have very different skin tones from each other, resulting in negative attitudes. Typically individuals with darker skin tones are treated relatively harsher, and presumptions about negative traits, in contrast with individuals with lighter skin tones (Knight, 2015).

Unfortunately, the presence of hostility during childhood with parents and siblings will predict the kind of hostility that is salient or present in adult relationships. So what one is exposed to as a child may become replicated in adult life, that is, without therapy or intervention. This is where/how therapy can be incredibly powerful in helping people understand the impact that childhood and youthful hostility (including physical and emotional abuse) and how this plays out in current relationships. How couples and families resolve conflicts also is very important to mental well being and relationship satisfaction. The reality is that conflicts are a normative and unavoidable part of relationships. Developing skills and attitudes surrounding conflicts are instead a more constructive and effective approach for conflict resolution. Thus, if a couple mainly uses aggressive methods that increase anger, anxiety, and so on, over time these methods will have a negative impact on both individual and family functioning. Instead, the more up front and open communication with supportive features are engaged, the more successful the relationship may be.

Another aspect of family relationships is that in addition to gender roles, people also play other kinds of roles in their families, although gender can come into play in terms of who engages in emotional labor (Hackman, 2023), who is the peacemaker, who puts others' needs first, and who is willing or able to share their true feelings. All of those are an interplay of people's own individual senses of self as well as the socialized roles of, for example, putting other people's needs first rather than sharing one's own true feelings.

Not surprisingly, gender also is highlighted in most families, with traditional gender role socialization being emphasized, for example, the father as the authoritative figure to the external world, whereas the mother most commonly is the authoritative figure in the internal world of the family, albeit in deference to the father as the ultimate power figure. Dobbins et al. (2014) notes that much of the research is focused on heteronormative families, so that families who come from distinct backgrounds, especially same gender or transgender families are still largely unaccounted for in the literature. Dobbins et al. developed a model, the DIMGREP model that explores the complexities of multiple identities that are developed within a family context, along with an emphasis on the importance of parenting competencies (see Fig. 9.1).

The DIMGREP model, which emphasizes inclusivity of diverse family structures, distinguishes among different types of parenting styles and competencies, including the distinction of control versus nurturing versus objective styles as well as competencies that stretch across a variety of family relationships (e.g., male and female siblings). Dobbins et al. further suggest that most parents use a mix of parenting styles, typically described as warm or nurturant, controlling (coercive), and objective (inclusive of developmental stage of child). They also examined cultural/contextual issues, particularly gender and racial identity development, and their impact on both parents and children. Parenting competence refers to how parents use these various styles to promote healthy development of their children. The

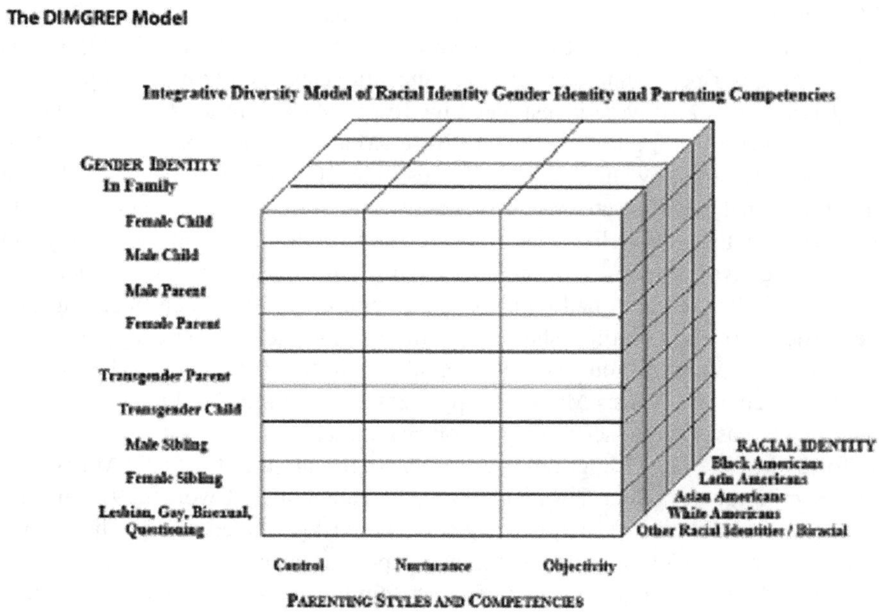

Fig. 9.1 The DIMGREP model

DIMGREP model also incorporates transgender and LGBT parents, again using a similar style and competence of control, nurturance and objectivity nestled within as well the racial-cultural identity of that particular family. Dobbins et al. further acknowledged that nuclear families predominate as a focus in much of the U.S., and that rigid, essentialist gender role assignment even in diverse families lean on the traditional roles of mother and father. Moreover, Dobbins et al. assert that family "is the place where stereotypes are likely learned and projected onto every other aspect of institutional and cultural life" (p. 141). And that can be particularly applicable when it comes to gender stereotypes and the kinds of essentialized gender roles that people are socialized to take on. Dobbins et al. highlight the role that nuclear family systems play in promoting men's role and power, while at the same time diminishing that of women's roles. Consequently, the complementary roles of husband and wife may end up being developed from the husband's perspective, as in the saying, "what I lack, my spouse (wife) makes up." Another way of saying this, per Dobbins et al. is "what I do not want to do, I delegate to the person who is less powerful than I am" (p. 144). They further emphasize the notion of "relationship dread" in which the woman/wife may end up taking responsibility for what is negative in the family in order to relieve the negative effect on herself and the children (emotional labor). Ultimately, Dobbins et al. suggest that the prime concern

> is not about bargaining for chores, or who is the man or the woman in post-modern constructions of family systems and structures. There is a fundamental understanding that both men and women can become trapped in socially constructed expectations about roles and power dynamics. (p. 146)

Children of single mothers. In Chap. 4, we described the socioeconomic and sociological struggles of single mothers, as investigated by Torres-Mackie (2020). In this section we describe the unique challenges and strategies of children of single mothers (COSM) that also were investigated by Torres-Mackie, at least in a more constructive and positive light. According to Torres-Mackie, approximately 17.5 million children were raised by single moms, and less than 50% of children in the U.S. live in a traditional nuclear family. Unfortunately, stigma continues regarding single mothers, such that 70% believe that single mothers can be detrimental to society and that 83% believe increases in the number of single mother families are considered a problem. Earlier research had emphasized an elimination argument meaning that the existence of such families should be minimized to the greatest extent possible, given the prevailing notion that single mother families are somehow harmful to society. In contrast, Torres-Mackie emphasizes that the more accurate concern is how society has failed to serve single-mother families.

Torres-Mackie (2020) engaged in a qualitative research study of COSM that featured semi-structured interviews with a total of 20 people (11 women, 9 men) in a racially, ethnically diverse sample using constructivist grounded theory. The themes that she found for COSM included context, experiences and strategies, and capacities. Regarding context, there were two types, familial and societal. Familial context was found to refer to single mother role strain (work overload due to fulfilling multiple roles) and the societal context in which COSM grow up, marked by negative perceptions and low expectations from others, affiliation with other stigmatized groups (e.g., per race), social exclusion and distancing, SM household invisibility (lack of positive images), and disparaging media depictions. Two types of experiences predominated for Torres-Mackie's participants, at-home, including responsibility overload, time alone, and getting an early dose of reality and internal experiences, such as feeling abnormal, experiencing shame, and having a lowered self-image. Strategies in which COSMs engaged to manage both context and experiences included observing parents and other role models, receiving support from one's parent, establishing other supportive relationships, utilizing creativity and playfulness, focusing on one's own strengths and actively resisting stigma.

Torres-Mackie (2020) also emphasized a more nuanced outcome of these experiences she called *capacities*, a construct born of challenging experiences that are highly nuanced strengths that can become assets but also may be "double edged swords" (p. 97). These capacities included internal well-being (reflectiveness, empowerment, freedom from convention), adversity management (adaptability, resourcefulness, acceptance of reality, and self-sufficiency), ability to achieve (diligence, perseverance, and self-efficacy), interpersonal functioning (empathy, social justice mindset, and maturity). Another capacity is relevant to the current chapter, gender role agency, in which COSMs develop democratized gender roles, an expanded sense of both masculinity and femininity, gender self-efficacy, and gender self-sufficiency. These latter two aspects were found primarily in women, daughters who learned they can do things for themselves without necessarily having to be married.

Latina Socialization

Another example of a culturally framed approach to gender, relationships, and families comes from the work of Alberta Gloria and Jeanette Castellanos (2016). They defined the term *Latina poderosas*, which means Latina empowerment, beginning with the basic question of *Quien somos?* (Who are we as Latinas?). Gloria and Castellanos described the gendered racist stereotypes for Latinas of the sinner, saint, sex worker, mother, wife, and caretaker (Miville & Ferguson, 2014). But the simple truth is that there is no "typical" Latina and that, instead, the core belief is that individuals are interconnected more broadly to the environment and to others, physically, mentally, energetically, or spiritually. Gloria and Castellanos also emphasize the cultural values of *familismo* and *la comunidad*, that is, the family and the community in which one is born and raised. La Familia is "the primary natural support system that provides physical, emotional, and social support" for many Latine families. According to Gloria and Castellanos, it is the "chief cultural structure, mutual support system and source of resource" (p. 95) for Latinas. Familismo refers to "solidarity, loyalty, reciprocity, and interdependence" (p. 95). Most Latinas are socialized to focus on "todo para la familia," that is, everything for the family, so that the family comes first, as does taking responsibility for others within that family. Thus, "the care of and obligation to family creates and expands responsibility of interconnection to the broader community, leading to the development of a collective family identity that is broad and serves to integrate and connect with one's community" (p. 96).

Being a part of la comunidad leads to a type of co-parenting common in many Latine families, *compadrazgo*, which occurs by giving responsibility to *padrinos* (godfathers) and *madrinas* (godmothers) to assist with various aspects of childcare (e.g., financial, spiritual) (Gloria & Castellanos, 2016). The practice of compadrazgo builds both family and community because there is both a family of origin (which is extended rather than nuclear) and one's close friends to whom one entrusts some aspects of care for their children. Compadrazgo links individuals and families in lifelong relationships, where families hold a collective responsibility for the welfare of the whole group. This represents a fairly distinctive approach to family socialization that is quite distinct from the nuclear families that Dobbins et al. (2014) critiqued, which emphasizes individuality and competition.

A number of cultural values help to sustain Latine families and communities since familism and community drive a variety of connections and interactions (Gloria & Castellanos, 2016). For example, *personalismo* is "a cultural script or orientation in which the personal exchanges are centralized and embodied by *respeto* (respect) and *dignidad* (dignity) regardless of personal or social statuses" (p. 96). So respect and dignity are a hallmark of relationships within the Latine community. Another value is *simpatía*, which is the "process of maintaining cordial and positive relationships" to the point that sometimes non-Latine folks across many races may wonder about the sincerity and genuineness because Latine people are always presenting a cordial and positive foot and face forward. Simpatía helps drive the creation of the trust (*confianza*), intimacy, and familiarity among people that is critical to maintaining one's family and community. Another aspect of Latine relationships is interacting with others with *cariño* (affection) verbally (e.g., use of nicknames and endearments) and nonverbally (hugs and kisses) (Gloria and Castellanos).

Conclusion

In this chapter, we described unique challenges and opportunities regarding individuals' navigation of gender and relationships. Many if not most individuals are still socialized regarding traditional roles that may affect the nature and duration of significant relationships throughout the lifespan. Today much more emphasis on the normative nature of the flexibility and fluidity of relationships has become more centralized in psychology, including for research and practice. Our own reflections regarding what *healthy relationships for all* people within these newer approaches mirror much of the thinking that has gone before. Issues such as trust, communication, emotional openness, balancing interdependence and independence, and intimacy are critical to establishing in any intimate relationship. Attending to each person's expectations, beliefs, and practices about what each of these mean will be critical to bridging the gaps between individuals and within families about what a healthy relationship can be.

Case Study

Nour is a 32 year old bisexual nonbinary Iraqi person who is Muslim and was assigned "female" at birth. They are currently living in San Francisco, CA and sought counseling services reporting difficult dynamics with their family of origin. They relay that the majority of their life has been spent identifying as a woman, but they have recently started identifying as transgender, nonbinary as they are exposed to narratives that they feel fit their understanding of themself. This has created an upheaval of their family life as their mother, father, and brother are all Muslim. They explain that their family does not understand this decision, views them as a woman, and insists that they rethink their decision to engage in Hormone Replacement Therapy (HRT). They strongly believe in maintaining contact with their family and want to both honor themself and their family and faith. In the first few sessions, they state that "cutting their family off is not an option" and they would like to try finding a balance between them. They are particularly nervous about sustaining their close relationship with their brother's children. When asked, Nour shares that they do not worry about money as they are able to sustainably support themself and has a strong support network with friends.

Discussion Questions

1. In Nour's relationships with their loved ones, how do the distinct gender roles discussed in the chapter—such as peacemaker, caregiver, and provider—play out? Describe how Nour's transition may have affected or tested these responsibilities.
2. To what extent may Nour's self-esteem and relationship satisfaction be affected by ideas like gender intensification and self-objectification within the framework of their experiences? Think about how Nour's nonbinary identity could make these concerns unique.
3. Consider the impact of Nour's family's reaction to their gender identity on their relationship satisfaction and self-esteem. How do you think their sense of self fits into all of this?
4. How is Nour's ancestral background influencing their present and future relationships? Dig deeper into how Nour's emotional and mental health may have been affected by their family's rejection in the long run.
5. What approaches could Nour take to strike a balance between being themselves and fulfilling their family responsibilities, taking into account their strong desire to stay connected to family while also being true to themselves?
6. Amidst the difficulties brought about by family dynamics, how does Nour's support system aid them? Discuss how other people's support systems can help those going through the same thing.
7. How do Nour's ethnicity and race make it difficult for them to conform to traditional gender norms? Describe how these relate to Nour's gender identity and the pressures they feel to conform to society norms.

References

Ayoola, E. (2021, July). How introverts can best manage their mental health. *Essence*. https://www.essence.com/lifestyle/how-introverts-can-best-manage-their-mental-health/

Barroso, A. (2020, July). *61% of U.S. women say 'feminist' describes them well; many see feminism as empowering, polarizing*. Pew Research Center. https://www.pewresearch.org/short-reads/2020/07/07/61-of-u-s-women-say-feminist-describes-them-well-many-see-feminism-as-empowering-polarizing/

Berrin, D. (2020, September). Mark Zuckerberg created Facebook to get non-Jewish girls. *HuffPost*. https://www.huffpost.com/entry/the-social-network-mark-z_b_741914

Bühler, J. L., Krauss, S., & Orth, U. (2021). Development of relationship satisfaction across the life span: A systematic review and meta-analysis. *Psychological Bulletin, 147*(10), 1012–1053. https://doi.org/10.1037/bul0000342

Castañeda, D., & Burns-Glover, A. L. (2008). Women's friendships and romantic relationships. In F. L. Denmark & M. A. Paludi (Eds.), *Psychology of women: A handbook of issues and theories* (2nd ed., pp. 332–350). Praeger Publishers/Greenwood Publishing Group.

Dobbins, J. E., Beale, B., Thornton, A., & Porter, T. G. (2014). Exploring the intersection of parenting, ethnicity, race, and gender in the deconstruction of the nuclear family archetype. In M. L. Miville & A. D. Ferguson (Eds.), *Handbook of race-ethnicity and gender in psychology* (pp. 131–149). Springer Science + Business Media. https://doi.org/10.1007/978-1-4614-8860-6_7

Doyle, C. M., Rees, A. M., & Titus, T. L. (2015). Perceptions of same-sex relationships and marriage as gender role violations: An examination of gendered expectations (sexism). *Journal of Homosexuality, 62*(11), 1576–1598. https://doi.org/10.1080/00918369.2015.1073038

Frost, D. M., LeBlanc, A. J., de Vries, B., Alston-Stepnitz, E., Stephenson, R., & Woodyatt, C. (2017). Couple-level minority stress: An examination of same-sex couples' unique experiences. *Journal of Health and Social Behavior, 58*(4), 455–472. https://doi.org/10.1177/0022146517736754

Gallo, L. C., Troxel, W. M., Matthews, K. A., & Kuller, L. H. (2003). Marital status and quality in middle-aged women: Associations with levels and trajectories of cardiovascular risk factors. *Health Psychology, 22*(5), 453–463. https://doi.org/10.1037/0278-6133.22.5.453

Gloria, A. M., & Castellanos, J. (2016). Latinas poderosas: Shaping mujerismo to manifest sacred spaces for healing and transformation. In I. T. Bryant-Davis & L. Comas-Díaz (Eds.), *Womanist and mujerista psychologies: Voices of fire, acts of courage* (pp. 93–119). American Psychological Association. https://doi.org/10.1037/14937-005

Grieger, I. (2017). Women in intimate relationships: Theory, research, and implications for practice. In M. Kopala & M. Keitel (Eds.), *Handbook of counseling women* (2nd ed., pp. 352–369). Sage. https://doi.org/10.4135/9781506300290.n31

Hackman, R. (2023). *Emotional labor: The invisible work shaping our lives and how to claim our power*. Flatiron Books.

Hammack, P. L., Frost, D. M., & Hughes, S. D. (2019). Queer intimacies: A new paradigm for the study of relationship diversity. *Journal of Sex Research, 56*(4–5), 556–592. https://doi.org/10.1080/00224499.2018.1531281

Just Like Us. (2023, April). *A quarter of LGBT+ young adults go back into the closet after starting work, and many earn less than straight peers*. https://www.justlikeus.org/blog/2023/04/12/lgbt-work-jobs/

Kimmel, M. (2008). *Guyland: The perilous world where boys become men*. Harper.

Knight, D. (2015, August). "What's 'colorism'?" *Learning for Justice Magazine*. https://www.learningforjustice.org/magazine/fall-2015/whats-colorism

Knudson-Martin, C., & Mahoney, A. R. (Eds.). (2009). *Couples, gender, and power: Creating change in intimate relationships*. Springer. https://doi.org/10.1891/9780826117564

Mendez, N. (2021). *Afro-Latinx Caribbean women's body image: A mixed methodology inquiry on gender, race, and culture*. Doctoral dissertation, Columbia University. Columbia Academic Commons. Retrieved from: https://academiccommons.columbia.edu/doi/10.7916/d8-hqer-4d14.

Mills, M., Rindfuss, R. R., McDonald, P., te Velde, E., & ESHRE Reproduction and Society Task Force. (2011). Why do people postpone parenthood? Reasons and social policy incentives. *Human Reproduction Update, 17*(6), 848–860. https://doi.org/10.1093/humupd/dmr026

Miville, M. L., & Ferguson, A. D. (2014). Intersections of race-ethnicity and gender on identity development and social roles. In M. L. Miville & A. D. Ferguson (Eds.), *Handbook of race-ethnicity and gender in psychology* (pp. 3–21). Springer. https://doi.org/10.1007/978-1-4614-8860-6_1

Smiler, A. P., & Heasley, R. (2016). Boys' and men's intimate relationships: Friendships and romantic relationships. In Y. J. Wong & S. R. Wester (Eds.), *APA handbook of men and masculinities* (pp. 569–589). American Psychological Association. https://doi.org/10.1037/14594-026

Thomeer, M. B., Umberson, D., & Reczek, C. (2020). The gender-as-relational approach for theorizing about romantic relationships of sexual and gender minority mid- to later-life adults. *Journal of Family Theory & Review, 12*(2), 220–237. https://doi.org/10.1111/jftr.12368

Torres-Mackie, N. (2020). *Cultivating capacities: How children of single mothers manage stigma and endure strain*. Doctoral dissertation, Columbia University. Columbia Academic Commons. https://academiccommons.columbia.edu/doi/10.7916/d8-10ya-je80

University of British Columbia. (2016, January). *Gay couples face pressure to marry, conform to relationship status quo*. https://phys.org/news/2016-01-gay-couples-pressure-conform-relationship.html

Vélez-Ibáñez, C. G., & Greenberg, J. B. (1992). Formation and transformation of funds of knowledge among U.S.-Mexican Households. *Anthropology & Education Quarterly, 23*(4), 313–335.

Vink, M., Derks, B., Ellemers, N., & van der Lippe, T. (2022). Penalized for challenging traditional gender roles: Why heterosexual relationships in which women wear the pants may be more precarious. *Sex Roles: A Journal of Research*. Advance online publication. https://doi.org/10.1007/s11199-022-01339-5

Chapter 10
Health and Wellness

Gender and Physical Health

Sex and gender play a role in how health and disease affect individuals. Historically, researchers studied men and applied those findings to women, often without regard for potential gender differences that may need to be incorporated. "We have learned that there are distinct biological differences between women and men," explains Dr. Janine Austin Clayton, who heads research on women's health at the National Institute of Health (NIH) (2014; NIH, n.d.). For example, women and men have different hormones, organs, and cultural influences, which can lead to significant differences in health maintenance and promotion.

Unfortunately, the disparities of research on gender differences and the unique impact of gender were lacking for many decades in the U.S., with most studies using male-only samples. The U.S. Congress passed a law in 1992 (the first "Year of the Woman" regarding the election of women representatives) requiring medical researchers to include women in future studies systematically. Ironically, 30 years later, researchers found that if same-gender-only samples are used in universalized paradigms, women, rather than men, represent more stable presentations and concerns of humans, an important feature for research designs. In contrast, males may present more often with atypical features or symptoms (Rabin, 2014). Another primary concern with medical research has been the lack of systematic study of developmental processes, diseases and syndromes that only affect women, including endometriosis ("in which tissue similar to the lining of the uterus grows outside the uterus causing extensive pelvic pain;" World Health Organization, 2023), hyperemesis gravidarum or extreme nausea during pregnancy, pre-eclampsia (extremely high blood pressure during pregnancy and birth), and menopause (e.g., cause and prognoses of outcomes such as hot flashes as well as effective treatments). Recent advances in research have begun to address some of these concerns regarding their etiology and treatment (Gross, 2021; Rabin, 2023).

M. L. Miville et al., *Counseling and Gender*,
https://doi.org/10.1007/978-3-031-69172-0_10

Sex is considered a biological classification encoded in DNA. Females are usually assigned two copies of the X chromosome, while males are assigned one X and one Y chromosome. At the time of birth, individuals assigned as females also typically have elevated levels of estrogen and progesterone, whereas those assigned males have higher levels of testosterone. The prevailing perception in society is that maleness and femaleness are strictly defined as a biological binary; however, there are concerns regarding this differentiation, as described in Chap. 6. For example, the chromosomal markers may not always have distinct boundaries. Certain male babies are born with a condition known as Klinefelter syndrome, where they have two or three X chromosomes. Similarly, some female babies are born with a Y chromosome, a condition called Swyer syndrome (Newman, 2023). In addition, certain infants are born with atypical genitalia as a result of variations in sexual development. This particular distinction was formerly referred to as a "disorder of sex development"; however, this terminology presents certain issues. According to a 2015 survey (Lin-Su et al., 2015), the majority of participants had a negative perception of the term, with subsequent examination revealing that a significant number of individuals do not utilize it whatsoever, opting instead for the term "intersex" (Ainsworth, 2015, p. 288).

Intersex, or intersexuality, encompasses a range of diverse conditions and characteristics. For instance, an individual may possess genitalia or internal reproductive organs that deviate from conventional binary classifications. Alternatively, an individual may possess a distinct arrangement of chromosomes. Many individuals are unaware of their intersex condition until they enter puberty (Ainsworth, 2015). Biologists are engaging in discussions regarding the notion that sex could potentially exist on a spectrum. This idea is not novel but has gradually gained recognition among the general public (Ainsworth, 2015).

While sex typically pertains to the physical attributes a person possesses at the time of birth, *gender* refers to the socially constructed roles, behaviors, expressions, and identities of girls, women, boys, men, and gender diverse people. It influences how people perceive themselves and each other and how they act and interact. Gender in psychology has most often been conceptualized as binary (girl/woman and boy/man). However, most recent constructions, including this book, are more inclusive of the considerable diversity in how individuals and groups understand, experience, and express gender, as in the case of nonbinary individuals.

The following sections explore a variety of important examples that illustrate how sex and gender can impact physical health. Please note that this is not an exhaustive list but more illustrative of how sex and gender affect physical health. The complexities of how sex, typically understood as biological differences, and gender, encompassing socially constructed roles and expectations, impact health outcomes are extensive and multifactorial. We will delve into the effects of these factors on widespread diseases such as cardiovascular risk, osteoporosis, and knee arthritis, offering an understanding of how biological and societal elements interact to influence health. These examples shed light on the broader impact of sex and gender on physical health and emphasize the significance of taking both into account when it comes to healthcare delivery and policy.

Gender and Cardiovascular Risk

The connection between gender and cardiovascular risk (CVR) highlights significant disparities in the biological and social aspects that impact heart health. When considering the differences between men and women, it is worth noting that the blood vessels in a woman's heart tend to be smaller in diameter and have a more intricate branching pattern than men's (Hiteshi et al., 2014). There are certain differences in the way vessel blockage occurs in women compared to men, which can lead to distinct heart attack symptoms and patterns on heart-screening tests. As a result, these variations can lead to misdiagnosis or the failure to identify the symptoms of an approaching heart attack in women.

A poignant example of how impactful gender can be on CVR risks and accurate diagnoses was shared by comedian Rosie O'Donnell in her 2015 HBO/MAX television special, *A Heartfelt Stand-Up*. When Rosie was around 50, she suffered a severe type of heart attack, often called "the Widowmaker," due to its deadly impact on patients. Rosie was at a shopping mall helping another individual into their car when she suddenly began to feel hot, with back pains and sweating. Since health authorities did not usually cite these symptoms for a heart attack, Rosie did not immediately recognize what was happening to her. She even consulted with her mental health therapist, who similarly did not understand these gravity of these symptoms. It would be an entire week before Rosie sought medical help, resulting in a high-risk emergency heart bypass operation. As a result of this experience, Rosie mounted a public campaign regarding the kinds of unique CVR symptoms women may experience during a heart attack, using the acronym of HEPPP: Hot, Exhausted (flu-like fatigue, shortness of breath); Pain (in the chest, arms, back, neck, jaw, and stomach); Pale (clammy skin, nervous sweats); and Puke (nausea and vomiting; see also the American Heart Association guidelines at https://www.heart.org).

Societal roles and expectations have significant impacts on CVR health when viewed through a gender lens. It is common for women to take on the primary responsibilities of childcare, household management, and caring for aging family members. However, this can lead to a tendency for women to postpone prevention and treatment for chronic conditions such as heart disease, as was the case for Rosie in the example above. The decision to delay seeking medical attention is often influenced by societal expectations that place a greater emphasis on women prioritizing the needs of others over their own health. Healthcare professionals must be made aware of these societal pressures when evaluating and providing guidance to female patients regarding cardiovascular risk and treatment. These pressures highlight the importance of considering the broader context in healthcare decisions.

Gender and Osteoporosis

Osteoporosis provides another illustration of how sex and gender can impact health outcomes. From a biological standpoint, women have a higher susceptibility to osteoporosis compared to men, with one in three women and one in five men over the age of 50 years being affected. This risk is because women generally have less bone tissue and undergo a significant phase of bone loss during menopause, which is caused by hormonal changes. It is important to be more aware and take preventive measures for women, particularly as they approach and go through menopause, due to their increased vulnerability (Keen & Reddivari, 2023).

On the other hand, gender biases can also harm men. For example, osteoporosis is often seen as a condition that only affects women and can result in men over the age of 50 being overlooked and not receiving the necessary diagnosis and treatment. Even though osteoporosis may be present in this demographic, it is often overlooked or downplayed by both patients and healthcare providers because there is a prevailing belief that osteoporosis primarily affects women. This misunderstanding can lead to missed chances for early detection and intervention in men, making the impact of the prognosis of the disease worse.

Gender and Knee Arthritis/Knee Injuries

The study of knee arthritis, especially in the context of sports injuries, brings attention to the impact of sex and gender on health outcomes. When it comes to playing sports, women and girls have a higher vulnerability to knee injuries from a biological standpoint. Various factors, including variations in knee and hip anatomy, imbalances in leg muscle strength, and more flexible tendons and ligaments, all contribute to this heightened risk. Presumably "weaker" knees and hormonal differences have traditionally been mentioned as potential causes of these injuries. However, these age-old emphases on biology have begun to be critiqued, as in the case of women athletes. For example, rather than anatomical weaknesses, the actual equipment used in many sports recently has been identified as a potential cause of injuries, as in the case of footwear in which men's anatomies are used as the basis for design, after which women's shoes are made as simply smaller versions (Smith, 2023). Unfortunately, using a falsely universalized design for footwear does not incorporate the different physiques and their unique dynamics between women and men, including how balance and speed can be achieved within each gender group.

Moreover, women athletes may have more grueling sports schedules and fewer resources to support their physical health. As a result, far more injuries can be caused for women athletes (Smith, 2023). Developing osteoarthritis later in life is also a common concern for individuals who have experienced injuries such as anterior cruciate ligament (ACL) tears. When considering gender, it is important to acknowledge the impact of cultural norms on fashion and appearance, which can influence knee health. For example, walking in high-heeled shoes, primarily worn by women, puts additional strain on the knee joint, increasing the likelihood of developing osteoarthritis. This gendered aspect of knee health underscores the significance of taking into account both biological and societal factors in the effort to address and prevent conditions such as knee arthritis in women. Arthritis conditions also have been linked with autoimmune issues. Women are disproportionately impacted by autoimmune diseases, constituting 80% of cases, whereas men typically encounter more severe symptoms, including death (Goldman, 2024).

Gender and Life Expectancy

Another important measure of physical health is life expectancy (LE) rates (Yan et al., 2024). Sadly, in recent years, the overall LE in the United States has decreased from 78.8 in 2019 to 76.1 (Yan et al.). Much of this loss can be attributed to the widening gender gap in LE, estimated at 79.3 for women and 73.5 for men (Ghorayshi, 2023). According to Yan and his colleagues, their analyses found that primarily more deaths from COVID and drug overdoses were prime drivers of the burgeoning gap. They attributed the higher COVID deaths to underlying health issues (e.g., diabetes, heart disease), risky health behaviors, and SES factors, such as either lost or high-risk jobs, incarceration, and homelessness. The accidental nature of other deaths, from overdose and homicide/suicide, further "underscored twin crises of deaths from despair and firearm violence" (Yan et al., 2024, pp. 109–110).

Intersections with race-ethnicity provide further nuances in understanding LE rates. For example, in 2021, White Americans saw a relatively significant decline (76.4), relative to 2020 (77.4), whereas Black Americans had a similar but less steep decline in 2022, currently at 70.8 (Hill & Artiga, 2023; Rabin, 2022). The rate of decline in White LE was only lower than that of Native Americans. In contrast, Latine people saw a minor decline, though the previous year, the decline was four years, down to 77.9 from a high of 81.9 in 2019. Of all racial groups, Asian/Asian Americans had the longest LE, at 83.5 in 2022 (down just one month from 2019). The figures are alarming enough that health officials now refer to the *U.S. health disadvantage* due to "fragmented, profit-driven health care systems; poor diet and lack of physical activity, as well as pervasive risk factors such as smoking, widespread access to guns, poverty, and pollution" (Rabin, 2022).

Regarding TGNC populations, recent research (Hughes et al., 2022) demonstrated concerning LE rates and other health statistics for this population. For example, during the period of 2011 to 2019, TGNC people were "nearly twice as likely to die" as non-TGNC people (Hughes et al.). They also had higher rates of CVR, diabetes, and HIV. Moreover, among TGNC people, trans women and nonbinary individuals had lower LE rates than non-TGNC people or trans men. These differences were not found to be related with transitioning processes but behavioral health variables, such as substance abuse, depression, and suicidal ideation. Great exposure to violence also is linked with these health statistics (see also Chap. 11).

To summarize, these examples of gender-related health outcomes highlight the intricate relationship between sex and gender in health. Sex and gender each and together substantially impact disease susceptibility and advancement in different medical conditions. Furthermore, gender plays a significant role in determining not only the vulnerability to diseases, such as women being more susceptible to lung and heart disease, compared with men, but also the reasons behind drug use, responses to treatment, and patterns of relapse. Likewise, the frequency and consequences of different conditions differ depending on gender. Osteoarthritis is more prevalent in men below the age of 45 but becomes more common in women afterward. On the other hand, men are more prone to developing strokes overall, whereas women tend to experience strokes at an older age and have higher rates of mortality. Furthermore, medical conditions that specifically affect one gender, such as prostate and breast cancer, require customized treatments. These differences emphasize the significance of considering sex and gender in medical research and healthcare practices, as well as the importance of a comprehensive understanding of these factors in healthcare practice and policy to enhance prevention, diagnosis, and treatment for all genders.

Racial-Ethnic Considerations

The intersections with race-ethnicity as it relates to life expectancy harks back to Chap. 3, where Lopez and colleagues (2018) utilized the 2015 "Latino National Health and Immigration Survey" to investigate the correlation between physical and mental health and three aspects of race: street race (how others perceive one's race), ascribed race (how one's race is classified by others in the U.S.), and self-perceived race (how one classifies their race on questionnaires). Their study revealed a correlation between individuals' self-perceived race and physical well-being and a connection between socioeconomic status and mental well-being. Men who identified their street race as Latine or Arab experienced more pronounced mental health challenges, yet Latine men reported better physical well-being. When it comes to physical health, women who identified as Mexican reported worse physical well-being compared to other ethnic groups. However, there were no notable differences in mental health among women from different ethnic backgrounds. This study highlights the intricate connection between race, ethnicity, and mental health, shedding light on their impact on overall well-being.

Black Maternal Health

Maternal mental health within the Black community encompasses a wide range of complex issues that are frequently exacerbated by racial inequalities ingrained in the system (Prather et al., 2018). Statistics in the United States reveal an alarming disparity in pregnancy-related deaths, with Black women being three times more likely to experience such outcomes compared to their White counterparts (Center for Disease Control Office of Health Equity, 2008). This concerning discrepancy can be explained by various factors such as variations in the standard of healthcare provided, pre-existing long-term health conditions, systemic racism, and unconscious biases within the healthcare system (Prather et al., 2018). In addition, factors such as economic instability, limited access to healthcare services, and educational disparities pose challenges for many Black women in achieving optimal health outcomes during and after pregnancy.

The annual observance of Black Maternal Health Week from April 11–17 serves as a reminder of the urgent importance of addressing these issues. The week focuses on educating the public and healthcare providers about the significance of identifying urgent maternal warning signs and delivering timely and considerate care. For example, if a pregnant woman experiences severe headaches, extreme swelling of the hands or face, or heavy vaginal bleeding, she must seek immediate medical attention. Being aware of and responding correctly to these symptoms can help prevent a significant number of pregnancy-related deaths, the majority of which (80%) are considered preventable in the U.S. (Center for Disease Control Office of Health Equity).

Collaboration across various sectors is crucial in efforts to reduce Black maternal mortality (Prather et al., 2018). It is highly recommended that healthcare providers listen attentively to their patient's concerns, as this can significantly impact their well-being and potentially save lives. In addition, healthcare professionals need to have a comprehensive understanding of their patients' lives, including how to effectively address and manage chronic conditions like hypertension, diabetes, or depression. On a systemic level, hospitals and healthcare systems can prioritize identifying and eliminating unconscious bias, standardizing emergency responses, and enhancing prenatal and postpartum care. Community and state interventions can also significantly impact improving socio-economic conditions that influence maternal health outcomes, including housing, transportation, and access to nutritious food (Center for Disease Control Office of Health Equity, 2008).

Medical Gaslighting

Caron (2022), Moyer (2022) and others have begun to shed light on the concerning issue of *medical gaslighting*. This phenomenon occurs when doctors disregard or minimize their patients' symptoms, which can result in incorrect diagnoses or delays in receiving proper medical attention. This issue is more pervasive among women, who have a higher likelihood of being misdiagnosed compared to men. The concept of medical gaslighting captures the frustration and anger that women often face when their symptoms are dismissed or not given proper attention by healthcare professionals. This situation can have severe repercussions, including physical harm, and is regarded as a type of medical malpractice in instances where it results in patient injury. The literature highlights the prevalence of medical gaslighting in Black individuals and women of all backgrounds.

Because of biases in medical education and healthcare provision, symptoms in these groups are frequently disregarded or misunderstood. Take heart disease symptoms, for instance, as in the case of Rosie O'Donnell's story. It is interesting to note that these can vary between men and women, as well as among racial-ethnic groups (e.g., the differential impact of menopause on women of color). However, most medical literature and training tend to emphasize how these symptoms manifest in White men primarily. This bias results in women experiencing longer wait times for diagnoses of cancer and heart disease compared to men. Research has also shown the issue of inadequate pain treatment for both women and Black patients, highlighting the misconceptions and biases that exist among medical professionals (Hoffman et al., 2016). This theme highlights the importance of raising awareness and educating healthcare providers to prevent medical gaslighting. It is crucial to ensure that all patients receive fair and accurate medical treatment, regardless of their gender, race, or body size. See also Cleghorn (2021) for a more expanded history of these issues in medicine as well as Reid (2023) regarding the continuing gender disparities in medical research.

Impact of Sex and Gender on Mental Health

Depression: An Insight into Gender Differences

In addition to physical health, the relationship between sex and gender has a profound impact on the rates of mental health, particularly depression. Statistically, women have a higher likelihood of experiencing depression compared to men, estimated to be at least twice that of men. Women are more prone to experiencing mood symptoms that are often attributed to hormonal changes that happen during puberty, pregnancy, and perimenopause (Salk et al., 2017). Indeed, depression is so prevalent throughout the world that it is thought to represent 10% of all non-fatal illnesses among humans. In a recent meta-analytic analysis, adolescence was the predominant time of life in which gender differences appeared, after which the gap declined and stabilized during adulthood (Salk et al., 2017).

Salk et al. (2017) also found that although rates of depression were significantly lower for men, this population also needed attention regarding diagnosis and treatment considerations. Reasons for these gender differences, in addition to the traditional emphases on women's physical, particularly hormonal, makeup (i.e., "weakness), have focused on issues of poverty and the disparate ratio of women living in poverty, victimization (e.g., violence), as well as the social status of women relative to men (e.g., impact of policies emphasizing inequality). Salk et al. (2017)

found that globally nations with greater gender equality reflected a broader gap in depression rates, which they interpreted as an outcome of the downward comparison of women in relation to men.

The Gender Paradox in Suicide

In addition to depression, gender also affects suicide rates, where there is a *gender paradox* when it comes to the phenomenon of suicide (Moore et al., 2018). The paradox refers to the fact that although women express a higher prevalence of both suicidal thoughts and attempts, especially those under 25, it is men, particularly those over 65, who experience a higher rate of suicide fatalities. There is often a connection between this difference and the methods employed. Men tend to use methods with a higher likelihood of completion, resulting in death, such as firearms or hanging. Women, on the other hand, are more inclined to attempt suicide by less risky methods, such as drug overdose or poisoning, which have a higher likelihood of intervention and survival. Other gender differences that may lead to this disparity are experiences of chronic stressors and seeking support when experiencing suicidal ideation (Moore et al., 2018). The suicide gender paradox highlights the need for gender-sensitive approaches in suicide prevention and mental health care.

For TGNC people, some recent research (albeit with non-random samples) indicates that more than 40% of TGNC people in the U.S. have attempted suicide (Williams Institute, 2023), with between 32% and 50% attempting globally (Virupaksha et al., 2016). Moreover, the family setting is critical for well-being and self-acceptance, since a TGNC person with a non-accepting family is eight times more likely to have attempted suicide than an individual with an accepting family. Virupaksha et al. (2016) attribute these very concerning statistics to several factors, including discrimination, poverty and homelessness, gender-based violence and harassment, negative experiences with health systems, and resultant mental health symptoms, such as depression and anxiety. Virupaksha et al. also identified important protective factors, such as coping strategies, personal qualities such as self-advocacy, integrity, being open and friendly, formal education and higher income, and social support, especially from family of origin and friends. According to Myer (in Williams Institute Press, 2023):

> A lack of societal recognition and acceptance of gender identities outside of the binary of cisgender man or woman and increasing politically motivated attacks on transgender individuals, increase stigma and prejudice and related exposure to minority stress, which contributes to the high rates of substance use and suicidality we see among transgender people.

Gender and Stress: Increasing for Women

Researchers have often identified an important precursor for depression: stress (Moore et al., 2018). According to the APA's Stress in America survey (Bethune, 2023), there is a noticeable difference between men and women when it comes to reporting high levels of stress. Though they report similar average stress levels, women are more likely than men to report that their stress levels are on the rise. Women are also much more likely than men to report somatic and emotional symptoms of stress. When comparing women with each other, there also appear to be differences in the ways that married and single women experience stress. According to APA's recent survey (Bethune, 2023), the following was found:

- Women are more likely than men (28% vs. 20%) to report having a great deal of stress (8, 9 or 10 on a 10-point scale).
- Almost half of all women (49%) surveyed said their stress has increased over the past five years, compared to 4 in 10 (39%) men.
- Women are more likely to report that money (79% compared with 73% of men) and the economy (68% compared with 61% of men) are sources of stress, while men are far more likely to cite work as a source of stress (76% compared with 65% of women).
- Women are more likely to report physical and emotional symptoms of stress than men, such as having had a headache (41% vs. 30%), having felt as though they could cry (44% vs. 15%), or having had an upset stomach or indigestion (32% vs. 21%) in the past month.
- Married women report higher levels of stress than single women, with one-third (33 percent) reporting that they have experienced a great deal of stress in the past month (8, 9, or 10 on a 10-point scale) compared with one in five (22%) of single women. Similarly, significantly more married women report that their stress has increased over the past five years (56% vs. 41% of single women).
- Single women are more likely than married women to say they feel they are doing enough to manage their stress (63% vs. 51%).
- Married women are more likely than single women to report experiencing the following due to stress in the past month: feeling as though they could cry (54% vs. 33%), feeling irritable or angry (52% vs. 38%), having headaches (48% vs. 33%), and experiencing fatigue (47% vs. 35%).

As these data indicate, stress levels can be influenced by marital status; married women tend to report higher levels of stress compared to single women. Several factors contribute to this situation, such as feeling overwhelmed by various responsibilities and experiencing emotional strain. Women who are married tend to experience a higher prevalence of symptoms such as crying, irritability, headaches, and fatigue as a result of stress in comparison to those who are single. Recent research also indicates that biologically, women may respond differently to stress than men, with greater neural and biological reactivity and experience of stress in response to an environmental stimulus (Bangasser, 2016).

Women of Color and Mental Health: Gender, Race, and Stress

As mentioned in Chap. 3, the interplay of gender and race introduces an additional dimension of intricacy to the realm of stress and mental health. The "Strong Black Woman" archetype, for example, has profound effects on the mental well-being of Black women. It frequently results in the internalization of stress and a hesitancy to seek assistance (Simon, 2024). Microaggressions and systemic racism have a significant impact on the mental health of BIPOC women, adding to their stress and mental health struggles. Ultimately, the intricate connection between sex, gender, race, and mental health emphasizes the importance of a comprehensive understanding of these intertwined elements in the identification, management, and avoidance of mental health conditions. Recognizing and dealing with these intricacies are vital measures in enhancing mental health care and results among various populations.

When it comes to women of color and mental health, Beauboeuf-Lafontant (2007) described the *silencing paradigm* for women in which the pressure and relevant norms of feminine socialization lead to girls and women to be overly attuned to others' needs often at the high cost of one's own goals, desires, and feelings. This socialization can also exert a moral influence on how one views others and their decisions and behaviors (e.g., having a child as a single person). As a result, self-silencing can keep psychologically unacceptable thoughts, feelings, and needs from being known by others and then eventually by oneself. A woman can come to ignore her desires and feelings to the extent that it becomes a pattern that may be accompanied by feelings of sadness or mourning for women regarding their loss of self. Indeed, self-silencing may be a driver of depression for women, particularly women of color, in addition to objectification attitudes. That is, depression in the context of self-silencing becomes a period of voicelessness and fracturing from private thoughts that are repressed because they do not conform to one's internalized image of what is feminine or female, rather than letting those thoughts come out and dealing with the reality of these true thoughts and feelings. Through therapy, recovery from a silencing paradigm may involve reintegration, redefinition, and resistance in which women critically sit through cultural messages and determine what they will embrace and what they want.

Another pressure women of color may experience is the notion of "showing strength" (Taylor, 2002). This display may arise from gendered racist images and stereotypes that we addressed in Chap. 3. A key stereotype that drives many Black women is the notion of being strong so that the only time that a woman might take a break is by breaking down emotionally and physically. This may lead to what Taylor called the "Sisterella Complex," where "Sisterella suffers quietly… if you're trying to identify depression in Black women, one of the first things to look for is a woman who is working very hard and seems disconnected from her own needs" (Taylor, p. 9). It is an interesting parallel with the masculinity ideology, wherein strength becomes a masquerade that comes to be believed as real by that person and their families. This display shows how some women are even less likely to seek help for physical or mental health concerns than men because they are so used to being "strong" by not attending to their real feelings.

This mixture of self-silencing and pressure, both internally and from others, to appear strong, can result in depression when the person is leading a selfless life doing for others, and others do not notice the growing emptiness inside, until it just completely overwhelms them. Sometimes, one's community can facilitate these false images of strength. Taylor (1998) reported that responses from communities can be dismissive, asking the person, "What do you have to be depressed about? If our people can make it through slavery, we can make it through anything." By not acknowledging or recognizing the difficulties faced, one can develop an exterior emotional wall or internalizing processes, such as eating, drinking, and shopping. That is, people figure out a way, as one participant says, to not "let those feelings out to anybody... It's just the time bomb waiting to go off." Ultimately, by normalizing struggle and heavy caregiving demands while censoring women against acknowledging strength, discrepancy, experiences, and needs, "being strong"can enable the denial of fundamental inequities in a Black woman's life.

The dynamics of colorism and its effects on health, particularly among African Americans, reveal the significant influence of within-race phenotype heterogeneity. Monk's (2021) national survey delves into the nuanced interplay between skin color, discrimination, and health outcomes, demonstrating that self-perceived skin tone—or "embodied bodily social status"—is a more potent health outcome predictor than interviewer-assessed skin color. Notably, individuals at the extremes of the skin color spectrum face more intraracial discrimination than those with a medium skin tone. Monk's (2021) findings also suggest that self-rated skin color more strongly correlates with mental health than physical health, highlighting the more immediate mental health ramifications of racialization compared to its physical health impacts, which may emerge gradually. This study underscored the necessity of acknowledging skin color's "relationality," as the significance of race or phenotype can vary based on context and reference group, leading to complex interactions in health pathways influenced by racialization and embodiment, as further supported by research from Gravlee et al. (2005), Gravlee (2009), and Campbell & Troyer (2007).

Men and Health

According to Griffith and Thorpe (2016), being a man in the larger society and within healthcare brings many privileges, such as their overrepresentation in medical research and practice. Men have defined medical care interventions and problems to investigate, including only using men in research for many generations. Only by a federal law passed in 1992 were medical researchers legally required to have a gender balance of women and men; unfortunately, issues of inclusivity remain a concern 30 years later, according to a recent report (Reid, 2023).

Nevertheless, despite all these privileges, men remain more likely than women to die in their first year of life and then at every age across the remainder of the life course (Griffith & Thorpe, 2016). Men are not only more likely to die from all causes but are also more likely to die from the top 5 causes, at least in the Western world: heart disease, cancer, unintentional injuries (that sometimes mask suicidal behaviors), chronic lower respiratory diseases, and cerebral vascular diseases. Men in the United States have the lowest life expectancy out of the 22 highest-income countries, including Australia, Japan, the United Kingdom, etc. Worse, the sex differences in health outcomes and life expectancy are expected to widen, at least for now. For example, in the course of the past 50 to 60 years, the life expectancy gap between women and men have widened an entire year, from 5 years to 6 years (Ghorayshi, 2023). U.S. men die approximately seven years earlier than women, have a higher mortality rate for each of the fifteen leading causes of death, and experience more severe chronic illnesses overall. An essential factor in these variations is how people think and act concerning their health. The United States male population is disproportionately prone to risk-taking attitudes and actions, while the female population is more likely to engage in health-promoting and longevity-promoting behaviors (Courtenay, 2000).

Racial disparities further heighten these gender health disparities, especially for Black and Native American men. In contrast, Asian Asian American men have the lowest mortality rate of all men, as well as the lowest gender disparity of life expectancy rates between women and men. A key issue driving these male pattern disparities in health is the engagement, or lack thereof, of health-promoting behaviors, such as drinking alcohol to excess, inactivity, poor eating patterns, and poor sleep. Masculine ideology attitudes may potentially support these poor health behaviors since a major aspect of these attitudes is to "prove" one's masculinity to others (i.e., taking risks), as well as never showing if or when something is ailing them. Moreover, being socialized to believe in the strength and power of one's body may prevent some men from seeking help when they need it the most. The media, in their celebrations of athletic achievements and victories, even for activities like competitive eating, further provide social rewards for "never letting them see you sweat" when engaging in death-defying activities.

Conforming to Masculine Norms

Conforming to masculine norms (CMN) in men's health insinuates self-reliance, emotional control, the primacy of work, and the pursuit of status-winning at all costs. Contextual aspects reflect how conformity to masculinity norms is expressed, depending on race, ethnicity, and socioeconomic status. For example, for Asian American men, emotional control or restraint is a congruent cultural value rather than trying to cover up, and may have less negative impact. That is, there are healthy ways of restraining oneself that also could benefit many men. Wong, Hoang, and

Miller (2017) explored the overall impact of outcomes on persons, using various predictors such as race and age. They found that CMN was positively associated with adverse mental health, inversely related to positive mental health, inversely related to seeking psychological help, and unfavorably related to negative social functioning or relations than indicators of adverse mental health. As discussed in Chap. 9, the impact of these norms is prevalent on social functioning in the context of mental health and relationships. Overconformity to masculinity can damage one's ability to have positive relationships, which can then play a role in affecting mental health. This damage makes sense because conformity to masculine norms focuses on dominating women by winning emotional control, violence, self-reliance, and being the playboy. That is, CMN is linked both with establishing and expressing power and dominance over women, as well as disdain for LGB and TGNC people.

Another important aspect regarding CMN is that contexts and content matter. Wong et al. (2017) found that only developmental characteristics predicted links between conformity to masculine norms and mental health. In contrast, race, SES, and age did not. There was a negative link between conformity to masculine norms and positive mental health and psychological health seeking with non-college men and mixed samples versus only college men. It also may be that person-centered variables, age and SES were linked with finding. Regarding predictor-centered variables (CMN), three specific dimensions of CMN were significantly and unfavorably associated with adverse mental health: self-reliance, playboy, and power over women. The primacy of work was not related to these outcomes, so the role of being a provider or protector was not linked to masculinity norms. Rather it was the nature of relationships with other people, particularly how one sees themselves as a playboy who can dominate women, that most affected mental health.

Objectification Theory

Several theories drive health disparities among the genders as well as lead to particular gender-based concerns. For example, in exploring women's health, objectification theory, the notion that women's life experiences and their gender socialization routinely include objectification, including sexual objectification of themselves and others in which one's entire being is identified with the body, or worse, individual body parts (Moradi & Huang, 2008; Roberts et al., 2018). As we noted before, patriarchal societies socialize girls and women to treat themselves and each other as sexual objects to be looked upon and evaluated, based primarily upon bodily appearance. Self-objectification, in which a person internalizes objectifying ways, essentially denies one's personhood beyond physical appearance. One of the key symptoms or outcomes of being socialized to view oneself and others as objects is a persistent surveillance of one's body, a habitual monitoring of one's outward appearance.

Objectification theory has several mental health outcomes. For example, it promotes body shame when a person measures themselves against an internalized or cultural standard and often perceives that they are failing to meet that standard. Body shaming predicts higher levels of depression (Roberts et al., 2018), and constant body surveillance also promotes anxiety, which includes the anticipation of threats and fear about when and how one's body will be evaluated. Moreover, in the twenty-first century, with the advent of social media, many girls find themselves, especially in their adolescence and youth, a target of constant surveillance by peers, family members, and strangers. Social media can be a platform that promotes more intensified feelings of self-objectification, therefore resulting in body shame, anxiety, and depression as a result. Recent research indicates that youth, especially girls, can be quite harshly impacted by their interactions on social media. A recent study found that reducing social media exposure increased esteem in both appearance and weight for a group of primarily women youth experiencing emotional distress (Thai et al., 2023).

Self-objectification or sexual objectification also interferes with being able to have peak experiences and positive processes like flow, creativity, and innovativeness, and it can even impact one's awareness of internal bodily states. Because people feel shame, they feel depression and anxiety. Ultimately, individuals may choose to do fewer things in life, such as going to the beach or even applying for a job, because they fear that they do not measure up to whatever imagined bodily standard these actions require. Self-objectification can also intensify future experiences when one is treated as an object by others, such that it becomes a damaging cycle (Moradi & Huang, 2008).

Self-objectification can also appear with the following concerns (Nussbaum, 1995): a sense of instrumentality or transactionalism in which people are treated as tools. Doing so involves a denial of the autonomy of individuals, as one might imagine for the worst aspects of Hollywood film casting. Moreover, one may treat others with a level of inertness, being viewed as lacking agency to make their own decisions. Another outcome is fungibility, which means treating people as interchangeable objects lacking meaningful differentiation. Objectified people also may be treated as lacking viability, that it is permissible to violate, break apart, or even broken into. Thus, it is not hard to imagine how objectification processes of self and others can lead to violations, even violence or sexual assault. That comes because somebody is engaging and objectifying someone who does not appreciate their humanity and inviability. Therefore, violating or "breaking into" that person feels fine. On a worse level is ownership, wherein people are treated as things that are owned, implying they can be bought or sold in what is still an ongoing global crisis, human trafficking. Finally, objectification involves a denial of subjectivity wherein people are treated as things whose experiences, feelings, and internal states are not considered. Therefore, they are not part of any decision-making on how to treat people.

Roberts et al. (2018) provided a snapshot of the literature on objectification that shows important correlates and outcomes across several areas of life, such as health and physicality, cognitive and behavioral processes, the social and environmental context, and the motivational and affective components. In terms of health and physicality, self-objectification has been linked with self-injury, negative views of reproductive functions, less agency over one's self-care, less use of sexual protection, increased health risks, such as smoking and substance abuse, as well as increased trauma symptoms. Motivationally/affectively, correlates include increased negative emotions, lower life satisfaction, lower self-esteem, more body-based and often downward social comparisons, body guilt, and lower body esteem. Cognitive and behavioral components include more self-silencing, self-sexualization, choosing clothes more for fashion than comfort, poor physical performance, narrowed thinking since one is so focused on monitoring, and exercising for looks rather than health promotion. Finally, in the social, environmental area, correlates include increased hostility toward women and rape myth acceptance as well as fears of rape, lower feelings of authenticity and social interactions, views of sex as a source of personal power, and less support for egalitarian gender roles and social activism.

Objectification theory also applies to men and has been linked to men with body image, self-esteem, and health-promoting behaviors. Spirituality has been negatively linked with men's objectification attitudes, but not women's. Instead of becoming obsessed with thinness, as it may become for many women, especially White/Euro-American women, self-objectification for boys and men ends up focusing on building one's body into a muscular powerhouse, much like the Marvel superheroes that we see in the popular media (Boyd & Murnen, 2017). Gay and bisexual men, in particular, are at a higher risk of adopting self-objectification attitudes as well as attitudes toward others (Martins et al., 2007). There may be a role of internalized homophobia that can drive these internalized objectification attitudes, as in the case of someone who attempts to feel more accepted by others in both the gay social world as well as in the larger society.

Conclusion

The examination of how gender influences physical and mental well-being highlights the critical role that both biological sex and socially constructed gender have in shaping health outcomes. Understanding and acknowledging these variations is crucial for the progress of medical research and healthcare provision. For instance, the incorporation of women in clinical trials has brought attention to distinct cardiovascular risks and reactions to treatments that vary significantly from those observed in men. Similarly, gender plays a significant role in the distinct patterns exhibited by mental health issues such as depression and suicide. This difference highlights the need for tailored approaches to prevention and treatment, considering individuals' unique experiences and challenges.

In addition, the combination of gender with other demographic factors, such as race and ethnicity, brings about a multitude of complexities when it comes to health disparities. These intersections significantly impact a wide range of factors, including life expectancy, the occurrence of specific diseases, and the effectiveness of different treatments. Therefore, considering these intricacies can result in more efficient healthcare strategies, which can help decrease inequalities and enhance outcomes for various populations. As we progress, the health sciences must incorporate gender-specific insights to improve the accuracy and efficacy of medical care for all individuals.

Case Study

Sonia is a 35-year-old Afro-Latina genderqueer woman living in rural Maine. Recently, Sonia has referred herself to counseling due to emotional overwhelm, exhaustion, and feelings of depression. For the past ten years, she has experienced intense menstrual pain, fatigue, irregular periods, and pain during sex, all of which her male doctor indicates are natural. She suspects she has endometriosis but has been denied the diagnosis since her first consultation at the age of 24. Throughout her life, she has learned to cope with the pain and has avoided sexual intercourse to manage the symptoms. Through this, she learned that stress increases her pain and fatigue. It is difficult for her to find a doctor in-network in her area that she has not already seen, and she does not trust doctors to believe that her pain is unmanageable. She would like to try emotional coping strategies as she feels helpless to change her condition medically. Sonia is open to referrals but only to women doctors who are in-network and is largely focused on "making it to menopause," where she may experience a decrease in symptoms. In the intake, you learn she is currently experiencing a significant amount of stress as a result of her mother's declining health, which has caused her to ignore many of her own health concerns.

Discussion Questions

1. In Sonia's interactions with her doctors and how they interpret her symptoms, how do the biological and social concepts of sex and gender factor in? Describe how these things could affect how her suspected condition is diagnosed and treated.
2. How can we reframe Sonia's gender identity and depression experiences in light of the gender paradox in mental health and suicide that this chapter outlines? Is her genderqueer identity going to present her with other obstacles?
3. A major obstacle to Sonia getting the care she needs is her mistrust of medical experts. What roles do gender, race, and geography play in the perpetuation of healthcare disparities and mistrust?
4. Think about how gender norms and beliefs could make Sonia's health problems worse. How do these norms and expectations contribute to the fact that her doctors either ignored or downplayed the severity of her symptoms?

5. Sonia aims to manage her condition through emotional coping strategies. Taking into account the fact that her gender, race, and rural upbringing all interact with one another, what approaches could work for her?
6. Talk about the specific challenges that Sonia, an Afro-Latina genderqueer woman, faces in terms of her health. In what ways do these pressures make it even more difficult to take care of her mother's health problems and her own suspected medical condition?
7. In light of Sonia's remarks regarding "making it to menopause," what adjustments or interventions could be made to healthcare practices to provide better assistance to individuals who experience marginalization within the system, such as Sonia?

References

Ainsworth, C. (2015). Sex redefined. *Nature, 518*(7539), 288–291. https://doi.org/10.1038/518288a

American Heart Association. (2022). *Heart attack symptoms in women*. https://www.heart.org/en/health-topics/heart-attack/warning-signs-of-a-heart-attack/heart-attack-symptoms-in-women

Bangasser, D. A. (2016, November). Female stress—A faster, stronger response. *Scientific American*. https://www.scientificamerican.com/article/female-stress--faster-stronger-response/

Beauboeuf-Lafontant, T. (2007). "You have to show strength": An exploration of gender, race, and depression. *Gender and Society, 21*(1), 28–51. http://www.jstor.org/stable/27640945

Bethune, S. (2023). *Stress in America 2023: A nation recovering from collective trauma.* American Psychological Association. https://www.apa.org/news/press/releases/stress/2023/collective-trauma-recovery

Boyd, H., & Murnen, S. K. (2017). Thin and sexy vs. muscular and dominant: Prevalence of gendered body ideals in popular dolls and action figures. *Body Image, 21*, 90–96. https://doi.org/10.1016/j.bodyim.2017.03.003

Campbell, M. E., & Troyer, L. (2007). The implications of racial misclassification by observers. *American Sociological Review, 72*(5), 750–765. https://doi.org/10.1177/000312240707200505

Caron, C. (2022, July). Feeling dismissed? How to spot 'medical gaslighting' and what to do about it. *The New York Times*. https://www.nytimes.com/2022/07/29/well/mind/medical-gaslighting.html

Center for Disease Control Office of Health Equity. (2008, April). *Working together to reduce Black maternal mortality*. https://www.cdc.gov/healthequity/features/maternal-mortality/index.html

Cleghorn, E. (2021). Medical myths about gender roles go back to ancient Greece. Women are still paying the price today. *Time Magazine*. https://time.com/6074224/gender-medicine-history/

Courtenay, W. H. (2000). Constructions of masculinity and their influence on men's well-being: A theory of gender and health. *Social Science & Medicine (1982), 50*(10), 1385–1401. https://doi.org/10.1016/s0277-9536(99)00390-1

Ghorayshi, A. (2023, November 13). An 'unsettling' drop in life expectancy for men. *The New York Times*. https://www.nytimes.com/2023/11/13/health/men-life-expectancy-drops.html

Goldman, B. (2024). *Stanford Medicine-led study shows why women are at greater risk of autoimmune disease*. Stanford School of Medicine. https://med.stanford.edu/news/all-news/2024/02/women-autoimmune.html

Gravlee, C. C. (2009). How race becomes biology: Embodiment of social inequality. *American Journal of Physical Anthropology, 139*(1), 47–57. https://doi.org/10.1002/ajpa.20983

Gravlee, C. C., Dressler, W. W., & Bernard, H. R. (2005). Skin color, social classification, and blood pressure in southeastern Puerto Rico. *American Journal of Public Health, 95*(12), 2191–2197. https://doi.org/10.2105/AJPH.2005.065615

Griffith, D. M., & Thorpe, R. J., Jr. (2016). Men's physical health and health behaviors. In *APA handbook of men and masculinities* (pp. 709–730). American Psychological Association. https://doi.org/10.1037/14594-032

Gross, R. E. (2021, April 27). Endometriosis is more than a gynecological disease. *The New York Times*. https://www.nytimes.com/2021/04/27/health/endometriosis-griffith-uterus.html

Hill, L., & Artiga, S. (2023). What is driving widening racial disparities in life expectancy? *KFF*. https://www.kff.org/racial-equity-and-health-policy/issue-brief/what-is-driving-widening-racial-disparities-in-life-expectancy/

Hiteshi, A. K., Li, D., Gao, Y., Chen, A., Flores, F., Mao, S. S., & Budoff, M. J. (2014). Gender differences in coronary artery diameter are not related to body habitus or left ventricular mass. *Clinical Cardiology, 37*(10), 605–609. https://doi.org/10.1002/clc.22310

Hoffman, K. M., Trawalter, S., Axt, J. R., & Oliver, M. N. (2016). Racial bias in pain assessment and treatment recommendations, and false beliefs about biological differences between blacks and whites. *Proceedings of the National Academy of Sciences of the United States of America, 113*(16), 4296–4301. https://doi.org/10.1073/pnas.1516047113

Hughes, L. D., King, W. M., Gamarel, K. E., Geronimus, A. T., Panagiotou, O. A., & Hughto, J. M. W. (2022). Differences in all-cause mortality among transgender and non-transgender people enrolled in private insurance. *Demography, 59*(3), 1023–1043. https://doi.org/10.1215/00703370-9942002

Keen, M. U., & Reddivari, A. K. R. (2023). Osteoporosis in females. In *StatPearls*. StatPearls Publishing.

Lin-Su, K., Lekarev, O., Poppas, D. P., & Vogiatzi, M. G. (2015). Congenital adrenal hyperplasia patient perception of 'disorders of sex development' nomenclature. *International Journal of Pediatric Endocrinology, 2015*(1), 9. https://doi.org/10.1186/s13633-015-0004-4

López, N., Vargas, E. D., Juarez, M., Cacari-Stone, L., & Bettez, S. (2018). What's your "street race"? Leveraging multidimensional measures of race and intersectionality for examining physical and mental health status among Latinxs. *Sociology of Race and Ethnicity, 4*(1), 49–66. https://doi.org/10.1177/2332649217708798

Martins, Y., Tiggemann, M., & Kirkbride, A. (2007). Those speedos become them: The role of self-objectification in gay and heterosexual men's body image. *Personality & Social Psychology Bulletin, 33*(5), 634–647. https://doi.org/10.1177/0146167206297403

Monk, E. P., Jr. (2021). Colorism and physical health: Evidence from a national survey. *Journal of Health and Social Behavior, 62*(1), 37–52. https://doi.org/10.1177/0022146520979645

Moore, F., Taylor, S., Beaumont, J., Gibson, R., & Starkey, C. (2018). The gender suicide paradox under gender role reversal during industrialisation. *PLoS One, 13*(8), e0202487. https://doi.org/10.1371/journal.pone.0202487

Moradi, B., & Huang, Y.-P. (2008). Objectification theory and psychology of women: A decade of advances and future directions. *Psychology of Women Quarterly, 32*(4), 377–398. https://doi.org/10.1111/j.1471-6402.2008.00452.x

Moyer, M. W. (2022, March 28). Women are calling out 'medical gaslighting.' *The New York Times*. https://www.nytimes.com/2022/03/28/well/live/gaslighting-doctors-patients-health.html

National Institutes of Health. *NIH Inclusion Outreach Toolkit: How to engage, recruit, and retain women in clinical research*. https://orwh.od.nih.gov/toolkit/welcome/introduction

Newman, T. (2023, March). Sex and gender: What is the difference? *Medical News Today*. https://www.medicalnewstoday.com/articles/232363

Nussbaum, M. C. (1995). Objectification. *Philosophy & Public Affairs, 24*(4), 249–291.

Prather, C., Fuller, T. R., Jeffries, W. L., Marshall, K. J., Howell, A. V., Belyue-Umole, A., & King, W. (2018). Racism, African American women, and their sexual and reproductive health: A review of historical and contemporary evidence and implications for health equity. *Health Equity, 2*(1), 249–259. https://doi.org/10.1089/heq.2017.0045

Rabin, R. C. (2014, September). Health researchers will get $10.1 million to counter gender bias in studies. *New York Times*. https://www.nytimes.com/2014/09/23/health/23gender.html

Rabin, R. C. (2022, August). U.S. life expectancy falls again in 'historic' setback. *The New York Times*. https://www.nytimes.com/2022/08/31/health/life-expectancy-covid-pandemic.html

Rabin, R. C. (2023, July). A blood test predicts pre-eclampsia in pregnant women. *The New York Times*. https://www.nytimes.com/2023/07/03/health/pregnancy-preeclampsia-test.html

Reid, B. (2023). Despite decades of promises, health research still overlooks women. *The Guardian*. https://www.theguardian.com/science/2023/nov/20/women-health-research-jill-biden-white-house

Roberts, T.-A., Calogero, R. M., & Gervais, S. J. (2018). Objectification theory: Continuing contributions to feminist psychology. In *APA handbook of the psychology of women: History, theory, and battlegrounds* (Vol. 1, pp. 249–271). American Psychological Association. https://doi.org/10.1037/0000059-013

Salk, R. H., Hyde, J. S., & Abramson, L. Y. (2017). Gender differences in depression in representative national samples: Meta-analyses of diagnoses and symptoms. *Psychological Bulletin, 143*(8), 783–822. https://doi.org/10.1037/bul0000102

Simon, C. (2024). *Strong Black woman schema and its impact among Black women* (Publication No. 15493). Walden Dissertations and Doctoral Studies. Retrieved from https://scholarworks.waldenu.edu/dissertations/15493

Smith, R. (2023, July). The curse stalking women's soccer. *The New York Times*. https://www.nytimes.com/2023/07/19/sports/soccer/womens-world-cup-soccer-torn-acl.html

Taylor, S. L. (1998). Taking back our power. *Essence, 29*(1), 107–107.

Taylor, S. L. (2002). Passion for peace. *Essence, 33*(8), 9–9.

Thai, H., Davis, C. G., Mahboob, W., Perry, S., Adams, A., & Goldfield, G. S. (2023). Reducing social media use improves appearance and weight esteem in youth with emotional distress. *Psychology of Popular Media, 13*(1), 162–169. https://doi.org/10.1037/ppm0000460

Virupaksha, H. G., Muralidhar, D., & Ramakrishna, J. (2016). Suicide and suicidal behavior among transgender persons. *Indian Journal of Psychological Medicine, 38*(6), 505–509. https://doi.org/10.4103/0253-7176.194908

Williams Institute. (2023). *More than 40% of transgender adults in the US have attempted suicide*. Williams Institute Press Release. Retrieved from https://williamsinstitute.law.ucla.edu/press/transpop-suicide-press-release/

Wong, Y. J., Ho, M.-H. R., Wang, S.-Y., & Miller, I. S. K. (2017). Meta-analyses of the relationship between conformity to masculine norms and mental health-related outcomes. *Journal of Counseling Psychology, 64*(1), 80–93. https://doi.org/10.1037/cou0000176

World Health Organization. (2023). *Endometriosis*. https://www.who.int/news-room/fact-sheets/detail/endometriosis#:~:text=Endometriosis%20is%20a%20disease%20in,period%20and%20last%20until%20menopause

Yan, B. W., Arias, E., Geller, A. C., Miller, D. R., Kochanek, K. D., & Koh, H. K. (2024). Widening gender gap in life expectancy in the US, 2010–2021. *JAMA Internal Medicine, 184*(1), 108–110. https://doi.org/10.1001/jamainternmed.2023.6041

Chapter 11
Gender and Violence

Exploring the Spectrum of Gender-Based Violence

Gender-based violence (GBV) encompasses a broad spectrum of harm, including physical, emotional, and structural forms of aggression directed toward individuals on the basis of their gender identity or expression (Khanlou et al., 2022; Wirtz et al., 2020). This violence includes but is not limited to, coercion and threats, intimidation, stalking, emotional abuse (e.g., gaslighting), forced isolation, minimizing, blaming, using children and reproduction as forms of control, incorporating economic abuse, spiritual abuse, or power over the victim based on immigration status or cultural factors. Women of color and members of other oppressed groups confront additional challenges and dangers as a result of these intersectional impacts. For example, Indigenous women are victims of sexual assault at twice the rates of other women, and the plight of murdered and missing Indigenous women (MMIW), their third leading cause of death, only recently has been brought to light in the larger society (Lucchesi, 2018).

Depression, anxiety, and post-traumatic stress disorder (PTSD) are among the negative mental and physical health outcomes that can result from exposure to and experiences of GBV (Lever et al., 2022). More broadly, this pervasive issue manifests in various forms in the lifespan that this chapter will focus on, including child sexual abuse (CSA), intimate partner violence/domestic violence (IPV/DV), and even sexual harassment (SH) in different contexts (New York State Office for the Prevention of Domestic Violence n.d.).

Delving into the range of GBV uncovers a distressing array of abuses that impact people in various stages of life and social settings. Child Sexual Abuse (CSA) is a type of child abuse that involves engaging in sexual activity with a victim who is under the age of 18 years old (Rape, Abuse & Incest National Network [RAINN], 2021). Intimate Partner Violence (IPV), sometimes referred to as Domestic Violence (DV), includes physical or sexual violence, stalking, or psychological harm by a

M. L. Miville et al., *Counseling and Gender*,
https://doi.org/10.1007/978-3-031-69172-0_11

current or former intimate partner or spouse, which has a profound impact on victims from all walks of life (Breiding et al., 2015). It can sometimes occur within the same household (domestic) but does not need to. Lastly, according to the U.S. Equal Employment Opportunity Commission (EEOC, n.d.), sexual harassment encompasses a wide range of behaviors, including unwanted sexual advances, requests for sexual favors, and other forms of verbal or physical harassment that are sexual in both the workplace and educational settings, more recently having more global and cultural impact with the #MeToo movement (RAINN, n.d.).

Gender Based Violence as a Global Pandemic

It is crucial to understand that those with power have roles in GBV since there is a global scope of gender-based violence, with countries like Argentina, Turkey, and the United States reporting high levels of violence against women (UNODC, 2019); USDHS, 2024). Unfortunately, many nations still uphold cultural values and legislation that support and encourage the use of violence against women and gender minorities (World Bank, 2020). With this in mind, it is no wonder that GBV happens to 1 in 3 women worldwide across all races and ethnicities (World Health Organization, 2024); transgender (trans) people, particularly Black transwomen, may experience GBV throughout their lives. This chronic experience often is associated with blocked access to protective services and contributes to poor health outcomes and quality of life (Lanham et al., 2019).

While a minimum of 155 countries have enacted legislation regarding domestic violence, and 140 countries have laws explicitly addressing sexual harassment in the workplace (Abramowitz & Moran, 2012; Sanjel, 2013; UN Women, n.d.), there are still obstacles to effectively implementing these laws. These obstacles restrict women's and girls' ability to obtain safety and justice, and insufficient measures are taken to mitigate violence proactively. When the laws are implemented, perpetrators frequently manage to avoid legal consequences. With legal consequences avoided, this pattern can generationally continue. Unfortunately, research indicates that those who witness GBV in childhood are more likely to become survivors or perpetrators of future violence (Russo & Pirlott, 2006). IPV/DV has a significant economic impact as well, as victims frequently lose their jobs as a result of the disruptions caused by abuse (i.e., disrupted childcare, hospital visits, or other reasons). Similarly, workplace sexual harassment reflects gendered power dynamics, with serious consequences for women's employment and mental health. The intergenerational cycle of violence, in which early exposure to gender-based violence increases the likelihood of future victimization or perpetration, emphasizes the critical need to address child sexual abuse first.

Childhood Sexual Abuse: Historical Trauma and Next Steps

When it comes to psychology's acknowledgment of the existence of childhood sexual trauma, it is disturbing to look at the history of how long it took for the field to recognize, conduct research, and develop effective interventions specifically for abuse survivors. Childhood sexual abuse (CSA) remains a grievous issue with long-term consequences for survivors. According to Draucker and Martsolf (2006), there were three points in history in which the abuse of young people was brought to light. For at least the first century of this discussion, it only focused on girls and women as victims. The victimization of boys and men only began to be discussed professionally, primarily in this century. For example, on Nov. 5, 2010, the Oprah Winfrey Show invited 200 male molestation survivors to appear after sharing her own story of CSA (Jensen, 2021). This watershed episode has been recognized for how it challenged cultural norms about sexual abuse and male survivors. The gendered nature of this abuse and its aftermath calls for an in-depth analysis, considering how societal norms around masculinity and femininity influence the experiences and responses of men and women survivors. As researchers and mental health workers work with this population, analysis should be grounded in psychological and sociocultural frameworks to unpack the complex interplay of gender, power, and trauma, reframe the story, and facilitate recovery from CSA.

Three Discoveries with CSA

According to Draucker and Martsolf (2006), CSA first became identified in the late 1800s and early 1900s, near the start of the field of psychology. Prior to that, any sexual abuse within families, or in any kind of community, generally was met with many levels of denial. Ironically, it was Sigmund Freud who first "discovered" sexual violence from CSA in the many stories that his women patients would share. He would typically attribute these "wild" stories to hysteria or something wrong with the patient rather than something wrong with the situation in which the patient was living (Bulut, 2019). Freud and many psychoanalysts at the time denied any role that fathers or male relatives could play in these abuses and instead usually emphasized blame on distant men in a girl's life; sadly, most victims know their perpetrators personally. Even worse, though, Freud eventually blamed the stories on incestuous fantasies on the part of the patient rather than an actual event (Draucker & Martsolf, 2006).

The second time CSA became a focus for scholars was in the 1940s (Draucker & Martsolf, 2006), when the study of human sexuality began with the work of Kinsey, the very first researcher to seriously explore sexuality among people in the United States (Kinsey et al., 1981). Here, CSA was "discovered" yet again, with 20–30% of the women in his studies saying that they had been abused as children (Draucker & Martsolf, 2006). Some male participants also reported CSA as well, with up to a third of men saying that they had been victims of abuse; however, these male narratives were completely ignored at the time. Moreover, and unfortunately, Kinsey and many of his colleagues in the 1940s and 1950s failed to understand the toll and the psychological consequences that this kind of abuse had on the survivors; they had difficulty differentiating between harmless exploration among consenting adults, or exploitative acts like CSA (Allen et al., 2017). As a result, the early sexuality researchers did not do anything with the information once the data were reported, and no follow-through occurred regarding interventions or further research.

It was not until the third discovery in the 1970s that CSA and, more broadly, GBV became an issue of serious focus within psychology when women and people of color began to enter into the fields of psychology and counseling in much larger numbers (Draucker & Martsolf, 2006). As a result, these newer members of the field were "at the table" and began to highlight awareness about violence that occurs in many forms against women. Several public events occurred in the 1970s and 1980s to help raise this concern, such as *Take Back the Night* rallies where women would protest, saying they had the right to walk the city (TBTN, 2023). Fifty years later, protests about the same issue still occur today with protestors demanding that if there is violence against women, why do the police and law enforcement focus on women staying at home to be safe? Why is there a focus on the victims rather than the perpetrators? More will be said on this when we discuss the #MeTooMovement.

Research during the 1980s and 1990s continued to show a great deal of evidence regarding the wide-spread existence of GBV, in particular, CSA. Unfortunately, this awareness campaign was met with backlash and as a result, a denial movement questioned the construct of "recovered memories" as well as minimization of the fact that abuse, including sexual abuse, does happen (Prout & Dobson, 1998). As noted earlier, male survivors were largely ignored until this century. So, even though these denial movements occurred in the 80s and 90s in the more prominent media, attorneys, psychologists and counselors nonetheless continued to work with victims/survivors, continued to develop research, yet ignored men as victims. This denial was even codified into law so that men could not be legally assaulted (McLean et al., 2005; Thomas & Kopel, 2023). For example, after public pressure, the Federal Bureau of Investigation (FBI) updated its own definition of rape to include men in 2012 (Terkel, 2012), over 90 years after their original definition was created.

Reporting depends on how CSA is defined, who is sampled, and how the data are collected. The estimated number of young people who are abused ranges a great deal. For nonclinical samples, the range varies between 10–60% of cisgender women (Ellonen et al., 2022), indicating limited reporting. For cisgender men, it is somewhere between 3–16%. While the majority of girls experience abuse from males (88.4%), boys face abuse from both men (45.6%) and women (54.4%), with a significant majority of episodes among 10- to 17-year-olds going unreported to parents or any adult. Police reports are filed in approximately 19.1% of all cases. Gewirtz-Meydan and Finkelhor (2020) also suggest that children and young people experience sexual abuse and assault in diverse ways, highlighting the need to go beyond traditional stereotypes when addressing this issue and meeting survivors where they are at when they are ready to share their story.

Storying Childhood Sexual Abuse

Keeping CSA a secret is an archaic and distressing narrative. A clinician's role as a mental health provider is to help survivors begin to share that secret, but most importantly to feel safe enough to share that secret (Draucker & Martsolf, 2006, 2008). As a counselor or mental health professional, thinking about disclosure, especially if a client presents in this way, is a critical step to consider. A common scenario is that weeks or months into therapy, and then in the last five minutes of a session, a client makes their first disclosure on the way out the door.

The act of disclosure is a process rather than a single event. There can be intense feelings of shame and embarrassment, and there may be dysfunction in the family that socializes a person to silence themselves (Draucker & Martsolf, 2006). Fears of harm by that perpetrator feel authentic when they meet with a therapist and can still be alive within their emotional life if the person feels they must keep the secret to protect their families. Alternatively, the client may not even have a conscious memory of that event yet. The worse the abuse, the harder it may be for that individual to cope and disclose the event—a typical response. Confiding and sharing is a crucial step toward health and wellness. When it comes to children, adolescents, and other young people in general, there are two issues of concern: (1) *What is happening,* the events, especially if it is before puberty, and that there is any cognitive understanding of what is happening and (2) *Why is it happening,* especially to the young person? These questions, if managed delicately, can lead to sharing that event with others.

Draucker and Martsolf (2008) describe *telling the story* as a general process of discussing CSA or any assault story. This storytelling can ideally begin as children or when the survivor is an adult, with the critical aspect of this model being how people respond to that individual sharing their story. Further sharing can be prevented for a long time if there are aversive or an adverse reactions. The survivor may end up shielding the story to become the secret they hang on to. However, if the story is encouraged to be shared, it can help the survivor continue to share even more. This encouragement is the story's goal, which accounts for something that *happened* rather than something the survivor is afraid of or hiding from. The more times there is aversion in the reaction of a person they are telling, the more likely the story stays a secret (Fig. 11.1).

When a story is not yet told, the perpetrator may negatively influence if and how it gets told and include multiple plots to manipulate the survivor, often with the lie that it is the survivor's wrongdoing. The plots can focus on one cause (the survivor's fault) and one effect (the abuse). Including the antagonist may detract the child from sharing, especially if they feel the other person might challenge them. However, the constructed story provides a basic explanation of the abuse, leaving the child/survivor feeling shame. When a person begins to come out with this event or set of events that occurred as children, the child may start by only expressing discomfort being around or with the perpetrator, not yet comfortable saying why.

If the first response a survivor hears is negative, it could be even more years before that person discloses it to another person (Draucker & Martsolf, 2008). When

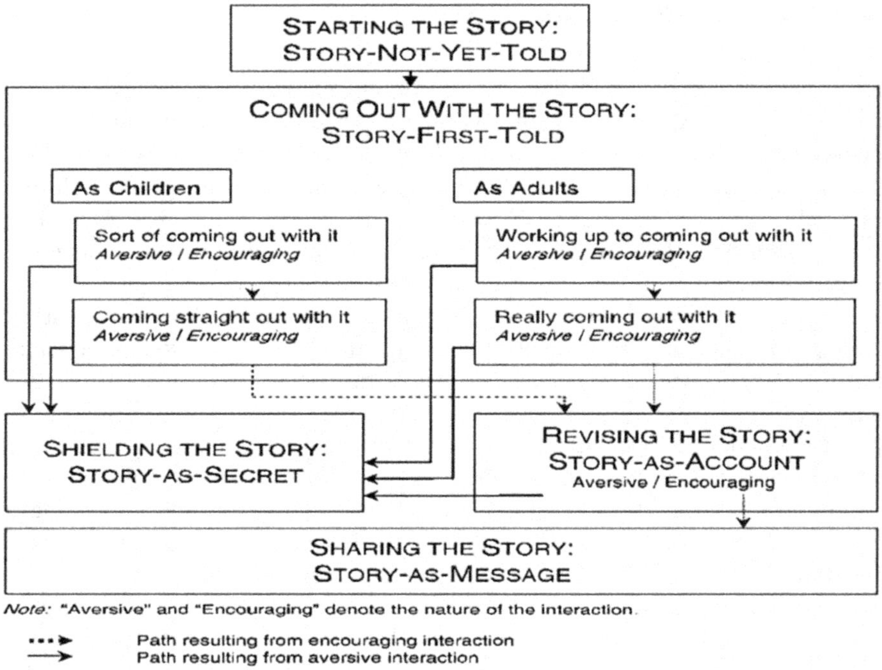

Fig. 11.1 The theoretical framework "Storying Childhood Sexual Abuse" (Draucker & Martsolf, 2008, p. 1039)

working with young people, it is important to stay cognizant and sensitive to how and what people are saying, what the symptoms they are presenting with, and what they might share in hidden or nonverbal ways to see how their therapist might respond. In adulthood, college counseling centers can be places where young people, for the first time, feel safe to share their stories because they are away from the originating setting, family member, or other person.

There are all kinds of reasons why people want to keep the story of their abuse secret; they may continue to believe that they were to blame, which is very common, or keeping the secret can be a way to keep a sense of control. In other words, if someone blames themselves, not telling becomes a way to maintain some kind of control over the event; the alternative for the survivor is much worse to consider, that this terrible thing happened and they had no control over it—a terrifying concept for somebody to accept. Recall that it is only recently, the past half century, that these stories have been expressed and supported by mental health professionals and others in the media.

Draucker and Martsolf gathered testimonies from survivors, with one survivor saying, "If you have never talked about it and you do not remember a lot about it, it is subconsciously beating you up" (2008, p. 1042). Survivors can be encouraged by somebody, ideally by a mental health professional, and with each telling and continuing supportive response may realize they are not to blame; it was the perpetrator (Draucker & Martsolf, 2008, p. 1043). By beginning to tell the story, by beginning that supportive response, and by putting it out into the open, that story begins to take shape differently and holds a different power in which the storyteller becomes the narrator of their own life.

Supporting the Client: What NOT to Say and What TO Say

Draucker and Martstolf (2006) explored the intricate aspects of how counselors should respond to clients who disclose trauma, specifically sexual abuse, and discussed various adverse reactions that counselors may unintentionally display, which can be counterproductive. These reactions include expressing shock in a manner that may intimidate the client into silence ("Oh my gosh, what your father did was disgusting!"), expressing disbelief that undermines the client's experience ("It sounds like you believe your father did these things to you even though you were so young. It is hard to know what happened"), assigning blame to the client ("Why didn't you tell your mother? Why did you let it go on for so long?"), downplaying the importance of the client's experiences ("You say this experience is past, and you coped with it, so let us move on"), displaying inappropriate curiosity about the details, or inappropriately diverting the conversation to less relevant topics like unrelated homework ("Wait, I gave you that homework for studying– what happened to that?"). The range of responses, from expressing shock and disgust to questioning why the client didn't inform their mother, not only lacks support for the client but can also worsen their trauma.

Draucker and Martstolf (2006) proposed a therapeutic approach emphasizing empathy, safety, and respect for the client's autonomy. Recognizing the significant bravery it requires for a client to share such profoundly personal experiences is vital, as is providing ongoing support and accessibility beyond the session. It is highly recommended for counselors to give clients the freedom to discuss their experiences of abuse at their own pace. This approach ensures that the client is in control of the conversation and that their emotional well-being is taken into consideration. Expressions such as "I'm interested in learning more about that experience whenever you're comfortable sharing" or "I admire your bravery for opening up to me" can help create a supportive and secure atmosphere. Therapists can create a supportive and validating space for clients by acknowledging their emotions and empowering them to take control of the disclosure process, promoting healing and empowerment.

Facilitating Recovery from CSA

Therapy with CSA survivors involves more than just sharing their story. It also focuses on the significance of formal training and addresses various trauma symptoms like flashbacks, nightmares, and intrusive thoughts (Draucker & Martstolf, 2006). Emphasizing the significance of staying grounded and practical is just as crucial as discussing effective strategies. Moreover, prioritize the current process instead of dwelling on the unsettling and risky aspects of the recovery framework. The process of therapy involves addressing emotional challenges, such as managing fluctuating emotions and building resilience to intense feelings.

Not surprisingly, there can be long-term effects of CSA. Some symptoms among girls include a heightened level of distress, depression, anxiety, post-traumatic effects such as disturbing memories or dreams, low self-esteem, substance abuse, eating disorders, self-harm (cutting) and other risky behaviors, somatization such that their anxiety gets expressed physically (stomach pains), and a lower sense of self of overall health for their physical well being. For boys, there may be similar effects, but, in addition, we can also see the use of externalizing behaviors, such as conduct disorders and acting out of sexual behaviors. If not treated, those effects may never change, or worse, the victim may come to identify with the abuser and come to abuse other people, although studies have not provided data on rates for children under the age of 11 (Ellonen et al., 2022; Barrocas et al., 2012).

One of the difficulties faced by individuals who have experienced abuse is the struggle with engaging in self-destructive behaviors, like using a blade to harm oneself and causing bleeding. Reported rates of nonsuicidal self-injury, which refers to self-harm without the intention of suicide, range from approximately 7% to 24% in studies involving both early and older adolescents (Barrocas et al., 2012; Salamon, 2023). It is crucial to address strategies for ensuring safety. Similarly, the therapy room provides a space to address homicidal ideation, where individuals can work through their feelings of rage towards their offender and find ways to manage it (Draucker & Martstolf, 2006). Engaging in activities like running or other forms of physical activity can evoke intense feelings of anger and frustration, whereas yoga and other similar activities may help develop a more calm focus. Addressing addictions and compulsions is an important aspect of supporting individuals who have endured abuse. Assisting the survivor in understanding the factors that contributed to their behavior, rather than solely highlighting negative or risky actions, involves discussing strategies for self-care. When it comes to nutrition and exercise issues, it iscrucial to highlight the survivor's autonomy in managing their own body and life. Equally important are matters concerning relationships: letting go of the patterns of abuse and victimization and embracing a new understanding of what it entails to have a healthy and mutually supportive bond with another person(Draucker & Martstoff).

In recent interviews with adult male survivors (Poirson et al., 2023; Lilley et al., 2023), survivors have expressed feelings of "damage" to their sense of masculinity as well as a "dread of homosexuality." This last aspect can occur if the perpetrator is a cisgender male, and the victim experiences pleasure during the abusive episode. This experience can create inner conflict, typical of abuse survivors of any gender who experience pleasure that then is at odds with accompanying negative feelings. Blaming oneself is also ubiquitous for all abuse survivors. For example, a clinician might see their woman survivor client try to blame themselves for provoking the abuse. In contrast, a male survivor may blame themselves for not being "man enough" or strong enough to stop it.

These reactions may align with how a patient identifies, and if they apply to the traditional feminine or masculine roles, that can also express itself in how one is negotiating as an abuse survivor. Following experiences of trauma, women may be more likely to suppress anger and aggression and in turn have higher rates of depression, whereas men may experience their anger as literally their only emotional outlet. There might also be an endorsement of really rigid, even binary gender roles, leading cisgender women to express these roles through verbal aggression, victimization, or engaging with powerful men (Poirson et al., 2023; Lilley et al., 2023). In comparison, a therapist might see male clients attempt to regain control by enacting violence themselves, with more recent evidence showing people of all genders engaging in these responses.

Overall, the main objective of therapy is to assist the client who has experienced CSA in confronting and understanding the abuse and trauma they have experienced while allowing them to process the associated emotions and physical reactions at a pace that feels comfortable and secure. It is not always easy to predict the outcome, so it is important to establish a strong and trusting relationship, marked by patience and understanding. Cole and Barney (1987) discussed the concept of the therapeutic window, which they argue is marked by a balance of distress and manageable symptoms. According to Cole and Barney, the counselor's role is to carefully assess the survivors' capacity to handle their memories and emotions. The therapist should carefully monitor the level of intensity and duration to ensure it remains within manageable limits, as stated in the research. Many mental health providers who work extensively with trauma survivors often question their effectiveness due to the complex and unpredictable nature of the healing process. It is a process that does not follow a straight path. This process can also be a continuous cycle, with clients pushing themselves back and forth.

Intimate Partner and Domestic Violence: Understanding the Dynamics

The counselor's role does not stop at CSA within the lifespan of GBV. It can continue to other forms of GBV such as Intimate Partner Violence (IPV) and Domestic Violence (DV), both distinct terms with unique definitions. DV refers to acts of violence within a household involving any two individuals residing in that household. In contrast, IPV exclusively occurs between individuals engaged in a romantic relationship, regardless of whether they cohabitate (Moorer, 2021; McHugh, 2005). IPV has been shown to disproportionately affect young women, especially those between the ages of 18 and 24; recent research showed that 20–45% of women-identified high school students reported experiencing IPV (Klencakova et al., 2023), making this issue one not only of adults, but girls and younger women as well. In the most severe cases, IPV can tragically result in homicide, with a significant number of women and men murder victims being killed by their intimate partners. These homicides have a devastating impact, reaching beyond just the victims themselves. They can profoundly affect the lives of family members, friends, neighbors, and even those who respond to the scene or happen to be nearby.

Extreme figures show that in the U.S., more than 10 million adults experience DV/IPV annually, with more than three women a day murdered by their significant other and 1 in 7 men having experienced IPV at all (National Coalition against Domestic Violence [NCADV], n.d.). The analysis of homicide by gender reveals a significant and apparent gender discrepancy in terms of both the perpetrators and the victims of these crimes, with 81% of IPV killings were perpetrated by men (UNODC, 2019). Typically, men who hold negative attitudes toward women, adhere to traditional gender roles, believe in hierarchical obedience, and approve of domestic violence in relationships are more likely to engage in IPV.

IPV and Marginalized Populations

IPV occurs across all socioeconomic and cultural groups. Therefore, when discussing more specific statistics relating to IPV, it is essential to note that those from marginalized and vulnerable populations are more at risk of IPV than the general population. For example, Rollè, Giardina, Caldarera, Gerino, and Brustia (2018) revealed that 43.7% of lesbian women and 23% of gay men have reported experiencing IPV. The CDC (Smith et al., 2018) also reported that this increase in prevalence extended across racial-ethnic lines as well, with 34% of Latina individuals and 30% of Latino men experiencing IPV, 45% of Black women and 40% of Black men experiencing IPV, and 18% of Asian women and 14% of Asian men experiencing IPV. Tragically, Black women face a threefold higher risk of being fatally harmed by their abuser compared to other demographics. Transgender individuals, especially Black trans women, are also particularly vulnerable to intimate partner violence, with studies showing between 31% and 50% elevated risk. This highlights the urgent need for specific interventions in these communities.

While alarming, these statistics may still not present the full picture when considering other vulnerable populations. Wright and Benson (2010) explored the *immigrant paradox*, a concept initially suggesting that cultural differences and strong social networks among immigrants accounted for their lower violence rates. Wright and Benson found that neighborhoods with greater concentrations of immigrants had lower levels of intimate partner violence. Unfortunately, just because IPV are reported does not mean it is not occurring. Follow-up studies later have revealed that Asian and Latine immigrant women may experience increased vulnerability as a result of immigration stressors (Frieze & Chen, 2010).

Perpetrators can utilize cultural (Liu et al., 2023; Strong Hearts, 2024) or spiritual abuse (Purcell, 1998) by using their partner's beliefs against them to instill terror, prevent the victim from participating in cultural traditions, or otherwise belittle the victim's beliefs, practices or traditions. Similarly, these immigration-related circumstances can be exploited by an abuser to coerce and manipulate their partner (Alsinai et al., 2023). As previously mentioned, a victim's immigration status when experiencing DV is exacerbated by limited access to social services, risk of deportation, family separation, distrust of systems, and limited English proficiency, which is further compounded by systemic discrimination based on race, ethnicity, gender, and sexuality (Alsinai et al., 2023; Lee, 2007; Weber, 2010; Rogerson, 2012; Reina & Lohman, 2015; Villalon, 2015; Abraham & Tastsoglou, 2016; Messing et al., 2017).

Perilla, Bakeman, and Norris (1994) explored how cultural beliefs might play a role in underreporting IPV among certain immigrant ethnic groups. Immigrants, particularly women from societies with unequal gender dynamics, often bring unique perspectives on relationships when they come to the United States. Immigration can also sometimes lead to increased reliance on male partners due to limited access to employment and education opportunities (Bui & Morash, 2008). This dependence, along with limited resources, can result in a scenario where women are at a higher risk of experiencing IPV as they become increasingly isolated, creating challenges for them to escape from an physically abusive relationship or willful intimidation (Abraham, 2000; Huerta, 2014; Morales-Campos et al., 2009).

Covert IPV

Physical violence is only one element of IPV/DV, yet some of the easiest to see from an outside perspective since there can be visible signs (e.g., bruises, blood, broken bones). However, the invisible injuries are more obscure and can leave deeper scars. *Gaslighting* is a specific type of emotional abuse that involves simultaneous attempts to convince a person of something untrue while also suggesting that they are wrong, crazy, or not seeing things clearly (Abramson, 2014; Hightower, 2017; Shafir, 2023). Beyond normal persuasion, gaslighting is the intentional act of misleading someone and using manipulative or deceptive tactics to undermine their perception of reality. Over time in a relationship, gaslighting is usually a recurrent pattern of behavior aimed at breaking down a person's ability to criticize, question, or challenge the other person now and in the future. Another type of abuse, *reproductive coercion*, is acknowledged as a form of GBV in certain states, such as New York and involves exerting control over an individual's reproductive choices by pressuring them to become pregnant, coercing them to terminate a pregnancy, or interfering with their use of birth control. (Office for the Prevention of Domestic Violence, n.d.). If children are already involved, they may also fear the perpetrator and be subjected to coercion and threats, leading the victim to stay longer or even pit the children against the victim, often minimizing, denying, or blaming them (Myhill, 2017).

Lastly, there is *economic abuse* (Postmus et al., 2020), or the deliberate pattern of control in which individuals interfere with their partner's ability to acquire, use, and maintain economic resources. The National Domestic Violence Hotline on average receives over 19,000 calls a day with victims of IPV losing a total of 8 million days of paid work. This is the equivalent to 32,000 jobs, costing the US economy between 5.8 billion and 12.6 billion each year due to IPV (Joseph, 2022). The impact of IPV on individuals' economic situation is significant, as a considerable percentage of victims experience job loss as a result of the abuse. This affects their financial stability and their ability to maintain independence.

Although not exhaustive, this list of invisible IPV begins to paint the picture for the nuanced ways IPV is informed when considering GBV. This willful intimidation, which may occur simultaneously with physical assault, battery, sexual assault, stalking, and abusive behavior that is a part of a systemic pattern of power and control, is a widespread issue that impacts individuals from all walks of life, irrespective of their nationality, age, socio-economic status, sexual orientation, gender, race, or religion. Therefore, mental health professionals need to be aware of some of the more insidious aspects of the cycle of violence clients may find themselves in and effectively assess IPV during a session, and identify the risk factors and the level of risk in order to create an effective safety plan with the client if necessary.

Cycle of Abuse in IPV/DV

Psychologist Lenore E. Walker (1979, 1989) famously conducted the initial documentation of the four primary stages of IPV/DV towards the "battered woman syndrome," which she referred to as the cycle of abuse. This 4-part cycle included: (1) Tension Building, (2) Violent Incident, (3) Reconciliation, and (4) Calm. Most victims or clients will share with their therapists that the relationship did not start with abuse and will often make references to their partner's initial charm and the unexpected nature of eventual violence. These ruminations often lead to self-blaming patterns where the client does not understand the cycle of violence that has been perpetuated (Sangeetha et al., 2022). The cycle begins with an initial calm phase that feels like a "honeymoon," where the violence has not yet erupted. In time, the tension building phase occurs as slight irritation forms, and the victim can feel like they are walking on eggshells. The perpetrator may call the victim names in front of friends and family and make other slights, catching the victim off guard. These instances may initiate infrequently (i.e., once a year or once a month), but the frequency and intensity inevitably increase.

The next stage is the explosion/violence phase. This stage is often when physical abuse is most likely to occur. However, similar to the tension-building phase, it may not occur as frequently when initiating the relationship, roping in the victim even further. These eruptions often occur when the abuser senses a loss of power or control, when the victim may be bringing up specific grievances, during intoxication, or seemingly out of nowhere. The trigger at this point may not always be clear and is never the victim's fault.

Following the explosion/violence phase is the makeup phase or another calm "honeymoon." At this phase, the perpetrator may feel guilt about their actions and try to compensate by apologizing, showering the victim with affection, gifts, and promises that it will never happen again. They may also justify their explosion or violent behavior by saying that they grew up in an abusive home, blame intoxication, or blame their partner for making them upset. This cycle then continues over time, decreasing the size of the cycle until the abuse is a daily occurrence, causing the victim to feel again as though they are walking on eggshells, lacking self-confidence, and otherwise feeling defeated.

Therapist Role in IPV

Suppose a therapist finds themselves working with someone in this cycle. In that case, the therapist's role is to assess, support, and provide adequate safety planning when evaluating and working with clients who have experienced IPV (Walker, 1989). Just because the client has come to therapy does not mean they are ready to leave their relationship. It behooves the therapist to follow the language and terminology the client uses and try to avoid the word "abuse" unless they use it first (Bagley & Diambra, 2016). Explore what it feels like for them and ask them to describe what they notice or experience in their body. Therapists should ensure that it is explicitly clear that they do not judge whether the client stays or leaves their relationship. The cycle of leaving and returning to an abusive partner is an intricate process, as victims often find themselves going back to their abuser multiple times, typically around five to seven instances on average (Halket et al., 2014). This cycle emphasizes the deep psychological, emotional, and sometimes financial control that abusers exert over their victims, making it difficult for them to find safety and regain their independence.

When engaging with a client who may be experiencing intimate partner violence (IPV), a therapist can adopt a sensitive and nonjudgmental approach to explore the client's relationship dynamics and feelings of safety within their partnership (Bagley & Diambra, 2016). Initially, the therapist might start the conversation by asking how the client and their partner manage disagreements or conflicts, inquiring if the client has ever felt uneasy about their partner's reactions. Questions like "How do you and your partner handle disagreements?" (Basile et al., 2007, p. 55) and "Have there been moments when you felt apprehensive about bringing up certain topics due to concern over your partner's reaction?" can open up the dialogue. The therapist can also delve into the client's physical and emotional responses during conflicts, asking, "How does your body react when there is tension or disagreement?" This question can help uncover somatic and psychological stress signs (Bagley &

Diambra, 2016). Further probing about the client's concerns regarding their partner's temper or the extent of monitoring in the relationship, such as questioning the client's whereabouts or activities, can provide deeper insights into the control dynamics at play (Basile et al., 2007).

To explore more deeply, the therapist might ask if the client has ever felt threatened or diminished by their partner. Questions like, "Has your partner ever threatened harm, monitored your communications, or made you feel belittled or coerced?" are critical to understanding the severity of the situation. The therapist can ask about any instances where the client was made to feel "crazy" or threatened with significant losses, like custody of children, due to alleged instability (Basile et al., 2007). These inquiries should be made with the utmost care, ensuring the client feels heard, validated, and safe within the therapeutic space. This care facilitates an environment where clients can disclose and discuss their experiences without fear of judgment or retribution.

Building on the foundation of trust and understanding established through initial questions about the client's current relationship dynamics, the therapist can smoothly transition to explore the influence of the client's family of origin on their present interpersonal relationships. This exploration can offer valuable insights into learned behaviors and emotional responses. The therapist might ask, "How do you think the relationship between your parents has influenced your current relationships?" and "Growing up, how did your parents deal with conflict?" Such questions can help the client reflect on the patterns and coping mechanisms they have observed and possibly internalized from their parents, providing a broader context for their current relationship dynamics (Basile et al., 2007).

Further deepening the exploration, the therapist can encourage the client to envision more empowering responses in their current relationship. Asking "How do you wish you could respond in situations of conflict?" and "What do you wish you could say to your partner during these moments?" can empower the client to identify and articulate their needs and desires that may have been suppressed (Bray, 2019). This reflective exercise fosters the client's self-awareness and promotes a sense of agency in navigating their relationship. To further enhance the client's sense of empowerment and self-expression, the therapist could introduce a creative and introspective activity: "I would like you to draw a picture of yourself feeling empowered." This exercise can be a powerful tool for the client to visualize and embody their strength and resilience, offering a tangible representation of their inner resources and desired state of being (Murray et al., 2017). Through this holistic approach, the therapist addresses the immediate concerns related to IPV and nurtures the client's broader emotional and psychological healing journey.

Lastly, it is imperative to check for nonverbal cues when asking these sensitive questions or when conducting assessments such as the Danger Assessment which also includes women in same-sex relationships (Campbell, 2019; Glass & Cambell, 2007), or the HITS (hurt, insult, threaten, scream) screen (Punukollu, 2003), among other tools (Basile et al., 2007; Northcott, 2012).

Safety Planning and Reducing Risk

Understanding the complex web of factors that may prevent individuals from leaving abusive relationships is crucial for clinicians. These factors vary widely, from financial dependencies and immigration status to profoundly ingrained fear. Clinicians must ensure they refrain from passing judgment or imposing our expectations on patients. Instead, therapists can focus on empowering and providing support as clients navigate their unique situations. Counselors can assist patients in recognizing and evaluating patterns of abuse, enabling them to identify early indications of escalation. Teaching strategies like "fawning," or attempting to appease whoever is causing the danger to prevent harm, can serve as a short-term safety measure in the face of a threat (Withers, 2021). It is important to consider practical safety tips, such as avoiding potentially dangerous accessories like scarves and being mindful of the location of weapons in the home. Introducing the "gray rock" technique can also be helpful, where the goal is to remain emotionally non-reactive and uninteresting to the abuser, reducing engagement and potential escalation (Villines, 2023).

Assisting patients in meticulous safety planning is also vital since victims are at the highest risk and danger when they decide to leave their partner. When clients are ready, clinicians can support patients in preparing their exit strategy, ensuring they have a detailed safety plan. The plan can assist in preparing the client, their surroundings, and, if applicable, their children before violence happens, what to do during a violent episode, and what to do after can provide a structured approach (Tracy, 2021; Women's Law, 2023). Many victims of IPV/DV may need to go into "hiding" or to move out of state for their safety. This planning also involves assessing the abuser's access to weapons and any connections they may have with law enforcement or military personnel. This safety planning should be thoughtful and customized to the patient's circumstances, acknowledging that their readiness to leave may change.

Explaining the concept of a restraining order (RO) or order of protection (OOP) to a patient is important as a legal measure provided by the court to enhance the victim's safety (Kippert & Thurrott, 2022). As mandated reporters, clinicians must be informed about the laws in their jurisdiction and the process of obtaining such orders (Hyman, 1997). It is important to emphasize that while restraining orders can provide protection, their effectiveness can vary, with 33–70% of victims who file an RO/OOP not being further violated.

Although domestic violence shelters provide a vital sanctuary for survivors, the environment within these shelters can present difficulties. Usually organized as spacious living spaces with communal amenities, they offer a temporary sanctuary. Nevertheless, residents frequently encounter major disruptions, including the need to interrupt their children's education, quit their jobs, and sever social ties in order to maintain secrecy and safety. Clients must be well-informed about the resources (Office on Women's Health, 2021) and the implications of seeking shelter to ensure their safety planning process is thorough.

As we navigate issues related to IPV/DV and GBV, it is important to tie in how these issues are informed in more modern times and what implicit messages are received. We turn next to women, and more specifically women of color, who have spearheaded new waves of support with the #MeToo movement.

#MeToo Movement and Sexual Harassment

The #MeToo movement emerged as a significant moment in the battle against gender-based violence, highlighting not only child sexual abuse and intimate partner violence but also sexual harassment within workplace settings. Legal frameworks, like the guidelines set by the Equal Employment Opportunity Commission (EEOC), state that *sexual harassment* encompasses a wide range of behaviors, including unwanted sexual advances, requests for sexual favors, and other forms of verbal or physical harassment that are sexual in both the workplace and educational settings, as well as the creation of a hostile environment (RAINN, n.d.). Sexual harassment is against the law, regardless of its impact on the victim's job or financial situation, highlighting the significance of the unwelcome nature of the harasser's behavior. The *#MeToo movement* is a third wave feminist movement begun formally in 2006, as coined by activist Tarana Burkey, which achieved global prominence in 2017 initially through social media, and then through legal procedures (Brown, 2022). At that time actor Alyssa Milano urged individuals to share their experiences of sexual harassment online, after which millions did, leading to the firing of hundreds of high profile, powerful men across a swath of settings, including sports, entertainment, food industries, religious institutions, the military, science, medicine, education, government, law, and journalism. The latest incursion has been through artificial intelligence, in which mostly young women, including children and adolescents in school settings, have been targeted regarding near-exact explicit images being distributed broadly within local communities and beyond; perpetrators have ranged from boys in the same school to strangers attempting to extort funds from these individuals and their families (Satter, 2023).

Although much focus of research and interventions typically center on men perpetrators/women victims, sexual harassment can occur between individuals of any gender, challenging the notion that it is limited to interactions between heterosexual individuals. The harasser could potentially be someone in a position of authority over the victim, a colleague, or even someone outside of the organization, showing different ways power can be misused. This movement goes beyond geographical and professional boundaries, indicating the widespread nature of sexual misconduct in various organizations and fields.

Typically, individuals who have experienced harassment are advised to clearly communicate their boundaries to the person responsible, making it known that the behavior is unwelcome and should stop (EEOC, n.d.). It is also recommended that they take advantage of any complaint mechanisms or grievance systems provided by their employer. Unwelcome sexual advances, requests for sexual favors, and other verbal or physical conduct of a sexual nature constitute sexual harassment when this conduct explicitly or implicitly affects an individual's employment, unreasonably interferes with an individual's work performance, or creates an intimidating, hostile, or offensive work environment. However, harassers can come from various positions, including supervisors, co-workers, or individuals who are not employed by the organization and come with varying levels of power making it more difficult for victims to come forward, indicating a deeper systemic problem.

An illustrative instance of this systemic problem was the scandal within USA Gymnastics, as reported by the New York Times (2018). Some gymnasts have bravely spoken out, revealing that the team doctor convicted of sexual misconduct, Dr. Larry Nassar's abhorrent actions with his patients were not isolated occurrences. Instead they were a reflection of a deeper, systemic issue within the sport, particularly in light of three more coaches who were accused of sexually abusing young gymnasts as well. The recent overturning of Harvey Weinstein's 2020 rape conviction in New York may appear to be a setback, but it only serves to strengthen the #MeToo movement's resolve and ongoing significance, said Tarana Burke (Davis, 2024). She saw this legal decision as a call to action and vigilance in the fight against sexual violence rather than a defeat. A recent opinion column by the New York prosecutor, Cyrus Vance (2024), pointed to the need for states to update their laws to allow evidence from previous sex crimes in court proceedings in order to establish a pattern of predatory behavior (as California currently has).

Despite legal challenges, the #MeToo movement's impact has not diminished, and it continues to inspire those fighting for a world free of sexual violence. Individuals like Burke, as well as supporters all over the world, remain engaged and determined to change not only the legal landscape but also societal attitudes toward sexual assault and harassment. The path to reform has been long and fraught with setbacks, but the #MeToo movement has a solid foundation driven by a community dedicated to justice and equality. Today more Americans support the movement than do not (Brown, 2022); as a young male participant observed: "Because we should all be free of sexual assault and harassment at work, and men in power should not be able to abuse those below them." This sustained effort demonstrates the movement's resilience and the hope that remains for survivors everywhere, advocating not only for momentary victories in high-profile cases but for long-term change that uplifts and heals.

Men and Gender-Based Violence

As we have described in this book, it is common for men, even those who do not engage in violence, to experience societal expectations that discourage them from expressing sensitivity or empathy. This expectation can perpetuate the false belief that masculinity and feminism are mutually exclusive (Precopio & Ramsey, 2017). This societal perspective often portrays nonviolence and gender equality as unmasculine, which can lead to boys and men becoming desensitized to the effects of violence in order to conform with others. Traditional male socialization also reinforces the notion that violence against women is only a concern for women rather than a problem that all people, including men, should address (Porter, 2016). The broader society's acceptance of male violence contributes to the downplaying of various harmful behaviors (Flood, 2015). Common phrases such as "boys will be boys" or "it is just locker room talk" normalize harmful actions instead of questioning or changing them. *Rape culture* is a clear illustration of this issue, where the sexual violence perpetrated by men is frequently disregarded or even glorified within certain male social circles (Barnett et al., 2018; Cole et al., 2020). The emphasis on conforming to societal expectations of masculinity can impede the growth of understanding individuals (Kimmel, 2018), especially when children are encouraged to suppress their nurturing instincts to reinforce damaging power dynamics. This socialization further harms boys and young men, since they too are commonly victims of sexual violence and other forms of GBV, and may not feel comfortable asking for help as a result of their socialization. To illustrate how pervasive GBV is among men victims, research indicates that 1 in 6 boys under 10 may be targets of CSA (Prevent Child Abuse of America, n.d.) and 1 in 9 men may experience sexual violence, physical violence and/or stalking by an intimate partner during their lifetime with 'IPV-related impact' such as being concerned for their safety, PTSD symptoms, injury, or needing victim services (NCADV, n.d.).

Fostering empathy through relationships is crucial (Jordan, 2017). Moreover, it is essential to address the connection between the socialized lack of empathy and the rise in GBV. This highlights the urgent requirement for fresh narratives that encourage compassion and empower boys and men to overcome cycles of violence and inequality. Men in positions of social, economic, and political influence must recognize this significance (Connell, 2005). Boys and men can develop a deeper understanding of power dynamics by fostering inclusive relationships that empower them to value diversity and actively choose to treat others with respect and dignity. These connections foster a sense of empathy, understanding, and social involvement (Adams & Frauenheim, 2020), involving men in challenging dominant forms of masculinity and reducing their impact (Di Bianca & Mahalik, 2022).

There is a pressing need to create and sustain programs that involve men in the fight against violence toward women and gender minorities (Brush & Miller, 2019; Dworkin & Barker, 2019). Nevertheless, despite the success of specific interventions in dispelling rape culture myths, there has not been a significant decrease in the occurrence of sexual assault within college environments (Wright et al., 2020). Prevention efforts are most effective when they go beyond just individual nonviolence. Boys and men need to come together and recognize their shared responsibility in stopping violence through actively listening to and learning from victims' experiences and holding their peers accountable for any harmful actions they may take (Flood, 2015; Porter, 2016). It is crucial to establish environments where men can engage in critical analysis and questioning of the societal expectations surrounding masculinity, especially those that promote sexual conquest, objectification, and aggression. In these settings, mentors and group facilitators have a crucial role to play. They can teach and embody nonviolent, feminist values in a way that empowers others. By doing so, they show how to positively influence men in their social circles (Bianca & Mahalik, 2022).

TGNC People and Gender-Based Violence

Gender-based violence against people of other genders, particularly those in the TGNC community, has received little attention in the field (Wirtz et al., 2020). Traditional definitions of gender-based violence frequently exclude an intersectional perspective that focuses on the unique needs of TGNC people who have survived GBV (Khanlou et al., 2022). According to a recent report, affirming services for TGNC people are sadly lacking throughout much of the U.S., except for large urban areas or university-based communities; barriers for care that were cited included: previous negative experiences with providers; fears of not being believed or shamed; being denied access to services based on gender identity; unavailability of TGNC oriented gender-based violence services; poorly informed systemic responses by law enforcement, and consequent distrust in the criminal and civil legal system; and fears of revictimization and further isolation (New York State Office for the Prevention of Domestic Violence, 2023).

Wirtz et al. (2020) described how various forms of GBV are relevant for TGNC people over their lives, including gender identity formation, transition and expression, as in the consequences of disclosure to family members and friends that may lead to physical violence as well as homelessness and unemployment, if the individual is forced to leave. Once outside one's family of origin, a TGNC person may then be exposed to any number of risky and potentially violent situations as they move to establish their own independent lives. IPV issues can also be a part of a TGNC person's experience, as this is estimated to affect about 1/3 of TGNC individuals. The term *trans panic* has been used to describe transphobic reactions of some partners and others in their violent response upon learning that a person is TGNC; this has been used as a legal defense, sometimes successfully (Wirtz et al., 2020). Other forms of GBV can include situations where a partner threatens to disclose identity information to employers. Conversely, some TGNC survivors may hesitate to call authorities or seek help due to fears of disclosure. Structural forms of GBV are quite pervasive and insidious, beginning with legal and public policy concerns that either deny or criminalize TGNC realities. They also may be targeted by authorities, or simply ignored by social services agencies. On a broader level, the multitude of anti-TGNC laws and policies of late create a general feeling of violation for many TGNC people.

Suggestions for providing assistance, support and advocacy for TGNC communities have recently been suggested by a number of scholars, for example, Burgess, Klemmer, Martin, and Srivastava (2021) who urged that anti-violence programs begin from childhood and youth, including teacher and peer programming addressing anti-bullying interventions, along with clear policies prohibiting such bullying. They also describe macro-level strategies aimed at changing laws and policies to be better informed and more accepting of TGNC people. Others (e.g., Singh & dickey, 2017) outlined general gender-affirmative strategies that could be used as a framework for treating survivors of GBV. Given the disproportionate numbers of TGNC individuals who have been targets of GBV, specific treatment guidelines for this diverse population are greatly needed.

Therapists and Vicarious Trauma

As a clinician it is important to remember that GBV stories are with real people and can affect themselves deeply. *Vicarious traumatization* (VT), as outlined by Pearlman and Saakvitne (1995), encapsulates the profound negative impact that arises from a therapist's deep empathetic engagement with their clients' traumatic experiences. This type of trauma induces a gradual but fundamental change in the therapist's inner world, affecting their meanings, beliefs, and schemas, and can even provoke imagery intrusions and sensory reactions, a phenomenon similar to emotional contagion (Hatfield et al., 1994). Unlike burnout, which is characterized by exhaustion, depersonalization, and reduced personal efficacy due to ongoing job-related stress, VT specifically alters the therapist's sense of self and worldview, potentially influencing their countertransference responses. Additionally, Secondary Traumatic Stress (STS) or Compassion Fatigue (CF) refer to the negative reactions experienced by those assisting trauma survivors, often mentioned in discussions alongside VT, yet with distinct nuances in their definitions and implications (Figley, 1995; Meichenbaum, 2007, p. 3).

It is important for a therapist to listen to their discomfort and triggers when working with victims of CSA, IPV, and SH and even transfer if necessary with this tough work, seeking any additional emotional support as needed (Figley, 1995; Meichenbaum, 2007). Trauma work is not for every therapist, and it is important for counselors to be mindful about managing VT, rather than avoiding it or worse, have the client begin to take care of the therapist. Useful tools are available that can help assess one's own quality of life and compassion fatigue with this work. One example is the Professional Quality of Life Scale (PROQOL) which assesses current work situations and potential experiences with compassion fatigue (Hudnall Stamm, 2009). Self-compassion, self-soothing and letting go of what is not personally applicable also are pertinent.

Many individuals who seek counseling have likely experienced GBV at some point in their lives and can appear in the offices of professionals who do not specialize in this area. To be sure, many clients seek counseling for other reasons, and then eventually their abuse history may come out, as is ideal for their healthy development. Therefore, we urge clinicians in the counseling profession to get formal training to professionally prepare for these individuals.

Conclusion

As we described here, it is clear that GBV is a widespread problem that affects people from all walks of life and is not limited to any particular gender, race, culture, social class, or economic status. In order to combat this worldwide epidemic, it is essential to raise awareness, educate the public, and establish comprehensive support systems. The many forms of gender-based violence, such as sexual harassment, intimate partner violence, and child sexual abuse, emphasize the critical importance of doing so. Even though the numbers are alarming, they show how much of an effect GBV has on people's lives, their families, and entire communities. Tackling GBV requires a multipronged strategy given its complexity, from the subtleties of personal experiences to the wider societal structures and consequences. An effective approach incorporates personal, social, cultural, and legal factors at once, prioritizes the empowerment of victims, the accountability of offenders, and the promotion of an equal and respectful society. Progress towards safer and more equitable environments for all individuals, regardless of their gender, is possible, despite the challenges that lie ahead in the journey to eradicate GBV if mental health professionals, lawmakers, and community stakeholders work together. In addition to illuminating the harsh facts of GBV, this chapter acts as a rallying cry, encouraging us to resolve to fight this deep-seated social problem through unwavering dedication to learning, advocacy, and support.

Case Study

Peggy, a 48 year old White American cisgender woman living in Denver, CO, has experienced domestic violence from her husband, Rick, for 28 years. She entered therapy for the first time as a result of a particularly difficult month consisting of financial abuse and physical harassment. She reports that she has never had a job as she married when she was young and depended financially on her husband. Additionally, she shares experiences where he will physically intimidate her, grab her wrists, and push her; the physical abuse has escalated to unidirectional hitting, but not for several years. Peggy says that she has no prospects of leaving him and feels no hope about the relationship improving and instead wants to "improve her mindset" about the seeming inevitabilities of her life. When prompted, she understands that gender plays a role in the relationship, but is unaware as to how, or what to do with that information. Her primary concern is managing feelings of "emptiness" and trying to connect with her two children, who do not contact her as much as she would like.

Discussion Questions

1. How do Peggy's experiences show typical patterns of domestic violence, especially when it comes to harassment and financial abuse? Discuss how long-term abuse affects a victim's mental health and how they see themselves.
2. Peggy knows that gender affects her relationship but does not know what that means. What are some ways that gender can play a role in the fact that Peggy is still experiencing domestic violence? How can therapists help clients like Peggy understand and deal with these issues?
3. Peggy has said that she feels trapped in her abusive marriage and has no plans to leave. What are some common psychological, social, and financial problems that people who are abused run into when they try to leave an abusive partner? How can these problems be addressed in therapy?
4. What can be done to use the #MeToo movement to help survivors like Peggy who may feel alone and hopeless, given how it has changed how people think about abuse and harassment?
5. What are effective therapeutic strategies for treating survivors of long-term domestic violence who do not see leaving as an option? Talk about giving clients the power to make decisions while respecting their choices.
6. Peggy wants to get back in touch with her kids, who have grown apart. In what ways can therapists help their clients deal with dysfunctional or abusive family relationships caused by domestic violence? What should be considered when considering the kids' experiences and points of view?
7. What does this case mean for social policy and advocacy? What changes could be made to social policy to protect clients like Peggy better and to give power to victims of domestic violence? How can people who work in mental health advocate for these changes?

References

Abraham, M. (2000). Isolation as a form of marital violence: The South Asian immigrant experience. *Journal of Social Distress & the Homeless, 9*(3), 221–236. https://doi-org.ezproxy.cul.columbia.edu/10.1023/A:1009460002177

Abraham, M., & Tastsoglou, E. (2016). Addressing domestic violence in Canada and the United States: The uneasy co-habitation of women and the state. *Current Sociology, 64*, 568–585. https://doi.org/10.1177/0011392116639221

Abramowitz, S., & Moran, M. H. (2012). International human rights, gender-based violence, and local discourses of abuse in postconflict Liberia: A problem of "culture"? *African Studies Review, 55*(2), 119–146. http://www.jstor.org/stable/43904825

Abramson, K. (2014). Turning up the lights on gaslighting. *Philosophical Perspectives, 28*(1), 1–30. https://doi.org/10.1111/phpe.1204

Adams, E. M., & Frauenheim, E. (2020). *Reinventing masculinity: The liberating power of compassion and connection*. Berrett-Koehler Publishers.

Allen, J. A., Allinson, H. E., Clark-Huckstep, A., Hill, B. J., Sanders, S. A., & Zhou, L. H. (2017). *The Kinsey Institute: The first seventy years*. Indiana University Press.

Alsinai, A., Reygers, M., DiMascolo, L., Kafka, J., Rowhani-Rahbar, A., Adhia, A., Bowen, D., Shanahan, S., Dalve, K., & Ellyson, A. M. (2023). Use of immigration status for coercive control in domestic violence protection orders. *Frontiers in Sociology, 8*, 1146102. https://doi.org/10.3389/fsoc.2023.1146102

Bagley, B., & Diambra, J. (2016, August 26). Counseling survivors of sexual assault. *Counseling Today*. Retrieved from https://ctarchive.counseling.org/2016/08/counseling-survivors-sexual-assault/.

Barnett, M. D., Sligar, K. B., & Wang, C. D. C. (2018). Religious affiliation, religiosity, gender, and rape myth acceptance: Feminist theory and rape culture. *Journal of Interpersonal Violence, 33*(8), 1219–1235. https://doi.org/10.1177/0886260516665110

Barrocas, A. L., Hankin, B. L., Young, J. F., & Abela, J. R. Z. (2012). Rates of nonsuicidal self-injury in youth: Age, sex, and behavioral methods in a community sample. *Pediatrics, 130*(1), 39–45. https://doi.org/10.1542/peds.2011-2094

Basile, K. C., Hertz, M. F., & Black, S. E. (2007). *Intimate partner violence and sexual violence victimization assessment instruments for use in healthcare settings* (Version 1). Centers for Disease Control and Prevention, National Center for Injury Prevention and Control. https://stacks.cdc.gov/view/cdc/44660

Bray, B. (2019, June). Addressing intimate partner violence with clients. *Counseling Today*. https://www.counseling.org/publications/counseling-today-magazine/article-archive/article/legacy/addressing-intimate-partner-violence-with-clients

Breiding, M., Basile, K. C., Smith, S. G., Black, M. C., & Mahendra, R. R. (2015). *Intimate partner violence surveillance: Uniform definitions and recommended data elements*. (Version 2.0.). National Center for Injury Prevention and Control, Centers for Disease Control and Prevention. https://stacks.cdc.gov/view/cdc/31292

Brown, A. (2022, September). *More than twice as many Americans support than oppose the #MeToo movement.* Pew Research Center. https://www.pewresearch.org/social-trends/2022/09/29/more-than-twice-as-many-americans-support-than-oppose-the-metoo-movement/

Brush, L. D., & Miller, E. (2019). Trouble in paradigm: "gender transformative" programming in violence prevention. *Violence Against Women, 25*(14), 1635–1656. https://doi-org.ezproxy.cul.columbia.edu/10.1177/1077801219872551

Bui, H., & Morash, M. (2008). Immigration, masculinity, and intimate partner violence from the standpoint of domestic violence service providers and Vietnamese-origin women. *Feminist Criminology, 3*, 191–215. https://doi.org/10.1177/1557085108321500

Bulut, S. (2019). Freud's approach to trauma. *Psychology and Psychotherapy Research Study, 3*(1). https://doi.org/10.31031/PPRS.2019.03.000554

Burgess, C., Klemmer, C. L., Martin, M., & Srivastava, A. (2021). Violence against sexual and gender minority youth: Social interventions of the twenty-first century. In E. M. Lund, C. Burgess, & A. J. Johnson (Eds.), *Violence against LGBTQ+ persons*. Springer. https://doi.org/10.1007/978-3-030-52612-2_5

Campbell, J. C. (2019). *Danger assessment.* https://www.dangerassessment.org/uploads/DA_NewScoring_2019.pdf

Cole, C. H., & Barney, E. E. (1987). Safeguards and the therapeutic window: A group treatment strategy for adult incest survivors. *The American Journal of Orthopsychiatry, 57*(4), 601–609.

Cole, B. P., Brennan, M., Tyler, E., & Willard, R. (2020). Predicting men's acceptance of sexual violence myths through conformity to masculine norms, sexism, and "locker room talk". *Psychology of Men & Masculinities, 21*(4), 508–517. https://doi.org/10.1037/men0000248

Connell, R. W. (2005). *Masculinities*. Polity.

Davis, A. (2024, April). MeToo founder Tarana Burke defiant after Harvey Weinstein ruling. *BBC*. https://www.bbc.com/news/world-us-canada-68904229.

Di Bianca, M., & Mahalik, J. R. (2022). A relational-cultural framework for promoting healthy masculinities. *American Psychologist, 77*(3), 321–332. https://doi-org.ezproxy.cul.columbia.edu/10.1037/amp0000929

Draucker, C., & Martsolf, D. S. (2006). *Counseling survivors of childhood sexual abuse*. Sage. https://doi.org/10.4135/9781446213681

Draucker, C. B., & Martsolf, D. S. (2008). Storying childhood sexual abuse. *Qualitative Health Research, 18*(8), 1034–1048. https://doi.org/10.1177/1049732308319925

Dworkin, S. L., & Barker, G. (2019). Gender-transformative approaches to engaging men in reducing gender-based violence: A response to Brush & Miller's "trouble in paradigm". *Violence Against Women, 25*(14), 1657–1671. https://doi.org/10.1177/1077801219872555

Ellonen, N., Horselenberg, R., Izura, C., Laajasalo, T., Wager, N. M., & (Eds.). (2022). *Child sexual abuse: Empirical research on understanding and helping victims and offenders*. Frontiers Media SA. https://doi.org/10.3389/978-2-88974-655-2

Equal Employment Opportunity Commission. (n.d.). *Sexual harassment*. https://www.eeoc.gov/sexual-harassment

Figley, C. R. (Ed.). (1995). Compassion fatigue: Coping with secondary traumatic stress disorder in those who treat the traumatized. Brunner/Mazel.

Flood, M. (2015). Work with men to end violence against women: A critical stocktake. *Culture, Health & Sexuality, 17*(Suppl 2), S159–S176. https://doi.org/10.1080/13691058.2015.1070435

Frieze, I. H., & Chen, K. Y. (2010). Intimate partner violence: Perspectives from racial/ethnic groups in the United States. In H. Landrine & N. F. Russo (Eds.), *Handbook of diversity in feminist psychology* (pp. 427–447). Springer.

Gewirtz-Meydan, A., & Finkelhor, D. (2020). Sexual abuse and assault in a large national sample of children and adolescents. *Child Maltreatment, 25*(2), 203–214. https://doi.org/10.1177/1077559519873975

Glass, N., & Campbell, J. C. (2007). *Danger Assessment-Revised for use in abusive female same-sex relationships*. Johns Hopkins University, School of Nursing. https://vawnet.org/material/danger-assessment-revised-use-abusive-female-same-sex-relationships-da-r.

Halket, M. M., Gormley, K., Mello, N., et al. (2014). Stay with or leave the abuser? The effects of domestic violence victim's decision on attributions made by young adults. *Journal of Family Violence, 29*(1), 35–49. https://doi.org/10.1007/s10896-013-9555-4

Hatfield, E., Cacioppo, J. T., & Rapson, R. L. (1994). *Emotional contagion*. Cambridge University Press.

Hightower, E. (2017). *An exploratory study of personality factors related to psychological abuse and gaslighting*. Doctoral dissertation, William James College. ProQuest. https://www.proquest.com/openview/0c6d2066bc1732bdd632be2194fad496/

Hudnall Stamm, B. (2009). *Professional Quality of Life: Compassion Satisfaction and Fatigue Version 5 (ProQOL)*. https://www.proqol.org

Huerta, D. I. (2014). Family related attitudes and beliefs influencing risk and support seeking among female victims of domestic and sexual violence in El Paso, Texas. Doctoral dissertation, University of Texas, El Paso. Texas ETD Collection for University of Texas, El Paso. http://digitalcommons.utep.edu/dissertations/AAI1583921

Hyman, A. (1997, November). Mandatory reporting of domestic violence by health care providers*: A policy paper.* Family Violence Prevention Fund. https://www.futureswithoutviolence.org/userfiles/file/HealthCare/mandatory_policypaper.pdf.

Jensen, E. (2021, May). "The me you can't see": Oprah talks about being molested as a child, breaks down in tears. *USA TODAY*. https://www.usatoday.com/story/entertainment/tv/2021/05/21/oprah-the-me-you-cant-see-talks-rape-and-trauma/5186682001/

Jordan, J. V. (2017). *Relational–cultural therapy* (2nd ed.). American Psychological Association.

Joseph, D'Andrea. (2022, October). *Understanding intimate partner violence: How to break the cycle*. Bulletin of the American College of Surgeons, 107(10). https://www.facs.org/for-medical-professionals/news-publications/news-and-articles/bulletin/2022/october-2022-volume-107-issue-10/understanding-intimate-partner-violence-how-to-break-the-cycle

Khanlou, N., Vazquez, L. M., Pashang, S., Connolly, J. A., Ahmad, F., & Ssawe, A. (2022). 2020 syndemic: Convergence of COVID-19, gender-based violence, and racism pandemics.

Journal of Racial and Ethnic Health Disparities, 9(6), 2077–2089. https://doi.org/10.1007/s40615-021-01146-w

Kimmel, M. (2018). Masculinity and our common humanity: "Real" men versus "good" men. In N. Way, C. Gilligan, P. Noguera, & A. Ali (Eds.), *The crisis of connection: Roots, consequences, and solutions* (pp. 173–187). New York University Press.

Kinsey, A. C., Pomeroy, W. B., Martin, C. E., & Gebhard, P. H. (1981). *Sexual behavior in the human female*. Indiana University Press.

Kippert, A., & Thurrott, S. (2022, July). *A guide to restraining orders: A comprehensive guide for survivors of domestic violence on getting an order of protection.* Domestic Shelters. https://www.domesticshelters.org/articles/legal/a-guide-to-restraining-orders

Klencakova, L. E., Pentaraki, M., & McManus, C. (2023). The impact of intimate partner violence on young women's educational well-being: A systematic review of literature. *Trauma, Violence & Abuse, 24*(2), 1172–1187. https://doi.org/10.1177/15248380211052244

Lanham, M., Ridgeway, K., Dayton, R., Castillo, B. M., Brennan, C., Davis, D. A., Emmanuel, D., Morales, G. J., Cheririser, C., Rodriguez, B., Cooke, J., Santi, K., & Evens, E. (2019). "We're going to leave you for last, because of how you are": Transgender women's experiences of gender-based violence in healthcare, education, and police encounters in Latin America and the Caribbean. *Violence and Gender, 6*(1), 37–46. https://doi.org/10.1089/vio.2018.0015

Lee, E. (2007). Domestic violence and risk factors among Korean immigrant women in the United States. *Journal of Family Violence, 22*, 141–149. https://doi.org/10.1007/s10896-007-9063-5

Lever, H., Baranowski, K. A., Ottenheimer, D., Atkinson, H. G., & Singer, E. K. (2022). Histories of pervasive gender-based violence in asylum-seeking women who have undergone female genital mutilation or cutting. *Journal of Traumatic Stress*, 1–13. https://doi.org/10.1002/jts.22791

Lilley, C., Willmott, D., Mojtahedi, D., & Labhardt, D. (2023). Intimate partner rape: A review of six core myths surrounding women's conduct and the consequences of intimate partner rape. *Social Sciences, 12*, 34. https://doi.org/10.3390/socsci12010034

Liu, K. J., Cook, A. N., & Jiang, R. (2023). Lessons from Canadian judgments: The consideration of culture in intimate partner violence legal cases involving Asian Canadians. *Journal of Interpersonal Violence, 38*(19–20), 11046–11066. https://doi.org/10.1177/08862605231178494

Lucchesi, A. (2018, November). *Murdered and missing Indigenous women and girls*. Urban Indian Health Institute. https://www.uihi.org/wp-content/uploads/2018/11/Missing-and-Murdered-Indigenous-Women-and-Girls-Report.pdf.

McHugh, M. C. (2005). Understanding gender and intimate partner abuse. *Sex Roles, 52*, 717–727. https://doi.org/10.1007/s11199-005-4194-8

McLean, I. A., Balding, V., & White, C. (2005). Further aspects of male-on-male rape and sexual assault in greater Manchester. *Medicine, Science and the Law, 45*(3), 225–232. https://doi.org/10.1258/rsmmsl.45.3.225

Meichenbaum, D. (2007). Self-care for trauma psychotherapists and caregivers: Individual, social and organizational interventions. *11th Annual Conference of the Melissa Institute for Violence Prevention and Treatment of Victims of Violence*, Miami. https://melissainstitute.org/

Messing, J. T., Vega, S., & Durfee, A. (2017). Protection order use among Latina survivors of intimate partner violence. *Feminist Criminology, 12*, 199–223. https://doi.org/10.1177/1557085116678924

Moorer. (2021). What is intimate partner domestic violence? [Webpage]. *YWCA Spokane*. https://ywcaspokane.org/what-is-intimate-partner-domestic-violence/#:~:text=Domestic%20Violence%20(DV)%20can%20occur,Partner%20Domestic%20Violence%20(IPDV)

Morales-Campos, D. Y., Casillas, M., & McCurdy, S. A. (2009). From isolation to connection: Understanding a support group for Hispanic women living with gender-based violence in Houston, Texas. *Journal of Immigrant and Minority Health, 11*, 57–65.

Murray, C. E., Moore, K., Stickl, J., & Crowe, A. (2017). See the Triumph Healing Arts workshops for survivors of intimate partner violence and sexual assault. *Journal of Creativity in Mental Health, 12*(2), 192–202. https://doi.org/10.1080/15401383.2016.1238791

Myhill, A. (2017). Measuring domestic violence: Context is everything. *Journal of Gender-Based Violence, 1*(1), 33–44. https://doi.org/10.1332/239868017X14896674831496

National Coalition Against Domestic Violence (NCADV). (n.d.). *Statistics*. Retrieved from https://ncadv.org/STATISTICS

New York City Anti-Violence Project & New York State Office for the Prevention of Domestic Violence. (2023, March). *The need for LGBTQI+-affirming gender-based violence services*. https://opdv.ny.gov/system/files/documents/2023/03/lgbtqi-ep-white-paper-3.23.pdf

New York State Office for the Prevention of Domestic Violence. (n.d.). *About gender-based violence*. https://opdv.ny.gov/about-gender-based-violence

New York Times. (2018). *Inside a 'culture of abuse' at U.S.A. Gymnastics* [Video]. YouTube. https://www.youtube.com/watch?v=mABPTdeFWLU

Northcott, M. (2012). *Intimate partner violence risk assessment tools: A review*. Department of Justice, Canada. https://www.justice.gc.ca/eng/rp-pr/cj-jp/fv-vf/rr12_8/rr12_8.pdf

Office on Women's Health. (2021). *Resources by state on violence against women*. Office of the Assistant Secretary for Health. https://www.womenshealth.gov/relationships-and-safety/get-help/state-resources#MA.

Pearlman, L. A., & Saakvitne, K. (1995). *Trauma and the therapist: Countertransference and vicarious traumatization in psychotherapy with incest survivors*. W. W. Norton.

Perilla, J., Bakeman, R., & Norris, F. H. (1994). Culture and domestic violence: The ecology of abused Latinas. *Violence and Victims, 9*, 325–339.

Poirson, L., Robin, M., Shadili, G., Lamothe, J., Corruble, E., Gressier, F., & Essadek, A. (2023). Male victims of sexual abuse: Impact and resilience processes, a qualitative study. *Healthcare (Basel, Switzerland), 11*(13), 1868. https://doi.org/10.3390/healthcare11131868

Porter, T. (2016). Breaking out of the "man box": The next generation of manhood. *Skyhorse*.

Postmus, J. L., Hoge, G. L., Breckenridge, J., Sharp-Jeffs, N., & Chung, D. (2020). Economic abuse as an invisible form of domestic violence: A multicountry review. *Trauma, Violence, & Abuse, 21*(2), 261–283. https://doi.org/10.1177/1524838018764160

Precopio, R. F., & Ramsey, L. R. (2017). Dude looks like a feminist! Moral concerns and feminism among men. *Psychology of Men & Masculinity, 18*(1), 78–86. https://doi-org.ezproxy.cul.columbia.edu/10.1037/men0000042.

Prevent Child Abuse America. (n.d.). *Fact sheet: Sexual abuse of boys*. https://preventchildabuse.org/images/docs/sexualabuseofboys.pdf

Prout, P. I., & Dobson, K. S. (1998). Recovered memories of childhood sexual abuse: Searching for the middle ground in clinical practice. *Canadian Psychology / Psychologie Canadienne, 39*(4), 257–265. https://doi-org.ezproxy.cul.columbia.edu/10.1037/h0086817

Punukollu, M. (2003). Domestic violence: Screening made practical. *The Journal of Family Practice, 52*(7), 537–543.

Purcell, B. C. (1998). Spiritual abuse. *American Journal of Hospice and Palliative Medicine®, 15*(4), 227–231. https://doi.org/10.1177/104990919801500409

Rape, Abuse & Incest National Network (RAINN). (2021). *Healing after child sexual abuse*. https://www.rainn.org/news/healing-after-csa#:~:text=Child%20sexual%20abuse%2C%20also%20known,age%20of%2018%20years%20old

Rape, Abuse & Incest National Network (RAINN). (n.d.). *Sexual harassment*. Retrieved from https://www.rainn.org/articles/sexual-harassment

Reina, A. S., & Lohman, B. J. (2015). Barriers preventing Latina immigrants from seeking advocacy services for domestic violence victims: A qualitative analysis. *Journal of Family Violence, 30*, 479–488. https://doi.org/10.1007/s10896-015-9696-8

Rogerson, S. (2012). Unintended and unavoidable: The failure to protect rule and its consequences for undocumented parents and their children: Unintended and unavoidable. *Family Court Review, 50*, 580–593. https://doi.org/10.1111/j.1744-1617.2012.01477.x

Rollè, L., Giardina, G., Caldarera, A. M., Gerino, E., & Brustia, P. (2018). When intimate partner violence meets same sex couples: A review of same sex intimate partner violence. *Frontiers in Psychology, 1506*. https://doi.org/10.3389/fpsyg.2018.01506

Russo, N. F., & Pirlott, A. (2006). Gender-based violence: Concepts, methods, and findings. *Annals of the New York Academy of Sciences, 1087*, 178–205. https://doi.org/10.1196/annals.1385.024

Salamon, M. (2023, May 31). *Cutting and self-harm: Why it happens and what to do*. Harvard Health. https://www.health.harvard.edu/blog/cutting-and-self-harm-why-it-happens-and-what-to-do-202305312940

Sangeetha, J., Mohan, S., Hariharasudan, A., & Nawaz, N. (2022). Strategic analysis of intimate partner violence (IPV) and cycle of violence in the autobiographical text: When I hit you. *Heliyon, 8*(6), e09734. https://doi.org/10.1016/j.heliyon.2022.e09734

Sanjel, S. (2013). Gender-based violence: A crucial challenge for public health. *Kathmandu University Medical Journal (KUMJ), 11*(42), 179–184. https://doi.org/10.3126/kumj.v11i2.12499

Satter, R. (2023, June). FBI says artificial intelligence being used for 'sextortion' and harassment. *Reuters*. https://www.reuters.com/world/us/fbi-says-artificial-intelligence-being-used-sextortion-harassment-2023-06-07/

Shafir, H. (2023, September). Gaslighting. *Choosing Therapy*. https://www.choosingtherapy.com/gaslighting/

Smith, S. G., Zhang, X., Basile, K. C., Merrick, M. T., Wang, J., Kresnow, M. J., & Chen, J. (2018). *The national intimate partner and sexual violence survey: 2015 data brief–updated release*. Centers for Disease Control. https://stacks.cdc.gov/view/cdc/60893.

Strong Hearts Native Helpline. (2024). *What is cultural abuse?* https://strongheartshelpline.org/abuse/what-is-cultural-abuse

Take Back The Night. (2023). *International history of TBTN*. https://takebackthenight.org/history/

Terkel, A. (2012, January). Eric Holder expands FBI's narrow, outdated definition of rape. *HuffPost*. https://www.huffpost.com/entry/eric-holder-fbi-rape_n_1189145

Thomas, J. C., & Kopel, J. (2023). Male victims of sexual assault: A review of the literature. *Behavioral Sciences (Basel, Switzerland), 13*(4), 304. https://doi.org/10.3390/bs13040304

Tracy, N. (2021, December 17). Battered women shelters: What are they? How to find one? *HealthyPlace*. https://www.healthyplace.com/abuse/domestic-violence/battered-women-shelters-what-are-they-how-to-find-one

U.S. Department of Homeland Security. (2024). *Combating gender-based violence*. https://www.dhs.gov/combating-gender-based-violence#:~:text=Specific%20forms%20of%20GBV%20may,%2C%20economic%2C%20and%20emotional%20abuse

UN Women. (n.d.). *Ending violence against women*. https://www.unwomen.org/en/what-we-do/ending-violence-against-women#:~:text=One%20in%20three%20women%20worldwide,can%20be%20devastating%2C%20including%20death

United Nations Office on Drugs and Crime (UNODC). (2019). *Global study on homicide 2019*. https://www.unodc.org/documents/data-and-analysis/gsh/Booklet1.pdf

Vance, C. (2024, May). What it takes to keep Harvey Weinstein, and men like him, behind bars. *New York Times*. https://www.nytimes.com/2024/05/14/opinion/cyrus-vance-harvey-weinstein.html

Villalon, R. (2015). Violence against immigrants in a context of crisis: A critical migration feminist of color analysis. *Journal of Social Distress and Homelessness, 24*, 116–139. https://doi.org/10.1179/1053078915Z.00000000017

Villines, Z. (2023). What is grey rocking? *Medical News Today*. Retrieved from https://www.medicalnewstoday.com/articles/grey-rock

Walker, L. E. (1979). *The battered woman*. Harper & Row.

Walker, L. E. (1989). Psychology and violence against women. *American Psychologist, 44*(4), 695–702. https://doi.org/10.1037/0003-066X.44.4.695

Weber, L. (2010). *Understanding race, class, gender, and sexuality: A conceptual framework* (2nd ed.). Oxford University Press.

Wirtz, A. L., Poteat, T. C., Malik, M., & Glass, N. (2020). Gender-based violence against transgender people in the United States: A call for research and programming. *Trauma, Violence & Abuse, 21*(2), 227–241. https://doi.org/10.1177/1524838018757749

Withers, M. (2021, February). It's more than just fight or flight: How trauma responses manifest in human trafficking survivors. *Psychology Today*. https://www.psychologytoday.com/us/blog/modern-day-slavery/202102/its-more-just-fight-or-flight

World Health Organization. (2024). Violence against women. https://www.who.int/news-room/factsheets/detail/violence-against-women

Women's Law. (2023, August). *Safety while living with an abuser*. Women's Law. https://www.womenslaw.org/safety-planning/domestic-violence-victims/safety-while-living-abuser

World Bank. (2020). *Women, business and the law 2020*. World Bank. https://doi.org/10.1596/978-1-4648-1532-4

Wright, E. M., & Benson, M. L. (2010). Immigration and intimate partner violence: Exploring the immigrant paradox. *Social Problems, 57*, 480–503.

Wright, L. A., Zounlome, N. O. O., & Whiston, S. C. (2020). The effectiveness of male-targeted sexual assault prevention programs: A meta-analysis. *Trauma, Violence, & Abuse, 21*(5), 859–869. https://doi-org.ezproxy.cul.columbia.edu/10.1177/1524838018801330

Chapter 12
Gender Affirmative Interventions: Theory and Practice Considerations

Competencies and Gender

This chapter will focus on gender and therapy, particularly gender affirmative approaches to therapy. We will discuss what affirmative approaches are as well as outline the different models that are currently used to centralize gender in the therapy room. Affirmative in the therapeutic setting means approaching clients in positive, supportive ways that take context into consideration as well as intersectionality (e.g., Singh & Dickey, 2017); more recently, liberatory frameworks, as inspired by Latin American psychology, have begun to be applied in therapy as well (Comas-Díaz, 2020). To fully understand the theory and practice of culturally competent interventions, it is also important to engage with the current backdrop of the field. A major source of information about working with diverse populations is drawn from the APA professional practice guidelines, developed each for TGNC people, women, and men (see next section). Another important strand is a brief review of the history of gender in therapeutic practice specifically.

We emphasize several *therapist responsibilities* to develop involve getting clarity and supervision with other therapists who can foster competence building and engage in vulnerability. Vulnerability is particularly important in clinical work when clinical disconnection occurs, when a therapist makes a mistake, or when engaging in self-disclosure. Clinical work involves the need to build distress tolerance, tolerance of ambiguity, and self-forgiveness, particularly because the work is nuanced enough to fundamentally include navigation of these issues. Lastly, therapist authenticity is important in being able to model to clients of all genders.

M. L. Miville et al., *Counseling and Gender*,
https://doi.org/10.1007/978-3-031-69172-0_12

APA Professional Practice Guidelines and Gender

Before exploring gender-centric approaches to therapeutic work, we discuss the practice guidelines that the APA has published for working respectively with women, men, and TGNC folx. The first set of guidelines for TGNC and cisgender boys and men were developed fairly recently (APA, 2015, 2018a), whereas the guidelines for cisgender girls and women were first published in 1978, and the latest in 2018 (APA, 2018b). These guidelines do not necessarily prepare counselors to do the actual work in the clinical setting. However they are helpful in orienting readers regarding the basic issues affecting a particular population or topic area. There are practice guidelines for many different populations, including race and ethnicity, aging, disability. Another point is that these guidelines are considered living documents, and are ostensibly in effect for about 10 or 15 years. At that point, if they continue to be relevant, APA creates a committee that updates and revises the guidelines for the next period of time. The approval of these practice guidelines is a long process of approval of all sections of APA (i.e., Directorates and the Council of Representatives). In addition to laying out basic areas of knowledge and areas of competency, another helpful component of these guidelines is the references listed at the end of each set. The next section reviews some of the foundational recommendations taken from the guidelines.

Guidelines for Boys and Men

The first set of practice guidelines for boys and men were only published in 2018, decades after similar work for girls and women was initially released. These guidelines, which contextualized gender issues for boys and men within historical and cultural frameworks, were greeted with some public controversy (Levant & McDermott, 2022), due to its emphasis that masculinity, like gender as a whole, is constructed based on social, cultural and contextual norms (APA, 2018a). The first guideline in the document acknowledges that for each person, there are individual aspects to how individuals construct their unique sense of gender. The second guideline states that boys and men integrate multiple aspects of their identity over the lifespan, and that power, privilege, and sexism have a major impact on the lives of boys and men (APA, 2018a). However, a surprising, but very important factor to understand is that male privilege often comes with a cost, as we have discussed throughout this book. As boys and men adhere to traditional masculine ideologies that promote sexist beliefs and a rigidity in attitudes about gender, this also leads to a restriction in boys' and men's abilities to function adaptively which can then affect both their mental and physical health (APA, 2018a).

One of the key aspects about the guidelines for boys and men is that the socialization practices that generally teach boys from an early age is to be self-reliant, strong, and to minimize and manage their problems on their own (APA, 2018a). One of the unfortunate consequences that can arise from this kind of socialization is that boys and men are going to be among the least likely individuals and groups to want to seek mental health treatment because this goes completely against most boys and men's socialization of how to be a man (APA, 2018a). Within the therapeutic setting, even when men and boys enter therapy, there exists implicit bias stemming from this socialization. For example, boys and men are less likely to be diagnosed with problems like depression (recall the gender differences of depression) despite the fact that more cisgender boys and men die by suicide than cisgender girls and women who attempt suicide far more often.

The guidelines also propose considerations for working with intersections within a group. For example when it comes to being a parent, being a father, there are over 70 million men in the United States who identify themselves as fathers, and approximately 80% of them see themselves as involved, and only 50% of men feel they're doing a "good job" at being a father (APA, 2018a). For example, in order to understand when a man who identifies as a father in the counseling setting, it is important to begin to ask them about how they see themselves and how they feel about the role of a parent, the strengths they bring to that, as well as their own anxieties and insecurities about their sense of being a father.

Regarding education, as we have been discussing in this book, men in general are falling behind their women peers in higher education (DiPrete & Buchmann, 2013). Relatedly, boys and men tend to have higher rates of developmental disabilities that may create difficulties for them to be successful in the educational setting. Another important fact to be aware of is that 90% of all violent crime is committed by boys or men (although 90% of boys and men are not violent). (Levant & McDermott, 2022; United States Department of Justice, 2011). This complicates the discussion on men and boys in education, as time spent within the prison industrial system in the U.S. is often not accounted for, particularly in Black and Latino communities (Federal Bureau of Prisons, 2024). This phenomenon has been coined by scholars as the school-to-prison pipeline (Mallett, 2015; see also Chaps. 4 and 8). When working with boys and men in therapy, it is imperative to engage with these considerations.

Regarding health related behavioral decisions, men tend to have significantly higher death rates than people of other gender groups, and that is typically true across all races and ethnicities (Gough & Robertson, 2017). As well, boys and men as a group tend to engage in higher levels of risk-taking behaviors such as substance abuse and driving faster than is recommended, and altogether, doing things that boys and men typically are socialized to do to prove they are "real men" (APA, 2018a). Another guideline regarding boys and men focuses on the importance of providing competent psychological services in understanding their development as well as the primary issues that men and boys may be presenting in the clinical setting. The final guideline urges advocacy at institutional and systemic levels.

Guidelines for Girls and Women

When it comes to the APA practice guidelines for girls and women, this is the gender group that has been the focus of practice guidelines for the longest period, beginning in 1978. There remains a tremendous need for these guidelines, as we have discussed in this book, due to significant biases in diagnosis, prognosis, and treatment of this wide-ranging population (APA, 2018b). The high incidence of trauma, particularly sexually based violence, and the diversity of girls and women are also important to understand, as are the impacts of intersections of race, ethnicity, religion, socio-economic status, disability, and so on.

Sexism and gender-based violence in its many forms have long been clinical issues emphasized in the guidelines, including even misconduct and abuse of women clients by their own therapists (APA, 2018b). The unique impact of terrorism, war, and refugee status on women also is suggested as important to understand (Björn et al., 2013). Manifestations of GBV that target girls and women create innate power dynamics within the clinical setting (APA). Media stereotypes promote either exoticized or sexualized images that reinforce submissive roles for girls and women (APA). Reproductive health and other health issues are also of concern, particularly now more than ever, given the recent Dobbs decision (Harvey et al., 2023). The discriminatory impact of being an older woman and a person who has disabilities increases, along with their traditionally-assigned roles and functions, considerations in the clinical setting also increase. Women are also more likely to develop disabilities for various reasons, including their relative longevity and unique gender related health issues, (Leveille et al., 2000; Murtagh & Hubert, 2004).

As a means of successfully navigating these significant concerns, the most recent guidelines (APA, 2018b) takes a strengths-based clinical approach, with the initial guideline urging counselors to honor and cultivate their clients' strengths and resilience. A related suggestion is to not over-pathologize their clients' presenting and long-term struggles. Other guidelines suggest, as we have in this volume, that clinicians appreciate that identity constructions of their clients (and themselves) are formed in social contexts of multiple, contradictory, and changing messages of what it means to be a woman. Structural disparities and discrimination (as in the case of health promotion) and long-time legacies of oppression and its impact on health are similarly critical to highlight. Moreover, the guidelines suggest that therapists examine their own socialization regarding gender (e.g., biases, values) and its intersections, particularly how this may affect the provision of effective (or ineffective) therapy.

Other considerations outlined in the guidelines are the use of evidence-based treatments that are known to be effective for girls and women, and attuning to the fact that what we consider as "evidence-based" needs to be inclusive of the unique experiences of girls and women, especially with an eye toward racial-cultural intersections and other important diverse experiences. As a whole, the guidelines provide information that is key to the goals of liberation-focused therapy: supporting initiative, instilling a sense of empowerment in one's life, and developing expanded alternatives and choices beyond what young girls are taught (Comas-Díaz, 2020). Considerations around psychological assessment and evaluation are also outlined in the guidelines (APA, 2018b), that is, clinicians are encouraged to diagnose only as needed or necessary, and understand the history of biases in these processes. The use of unbiased assessments is critical, as well as an understanding that context impacts all people, but in particular understanding how context impacts your women clients. Lastly, knowing the options for resources and social systems beyond the therapy room is critical for all clients, but particularly for those who are marginalized in the area of gender, such as women and girls.

Guidelines for TGNC People

We next turn our attention to the APA guidelines for TGNC people (2015). Since this population is a large and diverse group, the guidelines also establish a foundation of knowledge that clinicians should achieve, with much of that guidance involving attuning to difference and diversity (APA). The guidelines establish that clinicians should understand that gender is a construct and learn about the epistemology of gender as a nonbinary construct: not an "either or," but in many different ways of identifying that are fluid. Gender identity is distinguished from sexual orientation, but they may be increasingly interrelated with each generation. Similarly, understanding the multiple aspects of stigma, prejudice, discrimination, and violence on mental health as well as access to systems such as the medical-industrial complex is imperative with TGNC folks (APA).

As with cisgender girls and women and cisgender boys and men, the notion of institutional disparities and barriers, and the need for mental health professionals to be advocates is incredibly foundational to culturally competent work (APA, 2015). Also, understanding development and how it impacts identity is important, particularly when working with gender-questioning youth (APA). The guidelines encourage the use of research for groups within the community, such as youth and elders. For TGNC elders, it is important to consider the developmental factor of how social theory changes over time, i.e. some TGNC elders *may* subscribe to gender as a binary as this was prominent in social theory during their formative years (APA). The remaining guidelines focus on the impact of relationships to TGNC folks as parents and their roles as caregivers and in various family configurations. Of note, however, is that there are no current guidelines regarding childbearing concerns for TGNC people (APA). Lastly, the guidelines stress the importance of an interdisciplinary approach, one that involves a collaborative team of many people from different health professions (APA) to best serve TGNC clients because of how medicalized their existence has become for various communities within the TGNC umbrella. The need for research, as well as specific training and education for transgender and gender non conforming populations is made clear, as is true for the other guidelines we reviewed.

Integrating this review with the existing gender based therapies, there are clear themes that are parallel across all three guidelines: dealing with prejudice and discrimination, the need to understand socialization and identity development, the importance of looking at one's own biases as a clinician, and the need to engage as with institutional disparities as a significant source of stress. However, as these themes play out for individual clients, attending to the unique aspects of each client and their own issues, as well as their unique contexts, is the most important contribution from the guidelines.

Resistance and Liberation in Counseling

More recently in the field of counseling the terms "resistance" and "liberation" are used in clinical applications (Heitz, 2022). Many counselors strive not to actively engage with oppressive behaviors or align with oppressive structures, however there has been recent proliferation of calls for explicit resistance to oppressive institutions and forces *as a therapeutic tool* (Comas-Díaz, 2020). Ultimately, liberation means that collectively, individuals and communities do not have to be trapped in any kind of socialized process. Socialized processes will continue to happen and most likely remain an integral part of human society, though the power of socialized processes (in this case with gender) should be fluid and easily navigated or rejected without material consequences.

There are a number of affirming therapies that focus on *resistance strategies*, though it is important to note here that resistance has always been a part of gender throughout history (Wiesner-Hanks, 2011). To integrate knowledge passed down directly from resistance movements, we present a few sayings (or *dichos*) that develop the idea of resistance, politically and therapeutically.

- One example is a famous Mexican proverb "they tried to bury us, but they did not understand we are seeds." In other words, by trying to destroy a person or community through violence, instead what is created is the counterforce that will lead to resistance and the creation of a different way.
- Maya Angelou's saying of "you may trod me in the dirt but still like dust i rise." As with the first saying, force may be used to destroy someone, but like dust in the air, a person finds their way to survive and thrive.
- Another is a well-known Romani proverb often credited to Manush Romanov: "Bury me standing. I've been on my knees all my life." Here the emphasis is on long-term oppression, and the resilience of the Romani people and other communities who have been isolated and ostracized.

Each of these sayings beautifully express the fact that oppressive systems and oppressive forces can try to force people to be someone they do not want to be or do something they do not want to do. However, acts of coercion, i.e., "forcing" creates an alternate reaction that leads to strength, change, community, even improved health (consider the story of an IPV survivor). Robinson-Wood (2014) observed that *resistance* is not new to psychology, that it has always been a part of psychological theory and found in the makeup of the psychology of people. That being said, it has become a significantly more widespread word within the field of counseling. People, particularly people of color, have always had resistance strategies in response to oppressive circumstances (Robinson-Wood). Further, she distinguished between two types of resistance approaches: optimal and suboptimal. *Suboptimal resistance* is defined as "survival-oriented and refers to short-term cognitive and behavioral adaptations to chronic stress that, although do not serve women well in the long run, have immediate, short-term, numbing, soothing, and/or pleasure-inducing effects" (p. 63). Examples of these strategies include engaging in drug or alcohol use, or engaging in other kinds of behaviors, like self-injurious behaviors, isolation, and passive coping. In the long term, suboptimal resistance strategies are most likely not going to help people live authentically or feel connected to other people, community, or the world, but they can facilitate survival. *Optimal resistance* is defined as a "sociopolitical consciousness that embodies an awareness of chronic environmental stressors and institutional oppression along with a deliberate strategy of pushback through community connections, self-affirmation, and purpose" (p. 64). Engaging in optimal resistance is reflected in the use of longer term strategies that focus on wellness, not just for oneself, but family and community. Strategies, which Robinson-Wood frames within Afrocentric terms, include developing a support group or connecting to others in the struggle in a way to feel not just good about oneself but to organize and make change happen on systemic and institutional levels.

Comas-Díaz (2020) described liberatory psychotherapy for Latine populations as "a healing approach grounded in the lived experiences of oppressed individuals and communities" (p. 169) in which the goal is "the promotion of social justice action through the integration of Indigenous cultural healing and emancipatory approaches into mainstream psychotherapy" (p. 169). This approach to therapy emanates from the work of Latin American scholars, including Freire and his notion of *Conscientização* (conscientization): "a process of culling a critical sense of one's social reality through reflection and action that changes reality... In this process, people acquire social myths, which have a dominating effect so that learning is a process depending on uncovering real problems and actual needs" (Sanchez-Hucles, 2016, p. 81). Liberatory psychotherapists help clients "to become protagonists, instead of spectators," especially as they make changes in their personal lives that eventually lead to changes in their communities: "Simply put, when we heal individuals, we are healing the world" (Comas-Díaz, p. 169). A major aspect of this therapeutic approach is to reclaim one's historical memory (*conocimiento*) "and cultural consciousness as a source of power, healing, and liberation" (p. 179). Doing so helps clients transform oppressive narratives, as based on Western power-based hierarchies, into liberatory ones that emphasize resistance and resilience. An excellent example of a gender-based liberatory framework for Latinas was developed by Gloria and Castellanos (2016), centered on the construct of *poderosa* (empowerment). Their model includes four dimensions in which a Latina client begins with envisioning their transformation, applying their vision, and then acting with intent to advocate for oneself and one's community.

Feminist Therapy

Arguably the first Western therapy approach to address the cultural, social, and systemic effects of gender on psychology is Feminist Therapy (FT) (Brown, 1994, 2018). One unique aspect of FT is that during its inception, it was not formed by one, or even a few theorists, but instead was actively practiced by many counselors before a formal theory was established (Brown, 1994). This area of inquiry and practice started in the 1960s, though it has been noted that many clinicians had disclosed practicing from a feminist orientation for longer, though did not have theoretical language to call it anything (Brown, 1994; Evans et al., 2005). The FT approach necessitates a political view of how people develop and move through the world (Ballou et al., 2007). As Brown (2018) recently described,

> Feminist practice is psychology derived from the realities that lie outside, beneath, and at variance from the visions of the dominant patriarchal mainstream. It is a theory that not only listens to but privileges the voices and experiences of those who have been defined as "other" by dominant cultures. (p. 4)

Clinicians are encouraged to draw from philosophy and theory in disciplines outside of psychology, such as politics, sociology, and media studies. Feminist therapists are also encouraged to take on a *standpoint epistemology*, which is a philosophical stance that urges someone to view their perspective as influenced by their social positionalities–particularly in that they will be unable to see from another's standpoint and therefore must honor other ways of knowing than their own (Brown, 1994). This is reflected in therapy as the cyclical questioning of power dynamics, including from the therapist's own perspective and biases (Brown, 2018).

FT is a widely practiced therapeutic approach that incorporates various streams of theory and practice. It additionally centers a critique of "traditional" counseling practices (Evans et al., 2005). Among the several elements of traditional counseling that are critiqued through FT are: the philosophy of health and healing, the focus on the individual, the boundaries and constraints of the therapeutic relationship, and the process of diagnosis (Brown, 1994). FT holds true that healing is a holistic process, one that occurs not when the therapist determines, but when the client experiences it through the means that they decide (Ballou et al., 2007; Brown, 1994). Additionally, the traditional therapeutic relationship is critiqued as too power-laden to be healing and an alternative framing of striving towards egalitarianism is provided (Rader & Gilbert, 2005). Most importantly, the FT process is inherently intersectional–if a clinician does not account for the lived experiences of multiply marginalized people, they are not practicing in a truly feminist manner (Brown, 1994, 2018; Evans et al., 2005).

Relational Cultural Therapy

One of the most widely known and often used forms of gender affirmative therapy is *relational cultural therapy (RCT)*. Psychiatrist Jean Baker Miller developed RCT nearly a half century ago (1976) while working with psychologists in Boston. RCT was developed in response to traditional therapy, particularly the notion that therapy should emphasize individuation and autonomy as the ultimate goal of therapeutic work (Miller & Stiver, 1997). Health in the traditional therapeutic sense represents separating oneself from family and somehow distinguishing oneself from others (Jordan, 2018) and often has been associated with healthy psychological development of men and boys (see Chap. 9). However, according to RCT, separation and differentiation are not the most important aspect of health and maturation, and may even lead to damaging consequences, such as loneliness and isolation. Instead RCT centralizes relationships as important for healing, placing connection with others and the self at the center of what it means to be healthy and to thrive (Jordan). Rather than to separate oneself from others, health and healing are about connecting with others, or in other words, creating a sense of self in community with others. With this kind of approach to therapy, the responsibilities of the therapists are absolutely paramount since RCT requires an understanding of what one's level of relational competence is, including the ability to be authentic, and to take risks to understand what one's own possible relationship obstacles are.

RCT places a significant emphasis on the development of relationships, as well as tangible competence in relationship building that is important to foster throughout the lifespan. *Key components of RCT therapy* include: an egalitarian relationship with the client as much as can be, directly and explicitly attending to power dynamics that occur in relationships, and minimizing the power that counselors hold (e.g. in the room with clients, in society at large, especially in the medical industrial complex, and in the client's mind) (O'Donnell et al., 2014). RCT, along with other feminist and social justice-oriented approaches to care, reject the established–and enforced–tradition of privileging the knowledge and experience of a counselor over that of a client (Jordan, 2018). Instead RCT emphasized that what therapists should know is a particular set of knowledge and information pertaining to psychology, development, and the therapeutic process. Additionally, RCT aims to empower clients to embrace their own expertise on the topic of their life, placing connection with others and the self at the center of what it means to be healthy and to thrive. In this way, RCT is a reflection of long-held principles of feminist theory, for example, feminist therapists typically view clients as capable collaborators by privileging and centralizing client perspectives and their lives; this helps move clients to a strength based approach for change. For RCT in particular there is an emphasis on an egalitarian client-counselor relationship and concurrently an awareness of power differentials that exist.

Diversity and social justice are foundational to RCT (Jordan, 2018). Conceptually, relational cultural theory necessitates clinicians attend to issues of gender, race, ethnicity, social class, disability, and sexual orientation in addition to other social positionalities because RCT therapists incorporate these factors into their conceptualization (Comstock et al., 2008). This is partly why RCT is well-situated to engage gender in the counseling setting–for gender to be honored in its full complexity, as outlined through this book, the theories used in the clinical setting must embrace intersectionality.

RCT has now been practiced and researched with many populations and groups, not just with women or girls. Recently, Di Bianca and Mahalik (2022) described how RCT can be helpful in overcoming the harmful impacts of male socialization in the U.S. which "are shaped by the interpersonal and sociocultural disconnections that keep boys and men in rigid confines of what is expected of 'real men,'" (p. 321). For example, in response to the cultural expectation that men will be autonomous and independent, men may end up sacrificing relational skill development because of this emphasis on autonomy and achievement, or on actions. This would be focused on as a socialized expectation placed on men and the subsequent "treatment" would include developing authentic, emotionally deep, and interdependent relationships with others. For women who are socialized to carry the major responsibility for relationship development and maintenance, they are pressured to sacrifice authenticity. In other words, women are expected to present a certain face or sense of self to somebody else in order to develop or maintain a particular relationship, even if this is counter to their own thoughts and feelings. RCT does not posit a standardized treatment for any issue or group of people, and instead it encourages delving into the depths of socialization and political positionality to grasp the unique situations of our clients.

The *general course of RCT treatment* is to look at the relational and structural obstacles with the client, identify patterns of connection and disconnection, and work towards ameliorating obstructive relational patterns (Jordan, 2018; Walker, 2008). To become more relationally competent begins with the therapeutic relationship; being in therapy is a pathway for clients to develop healthy relationships beyond the clinic room. Helping the client to recognize how or if a relationship is unhealthy is a key aspect, as well as clients learning that they are worthy and deserving of healthier relationships. For example, a transgender woman in an emotionally abusive relationship with a straight, cisgender man (which we outlined in Chap. 6 is an unfortunate reality for many transgender people) may present with beliefs of deserving mistreatment, scarcity fear about who may be interested in her sexually, or feelings of disconnection from herself as encouraged by the system of cissexism. Utilizing an RCT approach with this case could be beneficial in that the client's ways of relating to others and herself are paramount to the therapeutic work, as are her sociopolitical positionalities.

Womanist Therapy

Through the development of feminist political and gender theory in the zeitgeist during the 1970s, *womanist therapy* was developed. Inspired by Alice Walker (1983), *womanism* is derived from Black feminist thought as a politically subversive reaction to hegemonically White feminist theory at the time. Sanchez-Hucles (2016) described womanist therapy, particularly with Black women, as a theoretical bridge to Afrocentric and feminist models of therapy. Alice Walker first defined a womanist as: "a woman who loves another woman sexually and or non sexually, she appreciates and prefers women's culture, women's emotional flexibility" (Walker, 1983, p. xi). In this sense, a womanist is committed to the survival and wholeness of an entire people, men and women (ideally of all genders). Womanist therapy does not promote separatism for women from men, since this is counter to promoting a healthy community; there may be periods when for reasons of health and safety, a time of separation may be needed. As with liberatory frameworks, womanist approaches to therapy emphasize activism, spirituality, and an ethical stance to breaking interlocking oppressions.

In womanist therapy, the ritual of life is unique and something to acknowledge and celebrate as shaped by the interactions of multiple identities (Sanchez-Hucles, 2016). It also emphasizes that women of color are inspired and strengthened by other women and men, including ancestors. Spirituality and belief are attended to in this approach, as it values pre-colonial history and practice as well as colonial resistance (Heath, 2006). Womanist therapists accept their clients, where they are, and work to help free clients from oppressive heterosexist, racist, sexist, and class and ability bound structures. There is the basic belief that all people are connected, even if people must work to view and comprehend our connection.

Womanist therapy theorizes that the majority of therapeutic work must be centered around socialization and identity, as women of color, especially Black women, are forced into impossible binds (Williams & Jackson, 2019). Part of this conceptualization stems from what womanist therapy refers to as a *soul wound*. Eduardo Duran (2006) originally outlined the concept of a soul wound regarding Indigenous people, and is defined as cultural traumas that have occurred throughout someone's life as well as across multiple generations. Embedded in these wounds are ungrieved losses, a sense of learned helplessness, and internalization of colonial narratives forced upon oneself, or what is called "adjust to oppression" (Duran et al., 1998).

Theory in womanist therapy states that to heal from soul wounds, *self care* is imperative. Although the term self care was proliferated within clinical, psychiatric, and medical settings in the 1950s, it was theorized and popularized as an essential act of political resistance by the Black Panther Party in the 1970s (Nelson, 2013). Self care as a womanist intervention strategy pushes beyond the concept of caring for oneself through gifts or acts of self-service materialistically (Zuckerwise, 2024). This can involve calling up ancestors, overcoming silencing, addressing shame at its political core, and working on overcoming soul wounds. Self care is a critical therapeutic framework within womanist therapy, as are coping strategies due to the larger societal expectation for Black women and other women of color to ignore their needs for the sake of keeping other people in positions of comfort (Sanchez-Hucles, 2016; Zuckerwise, 2024). Examples of womanist therapy coping strategies include breaking down stoicism and silencing, discarding that false notion of being a "superwoman", and challenging notions of strength. Womanist theory posits that putting significant effort into appearing strong can lead to harming oneself, particularly because the interlocking systems of sexism, racism, classism, and ableism encourage hyper-individualism (Campbell, 2008).

Central to womanist therapy theory is the framework of trauma in all forms: generational, colonial, and structural (Bryant-Davis, 2023). Trauma is recontextualized through womanist theory, especially in the framing that for some, trauma is a daily experience (Bryant-Davis, 2023; Lape, 2023). Black and Brown women and TGNC people in particular are consistently exposed to institutional, structural, and historical trauma in addition to the experiences of acute trauma (Bryant-Davis, 2023). In this reimagining of historical definitions of trauma, it is also important to consider factors of resilience. Resilience, someone's ability to survive, adapt, and thrive through traumatic experiences, is a consequence to continuous exposure to trauma at a systems-level (Lape, 2023). Without lauding resilience as a personal success, womanist therapy engages with it as a necessary component of healing. Womanist therapy also posits that marginalized communities enact a form of collective resistance, meaning the socially-based processes of coping and building trust simultaneously (Tummala-Narra, 2007).

Collective resistance is a foundational element of the healing process in womanist therapy, especially when attuning to specific intersections of identity. As such, womanist therapy encourages specific applications of womanist theory; for example, it has been applied to work specifically with Latine communities. This approach, developed in part through the work of Lillian Comas-Díaz (Bryant-Davis & Comas-Díaz, 2016), uses the term *mujerista* to describe the unique intersection of being Latina and being a woman. Mujerista therapy strategies include culture-specific practices such as *testimono*: a storytelling method that cultivates collective healing through sharing narrative with others (Fernández, 2022). Lastly, mujerista therapy encourages clinicians to go beyond the traditional boundaries of counseling practice and advocate for clients on systemic, institutional, and cultural levels (Bryant-Davis & Comas-Díaz, 2016).

Overarchingly, womanist therapy, stemming from womanist theory as a pivotal departure from mainstream White feminism, seeking to engage specifically with BIPOC communities. Taking a womanist therapy approach could be helpful when working with people who are multiply marginalized and can challenge deficit models of development for those at the intersections of racial and gendered oppression.

Positive Psychology/Positive Masculinity

Many of the approaches outlined in this chapter thus far involve specific theories dedicated to serving those who experience gender marginalization. The *Positive psychology/positive masculinity* (PPPM) approach examines the aspects of traditional masculine roles that are positive and strength based and to think about how they can improve the lives of men and those around them (Kiselica & Englar-Carlson, 2010). As bell hooks (in Di Bianca & Mahalik, 2022) poignantly suggested about change for men:

> Our work of love should be to reclaim masculinity and not allow it to be held hostage by patriarchal domination … those of us committed to ending patriarchy can touch the hearts of real men where they live, not by demanding that they give up manhood or maleness, but by asking that they allow its meaning to be transformed, that they become disloyal to patriarchal masculinity in order to find a place for the masculine that does not make it synonymous with dominance or the will do to violence. (p. 325)

Positive masculinity emphasizes the adaptive character, strengths, emotions, and virtues that promote well being and resilience in oneself, and as importantly, in others (McDermott et al., 2019). PPPM fosters an environment where men can be affirmed in therapy in addition to working towards facilitating a paradigm shift towards interdependence (Kiselica & Englar-Carlson, 2010). Positive masculinity can help people transcend rigid sexist oppressive socialization and work towards a more flexible enactment of masculinity. Additionally, PPPM can recognize existing strengths, capacities, and skills present in men, encourage the potential in men, and enhance the ability to see men for who they are rather than who they are not (Seager & Barry, 2019). This can assist in unpacking the stereotypes and rigid attitudes that some clients who are men may present with, as referenced throughout this book occurs as a process of put-upon socialized characteristics.

One way to reach men, especially those from working class or low income backgrounds, is to engage them in organically formed *communities of practice* based on activities like playing sports, being a father, or seeking a support group (Simpson & Richards, 2017) that provide space to discuss issues relevant to mental health. As one participant suggested, "Until we can talk as openly about mental health as we do physical health, there will be a stigma, and if I can talk about… the dark times… hopefully that touches someone else and makes them reach out for help." Or a social media post succinctly suggested: "Don't man up. Open up" (Simpson & Richards).

Positive psychology/positive masculinity approaches have also been applied to men of color, especially in the realm of community frameworks. One example is Homeboy Industries, a well-known initiative in East Los Angeles that serves young low-income Latinos involved in gang activities by emphasizing skills, jobs, and care (i.e., "Nothing stops a bullet like a job," Father Boyle, in Ojeda & Organista, 2016, p. 308). The programs emphasize men's unique roles in society and families; indeed, counseling work with some clients, especially those involved in IPV, can focus on positive aspects of machismo (*caballerismo*) and egalitarianism within this perspective.

TGNC Affirmative Therapy

The World Professional Association for Transgender Health (WPATH) issues specific guidelines for providers in all health and mental health disciplines working with TGNC people. The guidelines call for affirmative approaches to a person's gender identity (Coleman et al., 2012). This call reflects a larger trend towards affirmative therapy in the field of counseling due to rampant misinformation and lack of familiarity with TGNC populations (Korell & Lorah, 2007; Singh & Dickey, 2017). The need for affirmative therapy for TGNC is paramount, however, recent scholarship has attempted to push past affirmative practices to liberatory practices (Grzanka & Miles, 2016; Mosley et al., 2020; Singh, 2016). TGNC affirmative therapy is not a theoretical orientation, a style, or an intervention, it is a larger network of competencies that include various practices (Singh & Dickey, 2017). These practices could include using the correct pronouns with clients, writing gender support letters for the purposes of surgery or hormone replacement therapy (HRT), incorporating a non-binary view of gender into one's worldview, and actively deconstructing one's own sexism, cissexism, and heterosexism. Below we review some specific affirmative interventions available to clinicians.

TGNC Letter Writing

Due to the intense medicalization that TGNC people face in the United States, letter writing has become a staple requirement for clinicians working with this population (Drescher, 2018; Ducheny et al., 2017). Letters of support from mental health professionals for TGNC clients come in a few forms: letters indicating capacity to receive gender affirmation surgery, letters indicating capacity to receive HRT, and letters to support gender marker changes (Drescher). Although not a legal requirement, letters of support from mental health professionals or medical providers are often required by insurance companies to determine if gender affirmation surgery is "medically necessary". The requirements for letters depends upon the hospital system, the insurance company, and the purpose of the letter. A clinician's responsibility when seeing TGNC clients is to assess if their client demonstrates bare minimum capacity to understand the risks and benefits of surgery, as with any surgical procedure. However, we must also consider that most surgeries do not require a mental health professional to write support letters to determine capacity. The practice of requiring TGNC people to receive letters from mental health professionals is a gatekeeping device that upholds medicalization (Brown et al., 2020; Drescher, 2018). This means that clinicians hold an immense responsibility not to serve as further gatekeepers to proper TGNC care, particularly in the form of medical intervention and especially because levels of regret after gender affirmation surgeries are incredibly low (Bustos et al., 2021).

Conclusion

Gender is complex and the defining paradigms are constantly shifting and evolving–to do gender work is to lean into this change and incorporate some of the fundamental knowledge detailed in this book into counseling work. This book endeavors to create a thorough yet wide-ranging review of gender in the counseling setting. In implementing this goal, the culmination in a chapter focused on gender-competent interventions seems necessary. We have outlined the necessary benchmarks for foundational competencies, engaged with APA's gender-specific guidelines as well as themes of resistance and liberation, and introduced several gender-affirmative and liberatory approaches to clinical work. At the core, any counseling approach can attend to gender, what matters most is an intentional, historically-based, systemically-critical, intersectional, liberatory orientation to gender. Notable in its inclusion in most of the approaches outlined in this book is the focus on moving beyond the counseling room and into a more activist/advocate role. To truly engage in the subject of counseling and gender, one must stretch the traditional parameters of the field and work towards systemic change.

References

American Psychological Association. (2015). Guidelines for psychological practice with transgender and gender nonconforming people. *American Psychologist, 70*(9), 832–864. https://doi.org/10.1037/a0039906

American Psychological Association (2018a). *APA guidelines for psychological practice with boys and men.* https://www.apa.org/about/policy/boys-men-practice-guidelines.pdf

American Psychological Association. (2018b). *APA guidelines for psychological practice with girls and women.* https://www.apa.org/about/policy/psychological-practice-girls-women.pdf

Ballou, M., Hill, M., & West, C. (Eds.). (2007). *Feminist therapy theory and practice: A contemporary perspective* (1st ed.). Springer.

Björn, G. J., Bodén, C., Sydsjö, G., & Gustafsson, P. A. (2013). Brief family therapy for refugee children. *The Family Journal, 21*(3), 272–278.

Brown, L. S. (1994). *Subversive dialogues: Theory in feminist therapy*. Basic Books.

Brown, L. S. (2018). *Feminist therapy* (2nd ed., pp. xvi, 188). American Psychological Association. https://doi.org/10.1037/0000092-000

Brown, H. M., Rostosky, S. S., Reese, R. J., Gunderson, C. J., Kwok, C., & Ryser-Oatman, T. (2020). Blessing or BS? The therapy experiences of transgender and gender nonconforming clients obtaining referral letters for gender affirming medical treatment. *Professional Psychology: Research and Practice, 51*(6), 571–579. https://doi-org.ezproxy.cul.columbia.edu/10.1037/pro0000274

Bryant-Davis, T. (2023). Healing the trauma of racism and sexism: Decolonization and liberation. *Women & Therapy, 46*(3), 246–260. https://doi.org/10.1080/02703149.2023.2275935

Bryant-Davis, T., & Comas-Díaz, L. (2016). Introduction: Womanist and mujerista psychologies. In T. Bryant-Davis & L. Comas-Díaz (Eds.), *Womanist and mujerista psychologies: Voices of fire, acts of courage* (pp. 3–25). American Psychological Association. https://doi.org/10.1037/14937-001

Bustos, V. P., Bustos, S. S., Mascaro, A., Del Corral, G., Forte, A. J., Ciudad, P., Kim, E. A., Langstein, H. N., & Manrique, O. J. (2021). Regret after gender-affirmation surgery: A systematic review and meta-analysis of prevalence. *Plastic and Reconstructive Surgery. Global Open, 9*(3), e3477. https://doi.org/10.1097/GOX.0000000000003477

Campbell, F. A. K. (2008). Exploring internalized ableism using critical race theory. *Disability & Society, 23*(2), 151–162. https://doi.org/10.1080/09687590701841190

Coleman, E., Bockting, W., Botzer, M., Cohen-Kettenis, P., DeCuypere, G., Feldman, J., Fraser, L., Green, J., Knudson, G., Meyer, W. J., Monstrey, S., Adler, R. K., Brown, G. R., Devor, A. H., Ehrbar, R., Ettner, R., Eyler, E., Garofalo, R., Karasic, D. H., et al. (2012). Standards of care for the health of transsexual, transgender, and gender-nonconforming people (Version 7). *International Journal of Transgenderism, 13*(4), 165–232. https://doi.org/10.1080/15532739.2011.700873

Comas-Díaz, L. (2020). Liberation psychotherapy. In L. Comas-Díaz & E. T. Rivera (Eds.), *Liberation psychology: Theory, method, practice, and social justice* (pp. 169–185). American Psychological Association. https://doi.org/10.1037/0000198-010

Comstock, D., Hammer, T., Strentzsch, J., Cannon, K., Parsons, J., & Gustavo, S., II. (2008). Relational-cultural theory: A framework for bridging relational, multicultural, and social justice competencies. *Journal of Counseling & Development, 86*. https://doi.org/10.1002/j.1556-6678.2008.tb00510.x

Di Bianca, M., & Mahalik, J. R. (2022). A relational-cultural framework for promoting healthy masculinities. *American Psychologist, 77*(3), 321–332. https://doi.org/10.1037/amp0000929

DiPrete, T. A., & Buchmann, C. (2013). *The rise of women: The growing gender gap in education and what it means for American schools*. Russell Sage Foundation. https://www.russellsage.org/publications/rise-women

Drescher, J. (2018). Letter writing. In E. Yarbrough (Ed.), *Transgender mental health* (pp. 77–88). American Psychiatric Association.

Ducheny, K., Hendricks, M. L., & Keo-Meier, C. L. (2017). TGNC-affirmative interdisciplinary collaborative care. In A. A. Singh & L. M. Dickey (Eds.), *Affirmative counseling and psychological practice with transgender and gender nonconforming clients* (pp. 69–93). American Psychological Association. https://doi.org/10.1037/14957-004

Duran, E. (2006). *Healing the soul wound: Counseling with American Indians and other native peoples* (pp. xii, 147). Teachers College Press.

Duran, E., Duran, B., Brave Heart, M., & Horse-Davis, S. (1998). *Healing the American Indian soul wound* (pp. 341–354). https://doi.org/10.1007/978-1-4757-5567-1_22

Evans, K. M., Kincade, E. A., Marbley, A. F., & Seem, S. R. (2005). Feminism and feminist therapy: Lessons from the past and hopes for the future. *Journal of Counseling & Development, 83*(3), 269–277. https://doi.org/10.1002/j.1556-6678.2005.tb00342.x

Federal Bureau of Prisons. (2024, May). *BOP statistics: Average inmate age*. https://www.bop.gov/about/statistics/statistics_inmate_age.jsp

Fernández, J. (2022). A *mujerista* liberation psychology perspective on *testimonio* to cultivate decolonial healing. *Ethnic Studies*. https://doi.org/10.1080/02703149.2022.2095101

Gloria, A. M., & Castellanos, J. (2016). Latinas poderosas: Shaping mujerismo to manifest sacred spaces for healing and transformation. In T. Bryant-Davis & L. Comas-Díaz (Eds.), *Womanist and mujerista psychologies: Voices of fire, acts of courage* (pp. 93–119). American Psychological Association. https://doi.org/10.1037/14937-005

Gough, B., & Robertson, S. (2017). A review of research on men's health. In R. F. Levant & Y. G. Wong (Eds.), *The psychology of men and masculinities* (pp. 197–228). American Psychological Association.

Grzanka, P. R., & Miles, J. R. (2016). The problem with the phrase "intersecting identities:" LGBT affirmative therapy, intersectionality, and neoliberalism. *Sexuality Research & Social Policy, 13*(4), 371–389. https://doi.org/10.1007/s13178-016-0240-2

Harvey, S. M., Larson, A. E., & Warren, J. T. (2023). The Dobbs decision—Exacerbating U.S. health inequity. *The New England Journal of Medicine, 388*(16), 1444–1447. https://doi.org/10.1056/NEJMp2216698

Heath, C. D. (2006). A womanist approach to understanding and assessing the relationship between spirituality and mental health. *Mental Health, Religion & Culture, 9*(2), 155–170. https://doi.org/10.1080/13694670500116938

Heitz, H. K. (2022). Liberation psychology: Drawing on history to work toward resistance and collective healing in the United States. *Psychology from the Margins, 4*, Article 4. https://ideaexchange.uakron.edu/psychologyfromthemargins/vol4/iss1/4

Jordan, J. V. (2018). *Relational–cultural therapy* (2nd ed.). American Psychological Association. https://doi.org/10.1037/0000063-000

Kiselica, M. S., & Englar-Carlson, M. (2010). Identifying, affirming, and building upon male strengths: The positive psychology/positive masculinity model of psychotherapy with boys and men. *Psychotherapy: Theory, Research, Practice, Training, 47*(3), 276–287. https://doi.org/10.1037/a0021159

Korell, S. C., & Lorah, P. (2007). An overview of affirmative psychotherapy and counseling with transgender clients. In K. J. Bieschke, R. M. Perez, & K. A. DeBord (Eds.), *Handbook of counseling and psychotherapy with lesbian, gay, bisexual, and transgender clients* (2nd ed., pp. 271–288). American Psychological Association. https://doi.org/10.1037/11482-011

Lape, J. C. (2023). Gendering trauma: A womanist psychospiritual analysis of stress, trauma, and resilience. *Pastoral Psychology, 72*(3), 353–366. https://doi.org/10.1007/s11089-023-01075-x

Levant, R., & McDermott, R. (2022, October). Clarifying the American Psychological Association's guidelines for boys and men. *Newsweek*. https://www.newsweek.com/clarifying-american-psychological-associations-guidelines-boys-men-opinion-1749228

Leveille, S. G., Resnick, H. E., & Balfour, J. (2000). Gender differences in disability: Evidence and underlying reasons. *Aging Clinical and Experimental Research, 12*(2), 106–112. https://doi.org/10.1007/BF03339897

Mallett, C. (2015). *The school-to-prison pipeline*. Springer. https://www.springerpub.com/the-school-to-prison-pipeline-9780826194589.html

McDermott, R. C., Pietrantonio, K. R., Browning, B. R., McKelvey, D. K., Jones, Z. K., Booth, N. R., & Sevig, T. D. (2019). In search of positive masculine role norms: Testing the positive psychology positive masculinity paradigm. *Psychology of Men & Masculinities, 20*(1), 12–22. https://doi.org/10.1037/men0000160

Miller, J. B., & Stiver, I. P. (1997). *The healing connection: How women form relationships in therapy and in life* (pp. xi, 231). Beacon Press.

Mosley, D. V., Jean, P. L., Bridges, B., Sobrino, M., Mejia, J., Adam, S., Ross, G., & Abreu, R. (2020). Moving psychology toward anticolonial queer futures. In L. Comas-Díaz, Lillian & E. Torres Rivera (Eds.), Decolonial psychology: Toward anticolonial theories, research, training, and practice (pp. 369–388). American Psychological Association. https://doi.org/10.1037/0000376-016

Murtagh, K. N., & Hubert, H. B. (2004). Gender differences in physical disability among an elderly cohort. *American Journal of Public Health, 94*(8), 1406–1411. https://doi.org/10.2105/ajph.94.8.1406

Nelson, A. (2013). *Body and soul*. UMN Press. https://www.upress.umn.edu/book-division/books/body-and-soul

O'Donnell, M., Bentele, C., Grossman, H., Le, Y., Jang, H., & Steger, M. (2014). You, me, and meaning: An integrative review of connections between relationships and meaning in life. *Journal of Psychology in Africa, 24*, 44–50. https://doi.org/10.1080/14330237.2014.904097

Ojeda, L., & Organista, K. C. (2016). Latino American men. In Y. J. Wong & S. R. Wester (Eds.), *APA handbook of men and masculinities* (pp. 299–318). American Psychological Association. https://doi.org/10.1037/14594-014

Rader, J., & Gilbert, L. A. (2005). The egalitarian relationship in feminist therapy. *Psychology of Women Quarterly, 29*(4), 427–435. https://doi.org/10.1111/j.1471-6402.2005.00243.x

Robinson-Wood, T. (2014). Measuring resistance in black women: The resistance modality inventory. *Journal of Systemic Therapies, 33*(2), 62–77. https://doi.org/10.1521/jsyt.2014.33.2.62

Sanchez-Hucles, J. V. (2016). Womanist therapy with black women. In T. Bryant-Davis & L. Comas-Díaz (Eds.), *Womanist and mujerista psychologies: Voices of fire, acts of courage* (pp. 69–92). American Psychological Association. https://doi.org/10.1037/14937-004

Seager, M., & Barry, J. A. (2019). Positive masculinity: Including masculinity as a valued aspect of humanity. In J. A. Barry, R. Kingerlee, M. Seager, & L. Sullivan (Eds.), *The Palgrave handbook of male psychology and mental health* (pp. 105–122). Palgrave Macmillan. https://doi.org/10.1007/978-3-030-04384-1_6

Simpson, P., & Richards, M. (2017, October 5). Macho myth busting: Working class men aren't all too tough to seek help. *The Conversation*. https://theconversation.com/macho-myth-busting-working-class-men-arent-all-too-tough-to-seek-help-85149

Singh, A. A. (2016). Moving from affirmation to liberation in psychological practice with transgender and gender nonconforming clients. *American Psychologist, 71*(8), 755–762. https://doi.org/10.1037/amp0000106

Singh, A. A., & Dickey, L. M. (2017). Affirmative counseling with transgender and gender nonconforming clients. In A. A. Singh & L. M. Dickey (Eds.), *Handbook of sexual orientation and gender diversity in counseling and psychotherapy* (pp. 157–182). American Psychological Association. https://doi.org/10.1037/15959-007

Tummala-Narra, P. (2007). Conceptualizing trauma and resilience across diverse contexts: A multicultural perspective. *Journal of Aggression, Maltreatment & Trauma, 14*(1–2), 33–53. https://doi.org/10.1300/J146v14n01_03

United States Department of Justice. (2011). *Homicide trends in the United States: 1993–2022*. https://bjs.ojp.gov/%3Cfront%3E

Walker, A. (1983). *In search of our mothers' gardens: Womanist prose* (Reprint ed.). Mariner Books.

Walker, M. (2008). Power and effectiveness: Envisioning an alternate paradigm. *Women & Therapy, 31*(2–4), 129–144. https://doi.org/10.1080/02703140802146266

Wiesner-Hanks, M. E. (2011). *Gender in history: Global perspectives* (2nd ed.). Wiley-Blackwell.

Williams, W., & Jackson, L. (2019). Feminist/womanist/intersectional approaches to interventions with Black girls and women. *Women & Therapy, 42*, 1–5. https://doi.org/10.1080/02703149.2019.1622907

Zuckerwise, L. (2024). "I am writing you in reference to myself": White wellness, Black feminism, and the politics of self-care. *Signs: Journal of Women in Culture and Society, 49*. https://doi.org/10.1086/727990

Index

M. L. Miville et al., *Counseling and Gender*, https://doi.org/10.1007/978-3-031-69172-0

GPSR Compliance
The European Union's (EU) General Product Safety Regulation (GPSR) is a set of rules that requires consumer products to be safe and our obligations to ensure this.

If you have any concerns about our products, you can contact us on

ProductSafety@springernature.com

In case Publisher is established outside the EU, the EU authorized representative is:

Springer Nature Customer Service Center GmbH
Europaplatz 3
69115 Heidelberg, Germany

www.ingramcontent.com/pod-product-compliance
Lightning Source LLC
Chambersburg PA
CBHW070412010726
47387CB00003BA/133
* 9 7 8 3 0 3 1 6 9 1 7 1 3 *